Also by Paul Celan

Breathturn into Timestead: The Collected Later Poetry
(Translated and with commentary by Pierre Joris)

MEMORY ROSE INTO THRESHOLD SPEECH

MEMORY ROSE

THE COLLECTED EARLIER POETRY

A BILINGUAL EDITION

TRANSLATED FROM THE GERMAN BY PIERRE JORIS

WITH COMMENTARY BY PIERRE JORIS

AND BARBARA WIEDEMANN

FARRAR STRAUS GIROUX NEW YORK

Paul Celan

INTO THRESHOLD SPEECH

FARRAR, STRAUS AND GIROUX
120 Broadway, New York 10271

Published in 2020 by Farrar, Straus and Giroux
First paperback edition, 2022

Grateful acknowledgment is made to Barbara Wiedemann and Suhrkamp Verlag
for permission to incorporate the commentaries of Barbara Wiedemann in the work.

Library of Congress Control Number: 2020942468
Paperback ISBN: 9780374603236

Designed by Crisis

P1

Contents

SPRACHGITTER / SPEECHGRILLE

IV

V

Die Niemandsrose / NoOnesRose

I

II

IV

Introduction

This year—2020—marks the hundredth anniversary of Paul Celan's birth, and the fiftieth of his death. Introducing the previous, companion volume, *Breathturn into Timestead*, I suggested that Paul Celan is considered "the major German language poet of the period after 1945, and by some (George Steiner, for example) even as the major European poet of that period. Only Rilke, among last century's German-language poets, can conceivably match his fame and impact on German and world-poetry." Reader interest in this country, across Europe and beyond, judged by the vast number of editions and translations of his work, is testimony to this point beyond a doubt—even without enumerating the various critical and/or philological editions, the sixteen or seventeen volumes of correspondence published to date, the hundred plus books on one or the other aspect of Celan's poetry and poetics, and the several thousand—six thousand? seven thousand? it is nearly impossible to keep track worldwide—articles and essays that have appeared and keep appearing at a dizzying rate.[1]

The title I gave this book was composed with one eye on the title of the previous gathering—*Breathturn into Timestead*—which consisted of the titles of the first and last of the five volumes collected. But on the present occasion such a parallelism didn't work as neatly and this in fact tells us something about the difference between earlier and later Celan: if Celan's late volumes had (very Celanesque and often neologic) single compound words as titles, the early ones were still more expansive, at least the first two, which consisted each of two nouns joined by conjunctions, the earliest one (late 1952, early 1953) being *Poppy and Memory* and the second one *Threshold to Threshold* (1955). But a certain tightening starts to occur in the later fifties—on which more below—and the next collection, *Speechgrille* (1959), for the first time uses such a compound word creation, to be followed in 1963 by *NoOnesRose*, which both concludes the earlier phase and opens up into the later and final phases. I had to create a title based on those earlier ones and tried to show the differences in the work not by making up compound words, but by taking one word from each one of the four titles, thus: *Memory Rose into Threshold Speech.* A quick way of stating the difference would be to say that early Celan uses metaphors or metaphorical images in a more classically traditional poetic sense, whereas in later Celan the author's intent is to fuse, coagulate, join, transmute—however you want to speak of it, and you can speak of it from several different areas or fields of endeavor—those juxtaposed images into a concrete whole, or, as I put it elsewhere, "into the actual cornerstones of a new universe Celan was proposing, for him a necessary new universe after the Holocaust." But before addressing the poetry and poetics of the early volumes, permit me to insert my brief account of Paul Celan's life from the earlier book.

Born Paul Antschel in Czernowitz (today Chernivtsi, in the Ukraine), the capital of the Bukovina, a province of the Habsburg Empire that fell to Romania in 1920, the year of his birth, Celan was raised in a Jewish family that insisted both on young Paul receiving the best secular education—with the mother inculcating her love of the German language and culture—and on his Jewish roots: both his parents came from orthodox and, on one side, Hasidic family backgrounds. The languages were multiple: besides the usual Czernowitz languages—Romanian, Ukrainian, and Yiddish—the family at home spoke High German, somewhat different from the Czernowitzian dialectical German with "its Austrian informality and Slavic breadth, and interwoven with yiddish idioms."[2] Following his father's Zionistic ideals, young Paul attended the local Hebrew grade school Safah-Ivriah for three years, though moving eventually to the Romanian high school where he showed great interest in botany and French. Because of growing anti-Semitism, he moved to another state high school, where he added Italian, Latin, and ancient Greek to his studies. As a German-speaking student, he studied primarily the classics of German literature, supported in this by his mother and from 1937 on by his friend Edith Horowitz, whose father, a scholar of German literature, had a library very rich in this field. After his bar mitzvah Paul stopped studying Hebrew and began distancing himself from his father's ideological leanings. At this time he also began to take part in meetings of communist youth groups, got involved in antifascist activities, and read intensely in the classics of socialist literature.[3]

Celan, always reticent of speaking of private matters, left little autobiographical information, and the only somewhat expansive statement concerning his homeland occurs in the so-called Bremen speech, where he writes:

> The region from which I come to you—with what detours! but then, is there such a thing as a detour?—will be unfamiliar to most of you. It is the home of many of the Hassidic stories which Martin Buber has retold in German. It was—if I may flesh out this topographical sketch with a few details which are coming back to me from a great distance—it was a landscape where both people and books lived. There, in this former province of the Habsburg monarchy, now dropped from history, I first encountered the name of Rudolf Alexander Schröder while reading Rudolf Borchardt's "Ode with Pomegranate" . . . Within reach, though far enough, what I could aim to reach, was Vienna. You know what happened, in the years to come, even to this nearness.[4]

On November 9, 1938, the night that came to be known as Kristallnacht and that saw the first major Nazi pogrom against Jews in Germany and parts of Austria, Paul Celan traveled by train through Germany, an occasion remembered in the poem "La Contrescarpe," where he writes: "Via Kraków / you came, at the Anhalter / railway station / a smoke flowed toward your glance, / it already belonged to tomorrow." He was on his way via Paris to Tours, France, to study medicine at the local university, obedient to his parents' wishes. During this year in France he came in contact with a range of contemporary French literature and, in fact, spent much time on literary matters while slowly turning away from his premed studies. He had started to write poetry a few years earlier already, and in the summer of 1939, after returning to Czernowitz, and unable to return to Tours and medical studies due to the outbreak of the war, Celan decided on a major career change, enrolling in Romance studies at his hometown's university. The oldest surviving poems date from 1939 but would be published only posthumously.

The following year Soviet troops occupied his hometown, only to be replaced in 1941 by Romanian and German Nazi troops—specifically, Einsatzgruppe D, led by SS-Brigadeführer Ohlendorf, which reached Czernowitz on July 6. The SS had one essential job to fulfill—"Energisch durchgreifen, die Juden liquidieren" (to intervene energetically and liquidate the Jews), as they didn't trust the Romanians to do the job thoroughly enough. On July 7, the Great Temple went up in flames and for the next three days the hunt was open: 682 Jews were murdered. By late August, Ohlendorf triumphantly reported to Berlin that more than 3,000 had been killed. On October 11, the ghetto was created—the first one in the history of the Bukovina and of Czernowitz. Then began the *Umsiedlung* (relocation) of most Jews to Transnistria. The Romanians managed to argue with the Germans and to retain 15,000 Jews in Czernowitz to keep the city functioning. The Antschel family were among those who, at least for the time being, remained in the ghetto. Paul was ordered to forced labor on construction sites. Then, in June 1942, a new wave of arrests and deportations began, taking place primarily on Saturday nights. With the help of his friend Ruth Lackner, Paul had found a large and comfortable hideout, but his parents refused adamantly to take refuge there, preferring to remain in their own house—where Celan's mother did prepare rucksacks in case they should be deported. On one of those nights, disobeying his parents' orders, Paul left the house and decided to spend the night in the hideout. When he returned the next morning he found his home sealed off: his parents had been deported.

Celan continued to work in forced labor camps, where, in the late fall of 1942, he learned that his father, physically broken by the slave labor he was subjected to, had been killed by the SS. Later that winter the news reached him that his mother too had been shot by the Nazis. These killings, especially that of his mother, were to remain the core experience of his life. He was released in February 1944, when the labor camps were closed. In April, Soviet troops occupied Czernowitz without a fight. Celan was put to work as a medical auxiliary in a psychiatric clinic and made one trip as an ambulance assistant to Kiev. He remained in Czernowitz for one more year, enrolled at the now Ukrainian-Russian university there, studying English literature, while working as a translator for local newspapers. In February 1944 he had put together a first typescript of poems, expanding it in the fall of that year to include the poems written during the labor camp days. He entrusted this manuscript to his friend Ruth Kraft, who took it with her to Bucharest to present it to the poet Alfred Margul-Sperber. (This book would be published posthumously in 1986 as *Gedichte 1938–1944*, with a foreword by Ruth Kraft.) In April 1945 he left his hometown, Czernowitz, never to return. But the Bukovinian "meridian" (to use one of his favorite lines of orientation) would always be present; he mentioned "my (Czernowitz) meridian"[5] in a letter to Gideon Kraft as late as 1968, as he spoke of Gustav Landauer and Leon Kellner, two elder Bukovinians who had been important to him. As one commentator put it: "Celan's poetry transforms the main characteristic of Bukovina's culture into a structural principle. It is the legendary Bukovinian receptivity to heterogeneous ethnic traditions with which Celan infuses the rich intertextuality of his entire oeuvre."[6]

For two years he settled in Bucharest, making a living as a translator (mainly from Russian into Romanian), and working at becoming a poet, remaining true to his mother's language, German, as he would do all his life, but also trying his hand briefly at poems in Romanian. He was clear about this choice, stating on a number of occasions that there is no such thing as bilingual poetry, that the poet has to write in his mother tongue. The strongest formulation of this conviction was reported by Ruth Lackner to whom he said: "Only in the mother tongue can one speak one's own truth, in a foreign language the poet lies."[7] It is, however, in Bucharest and in a Romanian translation by his friend Petre Solomon that the poem that would make his fame—"Todesfuge" (Death-fugue)—was first published in May 1947 in the magazine *Contemporanul*, as "Tangoul Mortii" ("Tango of death"). It is also here that Paul Antschel, who signed many of the translations of that time with various pseudonyms, decided to change his name and anagrammatically transformed the Romanian spelling of Antschel, Ançel, into Celan. A change first suggested, so Ruth Kraft has it in her preface to the early poems, by Margul-Sperber's wife.

But Vienna, the old Hapsburg capital, to which the German-cultured Bukovinians and Czernowitzians had always looked up to as *their* cultural center, beckoned, and in December 1947 Celan clandestinely crossed over to Austria via Hungary—from the little information we have, an arduous journey but one made necessary by the tightening of the Iron Curtain. The only German-speaking place the poet was ever to live in, the Vienna of those years[8]—Orson Welles's *The Third Man* comes close to what it must have felt like to Celan—was relatively hospitable to the young poet, though the minimal and superficial denazification program it had submitted itself to must have left the survivor uneasy, to say the least. Through an introduction from Margul-Sperber he met Otto Basil, the editor of the avant-garde literary magazine *Der Plan*, in which he would publish a number of poems, and at some point he went to meet Ludwig von Ficker, who had been a close friend of Georg Trakl's, and who celebrated the young Bukovinian poet as "heir to Else Lasker-Schüler." The meeting with the surrealist painter Edgar Jené led to the writing of the first essay by Celan that we have, "Edgar Jené and the Dream of the Dream," composed as a foreword to a Jené exhibition catalogue. He also met a number of people who would remain lifelong friends, among them Nani and Klaus Demus, and maybe most important, the young poet Ingeborg Bachmann, who even after their early love affair faded, was to remain a close friend and a staunch defender in the later, darker days of the Goll affair. It was also in Vienna that Celan readied his first book, *Der Sand aus den Urnen* (*The Sand from the Urns*), for publication.

From Hölderlin's hallucinatory walk to the Bordelais and back, to von Horvath's strange death (a branch severed by lightning killed him on the Champs-Élysées), France has always proved a point of focal, not to say fatal, attraction—and certainly often enough, a point of rupture—for poets and writers of the German language: suffice it to add in this context the names of Heinrich Heine, Rainer Maria Rilke, and Walter Benjamin. For most of these, their stays in France were limited, and freely chosen. But often also they were a matter of political and/or intellectual exile. Few of them, however, had as symbiotic and long-term a relationship with France as Paul Celan. The latter clearly had not found what he was looking for in Vienna, and after less than a year—and even before his first book came out—he left Austria to head for Paris, where he arrived in July 1948. The city by the Seine, the *ville lumière*, was to remain his home until his death in late April 1970. It was not easy for him to adapt and make a living at first, but while doing this he never lost sight of his and poetry's aim: he worked tirelessly at getting his poetry published and known in the German language areas, be it Austria or Germany. In early 1952 he was invited by the already well-known Gruppe 47 to read in their yearly gathering in Niendorf, and this started a pattern of forays into Germany that would continue until just a few months before his death. His first major volume of poems, *Mohn und Gedächtnis*, was published later that year by the German publisher DVA (Deutsche Verlags-Anstalt) in Stuttgart, and brought instant recognition, as well as a measure of fame, due in no small part to what was to become one of the best-known and most-anthologized poems of the postwar era, "Todesfuge." A new volume of poems followed roughly every four years, with that rhythm accelerating during the last years of his life.

In Paris, he made contact with the literary scene and soon met a number of writers who were to stay important for him. Among them was the poet Yves Bonnefoy, who recalls Celan in those days:

> . . . His gestures, above all in the first years after Vienna—at the time of the room in *rue des Ecoles*, of the cheap university restaurants, of the archaic typewriter with a Greek-temple peristyle, of destitution—had nonchalance, and his head had a graceful movement towards the shoulder: as if to accompany, for a stretch, along the summer streets after a lively night's conversation, the friend being left for a whole day. (Bonnefoy 1988, 12)

It was Bonnefoy who introduced Celan, on the latter's insistence, to Yvan Goll in November 1949. This encounter would much later produce terrible results: festering throughout the fifties, the "Goll affair"—in which Claire Goll, the poet's widow, falsely accused Celan of plagiarism, and, shockingly, a range of German newspapers and reviews uncritically accepted and spread those false accusations—broke in 1960 and does indeed mark a traumatic turning point.[9]

Celan does not seem ever to have seriously thought about moving elsewhere, and certainly not after meeting the French graphic artist Gisèle Lestrange in the fall of 1951, and marrying her in late 1952. He became a naturalized French citizen in 1955, and it was as a French citizen and a Parisian literary person that he spent the rest of his life, employed as a teacher of German language and literature at the École Normale Supérieure on the rue d'Ulm, summering from 1962 on in the little farmhouse the Celans bought in Normandy. A first child, François, died shortly after birth in 1953, but 1955 saw the birth of his son Eric, with whom Celan would be very close. The last years brought a separation from his wife and son, and from 1967 to 1970, Celan lived alone in Paris.

During this final decade of his life, his latent psychic troubles had come to the fore, exacerbated by the false accusations of plagiarism leveled by Claire Goll. Celan the survivor's already tenuous psychic health was seriously endangered, and would increasingly necessitate medical attention. He had been in self-imposed psychiatric care some time around May 1965, and was forcibly put in psychiatric confinement in November 1965 after a life-threatening knife attack on his wife. Further hospitalizations followed from December 1965 to early June 1966. The following year started ominously with the chance encounter on January 25 at a literary event at the Paris Goethe Institute with Claire Goll, triggering deep psychic turmoil. Five days later, on January 30, Celan, after threatening the life of his wife, who then demanded a separation, tried to kill himself with a knife—or a letter opener—that missed his heart by an inch. Saved by his wife in extremis, he was transported to the Hôpital Boucicaut and operated on immediately, as his left lung was gravely wounded. He was in and out of psychiatric institutions from February 1967 to October of that year, even though by the middle of May he had started teaching again at the École Normale. These stays involved drug and shock therapy, and old friends who saw him during or after those days reported major changes in the man. Thus Petre Solomon visiting Paris that summer found Celan "profoundly altered, prematurely aged, taciturn, frowning . . . 'They are doing experiments on me,' he said in a stifled voice, interrupted by sighs."[10] One can hear this "stifled" voice, deeper though no less resonant—and perceive behind it the psychic pain probably muffled by medication—by listening to the 1967 recordings of poems from *Threadsuns.*[11]

Despite all this, Celan's last years were extremely active ones: the writing—contrary to a widespread belief that he came close to a *Verstummen*, a falling silent—kept on unabated with long productive periods that saw the composition of poems on a near-daily basis, with a number of days that brought several poems. He kept traveling: to Switzerland for holidays and meetings with old friends; to Germany for readings, recordings, and encounters (with the philosopher Martin Heidegger, among others;) and to Israel in 1969—though he broke that trip off after two weeks to return precipitately to Paris.[12] He had moved from his small studio apartment on rue Tournefort in the fifth arrondissement to an apartment on the avenue Émile Zola in late 1969, and on the night of April 19–20, 1970, he succumbed to his psychic demons: the Pont Mirabeau, close to his apartment at the end of avenue Émile Zola, is probably where he decided to put an end to his life by going into the Seine. His body was found farther downstream on May 1. He was buried in the Thiais cemetery on the outskirts of Paris where his son François already rested and where his wife, Gisèle, would join him in December 1991.

On his desk Paul Celan had left Wilhelm Michael's biography of Hölderlin, *Das Leben Friedrich Hölderlins*, lying open to page 464. He had underlined the following sentence from a letter by Clemens Brentano: "Sometimes this genius goes dark and drowns in the bitter well of his heart."

The four books that make up this volume are the four volumes Paul Celan put together and published in his adopted hometown of Paris between 1952 and 1963. There are some earlier poems, from the late thirties to the midforties, not published by him but that came out posthumously,[13] as mentioned above. There was, as well, his first actual book, *Der Sand aus den Urnen* (*The Sand from the Urns*), published in Vienna in October 1948 a few months after Celan had moved to Paris.

As it had not been proofread by the author, the book was so full of sense-disfiguring typos that Celan had the book recalled and destroyed. Of the forty-eight poems of that book, twenty-six—including "Deathfugue"—would be taken up in *Poppy and Memory*.

Rereading these four books in their order of composition (after decades spent concentrating on reading, translating, and writing about the later books) was a revelation in that such a chronological reading allowed me—and I hope will allow the readers of this book—to see and experience, thus to witness (to use one of Celan's own core terms), the development of his work from its earliest incarnations to its full-blown mature flowering. This development is, for example, easily visible if the reader compares the early masterpiece, "Deathfugue," and its later rewriting in the longest of Celan's poems, "Stretto." It is also made visible in those most culturally explicit and richest poems of the final volume, *NoOnesRose,* where for the first and last time Celan lays bare his sources, methods, affiliations, and associations, from Osip Mandelstam to Gershom Scholem, from Nelly Sachs to Margarete Susman, et cetera. Esther Cameron suggests[14] that this book is "perhaps the most open of Celan's books, although its openness was not necessarily [visible] to his contemporary audience." It certainly is today, and not only because of the accomplishments of scholarly research and analysis by Cameron and others. Time itself makes complex poems more readable, and in this case the range of materials that Celan himself brought to bear, visibly or invisibly, on the poems stand out as clearer and more available. Cameron goes on:

> Indeed, [the book] sometimes seems addressed to the assembly of poets ("all poets are Jews") from all time, with one rabbi—Rabbi Loew, the Maharal of Prague—included in the company, and the masters of the Kabbalah, through the influence of Gerschom Scholem, also present. Celan had at one point considered an epigraph from Dante ("That from the fact the word is not diverse"), and Dante, though

unnamed, is certainly present in the book along with Petrarch, Tsvetayeva and Hölderlin. The book is dedicated to the memory of Ossip Mandelstam, a Jewish poet (and devotee of Dante) who fell victim to Stalin's purges; it is pervaded by the emotional influence of Nelly Sachs, who had written to Celan on October 28, 1959: "Dear Paul Celan, let us continue to pass truth over to each other. Between Paris and Stockholm runs the meridian of pain and consolation." But Nelly Sachs was the last contemporary poet to whom Celan would dedicate a poem, and she was older than Celan by nearly a generation.

What we witness then in these four volumes is a great variety of riches and their near-alchemical transformation over this decade and a half, from the early Rilkean, metaphorically rich and driven verse, still close to a certain romantic *Naturlyrik*, a nature poetry, in often nearly classical (some poems actually rhyme) modes, to the later poems, just as rich though in a different, more content-referential manner. What is added, in that sense, to the always-already present knowledge of the experience of *khurbn* that underlies his life are literary, scientific, cabalistic, cultural informations and experiences searched for and gathered in. But added too are ricochets—often from hidden political motivations—triggered by the reception of his poetry in Germany, specifically, as during those years he became one of the most publicly successful poets writing in German. This success, however, had also brought with it the awareness on Celan's part, via reviews and critical essays, of the fact that his poetry was being misread and could thus also be misused. This misreading was easy enough to do for a reader with bad intentions, because of the early poems' lush near-surrealist language, mirroring the cultural richness of his origins, that gone world of an Austro-Hungarian Bukovina, augmented by his interest in twentieth-century avant-garde poetries such as that of the French surrealists, some of whom he translated during those years.

The "Deathfugue," for example, had been called by one major German critic—Hans Egon Holthusen—a gorgeous dreamlike surrealist fantasy with no reference to the actual world. Holthusen added: "With very few simple paradoxes Celan was able to master a theme that exceeds all human composure and all artistic imagination: by making it very 'light' and transcending it through a dreamy surrealism already beyond language, it could escape the bloody chamber of horrors of history and rise up into the ether of pure poetry." Celan realized how the image- and metaphor-richness his earlier poems still worked with could easily be misread—often purposefully so, as in the case of Holthusen, who, it turned out, had been an SS officer during the war—and that poetry post-*khurbn* had to become barer, that lush metaphors were an inappropriate luxury for these times, and that even the concept of metaphor, of something standing for something else, if historically an essential poetic device, was in need of revision.

Celan seems to have signaled that a change in his poetics had started to take place as far back as 1958, when he suggested that for him poetry was no longer a matter of "transfiguring" (*verklären*). The statement came in a short text written as a reply to a questionnaire from the Flinker bookstore in Paris, and needs quoting more fully, as it shows Celan already thinking about changes that will only be implemented in the poetry of the sixties, and which the volume *Speechgrille*, to be published the following year, foreshadows without as yet fully developing. Given "the sinister events in its memory," writes Celan, the language of German poetry has to become "more sober, more factual . . . 'grayer.'" This greater factuality checks a core impulse of the lyrical tradition, its relation to the 'lyre,' to music: "it is . . . a language which wants to locate even its 'musicality' in such a way that it has nothing in common with the 'euphony' which more or less blithely continued to sound alongside the greatest horrors." The direct effect of giving up this 'euphony' is to increase the accuracy of the language: "It does not transfigure or render 'poetical'; it names, it posits, it tries to measure the area of the given and the possible."

Also, in 1960 Claire Goll, to buttress the statements according to which Celan was supposed to have stolen from her husband's poetry, made more tentatively from 1953 on, now faked manuscripts in order to prove her accusations of plagiarism, and published letters to that effect in the Munich magazine *Baubudenpoet*, further claiming that the murder of Celan's parents was a "legend," while simultaneously using the cliché of the avaricious uncreative Jew (though she herself was Jewish) to cast doubt on what had been an enriching reciprocal relation between Yvan Goll in his last year and the younger poet.[15] This caused untold pain and psychic harm to Celan and was, I believe, one of the triggers of his suicide in 1970. But we are not there yet: the period we are looking at here is the period of his strongest response to those accusations.

To both the Holthusen type of attacks and denials of political facts veiled as literary criticism and the loudly screeched Gollian defamatory assaults on his personal and literary honesty, Celan's response was not any kind of public statement—though he helped some of his friends formulate such statements, while never satisfied with these and even turning away from supposed friends who, he thought, didn't defend him clearly and effectively enough. No, his response was a quest for a new poetics, foreshadowed and developed in *Speechgrille* and *NoOnesRose* and finding its full expression in the books from *Breathturn* on.

Also important here, for the reader who would like to get to the more theoretical aspects of Celan's poetics, is the Meridian speech (delivered on the occasion of receiving the Georg Büchner Prize in Darmstadt, October 22, 1960), Celan's most important and extended statement on poetics.[16] It is here that we have to look for the theoretical base of the changes from the early to later work. I will not go into detail here, as I went into some depth on these matters in the introduction to *Breathturn into Timestead*. Suffice it to say that from *Speechgrille* on, some of the poems are clearly what has been called *Widerrufe*: attempts at retracting, countermanding, disavowing previous poetics—those of other poets, but also his own earlier stance. The poem "Tenebrae," for example, is a carefully constructed refutation of Hölderlin's "Patmos" hymn, which, as Götz Wienold has shown,[17] negates the (Christian/pagan) hope for salvation expressed in Hölderlin's lines "Nah ist / Und schwer zu fassen der Gott. / Wo aber Gefahr ist, wächst / Das Rettende auch" ("Close / and difficult to grasp is God. / But where danger lurks, that which saves / also grows"); simultaneously the poem inverts and negates the (Judaic) hopes regarding God's promises as expressed in the psalms, specifically Psalm 34, and in other places of the Bible that are alluded to, mainly Isaiah 43:20 and Leviticus 17. In a similar vein, the title poem, "Sprachgitter," takes issue both with Gottfried Benn's famous essay *Probleme der Lyrik* and with the optimism of Psalm 126. I have already mentioned the rewriting of "Deathfugue" in "Stretto," maybe the most essential of such an autocritical reworking of the author's poetics. The reader will find further information on these and related matters in the commentaries to the poems.

Having translated all the later poetry, a project I had started in 1968, as well as a range of Celan's essays—including *The Meridian*—and posthumous prose,[18] I came to this project as a late but necessary endeavor that would permit me to complete a translation of all of Celan's literary works. I have spoken to the question (the difficulties and the enchantments) of translating Celan in the introduction to *Breathturn into Timestead*, as well as in a range of further essays published elsewhere over the years—references to most of which the reader can find in this volume. I will therefore limit myself here to a few quick remarks.

Reading a poem of Celan's at any kind of depth that will honor the poem's complexity, and translating it, are similar acts with a similar problematic. As the literary scholar and Celan friend Peter Szondi put it: "Anyone who has learned to 'read' Celan's text knows that it is not a question of deciding on any one meaning, but of realizing that these are not different, they are one. Ambiguity, having become the means of awareness, makes visible the unity of that which only appeared to be difference. It serves precision."[19] Such ever-present ambiguity—though to avoid the smell of negativity that inheres in the word "ambiguity," I prefer to call it polysemous richness—is easy enough for the knowledgeable reader to hold in mind, but difficult in most cases for the translator to resolve. For example, in one poem Celan, the German-language poet living in France and thus also in and with the French language, uses the word *Neige*, which means "inclination," "declination," even "shortage" in German, but is also and simultaneously readable homophonically as the French word *neige*, meaning "snow," and an attentive Celan reader will be aware of the symbolic importance of snow in Celan's universe. Translation, even trying to wield as just a Solomonic sword or scalpel pen as possible, can only cut the baby in two, as no mother tongue will come forth and give up her right to the word's meaning in order to save it—given that both languages are right, and trying to keep their baby alive, both can only step back and leave the Solomonic decision up to the translator who has to choose (*trancher*, as the French would have it, meaning literally "to cut," "to slice.") Such examples are plentiful throughout Celan's oeuvre, and the translator, unable to find the one word in the target language that reproduced the original polysemous meaning, has to choose a less-than-perfect word—and/or write an essay or at least a commentary laying out the richness of the original and the loss inherent in the translation.

I will lay out just one more such complex word, but one of major importance in this book: the title of the last volume included, *Die Niemandsrose*, most often and most literally rendered as *The No One's Rose*. I have already pointed to the importance in Celan's poetological development of the word-condensations, so that at the point in the late fifties when he creates the concept of the *Niemandsrose*—which first appeared in a poem before being elevated and made the title of the collection—this is meaningful enough for me not to want to use a title made of several separate words or word-elements. Trying to think through this (while playfully doodling variations of condensations in my notebook) while trying also to estrange Celan's word, which, since he had used it as a title, had become an all too familiar (if untranslatable? in every meaning of that word) concept, I thought it important to get a good grasp of what the two elements that make up the compound stood for and referred to in Celan's universe, and what brought them together.

The rose is, of course, one of the most classical images in poetry of all times and places, and in the context of Celan's referential universe, from the Bible on to, say, Rilke. Concerning the rose in the context of Judaism, Celan had made reference to it, in an early poem from *Der Sand aus den Urnen*, not retained in *Poppy and Memory*, where verse 8 reads: "Dein Haus ritt die finstere Welle, doch barg es ein Rosengeschlecht;" | "Your house rode the wave of darkness, though saved by a rose-lineage/house/family." (See elsewhere in the commentaries for a discussion of the difficulties in translating the word *Geschlecht*.) In the German translation of the Old Testament, Israel is compared to a rose in Hosea 14:6, though in English versions of the Bible, the rose is replaced by the lily. In the years of writing *Die Niemandsrose*, Celan, as we can see from his readings, was also interested in a range of esoteric matters, especially alchemy, and in that context one could think of the connection between the rose and the cross in the alchemical secret society of the Rosicrucians, as mentioned by Ernst Bloch, whom Celan read closely: "Cross and rose, the first the symbol of pain and dissolution, the second the symbol of love and life, thus united allegorically in the 'work of perfection.'"[20]

But more to the point: Celan was a close reader of Rilke, and in a draft of the poem "Walliser Elegie" (not included in any volume put together by Celan, and thus not reproduced here) from 1962 he quotes Rilke's epigraph: "Rose, oh reiner Widerspruch, Lust, | Niemandes Schlaf zu sein unter soviel | Lidern" | | "Rose, oh pure contradiction, desire | to be no one's sleep under so many | lids" (my translation). One could be tempted to see the *Niemandsrose* as exactly that rose of pure contradiction wanting to be "no one's sleep." But the *Niemand* is not simply taken over from Rilke—Celan has a range of references and sources here too.

The word itself—*Niemand*—first appears in "Count the almonds," a poem from 1952, in the line "I searched for your eye, when you opened it and no one [*Niemand*] looked at you," to be repeated later in the poem as "a saying that found its way to no one's [*niemandes*] heart." The word returned in the 1957 poem "Ein Tag und noch einer" | "One Day and One More," in the line "ich stürzte / alles in niemandes Hand" | "I crashed / everything into no-one's hand." In the 1961 poem "Psalm" | "Psalm," line 4 reads: "Gelobt seist du, Niemand" | "Praised be thou, NoOne" which is an allusion to verse 15 of "Es war Erde in ihnen" | "There was earth inside them": "o one, o no one, o noone, o you."

Another interesting strand to follow concerns Osip Mandelstam, the Russian poet of Jewish descent to whom the volume *Die Niemandsrose* is dedicated. Born in Warsaw in 1891, Mandelstam did not die, as Celan had assumed until he learned differently in 1961, in a German concentration camp, but in one of Stalin's transit camps near Vladivostok in 1938. In 1959 S. Fischer Verlag published a selection of Mandelstam's poems in Celan's translation. The publication of six poems from *Die Niemandsrose* in the first 1963 issue of the journal *Neue Rundschau* is preceded by two Mandelstam poems in translation, and is dedicated to Osip Mandelstam. Celan not only thinks of him as the greatest Russian poet, but considers Mandelstam his brother, as he makes clear in a poem fragment:[21]

Brother Osip

Pain plays with words
he plays at giving it names
he searches for the No-one's Places,
and there, there you wait.
You are the Russianjew,
the Jewrussian, and

To his son Eric, Celan called the book "La Rose de Personne" or "La RoseNulle," as French title variations.[22] On a sheet added to a notebook of reading notes dated April 1966, one can read: "LA ROSE NULLE" (The null [The nothing] rose).

The change of the pronoun *niemand* (no one) into a name easily brings to mind Odysseus's ruse to overcome the giant Polyphemus in Homer's epic, though one should also think back on the Kafka—one of Celan's favorite authors—story "Der Ausflug ins Gebirge" ("The Excursion into the Mountains"), translated into Romanian by Celan, a passage here in English by Michael Hofmann: "'I don't know,' I cried in a toneless voice, 'I really don't know. If nobody comes, then nobody comes. I've done nobody any harm, nobody ever did me any harm, yet nobody wants to come to my aid. Nobody upon nobody. But that's not it either. Only nobody comes to help me—nobody upon nobody would be fine. I would quite like—and why wouldn't I?—to go on an excursion with a crowd of nobodies. Into the mountains, of course, where else? The way those nobodies would crowd together, all their crossed and linked arms, their many feet, separated by minute steps!'"

See also Celan's prose story "Conversation in the Mountains": "They do not talk, they speak, and who speaks does not talk to anyone, cousin, he speaks because nobody hears him, nobody and Nobody"[23] (as translated by Rosmarie Waldrop). Finally, in *Microliths They Are, Little Stones: Posthumous Prose* (Contra Mundum Press, 2020), we find this, from the fragmentary dialogue #148: "Karl: Understood. So, I hear no one. (After a pause, with irony) Den Herrn Niemand. *Mister Nobody,* thus."

Please, reader, forgive what may feel like an overlong digression but is a meandering meditation necessary for the translator to come to his or her conclusion. Obviously the word "nobody," despite the fact that it is one word like *niemand*, does not work in this complex context—the meaning goes toward "no one." But how to make this word a Celanian compound in itself and add the word "rose"? For a while I tried out a simple compaction: Noone, then Noonesrose. Although I got somewhat used to it, it always felt heavy and in need of too much of a double take by the reader, as the "noon" in the compound was unavoidable. I wrote down all possible versions of the title I could come up with, including the one I finally settled on—possibly backed by Celan's own playful French version, *La RoseNulle*—just as the deadline for this book closed in: *NoOnesRose*.

This book concludes my fifty-year involvement with translating Paul Celan. I would like to thank all of those, innumerable and impossible to thank by name, who helped me over that half century to read and understand and translate his immense oeuvre. Special thanks are due to my wife, Nicole Peyrafitte, who has accompanied, nourished, counseled, and sustained me in this labor for the last three decades. Of course, it is I who am responsible for any and all remaining errors.

NOTES TO THE INTRODUCTION

1. For a more detailed record of Celan's life and work—though concentrated more on the later volumes—and of my relation to it and the long process of translating Celan, I would like to refer the reader to the more extensive introduction available in *Breathturn into Timestead.* I apologize for the inevitable fact that the introduction to this volume repeats, at times verbatim, a range of information already given in the previous book.

2. Israel Chalfen, *Paul Celan: A Biography of His Youth* (New York: Persea Books, 1991), p. 13.

3. Much detail here is taken from *Celan Handbuch: Leben, Werk, Wirkung*, ed. Markus May, Peter Goßens, and Jürgen Lehmann (Stuttgart: J. B. Metzler, 2008), pp. 7–9.

4. Paul Celan, *Collected Prose*, trans. Rosmarie Waldrop (Manchester: Carcanet Press, 1986), pp. 33–34.

5. Chalfen, *Paul Celan*, p. 180.

6. Amy D. Colin, "Paul Celan," in *Holocaust Literature: An Encyclopedia of Writers and Their Work*, ed. S. Lillian Kremer (New York: Routledge, 2003), I:216.

7. Chalfen, *Paul Celan*, p. 184.

8. For a detailed account of those years, see *"Displaced": Paul Celan in Wien, 1947–1949*, ed. Peter Goßen and Marcus G. Patka (Frankfurt am Main: Suhrkamp Verlag, 2001).

9. For a full treatment of this affair, see Barbara Wiedemann, *Paul Celan: Die Goll-Affäre* (Frankfurt am Main: Suhrkamp Verlag, 2000).

10. In Felstiner's citation and translation in *Paul Celan: Poet, Survivor, Jew* (New Haven, Conn.: Yale University Press, 1995), p. 243.

11. See especially side 3 of the double cassette edition of Paul Celan's readings *Ich hörte sagen: Gedichte und Prosa* (Munich: Der Hörverlag, Munich 1977).

12. For more details regarding the intersections between the life and the work, see the introductions to the various volumes of poems in the commentaries section at the end of this book; see also the introduction to my *Paul Celan: Selections* (Berkeley: University of California Press, 2005).

13. Paul Celan, *Gedichte, 1938–1944*, with a preface by Ruth Kraft (Frankfurt am Main: Suhrkamp Verlag, 1986).

14. Esther Cameron, *Western Art and Jewish Presence in the Work of Paul Celan: Roots and Ramifications of the "Meridian" Speech* (Lanham, Md.: Lexington Books, 2014), p. 264.

15. See a range of the commentaries to the poems, especially those for the last volume; see also the section "Texts on the Goll Affair" for Celan's own responses (mostly unpublished) to the affair in my *Microliths They Are, Little Stones: Posthumous Prose* (New York: Contra Mundum Press, 2020).

16. See Paul Celan, *The Meridian: Final Version—Drafts—Materials*, ed.

Bernhard Böschenstein and Heino Schmull; tr. Pierre Joris (Palo Alto, Calif.: Stanford University Press, 2011).

17. Götz Wienold, "Paul Celans Hölderlin-Widerruf" ("Paul Celan's Hölderlin Revocation"), *Poetica* 2, no. 2 (April 1968), 216–28.

18. Paul Celan, *Microliths They Are, Little Stones: Posthumous Prose*, trans. Pierre Joris (New York: Contra Mundum Press, 2020).

19. Peter Szondi, D. Caldwell, and S. Esh, *Reading, "Engführung": An Essay on the Poetry of Paul Celan*, *boundary 2*, vol. 11, no. 3, The Criticism of Peter Szondi (Spring 1983), 231–264.

20. Ernst Bloch, *The Principle of Hope*, vol. 2, trans. Neville Plaice, Stephen Plaice, and Paul Knight (Cambridge, Mass.: MIT Press, 1986), p. 637).

21. Published in the notes to *Paul Celan: Die Gedichte aus dem Nachlaß*, Hg. v. Bertrand Badiou u.a., Frankfurt a. M. 1977, 371.

22. On April 12, 1966. See Paul Celan/Gisèle Celan-Lestrange, *Correspondance*, éditée et commentée par Bertrand Badiou avec le concours d'Eric Celan (Paris: Editions du Seuil, 2001) vol. 1, p. 405, letter #406.

23. Originally in *Paul Celan: Gesammelte Werke in fünf Bänden*. Hg. v. Beda Allemann u.a. (Frankfurt a. M.: Suhrkamp Verlag, 1983), vol. III, 171.

Mohn und Gedächtnis

Poppy and Memory

Der Sand aus den Urnen

The Sand from the Urns

EIN LIED IN DER WÜSTE

Ein Kranz ward gewunden aus schwärzlichem Laub in der Gegend
von Akra:
dort riß ich den Rappen herum und stach nach dem Tod mit dem
Degen.
Auch trank ich aus hölzernen Schalen die Asche der Brunnen von Akra
und zog mit gefälltem Visier den Trümmern der Himmel entgegen.

Denn tot sind die Engel und blind ward der Herr in der Gegend von
Akra,
und keiner ist, der mir betreue im Schlaf die zur Ruhe hier gingen.
Zuschanden gehaun ward der Mond, das Blümlein der Gegend von
Akra:
so blühn, die den Dornen es gleichtun, die Hände mit rostigen Ringen.

So muß ich zum Kuß mich wohl bücken zuletzt, wenn sie beten in
Akra . . .
O schlecht war die Brünne der Nacht, es sickert das Blut durch die
Spangen!
So ward ich ihr lächelnder Bruder, der eiserne Cherub von Akra.
So sprech ich den Namen noch aus und fühl noch den Brand auf den
Wangen.

NACHTS ist dein Leib von Gottes Fieber braun:
mein Mund schwingt Fackeln über deinen Wangen.
Nicht sei gewiegt, dem sie kein Schlaflied sangen.
Die Hand voll Schnee, bin ich zu dir gegangen,

und ungewiß, wie deine Augen blaun
im Stundenrund. (Der Mond von einst war runder.)

A SONG IN THE DESERT

A wreath was woven from blackening leafage in the region of Acra:
there I pulled my black stallion around and jabbed at death with my rapier.
And from wooden vessels did I drink the ash of the wells of Acra
while with lowered visor I rode toward the ruins of the heavens.

For dead are the angels and blinded was the Lord in the region of Acra,
and there is no one who would guard while I sleep those laid to rest here.
Battered and profaned, the moon, the little flower from the region of Acra:
thus bloom, just as the thorns do, the hands with their rusty rings.

Thus in the end I'll have to bend down for the kiss, when they pray in Acra . . .
O flawed was night's brigandine, the blood is seeping through the clasps!
Thus became I her smiling brother, the iron cherub of Acra.
Thus do I still utter the name and still feel the burn on the cheeks.

AT NIGHT your body's brown from God's fever:
my mouth swings torches above your cheeks.
Be not swayed, to whom no lullaby's sung.
The hand full of snow, I came to you,

and unsure, how your eyes go blue
in the hours' round. (The erstwhile moon was rounder.)

Verschluchzt in leeren Zelten ist das Wunder,
vereist das Krüglein Traums – was tuts?

Gedenk: ein schwärzlich Blatt hing im Holunder –
das schöne Zeichen für den Becher Bluts.

Umsonst malst du Herzen ans Fenster:
der Herzog der Stille
wirbt unten im Schloßhof Soldaten.
Sein Banner hißt er im Baum – ein Blatt, das ihm blaut, wenn es herbstet;
die Halme der Schwermut verteilt er im Heer und die Blumen der Zeit;
mit Vögeln im Haar geht er hin zu versenken die Schwerter.

Umsonst malst du Herzen ans Fenster: ein Gott ist unter den Scharen,
gehüllt in den Mantel, der einst von den Schultern dir sank auf der Treppe, zur Nachtzeit,
einst, als in Flammen das Schloß stand, als du sprachst wie die Menschen: Geliebte . . .
Er kennt nicht den Mantel und rief nicht den Stern an und folgt jenem Blatt, das vorausschwebt.
›O Halm‹, vermeint er zu hören, ›o Blume der Zeit‹.

Sobbed out in empty tents is the wonder,
iced over the little jar of dreams—what does it do?

Remember: a blackening leaf hung in the elder—
the alluring sign for the beaker of blood.

For naught you draw hearts on the window:
The Duke of Stillness
recruits soldiers in the castle courtyard.
He hoists his banner in the tree—a leaf that blues for him when it autumns;
he shares the stalks of melancholy among the host and the flowers of time;
with birds in the hair he goes forth to bury the swords.

For naught you draw hearts on the window: there's a God among the hosts,
wrapped in the coat that once sank from your shoulders on the staircase, at night time,
once, when the castle stood in flames, when you spoke like the humans: Beloved . . .
He knows not the coat and didn't call the star and follows the leaf that floats ahead.
"O stalk," he thinks he hears, "O flower of time."

MARIANNE

Fliederlos ist dein Haar, dein Antlitz aus Spiegelglas.
Von Auge zu Aug zieht die Wolke, wie Sodom nach Babel:
wie Blattwerk zerpflückt sie den Turm und tobt um das
Schwefelgesträuch.

Dann zuckt dir ein Blitz um den Mund – jene Schlucht mit den
Resten der Geige.
Mit schneeigen Zähnen führt einer den Bogen: O schöner tönte das
Schilf!

Geliebte, auch du bist das Schilf und wir alle der Regen;
ein Wein ohnegleichen dein Leib, und wir bechern zu zehnt;
ein Kahn im Getreide dein Herz, wir rudern ihn nachtwärts;
ein Krüglein Bläue, so hüpfest du leicht über uns, und wir schlafen . . .

Vorm Zelt zieht die Hundertschaft auf, und wir tragen dich zechend
zu Grabe.
Nun klingt auf den Fliesen der Welt der harte Taler der Träume.

TALGLICHT

Die Mönche mit haarigen Fingern schlugen das Buch auf: September.
Jason wirft nun mit Schnee nach der aufgegangenen Saat.
Ein Halsband aus Händen gab dir der Wald, so schreitest du tot übers
Seil.
Ein dunkleres Blau wird zuteil deinem Haar, und ich rede von Liebe.
Muscheln red ich und leichtes Gewölk, und ein Boot knospt im Regen.
Ein kleiner Hengst jagt über die blätternden Finger –

MARIANNE

Your hair lacks lilacs, your face is mirror-glass.
From eye to eye the cloud drifts, like Sodom toward Babel:
like leafage it shreds the tower and rages around the sulfur-bush.

Then lightning flickers at your mouth—that ravine with the violin's remnants.
With snowy teeth someone guides the bow: oh the sedge sounded finer!

Beloved, you too are the sedge and we all, the rain;
your body a wine sans pareil, and we're ten who imbibe;
a boat in the grains of your heart, we row it nightward;
a little jug of blueness, so you hop over us lightly, and we sleep . . .

Before the tent the hundred pull up, and carousing we carry you to the grave.
Now the hard thaler of dreams resounds on the flagstones of the world.

TALLOWLIGHT

The monks with hairy fingers laid open the book: September.
Jason now throws snow at the sprouting seed.
A necklace of hands the forest gave you, so dead you walk the rope.
A darker blue becomes part of your hair, and I speak of love.
Shells I speak and light clouds, and a boat buds in the rain.
A little stallion gallops over the leaf-turning fingers—

Schwarz springt das Tor auf, ich singe:
Wie lebten wir hier?

DIE HAND voller Stunden, so kamst du zu mir – ich sprach:
Dein Haar ist nicht braun.
So hobst du es leicht auf die Waage des Leids, da war es schwerer als ich . . .

Sie kommen auf Schiffen zu dir und laden es auf, sie bieten es feil auf den Märkten der Lust –
Du lächelst zu mir aus der Tiefe, ich weine zu dir aus der Schale, die leicht bleibt.
Ich weine: Dein Haar ist nicht braun, sie bieten das Wasser der See, und du gibst ihnen Locken . . .
Du flüsterst: Sie füllen die Welt schon mit mir, und ich bleib dir ein Hohlweg im Herzen!
Du sagst: Leg das Blattwerk der Jahre zu dir – es ist Zeit, da du kommst und mich küssest!

Das Blattwerk der Jahre ist braun, dein Haar ist es nicht.

HALBE NACHT

Halbe Nacht. Mit den Dolchen des Traumes geheftet in sprühende Augen.
Schrei nicht vor Schmerz: wie Tücher flattern die Wolken.
Ein seidener Teppich, so ward sie gespannt zwischen uns, daß getanzt sei von Dunkel zu Dunkel.

Black the gate leaps open, I sing:
How did we live here?

THE HAND full of hours, so did you come to me—I said:
Your hair is not brown.
So you lifted it easily onto the scales of grief; there it lay, heavier than I . . .

They come to you on ships loaded down with it, they put it up for sale on the markets of lust —
You smile at me from the depths, I weep toward you from the scale that stays light.
I weep: Your hair is not brown, they offer the water of the sea, and you give them locks of hair . . .
You whisper: They do fill the world with me now, and for you I remain a narrow pass through the heart!
You say: Treat yourself to the foliage of the years—it's time you came closer and kissed me!

The foliage of the years is brown, your hair is not.

HALF NIGHT

Half night. With the daggers of the dream fixed in the spitting eyes.
Don't scream from pain: the clouds flutter like towels.
Like a silken rug it was stretched between us, so that there be dancing from darkness to darkness.

Die schwarze Flöte schnitzten sie uns aus lebendigem Holz, und die
Tänzerin kommt nun.
Aus Meerschaum gesponnene Finger taucht sie ins Aug uns:
eines will hier noch weinen?
Keines. So wirbelt sie selig dahin, und die feurige Pauke wird laut.
Ringe wirft sie uns zu, wir fangen sie auf mit den Dolchen.
Vermählt sie uns so? Wie Scherben erklingts, und ich weiß es nun
wieder:
du starbst nicht
den malvenfarbenen Tod.

DEIN HAAR ÜBERM MEER

Es schwebt auch dein Haar überm Meer mit dem goldnen
Wacholder.
Mit ihm wird es weiß, dann färb ich es steinblau:
die Farbe der Stadt, wo zuletzt ich geschleift ward gen Süden . . .
Mit Tauen banden sie mich und knüpften an jedes ein Segel
und spieen mich an aus nebligen Mäulern und sangen:
›O komm übers Meer!‹
Ich aber malt als ein Kahn die Schwingen mir purpurn
und röchelte selbst mir die Brise und stach, eh sie schliefen, in See.
Ich sollte sie rot dir nun färben, die Locken, doch lieb ich sie
steinblau:
O Augen der Stadt, wo ich stürzte und südwärts geschleift ward!
Mit dem goldnen Wacholder schwebt auch dein Haar überm Meer.

They carve for us a black flute from living wood, and now the dancer comes.
Fingers spun from spume she dips into our eye:
would one eye still want to weep?
None. So she blissfully whirls around, and the fiery drum resounds.
Rings she throws at us, we catch them with our daggers.
Is that how she weds us? It sounds like shards, and I know it once again:
you did not die
the mallow-colored death.

YOUR HAIR OVER THE SEA

Your hair too hovers above the sea with the golden juniper.
With it, it turns white, then I dye it stone-blue:
the color of the city where last I was dragged to the south . . .
With ropes they bound me and tied a sail to each one
and spat upon me from foggy mouths and sang:
"O come over the sea!"
But I as a pinnace paint the wings purple
and rattled the breeze to myself and, ere they slept, put to sea.
I was to dye them red, your locks, but loved them stone-blue:
O eyes of the city, where I fell and was dragged southward!
With the golden juniper your hair too hovers above the sea.

Espenbaum, dein Laub blickt weiß ins Dunkel.
Meiner Mutter Haar ward nimmer weiß.

Löwenzahn, so grün ist die Ukraine.
Meine blonde Mutter kam nicht heim.

Regenwolke, säumst du an den Brunnen?
Meine leise Mutter weint für alle.

Runder Stern, du schlingst die goldne Schleife.
Meiner Mutter Herz ward wund von Blei.

Eichne Tür, wer hob dich aus den Angeln?
Meine sanfte Mutter kann nicht kommen.

ASCHENKRAUT

Zugvogel Speer, die Mauer ist längst überflogen,
der Ast überm Herzen schon weiß und das Meer über uns,
der Hügel der Tiefe umlaubt von den Sternen des Mittags –
ein giftleeres Grün wie des Augs, das sie aufschlug im Tode . . .

Wir höhlten die Hände zu schöpfen den sickernden Sturzbach:
das Wasser der Stätte, wo's dunkelt und keinem gereicht wird der
Dolch.
Du sangst auch ein Lied, und wir flochten ein Gitter im Nebel:
vielleicht, daß ein Henker noch kommt und uns wieder ein Herz
schlägt;

ASPEN TREE, your leaves gaze white into the dark.
My mother's hair ne'er turned white.

Dandelion, so green is the Ukraine.
My fair-haired mother did not come home.

Rain cloud, do you dally by the well?
My quiet mother weeps for all.

Round star, you coil the golden loop.
My mother's heart was seared by lead.

Oaken door, who ripped you off your hinges?
My gentle mother cannot return.

CINERARIA

Migrant bird spear, the wall flown over long ago,
the branch above the heart white already and the sea above us,
the hill of the depth enleafed by the stars of noonday—
a poison-empty Green like that of the eye she opened in death . . .

We hollowed the hands to scoop the oozy torrent:
the water of the places where it's dark and the dagger is handed
to no one. You sang a song too, and we wove a lattice in fog:
maybe a hangman will still come and make our heart beat again;

vielleicht, daß ein Turm sich noch wälzt über uns, und ein Galgen wird
johlend errichtet;
vielleicht, daß ein Bart uns entstellt und ihr Blondhaar sich rötet . . .

Der Ast überm Herzen ist weiß schon, das Meer über uns.

DAS GEHEIMNIS DER FARNE

Im Gewölbe der Schwerter besieht sich der Schatten laubgrünes Herz.
Blank sind die Klingen: wer säumte im Tod nicht vor Spiegeln?
Auch wird hier in Krügen kredenzt die lebendige Schwermut:
blumig finstert sie hoch, eh sie trinken, als wär sie nicht Wasser,
als wär sie ein Tausendschön hier, das befragt wird nach dunklerer
Liebe,
nach schwärzerem Pfühl für das Lager, nach schwererem Haar . . .

Hier aber wird nur gebangt um den Schimmer des Eisens,
und leuchtet ein Ding hier noch auf, so sei es ein Schwert.
Wir leeren den Krug nur vom Tisch, weil uns Spiegel bewirten:
einer springe entzwei, wo wir grün sind wie Laub!

DER SAND AUS DEN URNEN

Schimmelgrün ist das Haus des Vergessens.
Vor jedem der wehenden Tore blaut dein enthaupteter Spielmann.
Er schlägt dir die Trommel aus Moos und bitterem Schamhaar;
mit schwärender Zehe malt er im Sand deine Braue.

maybe a tower will roll over us still, and a gallows will raise the roof;
maybe a beard will disfigure us and her fair hair turn red . . .

The branch over the heart is white already, the sea over us.

THE SECRET OF THE FERNS

In the vault of swords the shadows' leafgreen heart gazes at itself.
Naked are the blades: who in death wouldn't linger before mirrors?
Here too live melancholia's served up in jars:
flowery it darkens upward before they drink, as if it were not water,
as if it were a daisy here, queried for a darker love,
for a blacker pillow for the bunk, for heavier hair . . .

But here there's dread only for the shimmer of the iron,
and if anything still shines here, let it be a sword.
We empty the jar from the table only because mirrors host us:
let one of them split in twain where we're green as the leaves.

THE SAND FROM THE URNS

Moldgreen is the house of forgetting.
Before each of the blowing gates your beheaded minstrel blues.
For you he beats the drum made of moss and bitter pubic hair;
with festering toe he draws your brow in the sand.

Länger zeichnet er sie als sie war, und das Rot deiner Lippe.
Du füllst hier die Urnen und speisest dein Herz.

DIE LETZTE FAHNE

Ein wasserfarbenes Wild wird gejagt in den dämmernden Marken.
So binde die Maske dir vor und färbe die Wimpern dir grün.
Die Schüssel mit schlummerndem Schrot wird gereicht über
Ebenholztische:
von Frühling zu Frühling schäumt hier der Wein, so kurz ist das Jahr,
so feurig der Preis dieser Schützen – die Rose der Fremde:
dein irrender Bart, die müßige Fahne des Baumstumpfs.

Gewölk und Gebell! Sie reiten den Wahn in den Farn!
Wie Fischer werfen sie Netze nach Irrlicht und Hauch!
Sie schlingen ein Seil um die Kronen und laden zum Tanz!
Und waschen die Hörner im Quell – so lernen sie Lockruf.

Ist dicht, was du wähltest als Mantel, und birgt es den Schimmer?
Sie schleichen wie Schlaf um die Stämme, als böten sie Traum.
Die Herzen schleudern sie hoch, die moosigen Bälle des Wahnsinns:
o wasserfarbenes Vlies, unser Banner am Turm!

EIN KNIRSCHEN von eisernen Schuhn ist im Kirschbaum.
Aus Helmen schäumt dir der Sommer. Der schwärzliche Kuckuck
malt mit demantenem Sporn sein Bild an die Tore des Himmels.

Longer he draws it than it was, and the red of your lip.
You fill up the urns here and nourish your heart.

THE LAST FLAG

A water-colored quarry is hunted in the dusking Marches.
So tie on the face mask and dye your eyelashes green.
The dish with dozing shot is proferred over ebony tables:
wine foams here from spring to spring, so short is the year,
so fiery the prize of these sharpshooters—the rose of the unknown:
your erring beard, the tree stump's idle flag.

Cloud-billows and baying! They're riding delusion into the ferns!
Like fishermen they cast nets after will-o'-the-wisp and thin air!
They sling a rope around the crowns and invite to the dance!
And wash the horns in the spring—thus they learn lure-calls.

Is what you choose as coat leak-proof and does it salvage the
radiance?
They slink like sleep around the trunks, as though offering dream.
The hearts they fling up high, the mossy balls of madness:
O water-colored fleece, our own banner on the tower.

A CRUNCHING of iron shoes there is in the cherry tree.
Out of helmets summer foams up for you. The blackish cuckoo
with diamantine spur draws his image on the gates of the sky.

Barhaupt ragt aus dem Blattwerk der Reiter.
Im Schild trägt er dämmernd dein Lächeln,
genagelt ans stählerne Schweißtuch des Feindes.
Es ward ihm verheißen der Garten der Träumer,
und Speere hält er bereit, daß die Rose sich ranke . . .

Unbeschuht aber kommt durch die Luft, der am meisten dir gleichet:
eiserne Schuhe geschnallt an die schmächtigen Hände,
verschläft er die Schlacht und den Sommer. Die Kirsche blutet für ihn.

DAS GASTMAHL

Geleert sei die Nacht aus den Flaschen im hohen Gebälk der
Versuchung,
die Schwelle mit Zähnen gepflügt, vor Morgen der Jähzorn gesät:
es schießt wohl empor uns ein Moos noch, eh von der Mühle sie hier
sind,
ein leises Getreide zu finden bei uns ihrem langsamen Rad . . .

Unter den giftigen Himmeln sind andere Halme wohl falber,
wird anders der Traum noch gemünzt als hier, wo wir würfeln um Lust,
als hier, wo getauscht wird im Dunkel Vergessen und Wunder,
wo alles nur gilt eine Stunde und schwelgend bespien wird von uns,
ins gierige Wasser der Fenster geschleudert in leuchtenden Truhen –:
es birst auf der Straße der Menschen, den Wolken zum Ruhm!

So hüllet euch denn in die Mäntel und steiget mit mir auf die Tische:
wie anders sei noch geschlafen als stehend, inmitten der Kelche?
Wem trinken wir Träume noch zu, als dem langsamen Rad?

Bareheaded the rider towers above the foliage.
On his shield he bears your dusking smile
nailed to the enemy's steel sweatband.
He was promised the garden of the dreamers,
and spears he holds at the ready, that the rose may ramble . . .

But shoeless through the air comes he who resembles you most:
iron shoes strapped to frail hands,
he sleeps through the battle and summer. The cherry bleeds for him.

THE BANQUET

Drained be the night from the flasks in temptation's high rafters,
the threshold be ploughed with teeth, before dawn choler be sowed:
a moss may yet shoot up for us, before they'll arrive from the mill
to find a quiet grain among us, their slow wheel . . .

Under the poisonous skies there lie other, likely fallower, stalks,
there the dream is coined different than here where we throw dice
  for pleasure,
than here, where in darkness oblivion and wonder are traded,
where all's valid but for an hour and is spat at by us in our revels,
hurled into the windows's avid water in luminous coffers—:
it bursts on the pavement of humans, for the glory of clouds!

Now wrap yourselves in your coats and climb on the tables with me:
how else to sleep now except standing up, amidst the chalices?
To whom shall we still drink our dreams, if not to the slow wheel?

DUNKLES AUG IM SEPTEMBER

Steinhaube Zeit. Und üppiger quellen
die Locken des Schmerzes ums Antlitz der Erde,
den trunkenen Apfel, gebräunt von dem Hauch
eines sündigen Spruches: schön und abhold dem Spiel,
das sie treiben im argen
Widerschein ihrer Zukunft.

Zum zweitenmal blüht die Kastanie:
ein Zeichen der ärmlich entbrannten
Hoffnung auf Orions
baldige Rückkunft: der blinden
Freunde des Himmels sternklare Inbrunst
ruft ihn herauf.

Unverhüllt an den Toren des Traumes
streitet ein einsames Aug.
Was täglich geschieht,
genügt ihm zu wissen:
am östlichen Fenster
erscheint ihm zur Nachtzeit die schmale
Wandergestalt des Gefühls.

Ins Naß ihres Auges tauchst du das Schwert.

DER STEIN AUS DEM MEER

Das weiße Herz unsrer Welt, gewaltlos verloren wirs heut um die
Stunde des gilbenden Maisblatts:

DARK EYE IN SEPTEMBER

Stonehood Time. And lusher do
the locks of pain well up around earth's face,
the drunk apple, browned by the breath
of a sinful saying: fair and averse to the game
they play in the baleful
afterglow of their future.

A second time the chestnut blooms:
a sign of the poorly enkindled
hope for Orion's
quick return: the star-clear
fervor of heaven's blind friends
calls him near.

Unconcealed at the gates of the dream
a lonely eye contends.
What happens daily
is all it needs to know:
at the eastern window
nomad-figure of feeling.

Into the wet of its eye you dip your sword.

THE STONE FROM THE SEA

The white heart of our world, without violence did we lose it today
at the hour of the yellowing corn leaf:

ein runder Knäuel, so rollt' es uns leicht aus den Händen.
So blieb uns zu spinnen die neue, die rötliche Wolle des Schlafs an der sandigen Grabstatt des Traumes:
ein Herz nicht mehr, doch das Haupthaar wohl des Steins aus der Tiefe,
der ärmliche Schmuck seiner Stirn, die sinnt über Muschel und Welle.

Vielleicht, daß am Tor jener Stadt in der Luft ihn erhöhet ein nächtlicher Wille,
sein östliches Aug ihm erschließt überm Haus, wo wir liegen,
die Schwärze des Meers um den Mund und die Tulpen aus Holland im Haar.
Sie tragen ihm Lanzen voran, so trugen wir Traum, so entrollt' uns das weiße
Herz unsrer Welt. So ward ihm das krause
Gespinst um sein Haupt: eine seltsame Wolle,
an Herzens Statt schön.

O Pochen, das kam und das schwand! Im Endlichen wehen die Schleier.

ERINNERUNG AN FRANKREICH

Du denk mit mir: der Himmel von Paris, die große Herbstzeitlose . . .
Wir kauften Herzen bei den Blumenmädchen:
sie waren blau und blühten auf im Wasser.
Es fing zu regnen an in unserer Stube,
und unser Nachbar kam, Monsieur Le Songe, ein hager Männlein.
Wir spielten Karten, ich verlor die Augensterne;
du liehst dein Haar mir, ich verlors, er schlug uns nieder.

a round tangle, so it rolls easily from our hands.
What remains for us is to spin the new, the reddish wool of sleep at
the sandy burial site of the dream:
a heart no longer, though still the mane of the stone from the depth,
the meager ornament of its forehead, that thinks on mussel and
wave.

Maybe, so that at the gate of that city in midair a nightly will will
raise it,
opening its eastern eye above the house where we lie,
the blackness of the sea around our mouths and the tulips from
Holland in our hair.
They carry lances ahead, as we carried dream, as the white heart
of our world rolls from our hands. Thus the curly
gossamer around its head: a strange wool,
beautiful instead of a heart.

O knocking, it came and it left! In finitude, the veils wave.

REMEMBRANCE OF FRANCE

You, think with me: the sky of Paris, the great autumn crocus . . .
We bought hearts from the flower girls:
they were blue and blossomed in the water.
It started to rain in our room,
and our neighbor came, Monsieur le Songe, a thin little man.
We played cards, I lost the pupils of my eyes;
you lent me your hair, I lost it, he struck us down.

Er trat zur Tür hinaus, der Regen folgt' ihm.
Wir waren tot und konnten atmen.

CHANSON EINER DAME IM SCHATTEN

Wenn die Schweigsame kommt und die Tulpen köpft:
Wer gewinnt?
          Wer verliert?
                    Wer tritt an das Fenster?
Wer nennt ihren Namen zuerst?

Es ist einer, der trägt mein Haar.
Er trägts wie man Tote trägt auf den Händen.
Er trägts wie der Himmel mein Haar trug im Jahr, da ich liebte.
Er trägt es aus Eitelkeit so.

Der gewinnt.
          Der verliert nicht.
                    Der tritt nicht ans Fenster.
Der nennt ihren Namen nicht.

Es ist einer, der hat meine Augen.
Er hat sie, seit Tore sich schließen.
Er trägt sie am Finger wie Ringe.
Er trägt sie wie Scherben von Lust und Saphir:
er war schon mein Bruder im Herbst;
er zählt schon die Tage und Nächte.

He left by the door, the rain followed him.
We were dead and could breathe.

CHANSON OF A LADY IN THE SHADOWS

When Lady Taciturn comes and beheads the tulips:
Who wins?
          Who loses?
                    Who goes to the window?
Who says her name first?

There is someone who wears my hair.
He wears it as one wears the dead on one's hands.
He wears it as heaven wore my hair in the year when I loved.
He wears it that way out of vanity.

He's the one who wins.
          He doesn't lose.
                    He doesn't go to the window.
He does not say her name.

There is someone who has my eyes.
He has them ever since the gates closed.
He wears them on his fingers like rings.
He wears them like shards of lust and sapphire:
he was my brother in autumn already;
he's already counting the days and the nights.

Der gewinnt.
            Der verliert nicht.
                        Der tritt nicht ans Fenster.
Der nennt ihren Namen zuletzt.

Es ist einer, der hat, was ich sagte.
Er trägts unterm Arm wie ein Bündel.
Er trägts wie die Uhr ihre schlechteste Stunde.
Er trägt es von Schwelle zu Schwelle, er wirft es nicht fort.

Der gewinnt nicht.
            Der verliert.
                        Der tritt an das Fenster.
Der nennt ihren Namen zuerst.

Der wird mit den Tulpen geköpft.

NACHTSTRAHL

Am lichtesten brannte das Haar meiner Abendgeliebten:
ihr schick ich den Sarg aus dem leichtesten Holz.
Er ist wellenumwogt wie das Bett unsrer Träume in Rom;
er trägt eine weiße Perücke wie ich und spricht heiser:
er redet wie ich, wenn ich Einlaß gewähre den Herzen.
Er weiß ein französisches Lied von der Liebe, das sang ich im
    Herbst,
als ich weilte auf Reisen in Spätland und Briefe schrieb an den
    Morgen.

He's the one who wins.
He doesn't lose.
He doesn't go to the window.
He is the last to say her name.

There is someone who has what I said.
He wears it under his arm like a bundle.
He wears it like the watch wears its worst hour.
He wears it from threshold to threshold, he does not throw it out.

He does not win.
He loses.
He goes to the window.
He is the first to say her name.

He is beheaded with the tulips.

NIGHTBEAM

The hair of my evening beloved burned most brightly:
to her I sent the coffin made of the lightest wood.
It is swayed by waves like the bed of our dreams in Rome;
it wears a white wig like I and speaks hoarsely:
it talks like I do when I grant entry to hearts.
It knows a French song about love, I sang it in autumn,
when I tarried on journeys in Lateland and wrote letters to morning.

Ein schöner Kahn ist der Sarg, geschnitzt im Gehölz der Gefühle.
Auch ich fuhr blutabwärts mit ihm, als ich jünger war als dein Aug.
Nun bist du jung wie ein toter Vogel im Märzschnee,
nun kommt er zu dir und singt sein französisches Lied.
Ihr seid leicht: ihr schlaft meinen Frühling zu Ende.
Ich bin leichter:
ich singe vor Fremden.

DIE JAHRE VON DIR ZU MIR

Wieder wellt sich dein Haar, wenn ich wein. Mit dem Blau deiner
Augen
deckst du den Tisch unsrer Liebe: ein Bett zwischen Sommer und
Herbst.
Wir trinken, was einer gebraut, der nicht ich war, noch du, noch ein
dritter:
wir schlürfen ein Leeres und Letztes.

Wir sehen uns zu in den Spiegeln der Tiefsee und reichen uns
rascher die Speisen:
die Nacht ist die Nacht, sie beginnt mit dem Morgen,
sie legt mich zu dir.

LOB DER FERNE

Im Quell deiner Augen
leben die Garne der Fischer der Irrsee.

A gorgeous skiff is that coffin, carved from the timber of emotions.
I too sailed it downbloodstream, when I was younger than your eye.
Now you are as young as a dead bird in March snow,
now it comes to you and sings its French song.
You are light: you sleep my spring to its end.
I am lighter:
I sing before strangers.

THE YEARS FROM YOU TO ME

Your hair waves again when I weep. With the blue of your eyes
you set the table of our love: a bed between summer and autumn.
We drink what someone brewed, who was neither I, nor you, nor a
third:
we lap up an emptiness and a vastness.

We see ourselves in the mirrors of the deepsea and hand ourselves
the dishes faster:
the night is the night: it begins with the morning,
it lays me down next to you.

IN PRAISE OF DISTANCE

In the springs of your eyes
live the delirious sea's fishermen's nets.

Im Quell deiner Augen
hält das Meer sein Versprechen.

Hier werf ich,
ein Herz, das geweilt unter Menschen,
die Kleider von mir und den Glanz eines Schwures:

Schwärzer im Schwarz, bin ich nackter.
Abtrünnig erst bin ich treu.
Ich bin du, wenn ich ich bin.

Im Quell deiner Augen
treib ich und träume von Raub.

Ein Garn fing ein Garn ein:
wir scheiden umschlungen.

Im Quell deiner Augen
erwürgt ein Gehenkter den Strang.

DAS GANZE LEBEN

Die Sonnen des Halbschlafs sind blau wie dein Haar eine Stunde
vor Morgen.
Auch sie wachsen rasch wie das Gras überm Grab eines Vogels.
Auch sie lockt das Spiel, das wir spielten als Traum auf den Schiffen
der Lust.
Am Kreidefelsen der Zeit begegnen auch ihnen die Dolche.

In the springs of your eyes
the sea keeps its promise.

Here I, a heart
that dwelled among humans, throw
off my clothes and the luster of an oath:

Blacker in black, I am more naked.
Only as a renegade am I faithful.
I am you when I am I.

In the springs of your eyes
I drift and dream of plunder.

A net snared a net:
embracing, we separate.

In the springs of your eyes
a hanged man strangles the rope.

THE WHOLE LIFE

The suns of half sleep are blue like your hair an hour before dawn.
They too grow fast like the grass over the grave of a bird.
They too are tempted by the game we played as a dream on the ships
of desire.
At the chalk cliffs of time they too are met by the daggers.

Die Sonnen des Tiefschlafs sind blauer: so war deine Locke nur
einmal:
Ich weilt als ein Nachtwind im käuflichen Schoß deiner Schwester;
dein Haar hing im Baum über uns, doch warst du nicht da.
Wir waren die Welt, und du warst ein Gesträuch vor den Toren.

Die Sonnen des Todes sind weiß wie das Haar unsres Kindes:
es stieg aus der Flut, als du aufschlugst ein Zelt auf der Düne.
Es zückte das Messer des Glücks über uns mit erloschenen Augen.

SPÄT UND TIEF

Boshaft wie goldene Rede beginnt diese Nacht.
Wir essen die Äpfel der Stummen.
Wir tuen ein Werk, das man gern seinem Stern überläßt;
wir stehen im Herbst unsrer Linden als sinnendes Fahnenrot,
als brennende Gäste vom Süden.
Wir schwören bei Christus dem Neuen, den Staub zu vermählen
dem Staube,
die Vögel dem wandernden Schuh,
unser Herz einer Stiege im Wasser.
Wir schwören der Welt die heiligen Schwüre des Sandes,
wir schwören sie gern,
wir schwören sie laut von den Dächern des traumlosen Schlafes
und schwenken das Weißhaar der Zeit . . .

Sie rufen: Ihr lästert!

Wir wissen es längst.
Wir wissen es längst, doch was tuts?

The suns of deep sleep are bluer: your lock was such only once:
I sojourned as a nightwind in the venal lap of your sister;
your hair hung in the tree above us, but you were not there.
We were the world, and you were a shrub at the gates.

The suns of death are white like the hair of our child:
it stepped forth from the flood when you pitched a tent on the dune.
It wielded the knife of happiness above us with extinguished eyes.

LATE AND DEEP

Spiteful like golden speech this night begins.
We eat the apples of the mute.
We are doing a job one prefers to leave to one's star;
we stand in the autumn of our linden as a flag's pensive red,
as burning guests from the south.
We swear upon Christ the New to marry dust to dust,
the birds to the wandering shoe,
our heart to a stair in the water.
We swear to the world the holy oaths of the sand,
we swear them easily,
we swear them loudly from the rooftops of dreamless sleep
and wave the white mane of time . . .

They yell: You blaspheme!

We've known it all along.
We've known it all along, but so what?

Ihr mahlt in den Mühlen des Todes das weiße Mehl der Verheißung,
ihr setzet es vor unsern Brüdern und Schwestern –

Wir schwenken das Weißhaar der Zeit.

Ihr mahnt uns: Ihr lästert!
Wir wissen es wohl,
es komme die Schuld über uns.
Es komme die Schuld über uns aller warnenden Zeichen,
es komme das gurgelnde Meer,
der geharnischte Windstoß der Umkehr,
der mitternächtige Tag,
es komme, was niemals noch war!

Es komme ein Mensch aus dem Grabe.

CORONA

Aus der Hand frißt der Herbst mir sein Blatt: wir sind Freunde.
Wir schälen die Zeit aus den Nüssen und lehren sie gehn:
die Zeit kehrt zurück in die Schale.

Im Spiegel ist Sonntag,
im Traum wird geschlafen,
der Mund redet wahr.

Mein Aug steigt hinab zum Geschlecht der Geliebten:
wir sehen uns an,
wir sagen uns Dunkles,

You grind in the mills of death the white meal of the Promise,
you set it before our brothers and sisters—

We wave the white mane of time.

You caution us: You blaspheme!
We know it well,
let guilt come down on us.
Let guilt come down on us all our forewarning signs,
let the gurgling sea come,
the armored gust of the wind of a turning
the midnight day,
let come what never yet was!

Let a man come forth from the grave.

CORONA

Autumn eats its leaf out of my hand: we are friends.
We shell time from the nuts and teach it to walk:
time returns to the shell.

In the mirror is Sunday,
in the dream we sleep,
the mouth speaks true.

My eye goes down to my lover's sex:
we gaze at each other,
we speak of dark things,

wir lieben einander wie Mohn und Gedächtnis,
wir schlafen wie Wein in den Muscheln,
wie das Meer im Blutstrahl des Mondes.

Wir stehen umschlungen im Fenster, sie sehen uns zu von der Straße:
es ist Zeit, daß man weiß!
Es ist Zeit, daß der Stein sich zu blühen bequemt,
daß der Unrast ein Herz schlägt.
Es ist Zeit, daß es Zeit wird.

Es ist Zeit.

we love each other like poppy and memory,
we sleep like wine in the seashells,
like the sea in the moon's blood-beam.

We stand and embrace at the window, they watch us from the street:
it is time, for this to be known!
It is time that the stone took the trouble to bloom,
that unrest's heart started to beat.
It's time for it to be time.

It is time.

Todesfuge

Deathfugue

Schwarze Milch der Frühe wir trinken sie abends
wir trinken sie mittags und morgens wir trinken sie nachts
wir trinken und trinken
wir schaufeln ein Grab in den Lüften da liegt man nicht eng
Ein Mann wohnt im Haus der spielt mit den Schlangen der schreibt
der schreibt wenn es dunkelt nach Deutschland dein goldenes Haar
  Margarete
er schreibt es und tritt vor das Haus und es blitzen die Sterne er
  pfeift seine Rüden herbei
er pfeift seine Juden hervor läßt schaufeln ein Grab in der Erde
er befiehlt uns spielt auf nun zum Tanz

Schwarze Milch der Frühe wir trinken dich nachts
wir trinken dich morgens und mittags wir trinken dich abends
wir trinken und trinken
Ein Mann wohnt im Haus der spielt mit den Schlangen der schreibt
der schreibt wenn es dunkelt nach Deutschland dein goldenes Haar
  Margarete
Dein aschenes Haar Sulamith wir schaufeln ein Grab in den Lüften
  da liegt man nicht eng

Er ruft stecht tiefer ins Erdreich ihr einen ihr andern singet und spielt
er greift nach dem Eisen im Gurt er schwingts seine Augen sind blau
stecht tiefer die Spaten ihr einen ihr andern spielt weiter zum Tanz
  auf

Schwarze Milch der Frühe wir trinken dich nachts
wir trinken dich mittags und morgens wir trinken dich abends
wir trinken und trinken
ein Mann wohnt im Haus dein goldenes Haar Margarete
dein aschenes Haar Sulamith er spielt mit den Schlangen

Black milk of morning we drink you evenings
we drink you at noon and mornings we drink you at night
we drink and we drink
we dig a grave in the air there one lies at ease
A man lives in the house he plays with the snakes he writes
he writes when it darkens to Deutschland your golden hair Margarete
he writes and steps in front of his house and the stars glisten and he whistles his dogs to come
he whistles his jews to appear let a grave be dug in the earth
he commands us play up for the dance

Black milk of dawn we drink you at night
we drink you mornings and noontime we drink you evenings
we drink and we drink
A man lives in the house he plays with the snakes he writes
he writes when it turns dark to Deutschland your golden hair Margarete
Your ashen hair Shulamit we dig a grave in the air there one lies at ease

He calls out jab deeper into the earth you there and you other men sing and play
he grabs the gun in his belt he draws it his eyes are blue
jab deeper your spades you there and you other men continue to play for the dance

Black milk of dawn we drink you at night
we drink you at noon we drink you evenings
we drink you and drink
a man lives in the house your golden hair Margarete
your ashen hair Shulamit he plays with the snakes

Er ruft spielt süßer den Tod der Tod ist ein Meister aus
  Deutschland
er ruft streicht dunkler die Geigen dann steigt ihr als Rauch in die
  Luft
dann habt ihr ein Grab in den Wolken da liegt man nicht eng

Schwarze Milch der Frühe wir trinken dich nachts
wir trinken dich mittags der Tod ist ein Meister aus Deutschland
wir trinken dich abends und morgens wir trinken und trinken
der Tod ist ein Meister aus Deutschland sein Auge ist blau
er trifft dich mit bleierner Kugel er trifft dich genau
ein Mann wohnt im Haus dein goldenes Haar Margarete
er hetzt seine Rüden auf uns er schenkt uns ein Grab in der Luft
er spielt mit den Schlangen und träumet der Tod ist ein Meister aus
  Deutschland

dein goldenes Haar Margarete
dein aschenes Haar Sulamith

He calls out play death more sweetly death is a master from
Deutschland
he calls scrape those fiddles more darkly then as smoke you'll rise in
the air
then you'll have a grave in the clouds there you'll lie at ease

Black milk of dawn we drink you at night
we drink you at noon death is a master from Deutschland
we drink you evenings and mornings we drink and drink
death is a master from Deutschland his eye is blue
he strikes you with lead bullets his aim is true
a man lives in the house your golden hair Margarete
he sets his dogs on us he gifts us a grave in the air
he plays with the snakes and dreams death is a master from
Deutschland

your golden hair Margarete
your ashen hair Shulamit

Gegenlicht

Counterlight

AUF REISEN

Es ist eine Stunde, die macht dir den Staub zum Gefolge,
dein Haus in Paris zur Opferstatt deiner Hände,
dein schwarzes Aug zum schwärzesten Auge.

Es ist ein Gehöft, da hält ein Gespann für dein Herz.
Dein Haar möchte wehn, wenn du fährst – das ist ihm verboten.
Die bleiben und winken, wissen es nicht.

IN ÄGYPTEN

Du sollst zum Aug der Fremden sagen: Sei das Wasser.
Du sollst, die du im Wasser weißt, im Aug der Fremden suchen.
Du sollst sie rufen aus dem Wasser: Ruth! Noëmi! Mirjam!
Du sollst sie schmücken, wenn du bei der Fremden liegst.
Du sollst sie schmücken mit dem Wolkenhaar der Fremden.
Du sollst zu Ruth und Mirjam und Noëmi sagen:
Seht, ich schlaf bei ihr!
Du sollst die Fremde neben dir am schönsten schmücken.
Du sollst sie schmücken mit dem Schmerz um Ruth, um Mirjam und Noëmi.
Du sollst zur Fremden sagen:
Sieh, ich schlief bei diesen!

TRAVELING

There is an hour that makes dust your escort,
your house in Paris your hands' sacrificial altar,
your black eye the blackest eye.

There is a homestead where a team for your heart pulls up.
Your hair wants to waft when you ride—but that's forbidden.
Those who stay and wave don't know it.

IN EGYPT

You shall say to the eye of the stranger: Be the water.
You shall seek those you know to be in the water, in the stranger's
eye.
You shall call them forth from the water: Ruth! Naomi! Miriam!
You shall adorn them, when you lie with the stranger.
You shall adorn them with the stranger's cloudhair.
You shall tell Ruth and Miriam and Naomi:
See, I sleep with her!
You shall adorn the stranger next to you most beautifully.
You shall adorn her with the sorrow for Ruth, Miriam, and Naomi.
You shall tell the stranger:
See, I slept with these!

INS NEBELHORN

Mund im verborgenen Spiegel,
Knie vor der Säule des Hochmuts,
Hand mit dem Gitterstab:

reicht euch das Dunkel,
nennt meinen Namen,
führt mich vor ihn.

VOM BLAU, das noch sein Auge sucht, trink ich als erster.
Aus deiner Fußspur trink ich und ich seh:
du rollst mir durch die Finger, Perle, und du wächst!
Du wächst wie alle, die vergessen sind.
Du rollst: das schwarze Hagelkorn der Schwermut
fällt in ein Tuch, ganz weiß vom Abschiedwinken.

WER WIE DU und alle Tauben Tag und Abend aus dem Dunkel
    schöpft,
pickt den Stern aus meinen Augen, eh er funkelt,
reißt das Gras aus meinen Brauen, eh es weiß ist,
wirft die Tür zu in den Wolken, eh ich stürze.

Wer wie du und alle Nelken Blut als Münze braucht und Tod als Wein,
bläst das Glas für seinen Kelch aus meinen Händen,
färbt es mit dem Wort, das ich nicht sagte, rot,
schlägts in Stücke mit dem Stein der fernen Träne.

INTO THE FOGHORN

Mouth in the hidden mirror,
Knee before the column of pride,
Hand with the stanchion:

hand yourselves the darkness,
say my name,
lead me to him.

OF THE BLUE, that still seeks his eye, I'll be the first to drink.
From the trace of your foot I'll drink and I'll see:
you roll through my fingers, pearl, and you grow!
You grow like all who are forgotten.
You roll: melancholia's black hailstone
falls into a cloth, all white from waving goodbye.

WHO LIKE YOU and all doves scoops day and evening from the darkness,
picks the star from my eyes before it twinkles,
tears the grass from my eyebrows before it turns white,
slams the door shut in the clouds before I fall.

Who like you and all carnations needs blood as coin and death as wine,
blows the glass for its cup from my hands,
colors it red with the word I didn't say,
smashes it to pieces with the stone of the distant tear.

BRANDMAL

Wir schliefen nicht mehr, denn wir lagen im Uhrwerk der Schwermut
und bogen die Zeiger wie Ruten,
und sie schnellten zurück und peitschten die Zeit bis aufs Blut,
und du redetest wachsenden Dämmer,
und zwölfmal sagte ich du zur Nacht deiner Worte,
und sie tat sich auf und blieb offen,
und ich legt ihr ein Aug in den Schoß und flocht dir das andre ins Haar
und schlang zwischen beide die Zündschnur, die offene Ader –
und ein junger Blitz schwamm heran.

Wer sein Herz aus der Brust reißt zur Nacht, der langt nach der
Rose.
Sein ist ihr Blatt und ihr Dorn,
ihm legt sie das Licht auf den Teller,
ihm füllt sie die Gläser mit Hauch,
ihm rauschen die Schatten der Liebe.

Wer sein Herz aus der Brust reißt zur Nacht und schleudert es hoch:
der trifft nicht fehl,
der steinigt den Stein,
dem läutet das Blut aus der Uhr,
dem schlägt seine Stunde die Zeit aus der Hand:
er darf spielen mit schöneren Bällen
und reden von dir und von mir.

STIGMA

We slept no more, for we lay in melancholia's clockwork
and bent the hands like rods,
and they sprang back and whipped time and drew blood,
and you spoke a budding dusk,
and twelve times I said you to the night of your words,
and it opened and stayed ajar,
and I put one eye in its lap and braided the other into your hair
and looped the fuse between the two, the open vein —
and a young lightning bolt swam along.

HE WHO RIPS his heart from his breast at night, reaches for a rose.
His are its leaf and its thorn,
for him it lays its light on the plate,
for him it fills the glasses with breath,
for him whir the shadows of love.

He who rips his heart from his breast at night and hurls it upward:
he does not miss,
he stones the stone,
for him blood rings from the clock,
his hour knocks time out of his hand:
he may play with lovelier balls
and talk of you and of me.

KRISTALL

Nicht an meinen Lippen suche deinen Mund,
nicht vorm Tor den Fremdling,
nicht im Aug die Träne.

Sieben Nächte höher wandert Rot zu Rot,
sieben Herzen tiefer pocht die Hand ans Tor,
sieben Rosen später rauscht der Brunnen.

TOTENHEMD

Was du aus Leichtem wobst,
trag ich dem Stein zu Ehren.
Wenn ich im Dunkel die Schreie
wecke, weht es sie an.

Oft, wenn ich stammeln soll,
wirft es vergessene Falten,
und der ich bin, verzeiht
dem, der ich war.

Aber der Haldengott
rührt seine dumpfeste Trommel,
und wie die Falte fiel,
runzelt der Finstre die Stirn.

CRYSTAL

Not on my lips seek your mouth,
not outside the gate the stranger,
not in the eye the tear.

Seven nights higher, red wanders to red,
seven hearts lower, the hand knocks at the gate,
seven roses later, rustles the fountain.

SHROUD

What you of gossamer wove,
I wear in honor of stone.
When in the dark I wake the
screams, it wafts above them.

Often, when I should stammer,
it throws forgotten creases,
and who I am forgives
the one I was.

But the attleheapgod
beats his dullest drum,
and just as the crease runs,
the Dark One frowns.

AUF HOHER SEE

Paris, das Schifflein, liegt im Glas vor Anker:
so halt ich mit dir Tafel, trink dir zu.
Ich trink so lang, bis dir mein Herz erdunkelt,
so lange, bis Paris auf seiner Träne schwimmt,
so lange, bis es Kurs nimmt auf den fernen Schleier,
der uns die Welt verhüllt, wo jedes Du ein Ast ist,
an dem ich hänge als ein Blatt, das schweigt und schwebt.

ICH BIN ALLEIN, ich stell die Aschenblume
ins Glas voll reifer Schwärze. Schwestermund,
du sprichst ein Wort, das fortlebt vor den Fenstern,
und lautlos klettert, was ich träumt, an mir empor.

Ich steh im Flor der abgeblühten Stunde
und spar ein Harz für einen späten Vogel:
er trägt die Flocke Schnee auf lebensroter Feder;
das Körnchen Eis im Schnabel, kommt er durch den Sommer.

DIE KRÜGE

für Klaus Demus

An den langen Tischen der Zeit
zechen die Krüge Gottes.
Sie trinken die Augen der Sehenden leer und die Augen der
Blinden,
die Herzen der waltenden Schatten,
die hohle Wange des Abends.

ON THE HIGH SEAS

Paris, a tiny ship, lies at anchor in the glass:
and so I feast with you, drink to you.
I drink until my heart endarkens for you,
until Paris swims on its tear,
until it sets course for the distant veil
that shrouds the world for us, where every You is a branch,
from which I hang, a leaf, that in silence sways.

I AM ALONE, I put the ashflower
in the glass full of ripe blackness. Sistermouth,
you speak no word that survives before the windows,
and what I dreamed climbs soundlessly up on me.

I stand in the gauze-pile of the withered hour
and spare some pine sap for a late bird:
it carries the snowflake on a feather red as life;
a kernel of ice in the beak, it gets through summer.

THE JARS

for Klaus Demus

At the long tables of time
God's jars are boozing.
They drain the eyes of the seeing and the eyes of the blind,
the hearts of the governing shadows,
evening's hollow cheek.

Sie sind die gewaltigsten Zecher:
sie führen das Leere zum Mund wie das Volle
und schäumen nicht über wie du oder ich.

NACHTS, wenn das Pendel der Liebe schwingt
zwischen Immer und Nie,
stößt dein Wort zu den Monden des Herzens
und dein gewitterhaft blaues
Aug reicht der Erde den Himmel.

Aus fernem, aus traumgeschwärztem
Hain weht uns an das Verhauchte,
und das Versäumte geht um, groß wie die Schemen der Zukunft.

Was sich nun senkt und hebt,
gilt dem zuinnerst Vergrabnen:
blind wie der Blick, den wir tauschen,
küßt es die Zeit auf den Mund.

SO SCHLAFE, und mein Aug wird offen bleiben.
Der Regen füllt' den Krug, wir leerten ihn.
Es wird die Nacht ein Herz, das Herz ein Hälmlein treiben –
Doch ists zu spät zum Mähen, Schnitterin.

So schneeig weiß sind, Nachtwind, deine Haare!
Weiß, was mir bleibt, und weiß, was ich verlier!
Sie zählt die Stunden, und ich zähl die Jahre.
Wir tranken Regen. Regen tranken wir.

They are the mightiest boozers:
they raise to their lips the empty as well as the full
and don't brim over like you or I.

AT NIGHT, when the pendulum of love swings
between Always and Never,
your word accosts the moons of the heart
and your tempest-blue
eye hands heaven to the earth.

From afar, from a dream-blackened
grove the exhaled wafts about us,
and what's been neglected roams, large as future's outlines.

What now sinks and rises
is meant for what lies buried deep down:
blind like the gaze we exchange,
it kisses time on the mouth.

SO SLEEP, and my eye will remain open.
The rain filled the jar, we emptied it.
Night will grow a heart, the heart, a little stalk —
But it's too late to mow, reaperess.

So snow white is, nightwind, your hair!
White, what remains for me, white, what I lose!
She counts the hours, and I count the years.
We drank rain. Rain we drank.

So bist du denn geworden
wie ich dich nie gekannt:
dein Herz schlägt allerorten
in einem Brunnenland,

wo kein Mund trinkt und keine
Gestalt die Schatten säumt,
wo Wasser quillt zum Scheine
und Schein wie Wasser schäumt.

Du steigst in alle Brunnen,
du schwebst durch jeden Schein.
Du hast ein Spiel ersonnen,
das will vergessen sein.

DIE FESTE BURG

Ich weiß das abendlichste aller Häuser: ein
viel tiefres Aug als deines hält dort Ausschau.
Vom Giebel weht die große Kummerfahne:
ihr grünes Tuch – du weißt nicht, daß du's webtest.
Auch fliegts so hoch, als hättst nicht du's gewebt.
Das Wort, von dem du Abschied nahmst, heißt dich am Tor
willkommen,
und was dich hier gestreift hat, Halm und Herz und Blume,
ist längst dort Gast und streift dich nimmermehr.
Doch trittst in jenem Haus du vor den Spiegel,
so sehen drei, so sehen Blume, Herz und Halm dich an.
Und jenes tiefre Aug, es trinkt dein tiefes Auge.

So you have become
as I never knew you:
your heart beats everywhere
in a land of fountains,

where no mouth drinks and no
shape seams the shadows,
where water pretends to well
and presence like water foams.

You step into the fountains all,
you float through all pretense.
You have contrived a game
that wants to be forgotten.

THE MIGHTY FORTRESS

I know the most eveningly of all houses: an
eye much deeper than yours keeps lookout there.
From the gable the great sorrow-flag waves:
its green cloth—you don't know it's you who wove it.
And yet it flies so high as though it wasn't you who wove it.
The word from which you took leave welcomes you at the gate,
and what brushed against you here, stalk and heart and flower,
have long been guests there and will graze you never more.
But if in that house you face the mirror,
then the three, then flower, heart and stalk will gaze at you.
And that deeper eye, it drinks your deep eye.

Der Tauben weißeste flog auf: ich darf dich lieben!
Im leisen Fenster schwankt die leise Tür.
Der stille Baum trat in die stille Stube.
Du bist so nah, als weiltest du nicht hier.

Aus meiner Hand nimmst du die große Blume:
sie ist nicht weiß, nicht rot, nicht blau – doch nimmst du sie.
Wo sie nie war, da wird sie immer bleiben.
Wir waren nie, so bleiben wir bei ihr.

THE WHITEST OF DOVES took off: I may love you!
In the faint window sways the faint door.
The quiet tree stepped into the quiet parlor.
You're so near, as if you didn't dwell here.

From my hand you take the great flower:
It's neither white nor red nor blue—yet you take it.
Where it never was, there it will forever be.
We never were, so we will be with it.

Halme der Nacht

Night Stalks

SCHLAF UND SPEISE

Der Hauch der Nacht ist dein Laken, die Finsternis legt sich zu dir.
Sie rührt dir an Knöchel und Schläfe, sie weckt dich zu Leben und
Schlaf,
sie spürt dich im Wort auf, im Wunsch, im Gedanken,
sie schläft bei jedem von ihnen, sie lockt dich hervor.
Sie kämmt dir das Salz aus den Wimpern und tischt es dir auf,
sie lauscht deinen Stunden den Sand ab und setzt ihn dir vor.
Und was sie als Rose war, Schatten und Wasser,
schenkt sie dir ein.

DER REISEKAMERAD

Deiner Mutter Seele schwebt voraus.
Deiner Mutter Seele hilft die Nacht umschiffen, Riff um Riff.
Deiner Mutter Seele peitscht die Haie vor dir her.

Dieses Wort ist deiner Mutter Mündel.
Deiner Mutter Mündel teilt dein Lager, Stein um Stein.
Deiner Mutter Mündel bückt sich nach der Krume Lichts.

Augen:
schimmernd vom Regen, der strömte,
als Gott mir zu trinken befahl.

Augen:
Gold, das die Nacht in die Hände mir zählt',

SLEEP AND NOURISHMENT

Night's breath is your sheet, darkness lies down beside you.
It touches your ankle and temple, it wakes you to life and to sleep,
it tracks you in word, wish, and thought,
it sleeps with each one of these, it lures you out.
It combs the salt from your eyelashes and serves it up to you,
it listens for the sand in your hours and sets it in front of you.
And what it was as rose, shadow and water,
it pours for you.

THE TRAVELING COMPANION

Your mother's soul sails ahead.
Your mother's soul helps navigate the night, reef after reef.
Your mother's soul whips on the sharks before you.

This word is your mother's ward.
Your mother's ward shares your cot, stone by stone.
Your mother's ward bends down toward the crumb of light.

EYES:
shining from the rain streaming down
when God ordered me to drink.

Eyes:
gold, that night counted into my hands,

als ich Nesseln pflückt'
und die Schatten der Sprüche reutet'.

Augen:
Abend, der über mir aufglomm, als ich aufriß das Tor
und durchwintert vom Eis meiner Schläfen
durch die Weiler der Ewigkeit sprengt'.

DIE EWIGKEIT

Rinde des Nachtbaums, rostgeborene Messer
flüstern dir zu die Namen, die Zeit und die Herzen.
Ein Wort, das schlief, als wirs hörten,
schlüpft unters Laub:
beredt wird der Herbst sein,
beredter die Hand, die ihn aufliest,
frisch wie der Mohn des Vergessens der Mund, der sie küßt.

BRANDUNG

Du, Stunde, flügelst in den Dünen.

Die Zeit, aus feinem Sande, singt in meinen Armen:
ich lieg bei ihr, ein Messer in der Rechten.

So schäume, Welle! Fisch, trau dich hervor!
Wo Wasser ist, kann man noch einmal leben,

as I gathered nettles
and uprooted the sayings' shadows.

Eyes:
evening, that glowered above me as I tore open the gate
and, wintered through and through by my temples' ice,
hurtled through eternity's hamlets.

ETERNITY

Rind of the nighttree, rustborn knives
whisper the names, time, and hearts to you.
A word that slept, when we heard it,
slips under the foliage:
autumn will be eloquent,
more eloquent, the hand, that gathers it,
fresh like the poppy of forgetting, the mouth that kisses it.

BREAKERS

You, hour, you flutter in the dunes.

Time, made of fine sand, sings in my arms:
I lie next to it, a knife in my right hand.

Just foam, wave! Fish, dare come out!
Where there's water, one can live once more,

noch einmal mit dem Tod im Chor die Welt herübersingen,
noch einmal aus dem Hohlweg rufen: Seht,
wir sind geborgen,
seht, das Land war unser, seht,
wie wir dem Stern den Weg vertraten!

AUS HERZEN und Hirnen
sprießen die Halme der Nacht,
und ein Wort, von Sensen gesprochen,
neigt sie ins Leben.

Stumm wie sie
wehn wir der Welt entgegen:
unsere Blicke,
getauscht, um getröstet zu sein,
tasten sich vor,
winken uns dunkel heran.

Blicklos
schweigt nun dein Aug in mein Aug sich,
wandernd
heb ich dein Herz an die Lippen,
hebst du mein Herz an die deinen:
was wir jetzt trinken,
stillt den Durst der Stunden;
was wir jetzt sind,
schenken die Stunden der Zeit ein.

Munden wir ihr?
Kein Laut und kein Licht
schlüpft zwischen uns, es zu sagen.

once more in chorus with death to sing the world hither,
once more to call out from the defile: See,
we are salvaged,
see, the land was ours, see,
how we obstructed the star's path!

FROM HEARTS and brains
sprout the stalks of night,
and a word, spoken by scythes,
bends them into life.

Mute like them
we waft toward the world:
our gazes,
exchanged to be consoled,
fumble forward
beckon us darkly.

Gazeless
your eye into my eye now silences itself,
wandering
I raise your heart to my lips,
you raise my heart to yours:
what we drink now
quenches the thirst of hours,
what we are now,
the hours pour into time's cup.

Does it like how we taste?
No sound and no light
slips between us, to tell us.

O Halme, ihr Halme.
Ihr Halme der Nacht.

UNSTETES HERZ, dem die Heide die Stadt baut
inmitten der Kerzen und Stunden,
du steigst
mit den Pappeln hinan zu den Teichen:
im Nächtlichen schnitzt dort
die Flöte den Freund ihres Schweigens
und zeigt ihn den Wassern.
Am Ufer
wandelt vermummt der Gedanke und lauscht:
denn nichts
tritt hervor in eigner Gestalt,
und das Wort, das über dir glänzt,
glaubt an den Käfer im Farn.

SIE KÄMMT IHR HAAR wie mans den Toten kämmt:
sie trägt den blauen Scherben unterm Hemd.

Sie trägt den Scherben Welt an einer Schnur.
Sie weiß die Worte, doch sie lächelt nur.

Sie mischt ihr Lächeln in den Becher Wein:
du mußt ihn trinken, in der Welt zu sein.

Du bist das Bild, das ihr der Scherben zeigt,
wenn sie sich sinnend übers Leben neigt.

O stalks, you stalks.
You stalks of night.

UNSTEADY HEART, for which the heath builds the town
amidst the candles and the hours,
you step
with the poplars down to the ponds:
there at night the flute
whittles her silence's friend
and shows him to the waters.
On the shore
hooded thought wanders and listens:
for nothing
steps forth under its own shape,
and the word that shines above you
has faith in the beetle under the ferns.

SHE COMBS HER HAIR as one combs that of the dead:
she carries the blue shard under her shirt.

She carries the world shard on a string.
She knows the words, but only smiles.

She mixes her smile in the cup with the wine:
you have to drink it, to be in the world.

You are the image the shard shows to her,
when in contemplation she leans over this life.

DA DU GEBLENDET von Worten
ihn stampfst aus der Nacht,
den Baum, dem sein Schatten vorausblüht:
fliegt ihm das Aschenlid zu, darunter das Auge der Schwester
Schnee zu Gedanken verspann –

Nun ist des Laubes genug,
Windhauch und Spruch zu erraten,
und die Sterne, gehäuft,
stehn jetzt im Spiegel der Zeit.

Setze den Fuß in die Mulde, spanne das Zelt:
sie, die Schwester, folgt dir dahin,
und der Tod, aus der Lidspalte tretend,
bricht zum Willkomm euch das Brot,
langt nach dem Becher wie ihr.

Und ihr würzt ihm den Wein.

LANDSCHAFT

Ihr hohen Pappeln – Menschen dieser Erde!
Ihr schwarzen Teiche Glücks – ihr spiegelt sie zu Tode!

Ich sah dich, Schwester, stehn in diesem Glanze.

As you blinded by words
stamp it out of the night:
the tree, whose shadow blossoms ahead—
its ashlid slams shut, below it the sister's eye
spun snow into thoughts—

Now there's enough foliage,
to puzzle out windbreath and saying,
and the stars, heaped,
now stand in the mirror of time.

Set your foot in the hollow, rig the tent:
she, the sister, follows you there,
and death, stepping forth from the lidslit,
breaks bread to welcome you,
reaches for the cup as you do.

And you two spice his wine.

LANDSCAPE

You tall poplars—humans of this earth!
You black ponds of happiness—you mirror them to death!

I saw you, sister, stand in that radiance.

STILLE!

Stille! Ich treibe den Dorn in dein Herz,
denn die Rose, die Rose
steht mit den Schatten im Spiegel, sie blutet!
Sie blutete schon, als wir mischten das Ja und das Nein,
als wirs schlürften,
weil ein Glas, das vom Tisch sprang, erklirrte:
es läutete ein eine Nacht, die finsterte länger als wir.

Wir tranken mit gierigen Mündern:
es schmeckte wie Galle,
doch schäumt' es wie Wein –
Ich folgte dem Strahl deiner Augen,
und die Zunge lallte uns Süße . . .
(So lallt sie, so lallt sie noch immer.)

Stille! Der Dorn dringt dir tiefer ins Herz:
er steht im Bund mit der Rose.

WASSER UND FEUER

So warf ich dich denn in den Turm und sprach ein Wort zu den
Eiben,
draus sprang eine Flamme, die maß dir ein Kleid an, dein Brautkleid:

Hell ist die Nacht,
hell ist die Nacht, die uns Herzen erfand,
hell ist die Nacht!

SILENCE!

Silence! I drive the thorn into your heart,
because the rose, the rose
stands with the shadow in the mirror, and bleeds!
It bled already when we mixed the Yes and the No,
when we sipped it,
because a glass that jumped from the table rang out:
it rang in a night that darkened longer than we.

We drank with greedy mouths:
it tasted like bile,
yet it foamed like wine—
I followed the beam of your eyes,
and the tongue babbled something sweet . . .
(So it babbles, so it still and always babbles.)

Silence! The thorn drives deeper into your heart:
it is in league with the rose.

WATER AND FIRE

So I threw you in the tower and spoke a word with the yews,
from which shot a flame that measured you for a dress, your
wedding dress:

Bright is the night,
bright is the night that invented hearts for us,
bright is the night!

Sie leuchtet weit übers Meer,
sie weckt die Monde im Sund und hebt sie auf gischtende Tische,
sie wäscht sie mir rein von der Zeit:
Totes Silber, leb auf, sei Schüssel und Napf wie die Muschel!

Der Tisch wogt stundauf und stundab,
der Wind füllt die Becher,
das Meer wälzt die Speise heran:
das schweifende Aug, das gewitternde Ohr,
den Fisch und die Schlange –

Der Tisch wogt nachtaus und nachtein,
und über mir fluten die Fahnen der Völker,
und neben mir rudern die Menschen die Särge an Land,
und unter mir himmelts und sternts wie daheim um Johanni!

Und ich blick hinüber zu dir,
Feuerumsonnte:
Denk an die Zeit, da die Nacht mit uns auf den Berg stieg,
denk an die Zeit,
denk, daß ich war, was ich bin:
ein Meister der Kerker und Türme,
ein Hauch in den Eiben, ein Zecher im Meer,
ein Wort, zu dem du herabbrennst.

ZÄHLE DIE MANDELN,
zähle, was bitter war und dich wachhielt,
zähl mich dazu:

Ich suchte dein Aug, als du's aufschlugst und niemand dich ansah,
ich spann jenen heimlichen Faden,

It shines far over the sea,
it awakens the moons in the narrows and lifts them on foaming tables,
it washes them clean of time for me:
Dead silver, revive, be bowl and cup like the shell!

The table billows up and down the hours,
the wind fills the cups,
the sea rolls along the food:
the wandering eye, the storming ear,
the fish and the serpent—

The table billows night in, night out,
and above me the flags of the nations flutter,
and next to me humans are rowing the coffins ashore,
and under me it skys & it stars like once at home around St. John's!

And I look over at you,
the fire-besunned:
think of the time when night climbed the mountain with us,
think of the time,
think, that I was what I am:
a master of prisons and towers,
a breath in the yews, a reveler in the sea,
a word you burn down toward.

Count the almonds,
count what was bitter and kept you awake,
count me among them:

I searched for your eye, when you opened it and no one looked at you,
I spun that secret thread,

an dem der Tau, den du dachtest,
hinunterglitt zu den Krügen,
die ein Spruch, der zu niemandes Herz fand, behütet.

Dort erst tratest du ganz in den Namen, der dein ist,
schrittest du sicheren Fußes zu dir,
schwangen die Hämmer frei im Glockenstuhl deines Schweigens,
stieß das Erlauschte zu dir,
legte das Tote den Arm auch um dich,
und ihr ginget selbdritt durch den Abend.

Mache mich bitter.
Zähle mich zu den Mandeln.

along which the dew you thought
slid down to the jars,
watched over by a saying that found its way to no one's heart.

Only there did you wholly enter the name that is yours,
did you step sure-footed toward yourself,
did the hammers swing free in the belfry of your silence,
the overheard reach you,
the dead put its arm around you too,
and all three of you walked through the evening.

Make me bitter.
Count me among the almonds.

Von Schwelle zu Schwelle

für Gisèle

Threshold to Threshold

for Gisèle

Sieben Rosen später

Seven Roses Later

ICH HÖRTE SAGEN

Ich hörte sagen, es sei
im Wasser ein Stein und ein Kreis
und über dem Wasser ein Wort,
das den Kreis um den Stein legt.

Ich sah meine Pappel hinabgehn zum Wasser,
ich sah, wie ihr Arm hinuntergriff in die Tiefe,
ich sah ihre Wurzeln gen Himmel um Nacht flehn.

Ich eilt ihr nicht nach,
ich las nur vom Boden auf jene Krume,
die deines Auges Gestalt hat und Adel,
ich nahm dir die Kette der Sprüche vom Hals
und säumte mit ihr den Tisch, wo die Krume nun lag.

Und sah meine Pappel nicht mehr.

IM SPÄTROT

Im Spätrot schlafen die Namen:
einen
weckt deine Nacht
und führt ihn, mit weißen Stäben entlang-
tastend am Südwall des Herzens,
unter die Pinien:
eine, von menschlichem Wuchs,
schreitet zur Töpferstadt hin,
wo der Regen einkehrt als Freund

I HEARD IT SAID

I heard it said, there is
in the water a stone and a circle
and above the water a word
that lays the circle around the stone.

I saw my poplar go down to the water,
I saw its arm reach down into the depth,
I saw its roots beg skyward for night.

I did not hurry after it,
I picked up from the ground only the crumb
that has your eye's shape and nobility
I took the chain of sayings off your neck
and with it framed the table where the crumb now lay.

And saw my poplar no more.

IN LATE-RED

In late-red the names sleep:
one,
your night wakes
and leads, with white staffs groping
along the heart's south wall,
under the pine trees:
one, of human size,
walks toward the potter's town,
where rain comes to visit as friend

einer Meeresstunde.
Im Blau
spricht sie ein schattenverheißendes Baumwort,
und deiner Liebe Namen
zählt seine Silben hinzu.

LEUCHTEN

Schweigenden Leibes
liegst du im Sand neben mir,
Übersternte.

. . . .

Brach sich ein Strahl
herüber zu mir?
Oder war es der Stab,
den man brach über uns,
der so leuchtet?

GEMEINSAM

Da nun die Nacht und die Stunde,
so auf den Schwellen nennt,
die eingehn und ausgehn,

of a seahour.
In the blue
it speaks a shadow-promising treeword,
and your love's name
adds its own syllables.

TO SHINE

With body silent
you lie in the sand beside me,
you: starred-over.

. . . .

Did a beam break
through to me?
Or was it the staff
they broke over us
that shines so bright?

TOGETHER

As now night and the hour,
naming on the thresholds
what enters and leaves,

guthieß, was wir getan,
da uns kein Drittes den Weg wies,

werden die Schatten nicht
einzeln kommen, wenn mehr
sein soll als heute sich kundtat,

werden die Fittiche nicht
später dir rauschen als mir –

Sondern es rollt übers Meer
der Stein, der neben uns schwebte,
und in der Spur, die er zieht,
laicht der lebendige Traum.

MIT ÄXTEN SPIELEND

Sieben Stunden der Nacht, sieben Jahre des Wachens:
mit Äxten spielend,
liegst du im Schatten aufgerichteter Leichen
– o Bäume, die du nicht fällst! –,
zu Häupten den Prunk des Verschwiegnen,
den Bettel der Worte zu Füßen,
liegst du und spielst mit den Äxten –
und endlich blinkst du wie sie.

countenanced what we did,
as no third showed us the way,

the shadows will not
come singly, should there
be more than revealed itself today,

the wings won't roar
later for you than for me—

But over the sea the stone
shall roll, the one hovered near us,
and in the spoor it traces
the living dream spawns.

PLAYING WITH AXES

Seven hours of night, seven years of being awake:
playing with axes,
you lie in the shadow of erected corpses
—o trees that you don't fell!—
at their heads the pomp of the silenced,
the word trash at their feet,
you lie there and play with the axes—
and finally you blink like them.

DAS SCHWERE

Das Schwere, das du mir zuwarfst:
es macht mir den Stein nicht gewogen, der aufklafft,
wenn ich mit murmelndem Finger
in sein von Tiefen gekämmtes Haar greif.

Dich nur
neigt zu mir hin,
was du geworfen.

Rede von Blei.
Rede von Blei, sobald uns der Mond glänzt.
Strähle mein Pferd.
Strähle mein Pferd, wenn die Hand hier das Brot bricht.
Reit's an den Tisch hier zur Tränke.

EIN KÖRNCHEN SANDS

Stein, aus dem ich dich schnitzt,
als die Nacht ihre Wälder verheerte:
ich schnitzt dich als Baum
und hüllt dich ins Braun meines leisesten Spruchs
wie in Borke –

Ein Vogel,
der rundesten Träne entschlüpft,
regt sich wie Laub über dir:

THE LOAD

The load you threw at me:
it does not dispose me well toward the stone that gapes
when with murmuring finger
I grab for its depth-combed hair.

Only you're
bent toward me
by what you threw.

Speak of lead.
Speak of lead, as soon as the moon shines for us.
Curry my horse.
Curry my horse, when the hand here breaks the bread.
Ride it to the table here to the trough.

A GRAINLET OF SAND

Stone, from which I carved you,
while night wreaked havoc on its forests:
I carved you as a tree
I wrapped you into the brown of my softest saying
as if in bark—

A bird,
slipped out of the roundest tear,
stirs like foliage above you:

du kannst warten,
bis unter allen den Augen ein Sandkorn dir aufglimmt,
ein Körnchen Sands,
das mir träumen half,
als ich niedertaucht, dich zu finden –

Du treibst ihm die Wurzel entgegen,
die dich flügge macht, wenn der Boden von Tod glüht,
du reckst dich empor,
und ich schweb dir voraus als ein Blatt,
das weiß, wo die Tore sich auftun.

STRÄHNE

Strähne, die ich nicht flocht, die ich wehn ließ,
die weiß ward von Kommen und Gehen,
die sich gelöst von der Stirn, an der ich vorbeiglitt
im Stirnenjahr –:

dies ist ein Wort, das sich regt
Firnen zulieb,
ein Wort, das schneewärts geäugt,
als ich, umsommert von Augen,
der Braue vergaß, die du über mich spanntest,
ein Wort, das mich mied,
als die Lippe mir blutet' vor Sprache.

Dies ist ein Wort, das neben den Worten einherging,
ein Wort nach dem Bilde des Schweigens,
umbuscht von Singrün und Kummer.

you can wait,
until among all the eyes a sandgrain glimmers up to you,
a grainlet of sand
that helped me dream,
when I dove down to find you—

You drive the root toward it,
that fledges you, when the ground glows with death,
you rear up,
and I float ahead of you as a leaf
that knows where the gates open.

LOCK

Lock, that I didn't braid, that I let blow,
that turned white from coming and going,
that parted from the forehead, past which I slid
in the year of foreheads—:

this is a word that bestirs itself
for the love of firn,
a word that gazes snow-ward,
as I, ensummered by eyes,
forgot the brow you tautened above me,
a word that avoided me,
when my lip bled from language.

This is a word that walked along beside the words,
a word after the image of silence,
ambushed by evergreen and sorrow.

Niedergehn hier die Fernen,
und du,
ein flockiger Haarstern,
schneist hier herab
und rührst an den erdigen Mund.

AUS DEM MEER

Wir haben begangen das Eine und Leise,
wir schossen hinab in die Tiefe,
aus der man der Ewigkeit Schaum spinnt –
Wir haben ihn nicht gesponnen,
wir hatten die Hände nicht frei.

Sie blieben verflochten zu Netzen –
von obenher zerren sie dran . . .
O messerumfunkelte Augen:
wir fingen den Schattenfisch, seht!

ZWIEGESTALT

Laß dein Aug in der Kammer sein eine Kerze,
den Blick einen Docht,
laß mich blind genug sein,
ihn zu entzünden.

Here the distances descend,
and you,
a flaky comet's tail,
snow down, here,
and touch the earthy mouth.

OUT OF THE SEA

We have tread on the One and the Quiet,
we shot down into the depths,
from which one spins eternity's foam—
We did not spin it,
our hands were not free.

They were woven into nets—
from above they tug at them . . .
O eyes, knives flashing around you:
we caught the shadowfish, see!

BIFORM

Let your eye in the chamber be a candle,
the gaze a wick,
let me be blind enough
to light it.

Nein.
Laß anderes sein.

Tritt vor dein Haus,
schirr deinen scheckigen Traum an,
laß seine Hufe reden
zum Schnee, den du fortbliest
vom First meiner Seele.

FERNEN

Aug in Aug, in der Kühle,
laß uns auch solches beginnen:
gemeinsam
laß uns atmen den Schleier,
der uns voreinander verbirgt,
wenn der Abend sich anschickt zu messen,
wie weit es noch ist
von jeder Gestalt, die er annimmt,
zu jeder Gestalt,
die er uns beiden geliehn.

WO EIS IST

Wo Eis ist, ist Kühle für zwei.
Für zwei: so ließ ich dich kommen.

No.
Let it be otherwise.

Step out of your house,
harness your skewbald dream,
let its hoofs talk
to the snow that you blew off
the ridge of my soul.

DISTANCES

Eye to eye, in the cool,
let's also begin suchlike:
together
let's breathe the veil
that hides us from each other,
when evening sets up to measure
how far it still is
from each shape it assumes
to each shape
it has loaned us both.

WHERE THERE'S ICE

Where there's ice, it's cool for two.
For two: so I let you come.

Ein Hauch wie von Feuer war um dich –
Du kamst von der Rose her.

Ich fragte: Wie hieß man dich dort?
Du nanntest ihn mir, jenen Namen:
ein Schein wie von Asche lag drauf –
Von der Rose her kamst du.

Wo Eis ist, ist Kühle für zwei:
ich gab dir den Doppelnamen.
Du schlugst dein Aug auf darunter –
Ein Glanz lag über der Wuhne.

Nun schließ ich, so sprach ich, das meine –:
Nimm dieses Wort – mein Auge redet's dem deinen!
Nimm es, sprich es mir nach,
sprich es mir nach, sprich es langsam,
sprich's langsam, zögr es hinaus,
und dein Aug – halt es offen so lang noch!

VON DUNKEL ZU DUNKEL

Du schlugst die Augen auf – ich seh mein Dunkel leben.
Ich seh ihm auf den Grund:
auch da ists mein und lebt.

Setzt solches über? Und erwacht dabei?
Wes Licht folgt auf dem Fuß mir,
daß sich ein Ferge fand?

A breath as of fire was around you—
You came from where the rose is.

I asked: what did they call you back there?
You told it to me, that name:
a glare as of ashes coated it—
From where the rose is you came.

Where there's ice, it's cool for two:
I gave you the double name.
You opened your eye beneath it—
A luster lay over the hole in the ice.

Now I close, is what I said, my own—:
Take this word—my eye spoke it to yours!
Take it, repeat it after me,
repeat it after me, say it slowly,
say it slowly, draw it out,
and your eye—keep it open the while!

FROM DARKNESS TO DARKNESS

You opened your eyes—I see my darkness live.
I see to the bottom of it:
there too it's mine, and lives.

Does this carry across? And withal wake up?
Whose light follows on my heels,
that a ferryman was found?

IN GESTALT EINES EBERS

In Gestalt eines Ebers
stampft dein Traum durch die Wälder am Rande des Abends.
Blitzendweiß
wie das Eis, aus dem er hervorbrach,
sind seine Hauer.

Eine bittere Nuß
wühlt er hervor unterm Laub,
das sein Schatten den Bäumen entriß,
eine Nuß,
schwarz wie das Herz, das dein Fuß vor sich herstieß,
als du selber hier schrittst.

Er spießt sie auf
und erfüllt das Gehölz mit grunzendem Schicksal,
dann treibts ihn
hinunter zur Küste,
dorthin, wo das Meer
seiner Feste finsterstes gibt
auf den Klippen:

vielleicht
daß eine Frucht wie die seine
das feiernde Auge entzückt,
das solche Steine geweint hat.

IN THE SHAPE OF A BOAR

In the shape of a boar
your dream stomps through the woods at evening's edge.
Lighteningwhite
like the ice, from which it broke forth,
are its tusks.

A bitter nut
it rooted up from beneath the foliage,
that its shadow tore from the trees,
a nut,
as black as the heart, that your foot kicked along,
when you walked here yourself.

Spearing it
fills the thicket with grunting fate,
then something drives it
down to the coast,
where the sea
throws its darkest feast
on the cliffs:

maybe
a fruit like his
delights the feasting eye
that has wept such stones.

BRETONISCHER STRAND

Versammelt ist, was wir sahen,
zum Abschied von dir und von mir:
das Meer, das uns Nächte an Land warf,
der Sand, der sie mit uns durchflogen,
das rostrote Heidekraut droben,
darin die Welt uns geschah.

GUT

Gut, daß ich über dich hinflog.
Gut, daß auch ich mir erklang, als der Himmel dir quoll aus den
Augen.
Gut, daß ich sah, wessen Stern darin glomm –
Gut, daß ich dennoch nicht aufschrie.

Denn nun gellt dir die Stimme im Ohr,
die mich wild vor sich herstieß.
Und der mich peitschte, der Regen,
meißelt dir jetzt einen Mund,
der spricht, wenn die Sterne schrumpfen,
der schwillt, wenn die Himmel verebben.

BRETON BEACH

Gathered is what we saw,
from your and my leave-taking:
the sea that beached nights for us,
the sand that flew through them with us,
the rust-red heather above,
wherein the world happened for us.

GOOD

Good, that I flew above you.
Good, that I resounded for myself too when the sky welled from
 your eyes.
Good, that I saw whose star smoldered in there—
Good, that despite this I didn't cry out.

For now in your ear shrills the voice
that wildly pushed me ahead of itself.
And what whipped me, the rain,
now chisels you a mouth
that speaks when the stars shrink,
that swells when the heavens ebb away.

ZU ZWEIEN

Zu zweien schwimmen die Toten,
zu zweien, umflossen von Wein.
Im Wein, den sie über dich gossen,
schwimmen die Toten zu zwein.

Sie flochten ihr Haar sich zu Matten,
sie wohnen einander bei.
Du wirf deinen Würfel noch einmal
und tauch in ein Auge der Zwei.

DER GAST

Lange vor Abend
kehrt bei dir ein, der den Gruß getauscht mit dem Dunkel.
Lange vor Tag
wacht er auf
und facht, eh er geht, einen Schlaf an,
einen Schlaf, durchklungen von Schritten:
du hörst ihn die Fernen durchmessen
und wirfst deine Seele dorthin.

BY TWOS

The dead swim by twos,
by twos, girdled by wine.
In this girdle of wine,
the dead, they swim by twos.

They braided their hair into mats,
they live toward each other.
You, throw once more your die
and dive into the two's eye.

THE GUEST

Long before nightfall
the one who exchanged greetings with darkness stops over with you.
Long before daylight
he wakes
and kindles, before leaving, a sleep,
a sleep, echoing with footsteps:
you hear him surveying the distances
and throw your soul over there.

Mit wechselndem Schlüssel

With a Changing Key

GRABSCHRIFT FÜR FRANÇOIS

Die beiden Türen der Welt
stehen offen:
geöffnet von dir
in der Zwienacht.
Wir hören sie schlagen und schlagen
und tragen das ungewisse,
und tragen das Grün in dein Immer.

Oktober 1953

AUFS AUGE GEPFROPFT

Aufs Auge gepfropft
ist dir das Reis, das den Wäldern den Weg wies:
verschwistert den Blicken,
treibt es die schwarze,
die Knospe.

Himmelweit spannt sich das Lid diesem Frühling.
Lidweit dehnt sich der Himmel,
darunter, beschirmt von der Knospe,
der Ewige pflügt,
der Herr.

Lausche der Pflugschar, lausche.
Lausche: sie knirscht
über der harten, der hellen,
der unvordenklichen Träne.

EPITAPH FOR FRANÇOIS

Both doors of the world
stand open:
opened by you
in the twinight.
We hear them slam and slam
and bear uncertainty,
and bear the Green into your Ever.

October 1953

GRAFTED ON YOUR EYE

Grafted on your eye
is the shoot that showed the woods the way:
sister to the glances,
it sprouts the black one,
the bud.

Skywide the eyelid stretches toward this spring.
Lidwide the sky spreads,
below, sheltered by the bud,
the Eternal One ploughs,
the Lord.

Listen to the ploughshare, listen.
Listen: it grates
across the hard, the bright,
the immemorial tear.

DER UNS DIE STUNDEN ZÄHLTE

Der uns die Stunden zählte,
er zählt weiter.
Was mag er zählen, sag?
Er zählt und zählt.

Nicht kühler wirds,
nicht nächtiger,
nicht feuchter.

Nur was uns lauschen half:
es lauscht nun
für sich allein.

ASSISI

Umbrische Nacht.
Umbrische Nacht mit dem Silber von Glocke und Ölblatt.
Umbrische Nacht mit dem Stein, den du hertrugst.
Umbrische Nacht mit dem Stein.

  Stumm, was ins Leben stieg, stumm.
  Füll die Krüge um.

Irdener Krug.
Irdener Krug, dran die Töpferhand festwuchs.
Irdener Krug, den die Hand eines Schattens für immer verschloß.
Irdener Krug mit dem Siegel des Schattens.

HE WHO COUNTED THE HOURS FOR US

He who counted the hours for us,
he keeps on counting.
What's he counting, tell?
He counts and counts.

It doesn't get cooler,
nor more nightly,
nor moister.

Only what helped us listen:
it now listens
for itself alone.

ASSISI

Umbrian night.
Umbrian night with the silver of bell and olive leaf.
Umbrian night with the stone you carried hither.
Umbrian night with the stone.

  Dumb, what rose into life, dumb.
  Decant the jugs.

Earthen jug,
Earthen jug, onto which the potter's hand grew.
Earthen jug, which a shadow's hand plugged up forever.
Earthen jug with the seal of a shadow.

Stein, wo du hinsiehst, Stein.
Laß das Grautier ein.

Trottendes Tier.
Trottendes Tier im Schnee, den die nackteste Hand streut.
Trottendes Tier vor dem Wort, das ins Schloß fiel.
Trottendes Tier, das den Schlaf aus der Hand frißt.

Glanz, der nicht trösten will, Glanz.
Die Toten – sie betteln noch, Franz.

AUCH HEUTE ABEND

Voller,
da Schnee auch auf dieses
sonnendurchschwommene Meer fiel,
blüht das Eis in den Körben,
die du zur Stadt trägst.

Sand
heischst du dafür,
denn die letzte
Rose daheim
will auch heut abend gespeist sein
aus rieselnder Stunde.

Stone wherever you look, stone.
Let the donkey in.

Trotting animal.
Trotting animal in the snow the most naked hand spreads.
Trotting animal before the word that clicked shut.
Trotting animal that laps sleep from a hand.

Splendor, that will not console, splendor.
The dead—they're still begging, Francis.

TONIGHT TOO

Fuller,
as snow also fell on this
sun-soaked sea,
the ice blooms in the baskets
you carry to town.

Sand
you demand in exchange,
for the last
rose back home
wants to be fed tonight too
by a trickling hour.

VOR EINER KERZE

Aus getriebenem Golde, so
wie du's mir anbefahlst, Mutter,
formt ich den Leuchter, daraus
sie empor mir dunkelt inmitten
splitternder Stunden:
deines
Totseins Tochter.

Schlank von Gestalt,
ein schmaler, mandeläugiger Schatten,
Mund und Geschlecht
umtanzt von Schlummergetier,
entschwebt sie dem klaffenden Golde,
steigt sie hinan
zum Scheitel des Jetzt.

Mit nachtverhangnen
Lippen
sprech ich den Segen:

> Im Namen der Drei,
> die einander befehden, bis
> der Himmel hinabtaucht ins Grab der Gefühle,
> im Namen der Drei, deren Ringe
> am Finger mir glänzen, sooft
> ich den Bäumen im Abgrund das Haar lös,
> auf daß die Tiefe durchrauscht sei von reicherer Flut –,
> im Namen des ersten der Drei,
> der aufschrie,

IN FRONT OF A CANDLE

Of chased gold, just
as you bade me, mother,
I shaped the candlestick, from which
she darkens up to me amidst
splintering hours:
your
deadness's daughter.

A slender figure,
a slim almond-eyed shadow,
mouth and sex
danced around by sleep creatures,
she floats out of the gaping gold,
she soars up
to the peak of Now.

With nightdraped
lips
I speak the blessing:

> In the name of the three,
> who feud with each other until
> heaven dives down into the grave of feelings,
> in the name of the three whose rings
> shine at my finger, as often
> as I loosen the hair of the trees in the abyss,
> so that a richer flood roar through the depths—,
> in the name of the first of the three,
> who cried out

als es zu leben galt dort, wo vor ihm sein Wort schon gewesen,
im Namen des zweiten, der zusah und weinte,
im Namen des dritten, der weiße
Steine häuft in der Mitte, –
sprech ich dich frei
vom Amen, das uns übertäubt,
vom eisigen Licht, das es säumt,
da, wo es turmhoch ins Meer tritt,
da, wo die graue, die Taube
aufpickt die Namen
diesseits und jenseits des Sterbens:
Du bleibst, du bleibst, du bleibst
einer Toten Kind,
geweiht dem Nein meiner Sehnsucht,
vermählt einer Schrunde der Zeit,
vor die mich das Mutterwort führte,
auf daß ein einziges Mal
erzittre die Hand,
die je und je mir ans Herz greift!

MIT WECHSELNDEM SCHLÜSSEL

Mit wechselndem Schlüssel
schließt du das Haus auf, darin
der Schnee des Verschwiegenen treibt.
Je nach dem Blut, das dir quillt
aus Aug oder Mund oder Ohr,
wechselt dein Schlüssel.

when the need arose to go live where before him already his word
had been,
in the name of the second, who looked on and wept,
in the name of the third, who heaps
white stones in the center,—
I absolve you
of the Amen that deafens us,
of the icy light that bounds it,
there where tower-high it steps into the sea,
where the gray one, the dove,
pecks up the names
on either side of dying:
you remain, you remain, you remain
a dead woman's child,
hallowed to the No of my yearning,
wed to a fissure in time,
where the motherword led me,
so that just once
the hand might tremble
that again and again grasps at my heart!

WITH A CHANGING KEY

With a changing key
you unlock the house in
which the snow of the unsaid drifts.
Depending on the blood that spurts
from your eye or mouth or ear,
your key changes.

Wechselt dein Schlüssel, wechselt das Wort,
das treiben darf mit den Flocken.
Je nach dem Wind, der dich fortstößt,
ballt um das Wort sich der Schnee.

HIER

Hier – das meint hier, wo die Kirschblüte schwärzer sein will als dort.
Hier – das meint diese Hand, die ihr hilft, es zu sein.
Hier – das meint jenes Schiff, auf dem ich den Sandstrom heraufkam:
vertäut
liegt es im Schlaf, den du streutest.

Hier – das meint einen Mann, den ich kenne:
seine Schläfe ist weiß,
wie die Glut, die er löschte.
Er warf mir sein Glas an die Stirn
und kam,
als ein Jahr herum war,
die Narbe zu küssen.
Er sprach den Fluch und den Segen
und sprach nicht wieder seither.

Hier – das meint diese Stadt,
die von dir und der Wolke regiert wird,
von ihren Abenden her.

Your key changes change your word
allowed to drift with the flakes.
Depending on the wind that pushes you away,
the snow cakes around the word.

HERE

Here—that means here, where the cherry blossom wants to be
  blacker than there.
Here—that means this hand that helps it to be so.
Here—that means the ship on which I came up the sandstream:
towroped
it lies in the sleep you strewed.

Here—that means a man I know:
his temple is white
as the embers he doused.
He threw his glass at my forehead
and came,
after a year had passed,
to kiss the scar.
He uttered curse and benediction
and hasn't spoken since.

Here—that means this city,
that is governed by you and by the cloud,
from its evenings.

STILLEBEN

Kerze bei Kerze, Schimmer bei Schimmer, Schein bei Schein.

Und dies hier, darunter: ein Aug,
ungepaart und geschlossen,
das Späte bewimpernd, das anbrach,
ohne der Abend zu sein.

Davor das Fremde, des Gast du hier bist:
die lichtlose Distel,
mit der das Dunkel die Seinen bedenkt,
aus der Ferne,
um unvergessen zu bleiben.

Und dies noch, verschollen im Tauben:
der Mund,
versteint und verbissen in Steine,
angerufen vom Meer,
das sein Eis die Jahre hinanwälzt.

UND DAS SCHÖNE

Und das schöne, das du rauftest, und das Haar,
das du raufst:
welcher Kamm
kämmt es wieder glatt, das schöne Haar?
Welcher Kamm
in wessen Hand?

STILL LIFE

Candle by candle, shimmer by shimmer, glow by glow.

And this here, below it: an eye,
unpaired and closed,
lidding the late that dawned
without being evening.

Before it, the strange, whose guest you are here:
the lightless thistle,
with which darkness gifts its own,
from afar,
to remain unforgotten.

And this too, marooned in deafness:
the mouth,
petrified and doggedly sunk into stones,
summoned by the sea
that rolls its ice up the years.

AND THE BEAUTIFUL

And the beautiful you tore out, and the hair
you tear out:
what comb
combs it smooth again, the beautiful hair?
What comb
in whose hand?

Und die Steine, die du häuftest,
die du häufst:
wohin werfen sie die Schatten,
und wie weit?

Und der Wind, der drüber hinstreicht,
und der Wind:
rafft er dieser Schatten einen,
mißt er ihn dir zu?

WALDIG

Waldig, von Hirschen georgelt,
umdrängt die Welt nun das Wort,
das auf den Lippen dir säumt,
durchglüht von gefristetem Sommer.

Sie hebt es hinweg und du folgst ihm,
du folgst ihm und strauchelst – du spürst,
wie ein Wind, dem du lange vertrautest,
dir den Arm ums Heidekraut biegt:

wer schlafher kam
und schlafhin sich wandte,
darf das Verwunschene wiegen.

Du wiegst es hinab zu den Wassern,
darin sich der Eisvogel spiegelt,
nahe am Nirgends der Nester.

And the stones you heaped up,
that you heap up:
where do they cast their shadows,
and how far?

And the wind that sweeps over it,
and the wind:
does it grab one of these shadows,
does it allot it to you?

FORESTED

Forested, bellowed by stags' roars,
the world now besets the word
that, lingering, seams your lips,
annealed by an eked out summer.

It lifts it away and you follow it,
you follow it and stumble—you feel
that a wind you had trusted so long
bends your arm around the heather:

who came from sleep
and turned sleepward
may cradle the enchanted.

You cradle it down to the waters
where the kingfisher's mirrored,
close to the Nowhere of nests.

Du wiegst es hinab durch die Schneise,
die tief in der Baumglut nach Schnee giert,
du wiegst es hinüber zum Wort,
das dort nennt, was schon weiß ist an dir.

ABEND DER WORTE

Abend der Worte – Rutengänger im Stillen!
Ein Schritt und noch einer,
ein dritter, des Spur
dein Schatten nicht tilgt:

die Narbe der Zeit
tut sich auf
und setzt das Land unter Blut –
Die Doggen der Wortnacht, die Doggen
schlagen nun an
mitten in dir:
sie feiern den wilderen Durst,
den wilderen Hunger . . .

Ein letzter Mond springt dir bei:
einen langen silbernen Knochen
– nackt wie der Weg, den du kamst –
wirft er unter die Meute,
doch rettets dich nicht:
der Strahl, den du wecktest,
schäumt näher heran,

You cradle it down through the firebreak,
that deep in treeheat hungers for snow,
you cradle it over to the word,
that names what of you is already white.

EVENING OF THE WORDS

Evening of the words—dowser in stillness!
One step and another,
a third, whose trace
your shadow doesn't erase:

time's scar
opens
and floods the land with blood—
The mastiffs of Wordnight, those mastiffs
now bay right
inside you:
they celebrate the wilder thirst,
the wilder hunger . . .

One last moon leaps to your rescue:
but the long silver bone
—bare as the path you trod—
it throws among the hounds
doesn't save you:
the beam you woke up
foams toward you,

und obenauf schwimmt eine Frucht,
in die du vor Jahren gebissen.

DIE HALDE

Neben mir lebst du, gleich mir:
als ein Stein
in der eingesunkenen Wange der Nacht.

O diese Halde, Geliebte,
wo wir pausenlos rollen,
wir Steine,
von Rinnsal zu Rinnsal.
Runder von Mal zu Mal.
Ähnlicher. Fremder.

O dieses trunkene Aug,
das hier umherirrt wie wir
und uns zuweilen
staunend in eins schaut.

ICH WEISS

Und du, auch du –:
verpuppt.
Wie alles Nachtgewiegte.

and floating on top is a fruit
you bit into, years ago.

THE SLOPE

You live next to me, like me:
as a stone
in night's sunken cheek.

Oh this slope, beloved,
down which we ceaselessly roll,
we stones,
from runnel to runnel.
Rounder each time.
More alike. More alien.

Oh this drunken eye,
that roams around here as we do
and at times, amazed,
stares us into one.

I KNOW

And you, you too—:
pupated.
Like all that's night-cradled.

Dies Flattern, Flügeln rings:
ich hörs – ich seh es nicht!

Und du,
wie alles Tagenthobene:
verpuppt.

Und Augen, die dich suchen.
Und mein Aug darunter.

Ein Blick:
ein Faden mehr, der dich umspinnt.

Dies späte, späte Licht.
Ich weiß: die Fäden glänzen.

DIE FELDER

Immer die eine, die Pappel
am Saum des Gedankens.
Immer der Finger, der aufragt
am Rain.

Weit schon davor
zögert die Furche im Abend.
Aber die Wolke:
sie zieht.

This flitting, a-fluttering all around:
I hear it—I don't see it!

And you,
like all that's day-removed:
pupated.

And eyes that search for you.
And my eye among them.

A gaze:
one thread more that spins you in.

This late, late light.
I know: the threads shine.

THE FIELDS

Always the one, the poplar
at thought's seam.
Always the finger, raised at
field's margin.

Far before already
the furrow hesitates evenings.
But the cloud:
it drifts.

Immer das Aug.
Immer das Aug, dessen Lid
du aufschlägst beim Schein
seines gesenkten Geschwisters.
Immer dies Aug.

Immer dies Aug, dessen Blick
die eine, die Pappel umspinnt.

ANDENKEN

Feigengenährt sei das Herz,
darin sich die Stunde besinnt
auf das Mandelauge des Toten.
Feigengenährt.

Schroff, im Anhauch des Meers,
die gescheiterte
Stirne,
die Klippenschwester.

Und um dein Weißhaar vermehrt
das Vlies
der sömmernden Wolke.

Always the eye.
Always the eye, whose lid
you open at the gleam
of its closed sister.
Always this eye.

Always this eye, whose gaze
pupates the one, the poplar.

REMEMBRANCE

Fig-nourished be the heart
wherein the hour remembers
the dead one's almond-eye.
Fig-nourished.

Sheer, in sea's breath,
the shipwrecked
forehead,
the klippe-sister.

And around your white hair grows
the fleece
of the summering cloud.

Inselhin

Islandward

NÄCHTLICH GESCHÜRZT

für Hannah und Hermann Lenz

Nächtlich geschürzt
die Lippen der Blumen,
gekreuzt und verschränkt
die Schäfte der Fichten,
ergraut das Moos, erschüttert der Stein,
erwacht zum unendlichen Fluge
die Dohlen über dem Gletscher:

dies ist die Gegend, wo
rasten, die wir ereilt:

sie werden die Stunde nicht nennen,
die Flocken nicht zählen,
den Wassern nicht folgen ans Wehr.

Sie stehen getrennt in der Welt,
ein jeglicher bei seiner Nacht,
ein jeglicher bei seinem Tode,
unwirsch, barhaupt, bereift
von Nahem und Fernem.

Sie tragen die Schuld ab, die ihren Ursprung beseelte,
sie tragen sie ab an ein Wort,
das zu Unrecht besteht, wie der Sommer.

Ein Wort – du weißt:
eine Leiche.

PURSED AT NIGHT

for Hannah and Hermann Lenz

Pursed at night
the flowers' lips,
crossed and mingled
the spruces' trunks,
the moss, turned gray, the stone, shaken,
roused to infinite flight,
the jackdaws above the glacier:

this is the region where those
we caught up with rest:

they will not name the hour,
nor count the flakes,
nor follow the waters to the weir.

They stand apart in the world,
each one next to his night,
each one next to his death,
surly, bareheaded, frostbit
by all that's close and faraway.

They work off the guilt that ensouled their origin,
they hand it off to a word,
that exists unjustly, like summer.

A word—you know:
a corpse.

Laß uns sie waschen,
laß uns sie kämmen,
laß uns ihr Aug
himmelwärts wenden.

AUGE DER ZEIT

Dies ist das Auge der Zeit:
es blickt scheel
unter siebenfarbener Braue.
Sein Lid wird von Feuern gewaschen,
seine Träne ist Dampf.

Der blinde Stern fliegt es an
und zerschmilzt an der heißeren Wimper:
es wird warm in der Welt,
und die Toten
knospen und blühen.

FLÜGELNACHT

Flügelnacht, weither gekommen und nun
für immer gespannt
über Kreide und Kalk.
Kiesel, abgrundhin rollend.
Schnee. Und mehr noch des Weissen.

Let us wash it,
let us comb it,
let us turn its eye
toward the sky.

EYE OF TIME

This is the eye of time:
it looks askance
under seven-colored brow.
Its lid is washed by fires,
its tear is steam.

The blind star flies toward it
and melts on the hotter eyelash:
the world warms up,
and the dead
bud and bloom.

WINGNIGHT

Wingnight, come from afar and now
forever spanned
above chalk and limestone.
Gravel, rolling abyssward.
Snow. And still more of the white.

Unsichtbar,
was braun schien,
gedankenfarben und wild
überwuchert von Worten.

Kalk ist und Kreide.
Und Kiesel.
Schnee. Und mehr noch des Weissen.

Du, du selbst:
in das fremde
Auge gebettet, das dies
überblickt.

WELCHEN DER STEINE DU HEBST

Welchen der Steine du hebst –
du entblößt,
die des Schutzes der Steine bedürfen:
nackt,
erneuern sie nun die Verflechtung.

Welchen der Bäume du fällst –
du zimmerst
die Bettstatt, darauf
die Seelen sich abermals stauen,
als schütterte nicht
auch dieser
Äon.

Invisible,
what seemed brown,
thought-colored and wild
overgrown with words.

Limestone is, and chalk.
And gravel.
Snow. And more of the white.

You, yourself:
embedded in the alien
eye, that over-
looks all this.

WHICHEVER STONE YOU LIFT

Whichever stone you lift—
you lay bare
those in need of the stones' shelter:
naked,
they now renew the intertwining.

Whichever tree you fell—
you craft
the bedstead on which
the souls clot up again,
as if this eon too did not
convulse.

Welches der Worte du sprichst –
du dankst
dem Verderben.

IN MEMORIAM PAUL ÉLUARD

Lege dem Toten die Worte ins Grab,
die er sprach, um zu leben.
Bette sein Haupt zwischen sie,
laß ihn fühlen
die Zungen der Sehnsucht,
die Zangen.

Leg auf die Lider des Toten das Wort,
das er jenem verweigert,
der du zu ihm sagte,
das Wort,
an dem das Blut seines Herzens vorbeisprang,
als eine Hand, so nackt wie die seine,
jenen, der du zu ihm sagte,
in die Bäume der Zukunft knüpfte.

Leg ihm dies Wort auf die Lider:
vielleicht
tritt in sein Aug, das noch blau ist,
eine zweite, fremdere Bläue,
und jener, der du zu ihm sagte,
träumt mit ihm: Wir.

Whichever word you speak—
you thank
perdition.

IN MEMORIAM PAUL ÉLUARD

Lay the words into the dead man's grave
the words he spoke in order to live.
Pillow his head among them,
let him feel
the tongues of longing,
the tongs.

Lay the word on the dead one's lids,
the word he refused to the one
who said thou to him,
the word,
past which his heart's blood leaped,
when a hand, as naked as his own,
knotted the one who said
thou to him, into the trees of the future.

Put this word on his eyelids:
maybe
into his eye, which still is blue,
a second, stranger blueness will step,
and the one who said thou to him
dreams with him: We.

SCHIBBOLETH

Mitsamt meinen Steinen,
den großgeweinten
hinter den Gittern,

schleiften sie mich
in die Mitte des Marktes,
dorthin,
wo die Fahne sich aufrollt, der ich
keinerlei Eid schwor.

Flöte,
Doppelflöte der Nacht:
denke der dunklen
Zwillingsröte
in Wien und Madrid.

Setz deine Fahne auf Halbmast,
Erinnrung.
Auf Halbmast
für heute und immer.

Herz:
gib dich auch hier zu erkennen,
hier, in der Mitte des Marktes.
Ruf's, das Schibboleth, hinaus
in die Fremde der Heimat:
Februar. No pasarán.

Einhorn:
du weißt um die Steine,

SHIBBOLETH

Together with my stones,
wept large
behind bars,

they dragged me
into the market's midst,
there
where the flag I never swore
allegiance to unfurls.

Flute,
double flute of night:
think on the dark
twin redness
in Vienna and Madrid.

Fly your flag at half-mast,
memory.
At half-mast
today and forever.

Heart:
reveal yourself here too,
here, in the market's midst.
Cry out the shibboleth
into your homeland's alienness.
February. No pasarán.

Einhorn-Unicorn:
you know of the stones,

du weißt um die Wasser,
komm,
ich führ dich hinweg
zu den Stimmen
von Estremadura.

WIR SEHEN DICH

Wir sehen dich, Himmel, wir sehn dich.
Pocke um Pocke
treibst du hervor,
Pustel um Pustel.
So mehrst du die Ewigkeit.

Wir sehen dich, Erde, wir sehn dich.
Seele um Seele
setzest du aus,
Schatten um Schatten.
So atmen die Brände der Zeit.

KENOTAPH

Streu deine Blumen, Fremdling, streu sie getrost:
du reichst sie den Tiefen hinunter,
den Gärten.

you know of the water,
come,
come I'll lead you away
to the voices
from Estremadura.

WE SEE YOU

We see you, Heaven, we see you.
Pockmark by pockmark
you shoot forth
pustule by pustule.
Thus you increase eternity.

We see you, Earth, we see you.
Soul by soul
you set out,
shadow by shadow.
Thus they breathe, time's fires.

CENOTAPH

Strew your flowers, stranger, strew them confidently:
You hand them down to the depths,
the gardens.

Der hier liegen sollte, er liegt
nirgends. Doch liegt die Welt neben ihm.
Die Welt, die ihr Auge aufschlug
vor mancherlei Flor.

Er aber hielts, da er manches erblickt,
mit den Blinden:
er ging und pflückte zuviel:
er pflückte den Duft –
und die's sahn, verziehn es ihm nicht.

Nun ging er und trank einen seltsamen Tropfen:
das Meer.
Die Fische –
stießen die Fische zu ihm?

SPRICH AUCH DU

Sprich auch du,
sprich als letzter,
sag deinen Spruch.

Sprich –
Doch scheide das Nein nicht vom Ja.
Gib deinem Spruch auch den Sinn:
gib ihm den Schatten.

Gib ihm Schatten genug,
gib ihm so viel,

He who was supposed to lie here, lies
nowhere. But the world lies next to him.
The world that opened its eye
on all sorts of arrays.

He, however, having seen a lot, sided
with the blind:
he went and gathered too much:
he gathered the scent—
and those who saw it, did not forgive him.

Now he went and drank a peculiar dram:
the sea.
The fish—
did the fish run into him?

SPEAK, YOU TOO

Speak, you too,
speak last,
have your say.

Speak —
But do not split the No from the Yes.
Give your saying also meaning:
give it its shadow.

Give it enough shadow,
give it as much

als du um dich verteilt weißt zwischen
Mittnacht und Mittag und Mittnacht.

Blicke umher:
sieh, wie's lebendig wird rings –
Beim Tode! Lebendig!
Wahr spricht, wer Schatten spricht.

Nun aber schrumpft der Ort, wo du stehst:
Wohin jetzt, Schattenentblößter, wohin?
Steige. Taste empor.
Dünner wirst du, unkenntlicher, feiner!
Feiner: ein Faden,
an dem er herab will, der Stern:
um unten zu schwimmen, unten,
wo er sich schimmern sieht: in der Dünung
wandernder Worte.

MIT ZEITROTEN LIPPEN

Im Meer gereift ist der Mund,
dessen Worte der Abend hier nachspricht
im Angesicht seiner Länder.
Murmelnd spricht er sie nach,
mit zeitroten Lippen.

Mund, gezeitigt vom Meer,
vom Meer, wo der Thun schwamm
im Glanze,
der menschenher strahlt.

as you know to be parceled out between your
midnight and midday and midnight.

Look around:
see how it all comes alive—
At death! Alive!
Speaks true, who speaks shadows.

But now the place you stand on shrinks:
Where to now, shadow-stripped one, where to?
Climb. Grope your way up.
You'll grow thinner, more unrecognizable, finer!
Finer: a thread
along which it wants to alight, the star:
so as to swim further down, down
where it sees itself gleam: in the swell
of wandering words.

WITH TIME-RED LIPS

Ripened in the sea is the mouth,
its words evening repeats here
in the face of its lands.
It repeats them mumbling
with time-red lips.

Mouth, time-tamed by the sea,
by the sea where the tuna swam
in the shimmer
shining over from the human.

Silber des Thuns, den der Strahl traf,
Spiegelsilber des Thuns:
aufscheint den Augen
die zweite, die wandernde Glorie
der Stirnen.

Silber und Silber.
Doppelsilber der Tiefe.

Rudre die Kähne dorthin,
Bruder.
Wirf deine Netze danach,
Bruder.

Zieh es herauf,
wirf es uns in die Häuser,
wirf es uns auf die Tische,
wirf es uns auf die Teller –

Sieh, unsre Lippen schwellen,
zeitrot auch sie wie der Abend,
murmelnd auch sie –
und der Mund aus dem Meer
taucht schon empor
zum unendlichen Kusse.

Silver of the tuna the beam hit,
mirror-silver of the tuna:
lights up for the eyes
the second, the wandering glory
of the foreheads.

Silver and silver.
Double silver of the depths.

Row the boats over there,
brother.
Throw out the nets over there,
brother.

Pull it up,
throw it into our houses,
throw it onto our tables,
throw it onto our plates—

See, our lips swell,
time-red they too, like evening,
mumbling, they too—
and the mouth from the sea
already breaks surface
for the unending kiss.

ARGUMENTUM E SILENTIO

für René Char

An die Kette gelegt
zwischen Gold und Vergessen:
die Nacht.
Beide griffen nach ihr.
Beide ließ sie gewähren.

Lege,
lege auch du jetzt dorthin, was herauf-
dämmern will neben den Tagen:
das sternüberflogene Wort,
das meerübergossne.

Jedem das Wort.
Jedem das Wort, das ihm sang,
als die Meute ihn hinterrücks anfiel –
Jedem das Wort, das ihm sang und erstarrte.

Ihr, der Nacht,
das sternüberflogne, das meerübergossne,
ihr das erschwiegne,
dem das Blut nicht gerann, als der Giftzahn
die Silben durchstieß.

Ihr das erschwiegene Wort.

Wider die andern, die bald,
die umhurt von den Schinderohren,
auch Zeit und Zeiten erklimmen,
zeugt es zuletzt,

ARGUMENTUM E SILENTIO

for René Char

Shackled
between Gold and Forgetting:
Night.
Both grabbed for her.
Both she let have their way.

Lay,
you too now lay down what wants to a-
rise at dawn along with the days:
the word, star-overflown,
sea-drenched.

To each, the word.
To each the word that sang to him,
when the pack jumped him from behind—
To each the word, that sang to him and froze.

To her, to night,
the star-overflown, the sea-drenched,
to her, the word silence won,
whose blood did not curdle when the poison fang
pierced its syllables.

To her, the word silence won.

Against the others, who soon,
whored about by the knacker's ears,
climb time and eras too,
it bears witness at the last,

zuletzt, wenn nur Ketten erklingen,
zeugt es von ihr, die dort liegt
zwischen Gold und Vergessen,
beiden verschwistert von je –

Denn wo
dämmerts denn, sag, als bei ihr,
die im Stromgebiet ihrer Träne
tauchenden Sonnen die Saat zeigt
aber und abermals?

DIE WINZER

für Nani und Klaus Demus

Sie herbsten den Wein ihrer Augen,
sie keltern alles Geweinte, auch dieses:
so will es die Nacht,
die Nacht, an die sie gelehnt sind, die Mauer,
so forderts der Stein,
der Stein, über den ihr Krückstock dahinspricht
ins Schweigen der Antwort –
ihr Krückstock, der einmal,
einmal im Herbst,
wenn das Jahr zum Tod schwillt, als Traube,
der einmal durchs Stumme hindurchspricht, hinab
in den Schacht des Erdachten.

Sie herbsten, sie keltern den Wein,
sie pressen die Zeit wie ihr Auge,

at the last, when only chains ring out,
it bears witness to her who lies there
between Gold and Forgetting,
ensistered to both from the beginning—

For where
does it dawn, tell, except with her,
who in the river basin of her tears
shows the seed to diving suns
again and yet again?

THE VINTAGERS

for Nani and Klaus Demus

They harvest the wine of their eyes,
they press all the weepings, this too:
night wants it thus,
the night they lean on, the wall,
thus the stone demands it,
the stone, across which their walking cane speaks
into the answer's silence—
their walking cane that once,
once only in autumn,
when the year swells deathward, as a grape,
that once only speaks through muteness, down
into thought's mineshaft.

They harvest, they press the wine,
they press time like their eye,

sie kellern das Sickernde ein, das Geweinte,
im Sonnengrab, das sie rüsten
mit nachtstarker Hand:
auf daß ein Mund danach dürste, später –
ein Spätmund, ähnlich dem ihren:
Blindem entgegengekrümmt und gelähmt –
ein Mund, zu dem der Trunk aus der Tiefe emporschäumt, indes
der Himmel hinabsteigt ins wächserne Meer,
um fernher als Lichtstumpf zu leuchten,
wenn endlich die Lippe sich feuchtet.

INSELHIN

Inselhin, neben den Toten,
dem Einbaum waldher vermählt,
von Himmeln umgeiert die Arme,
die Seelen saturnisch beringt:

so rudern die Fremden und Freien,
die Meister vom Eis und vom Stein:
umläutet von sinkenden Bojen,
umbellt von der haiblauen See.

Sie rudern, sie rudern, sie rudern –:
Ihr Toten, ihr Schwimmer, voraus!
Umgittert auch dies von der Reuse!
Und morgen verdampft unser Meer!

they cellar the seepings, the weepings,
in the sungrave, readied
by nightstrong hand:
so that a mouth may thirst for it, later—
a latemouth, like to theirs:
bent toward blindness and lame—
a mouth to which the drink foams up from the depths, while
the sky descends into the waxen sea,
to shine from afar as a candle-stub,
when at last the lip moistens.

ISLANDWARD

Islandward, next to the dead,
to the dugout forest-wise wed,
arms vultured around by skies,
souls ringed saturninely:

thus row the strangers, the free,
the masters of ice and of stone:
chimed in by sinking buoys,
barked at by sharkblue seas.

They row, they row, they row—:
You the dead, you the swimmers, onward!
This too, trapped by the bownet!
And tomorrow our sea turns to steam!

Sprachgitter

Speechgrille

Stimmen, ins Grün
der Wasserfläche geritzt.
Wenn der Eisvogel taucht,
sirrt die Sekunde:

Was zu dir stand
an jedem der Ufer,
es tritt
gemäht in ein anderes Bild.

*

Stimmen vom Nesselweg her:

Komm auf den Händen zu uns.
Wer mit der Lampe allein ist,
hat nur die Hand, draus zu lesen.

*

Stimmen, nachtdurchwachsen, Stränge,
an die du die Glocke hängst.

Wölbe dich, Welt:
Wenn die Totenmuschel heranschwimmt,
will es hier läuten.

*

Stimmen, vor denen dein Herz
ins Herz deiner Mutter zurückweicht.
Stimmen vom Galgenbaum her,
wo Spätholz und Frühholz die Ringe
tauschen und tauschen.

Voices, scratched into
the water surface's green.
When the kingfisher dives,
the second saws:

What stood toward you
on each of the banks
steps
mown into another image.

*

Voices from the nettlepath:

Come to us on your hands.
Whoever is alone with the lamp,
has only the hand to read from.

*

Voices, night-veined, ropes
you hang the bell from.

Vault yourself, world:
When the deathmussel swims up,
the bell will want to chime.

*

Voices, from which your heart
recoils into your mother's heart.
Voices from the gallows tree,
where latewood and earlywood again
and again exchange their rings.

*

Stimmen, kehlig, im Grus,
darin auch Unendliches schaufelt,
(herz-)
schleimiges Rinnsal.

Setz hier die Boote aus, Kind,
die ich bemannte:

Wenn mittschiffs die Bö sich ins Recht setzt,
treten die Klammern zusammen.

*

Jakobsstimme:

Die Tränen.
Die Tränen im Bruderaug.
Eine blieb hängen, wuchs.
Wir wohnen darin.
Atme, daß
sie sich löse.

*

Stimmen im Innern der Arche:

Es sind
nur die Münder
geborgen. Ihr
Sinkenden, hört
auch uns.

*

*

Voices, throaty, in the debris
where Endlessness too shovels,
(heart-)
slimy runoff.

Child, lower the boats here
that I manned:

When midships the squall bestows itself,
the brackets will batten.

*

Jacobsvoice:

The tears.
The tears in the brothereye.
One hung in, grew.
We live in it.
Breathe, so
it can drop.

*

Voices inside the ark:

Only the
mouths are
salvaged. You
who drown, hear
us too.

*

Keine
Stimme – ein
Spätgeräusch, stundenfremd, deinen
Gedanken geschenkt, hier, endlich
herbeigewacht: ein
Fruchtblatt, augengroß, tief
geritzt; es
harzt, will nicht
vernarben.

No
voice—a
late noise, hour-estranged, gift
for your thoughts, here, at last
wakened here-ward: a
carpel, eye-sized, deeply
scratched,
resins, will not
scar over.

II

II

ZUVERSICHT

Es wird noch ein Aug sein,
ein fremdes, neben
dem unsern: stumm
unter steinernem Lid.

Kommt, bohrt euren Stollen!

Es wird eine Wimper sein,
einwärts gekehrt im Gestein,
von Ungeweintem verstählt,
die feinste der Spindeln.

Vor euch tut sie das Werk,
als gäb es, weil Stein ist, noch Brüder.

MIT BRIEF UND UHR

Wachs,
Ungeschriebnes zu siegeln,
das deinen Namen
erriet,
das deinen Namen
verschlüsselt.

Kommst du nun, schwimmendes Licht?

Finger, wächsern auch sie,
durch fremde,

CONFIDENCE

There will be one more eye,
a strange one, beside
ours: mute
under stone lid.

Come, drill your mineshaft!

There will be an eyelash,
turned inward in the stone,
steeled by the unwept,
the finest of spindles.

In front of you it does its work,
as if, because stone exists, there still were brothers.

WITH LETTER AND CLOCK

Wax,
to seal the unwritten
that guessed your
name,
that enciphers
your name.

Will you come now, swimming light?

Fingers, waxy they too,
pulled through

schmerzende Ringe gezogen.
Fortgeschmolzen die Kuppen.

Kommst du, schwimmendes Licht?

Zeitleer die Waben der Uhr,
bräutlich das Immentausend,
reisebereit.

Komm, schwimmendes Licht.

UNTER EIN BILD

Rabenüberschwärmte Weizenwoge.
Welchen Himmels Blau? Des untern? Obern?
Später Pfeil, der von der Seele schnellte.
Stärkres Schwirren. Näh're Glühen. Beide Welten.

HEIMKEHR

Schneefall, dichter und dichter,
taubenfarben, wie gestern,
Schneefall, als schliefst du auch jetzt noch.

Weithin gelagertes Weiß.
Drüberhin, endlos,
die Schlittenspur des Verlornen.

strange painful rings.
Melted away, the tips.

Will you come, swimming light?

Empty of time, the clock's honeycomb,
spousal, the bee-thousands,
ready to travel.

Come, swimming light.

BELOW A PAINTING

Crowswarmed wheatwave.
What sky's blue? The one below? The one above?
Late arrow, shot from the soul.
Stronger whirring. Nearer glowing. Both worlds.

HOMECOMING

Snowfall, thicker and thicker,
dove-colored, like yesterday,
snowfall, as if you were asleep even now.

Far layered whiteness.
Over it, endless,
the sledtracks of the lost.

Darunter, geborgen,
stülpt sich empor,
was den Augen so weh tut,
Hügel um Hügel,
unsichtbar.

Auf jedem,
heimgeholt in sein Heute,
ein ins Stumme entglittenes Ich:
hölzern, ein Pflock.

Dort: ein Gefühl,
vom Eiswind herübergeweht,
das sein tauben-, sein schnee-
farbenes Fahnentuch festmacht.

UNTEN

Heimgeführt ins Vergessen
das Gast-Gespräch unsrer
langsamen Augen.

Heimgeführt Silbe um Silbe, verteilt
auf die tagblinden Würfel, nach denen
die spielende Hand greift, groß,
im Erwachen.

Underneath, salvaged,
bulging up,
what hurts the eyes so much,
hill after hill,
invisible.

On each,
brought home into its today,
an I that slid into muteness:
wooden, a stake.

There: a feeling,
blown over here by the icewind,
fastening its dove-,
its snow-colored flagcloth.

BELOW

Brought home into forgetting
the host-conversation of our
slow eyes.

Brought home syllable by syllable, distributed
over the dayblind dice, the
gaming hand grabs for, large,
while waking up.

Und das Zuviel meiner Rede:
angelagert dem kleinen
Kristall in der Tracht deines Schweigens.

HEUTE UND MORGEN

So steh ich, steinern, zur
Ferne, in die ich dich führte:

Von Flugsand
ausgewaschen die beiden
Höhlen am untern Stirnsaum.
Eräugtes
Dunkel darin.

Durchpocht
von schweigsam geschwungenen Hämmern
die Stelle,
wo mich das Flügelaug streifte.

Dahinter,
ausgespart in der Wand,
die Stufe,
drauf das Erinnerte hockt.

Hierher
sickert, von Nächten beschenkt,
eine Stimme,
aus der du den Trunk schöpfst.

And the too-much of my talk:
taken up by the small
crystal tracht of your silence.

TODAY AND TOMORROW

So I stand, stony, to-
ward the distance I led you into:

By drift sand
washed out, the two
caves below the brow-seam.
Espied
darkness inside.

Beaten through
by silently swung hammers,
the spot,
where the wing'eye grazed me.

Behind,
recessed in the wall,
the step,
on which what's remembered squats.

From there
seeps, gifted by nights,
a voice,
from which you ladle the drink.

SCHLIERE

Schliere im Aug:
von den Blicken auf halbem
Weg erschautes Verloren.
Wirklichgesponnenes Niemals,
wiedergekehrt.

Wege, halb – und die längsten.

Seelenbeschrittene Fäden,
Glasspur,
rückwärtsgerollt
und nun
vom Augen-Du auf dem steten
Stern über dir
weiß überschleiert.

Schliere im Aug:
daß bewahrt sei
ein durchs Dunkel getragenes Zeichen,
vom Sand (oder Eis?) einer fremden
Zeit für ein fremderes Immer
belebt und als stumm
vibrierender Mitlaut gestimmt.

STREAK

Streak in the eye:
the lost caught half-
way by the gaze.
True-spun Never,
returned.

Paths, halfed—and the longest.

Threads walked on by souls,
glasspoor,
rolled backward
and now
by the Eye-you on the steady
star above you
veiled in white.

Streak in the eye:
that a sign
carried through darkness be salvaged
from the sand (or ice?) of a strange
time for an even stranger Always
enlivened and tuned as
a mutely vibrating consonant.

III

III

TENEBRAE

Nah sind wir, Herr,
nahe und greifbar.

Gegriffen schon, Herr,
ineinander verkrallt, als wär
der Leib eines jeden von uns
dein Leib, Herr.

Bete, Herr,
bete zu uns,
wir sind nah.

Windschief gingen wir hin,
gingen wir hin, uns zu bücken
nach Mulde und Maar.

Zur Tränke gingen wir, Herr.

Es war Blut, es war,
was du vergossen, Herr.

Es glänzte.

Es warf uns dein Bild in die Augen, Herr.
Augen und Mund stehn so offen und leer, Herr.
Wir haben getrunken, Herr.
Das Blut und das Bild, das im Blut war, Herr.

Bete, Herr.
Wir sind nah.

TENEBRAE

We are near, Lord,
near and graspable.

Grasped already, Lord,
clawed into each other, as if
each of our bodies was
your body, Lord.

Pray, Lord,
pray to us,
we are near.

Windbent we went there,
we went there to bend down
over crater and maar.

To the trough we went, Lord.

It was blood, it was
what you spilled, Lord.

It shone.

It cast your image into our eyes, Lord.
Eyes and mouths gape, so open and empty, Lord.
We have drunk, Lord.
The blood and the image that was in the blood, Lord.

Pray, Lord.
We are near.

BLUME

Der Stein.
Der Stein in der Luft, dem ich folgte.
Dein Aug, so blind wie der Stein.

Wir waren
Hände,
wir schöpften die Finsternis leer, wir fanden
das Wort, das den Sommer heraufkam:
Blume.

Blume – ein Blindenwort.
Dein Aug und mein Aug:
sie sorgen
für Wasser.

Wachstum.
Herzwand um Herzwand
blättert hinzu.

Ein Wort noch, wie dies, und die Hämmer
schwingen im Freien.

WEISS UND LEICHT

Sicheldünen, ungezählt.

Im Windschatten, tausendfach: du.
Du und der Arm,

FLOWER

The stone.
The stone in the air that I followed.
Your eye, as blind as the stone.

We were
hands,
we scooped the darkness empty, we found
the word that came up the summer:
flower.

Flower—a blindman's word.
Your eye and my eye:
they ensure
water.

Growth.
Heartwall by heartwall
refoliates.

One more word, like this one, and the hammers
will swing free.

WHITE AND LIGHT

Sickledunes, uncounted.

In the windshadow, a thousandfold: you.
You and the arm,

mit dem ich nackt zu dir hinwuchs,
Verlorne.

Die Strahlen. Sie wehn uns zuhauf.
Wir tragen den Schein, den Schmerz und den Namen.

Weiß,
was sich uns regt,
ohne Gewicht,
was wir tauschen.
Weiß und Leicht:
laß es wandern.

Die Fernen, mondnah, wie wir. Sie bauen.
Sie bauen die Klippe, wo
sich das Wandernde bricht,
sie bauen
weiter:
mit Lichtschaum und stäubender Welle.

Das Wandernde, klippenher winkend.
Die Stirnen
winkt es heran,
die Stirnen, die man uns lieh,
um der Spiegelung willen.

Die Stirnen.
Wir rollen mit ihnen dorthin.
Stirnengestade.

Schläfst du?

with which naked I grew toward you,
lost one.

The rays. They blow us into a heap.
We wear the shine, the pain and the name.

White,
what moves for us,
weightless,
what we barter.
White and light:
let it wander.

The distances, moon-close, as we are. They build.
They build the cliff, where
what wanders breaks,
they keep
building:
with lightspume and spraying wave.

What wanders, signaling from the cliffs.
The foreheads
it beckons,
the foreheads that were lent to us,
for the sake of the mirroring.

The foreheads.
We roll with them over there.
Forehead coasts.

Are you asleep?

Schlaf.

Meermühle geht,
eishell und ungehört,
in unsern Augen.

SPRACHGITTER

Augenrund zwischen den Stäben.

Flimmertier Lid
rudert nach oben,
gibt einen Blick frei.

Iris, Schwimmerin, traumlos und trüb:
der Himmel, herzgrau, muß nah sein.

Schräg, in der eisernen Tülle,
der blakende Span.
Am Lichtsinn
errätst du die Seele.

(Wär ich wie du. Wärst du wie ich.
Standen wir nicht
unter *einem* Passat?
Wir sind Fremde.)

Die Fliesen. Darauf,
dicht beieinander, die beiden

Sleep.

Seamill turns,
icebright and unheard,
in our eyes.

SPEECHGRILLE

Eyeround between the bars.

Flitterbug lid
rows upward,
frees a gaze.

Iris, swimmer, dreamless and dim:
the heavens, heartgray, must be near.

Slanted, in the iron socket
the smoldering splinter.
By its light-sense
you guess the soul.

(Were I like you. Were you like me.
Didn't we stand
under one trade wind?
We are strangers.)

The flagstone. On them,
close together, the two

herzgrauen Lachen:
zwei
Mundvoll Schweigen.

SCHNEEBETT

Augen, weltblind, im Sterbegeklüft: Ich komm,
Hartwuchs im Herzen.
Ich komm.

Mondspiegel Steilwand. Hinab.
(Atemgeflecktes Geleucht. Strichweise Blut.
Wölkende Seele, noch einmal gestaltnah.
Zehnfingerschatten – verklammert.)

Augen weltblind,
Augen im Sterbegeklüft,
Augen Augen:

Das Schneebett unter uns beiden, das Schneebett.
Kristall um Kristall,
zeittief gegittert, wir fallen,
wir fallen und liegen und fallen.

Und fallen:
Wir waren. Wir sind.
Wir sind ein Fleisch mit der Nacht.
In den Gängen, den Gängen.

heartgray pools:
two
mouthfuls of silence.

SNOWBED

Eyes, worldblind, in the deathcliffs: I come,
hardgrowth in the heart.
I come.

Moonmirror rockwall. Downward.
(Breathflecked lightglow. Blood streaks.
Clouding soul, once more near-shapely.
Tenfingershadow—gripclasped.)

Eyes worldblind,
eyes in the deathcliffs,
eyes, eyes.

The snowbed under us both, the snowbed.
Crystal after crystal,
meshed timedeep, we fall,
we fall and we lie and we fall.

And fall:
We were. We are.
We and the night are one flesh.
In the passageways, the passageways.

WINDGERECHT

Tafelwand, grau, mit dem Nachtfries.
Felder, windgerecht, Raute bei Raute,
schriftleer.
Leuchtassel klettert vorbei.

Gesänge:
Augenstimmen, im Chor,
lesen sich wund.
(Ungewesen und Da,
beides zumal,
geht durch die Herzen.)

Später:
Schneewuchs durch alle Gehäuse, frei
ein einziges Feld,
das ein Lichtschein beziffert: die Stimmen.

Die Stimmen:
windgerecht, herznah,
brandbestattet.

NACHT

Kies und Geröll. Und ein Scherbenton, dünn,
als Zuspruch der Stunde.

Augentausch, endlich, zur Unzeit:
bildbeständig,

WINDTRUE

Tablewall, gray, with nightfrieze.
Fields, windtrue, square after square
empty of writing.
Lightipede climbs past.

Chants:
Eyevoices, as choir,
read themselves sore.
(Never-been and Here,
both at once,
go through the hearts.)

Later:
snowgrowth through all enclosures, just
one field free,
it numbers a lightdazzle: the voices.

The voices:
wind true, heartnear,
cremation-buried.

NIGHT

Gravel and detrital. And a shardtone, thin,
the hour's exhortation.

Gaze-trade, finally, at untime:
imagefast,

verholzt
die Netzhaut –:
das Ewigkeitszeichen.

Denkbar:
droben, im Weltgestänge,
sterngleich,
das Rot zweier Münder.

Hörbar (vor Morgen?): ein Stein,
der den andern zum Ziel nahm.

MATIÈRE DE BRETAGNE

Ginsterlicht, gelb, die Hänge
eitern gen Himmel, der Dorn
wirbt um die Wunde, es läutet
darin, es ist Abend, das Nichts
rollt seine Meere zur Andacht,
das Blutsegel hält auf dich zu.

Trocken, verlandet
das Bett hinter dir, verschilft
seine Stunde, oben,
beim Stern, die milchigen
Priele schwatzen im Schlamm, Steindattel,
unten, gebuscht, klafft ins Gebläu, eine Staude
Vergänglichkeit, schön,
grüßt dein Gedächtnis.

lignified,
the retina—:
the eternity-sign.

Thinkable:
above, among the world-gears,
starlike,
the red of two mouths.

Audible (before dawn?): a stone,
that took the other as its aim.

MATIÈRE DE BRETAGNE

Gorselight, yellow, the slopes
pus skyward, the thorn
woos the wound, in it the bell
rings, it's evening, the Nothing
rolls its seas in worship,
the bloodsail heads toward you.

Dry, silted
up, the bed behind you, sedge-
choked, its hour, above,
next to the star, the milky
tidal inlets yack in the mud, stone-mussel
below, tufted, gapes into the blue, a shrub of
transience, pretty,
greets your memory.

(Kanntet ihr mich,
Hände? Ich ging
den gegabelten Weg, den ihr wiest, mein Mund
spie seinen Schotter, ich ging, meine Zeit,
wandernde Wächte, warf ihren Schatten – kanntet ihr mich?)

Hände, die dorn-
umworbene Wunde, es läutet,
Hände, das Nichts, seine Meere,
Hände, im Ginsterlicht, das
Blutsegel
hält auf dich zu.

Du
du lehrst
du lehrst deine Hände
du lehrst deine Hände du lehrst
du lehrst deine Hände
schlafen

SCHUTTKAHN

Wasserstunde, der Schuttkahn
fährt uns zu Abend, wir haben,
wie er, keine Eile, ein totes
Warum steht am Heck.

. . . .

(Did you know me,
hands? I walked
the forked path that you showed, my mouth
spit its gravel, I walked, my time,
a wandering snow cornice, cast its shadow—did you know me?)

Hands, the thorn-
wooed wound, it rings,
hands, the Nothing, its seas,
hands, in gorselight, the
bloodsail
heads toward you.

You
you teach
you teach your hands
you teach your hands you teach
you teach your hands to
                                        sleep

RUBBLE SCOW

Waterhour, the rubble scow
ferries us into evening, we,
like it, are in no hurry, a dead
Why stands at the stern.

. . . .

Geleichtert. Die Lunge, die Qualle
bläht sich zur Glocke, ein brauner
Seelenfortsatz erreicht
das hellgeatmete Nein.

Lightened. The lung, the jellyfish
swells into a bell, a brown
soul-extension reaches
the bright-breathed No.

IV

IV

KÖLN, AM HOF

Herzzeit, es stehn
die Geträumten für
die Mitternachtsziffer.

Einiges sprach in die Stille, einiges schwieg,
einiges ging seiner Wege.
Verbannt und Verloren
waren daheim.

Ihr Dome.

Ihr Dome ungesehn,
ihr Ströme unbelauscht,
ihr Uhren tief in uns.

IN DIE FERNE

Stummheit, aufs neue, geräumig, ein Haus –:
komm, du sollst wohnen.

Stunden, fluchschön gestuft: erreichbar
die Freistatt.

Schärfer als je die verbliebene Luft: du sollst atmen,
atmen und du sein.

COLOGNE, AM HOF

Hearttime, the dreamed
ones stand for
the midnight cipher.

Something spoke into the stillness, something was silent,
something went its way.
Exiled and Lost
were at home.

You cathedrals.

You cathedrals, unseen
you streams, unheard
you clocks, deep in us.

INTO THE DISTANCE

Muteness, anew, spacious, a house—:
come, you shall dwell.

Hours, staggered curse-handsome: within reach,
the sanctuary.

Sharper than ever the remaining air: you shall breathe,
breathe and be you.

EIN TAG UND NOCH EINER

Föhniges Du. Die Stille
flog uns voraus, ein zweites,
deutliches Leben.

Ich gewann, ich verlor, wir glaubten
an düstere Wunder, der Ast,
rasch an den Himmel geschrieben, trug uns, wuchs
durchs ziehende Weiß in die Mondbahn, ein Morgen
sprang ins Gestern hinauf, wir holten,
zerstoben, den Leuchter, ich stürzte
alles in niemandes Hand.

IN MUNDHÖHE

In Mundhöhe, fühlbar:
Finstergewächs.

(Brauchst es, Licht, nicht zu suchen, bleibst
das Schneegarn, hältst
deine Beute.

Beides gilt:
Berührt und Unberührt.
Beides spricht mit der Schuld von der Liebe,
beides will dasein und sterben.)

Blattnarben, Knospen, Gewimper.
Äugendes, tagfremd.
Schelfe, wahr und offen.

ONE DAY AND ONE MORE

Foehnish You. Stillness
flew ahead of us, a second,
clear life.

I won, I lost, we believed
in somber wonders, the branch,
quickly written into the sky, carried us, grew
through the drifting white into the moon-orbit, a
morning leaped up into yesterday, we retrieved
the candlestick, scattered, I crashed
everything into no-one's hand.

AT MOUTH LEVEL

At mouth level, palpable:
darkgrowth.

(Don't need to search for it, light, you
remain the snowsnare, you hold
your prey.

Both count:
the touched and the untouched.
Both speak with guilt about love,
both want to be and to die.)

Leafscars, buds, eyelashes.
Gazings, day-alien.
Involucre, true and open.

Lippe wußte. Lippe weiß.
Lippe schweigt es zu Ende.

EINE HAND

Der Tisch, aus Stundenholz, mit
dem Reisgericht und dem Wein.
Es wird
geschwiegen, gegessen, getrunken.

Eine Hand, die ich küßte,
leuchtet den Mündern.

ABER

(Du
fragst ja, ich
sags dir:)

Strahlengang, immer, die
Spiegel, nachtweit, stehn
gegeneinander, ich bin,
hingestoßen zu dir, eines
Sinnes mit diesem
Vorbei.

Lip knew. Lip knows.
Lip silences it to the end.

A HAND

The table, from hourwood, with
the rice dish and the wine.
There's
silence, eating, drinking.

A hand that I kissed
lights the way for the mouths.

BUT

(You
do ask, so I
tell you:)

Beampath, always, the
mirrors, nightwide, stand
against each other, I am,
pushed toward you, of one
mind with this
Done-With.

Aber: mein Herz
ging durch die Pause, es wünscht dir
das Aug, bildnah und zeitstark,
das mich verformt –:

die Schwäne,
in Genf, ich sah's nicht, flogen, es war,
als schwirrte, vom Nichts her, ein Wurfholz
ins Ziel einer Seele: soviel
Zeit
denk mir, als Auge, jetzt zu:
daß ichs
schwirren hör, näher – nicht
neben mir, nicht,
wo du nicht sein kannst.

ALLERSEELEN

Was hab ich
getan?
Die Nacht besamt, als könnt es
noch andere geben, nächtiger als
diese.

Vogelflug, Steinflug, tausend
beschriebene Bahnen. Blicke,
geraubt und gepflückt. Das Meer,
gekostet, vertrunken, verträumt. Eine Stunde,
seelenverfinstert. Die nächste, ein Herbstlicht,

But: my heart
crossed the interlude, wishes you
the eye, image-close and time-strong,
that distorts me—:

the swans
in Geneva, I didn't see, flew, it was
as if there whirred, out of the Nothing, a boomerang
targeting a soul: that much
time
allow me now, as an eye:
that I
may hear it whir, closer—not
next to me, not
where you cannot be.

ALL SOULS

What have I
done?
Inseminated the night, as if there
could be more, nightlier than
this one.

Birdflight, stoneflight, a thousand
described orbits. Gazes,
looted and plucked. The sea,
tasted, drunk dry, dreamed away. One hour
soul-eclipse. The next one, an autumn light,

dargebracht einem blinden
Gefühl, das des Wegs kam. Andere, viele,
ortlos und schwer aus sich selbst: erblickt und umgangen.
Findlinge, Sterne,
schwarz und voll Sprache: benannt
nach zerschwiegenem Schwur.

Und einmal (wann? auch dies ist vergessen):
den Widerhaken gefühlt,
wo der Puls den Gegentakt wagte.

ENTWURF EINER LANDSCHAFT

Rundgräber, unten. Im
Viertakt der Jahresschritt auf
den Steilstufen rings.

Laven, Basalte, weltherz-
durchglühtes Gestein.
Quelltuff,
wo uns das Licht wuchs, vor
dem Atem.

Ölgrün, meerdurchstäubt die
unbetretbare Stunde. Gegen
die Mitte zu, grau,
ein Steinsattel, drauf,
gebeult und verkohlt,
die Tierstirn mit
der strahligen Blesse.

burned offering to a blind
feeling that came this way. Others, many
placeless and heavy with themselves: glimpsed and dodged.
Erratics, stars,
black and full of language: named
after an oath silence-shredded.

And once (when? this too is forgotten):
the barbed hook, felt
where the pulse dared the counterbeat.

SKETCH FOR A LANDSCAPE

Roundgraves, below. In
quarter-time of yearspace on
the steep scarps all around.

Lavas, basalts, worldheart-
heattraversed rocks.
Calc-tufa,
where light grew for us, before
breath.

Oilgreen, seasprayed, the
inaccessible hour. To-
ward the center, gray,
a stonesaddle, on it,
warped and charred,
the beastbrow with
the radiant blaze.

V

V

EIN AUGE, OFFEN

Stunden, maifarben, kühl.
Das nicht mehr zu Nennende, heiß,
hörbar im Mund.

Niemandes Stimme, wieder.

Schmerzende Augapfeltiefe:
das Lid
steht nicht im Wege, die Wimper
zählt nicht, was eintritt.

Die Träne, halb,
die schärfere Linse, beweglich,
holt dir die Bilder.

Oben, geräuschlos, die
Fahrenden: Geier und Stern.

Unten, nach allem, wir,
zehn an der Zahl, das Sandvolk. Die Zeit,
wie denn auch nicht, sie hat
auch für uns eine Stunde, hier,
in der Sandstadt.

(Erzähl von den Brunnen, erzähl
von Brunnenkranz, Brunnenrad, von
Brunnenstuben – erzähl.

ONE EYE, OPEN

Hours, Maycolored, cool.
The no longer to be named, hot,
audible in the mouth.

No one's voice, again.

Painful eyeball-depth:
the lid
does not stand in the way, the lash
does not count what enters.

The tear, half,
the sharper lens, mobile,
brings you the images.

ABOVE, NOISELESS, the
travelers: vulture and star.

Below, after everything, we,
tallying ten, the sandpeople. Time
too, why shouldn't it,
has an hour for us, here,
in the sandcity.

(Tell of the wells, tell
of the well-wreath, well-wheel, the
well-parlors—tell.

Zähl und erzähl, die Uhr,
auch diese, läuft ab.

Wasser: welch
ein Wort. Wir verstehen dich, Leben.)

Der Fremde, ungebeten, woher,
der Gast.
Sein triefendes Kleid.
Sein triefendes Auge.

(Erzähl uns von Brunnen, von –
Zähl und erzähl.
Wasser: welch
ein Wort.)

Sein Kleid-und-Auge, er steht,
wie wir, voller Nacht, er bekundet
Einsicht, er zählt jetzt,
wie wir, bis zehn
und nicht weiter.

Oben, die
Fahrenden
bleiben
unhörbar.

DIE WELT, zu uns
in die leere Stunde getreten:

Tally and tell, the clock,
this one too, runs down.

Water: what
a word. We understand you, life.)

The stranger, unbidden, from where,
the guest.
His dripping garb.
His dripping eye.

(Tell us of wells, of—
tally and tell.
Water: what
a word.)

His garb-and-eye, he stands,
like us, full of night, he betokens
insight, he now counts,
as we do, up to ten
and no further.

Above, the
travelers
remain
inaudible.

THE WORLD, joining
us in the empty hour:

Zwei
Baumschäfte, schwarz,
unverzweigt, ohne
Knoten.
In der Düsenspur, scharfrandig, das
eine frei-
stehende Hochblatt.

Auch wir hier, im Leeren,
stehn bei den Fahnen.

Ein Holzstern, blau,
aus kleinen Rauten gebaut. Heute, von
der jüngsten unserer Hände.

Das Wort, während
du Salz aus der Nacht fällst, der Blick
wieder die Windgalle sucht:

– Ein Stern, tu ihn,
tu den Stern in die Nacht.

(– In meine, in
meine.)

Two
tree trunks, black,
unbranched, without
nodes.
In the contrail, sharp edged, the
one free-
standing spathe.

We too, here in the emptiness,
stand by the banners.

A WOODSTAR, blue,
built of small rhombs. Today, by
the youngest of our hands.

The word, while
you, salt, fell from the night, the gaze
again seeks the rainbow's lightfoot:

—A star, put it,
put the star into the night.

(—Into mine, into
mine.)

SOMMERBERICHT

Der nicht mehr beschrittene, der
umgangene Thymianteppich.
Eine Leerzeile, quer
durch die Glockenheide gelegt.
Nichts in den Windbruch getragen.

Wieder Begegnungen mit
vereinzelten Worten wie:
Steinschlag, Hartgräser, Zeit.

NIEDRIGWASSER. Wir sahen
die Seepocke, sahen
die Napfschnecke, sahen
die Nägel an unsern Händen.
Niemand schnitt uns das Wort von der Herzwand.

(Fährten der Strandkrabbe, morgen,
Kriechfurchen, Wohngänge, Wind-
zeichnung im grauen
Schlick. Feinsand,
Grobsand, das
von den Wänden Gelöste, bei
andern Hartteilen, im
Schill.)

Ein Aug, heute,
gab es dem zweiten, beide,
geschlossen, folgten der Strömung zu

SUMMER REPORT

The no longer trodden, the
skirted thyme-carpet.
An empty line, aslant
the cross-leaved heath.
Nothing carried into the windbreak.

Again, encounters with
single words like:
rockfall, hardgrass, time.

LOWWATER. We saw
the acorn-barnacle, saw
the limpet, saw
the nails on our hands.
No one cut the word from our heart wall.

(Tracks of green crab, tomorrow,
creep-furrows, crawlways, wind-
sketch in gray
ooze. Fine sand,
coarse sand, that
peeled off the walls, next
to other hard-parts, in the
shell-sediments.)

An eye, today,
gave it to the second, both
closed, followed the current to

ihrem Schatten, setzten
die Fracht ab (*niemand*
schnitt uns das Wort von der – –), bauten
den Haken hinaus – eine Nehrung, vor
ein kleines
unbefahrbares Schweigen.

BAHNDÄMME, WEGRÄNDER, ÖDPLÄTZE, SCHUTT

Lichtgewinn, meßbar, aus
Distelähnlichem:
einiges
Rot, im Gespräch
mit einigem Gelb.
Die Luftschleier vor
deinem verzweifelten Aug.
Das letzte
reitende Sandkorn.

(Die
Augärten, damals, das
gelächelte Wort
vom Marchfeld, vom
Steppengras dort.
Das tote Ringelspiel, kling.
Wir
drehten uns weiter.)

their shadow, set
down the freight (*no one
cut the word from our—— —*), built
the hook farther out—sand spit, before
a small
unnavigable silence.

EMBANKMENTS, ROADSIDES, VACANT LOTS, RUBBLE

Lightgain, measurable, out
of thistle-likeness:
some
red, in conversation
with some yellow.
The airveils before
your despairing eye.
The last
riding sandgrain.

(The
Augarten, back then, the
smiled word
about Marchfeld, the
steppe grass there.
The dead merry-go-round, ding.
We
kept on turning.)

Der Sandkornritt, das
Auge, ihm zugewandt.
Die Stundentür und
ihre Geräusche.

ENGFÜHRUNG

*

Verbracht ins
Gelände
mit der untrüglichen Spur:

Gras, auseinandergeschrieben. Die Steine, weiß,
mit den Schatten der Halme:
Lies nicht mehr – schau!
Schau nicht mehr – geh!

Geh, deine Stunde
hat keine Schwestern, du bist –
bist zuhause. Ein Rad, langsam,
rollt aus sich selber, die Speichen
klettern,
klettern auf schwärzlichem Feld, die Nacht
braucht keine Sterne, nirgends
fragt es nach dir.

*

Nirgends
Fragt es nach dir –

The sandgrain-ride, the
eye, turned toward it.
The hourdoor and
its noises.

STRETTO

*

Displaced into
the terrain
with the unmistakable track:

Grass, written asunder. The stones, white,
with the stalks' shadows:
Stop reading—look!
Stop looking—go!

Go, your hour
has no sisters, you are—
are at home. A wheel, slowly,
rolls out of itself, the spokes
climb,
climb on a blackish field, night
needs no stars, nowhere
are you asked after.

*

Nowhere
are you asked after—

Der Ort, wo sie lagen, er hat
einen Namen – er hat
keinen. Sie lagen nicht dort. Etwas
lag zwischen ihnen. Sie
sahn nicht hindurch

Sahn nicht, nein,
redeten von
Worten. Keines
erwachte, der
Schlaf
kam über sie.

*

Kam, kam. Nirgends
fragt es –

Ich bins, ich,
ich lag zwischen euch, ich war
offen, war
hörbar, ich tickte euch zu, euer Atem
gehorchte, ich
bin es noch immer, ihr
schlaft ja.

*

Bin es noch immer –

Jahre.
Jahre, Jahre, ein Finger
tastet hinab und hinan, tastet
umher:

The place where they lay, it has
a name—it has
none. They didn't lie there. Something
lay between them. They
didn't see through it.

Didn't see, no,
talked of
words. None
woke up,
sleep
came over them.

*

Came, came. Nowhere
asked after—

It's me, me,
I lay between you, I was
open, was
audible, I ticked toward you, your breath
obeyed, I
am still the one, as
you're asleep.

*

Am still the one—

Years.
Years, years, a finger
feels down and up, feels
around:

Nahtstellen, fühlbar, hier
klafft es weit auseinander, hier
wuchs es wieder zusammen – wer
deckte es zu?

*

Deckte es
zu – wer?

Kam, kam.
Kam ein Wort, kam,
kam durch die Nacht,
wollt leuchten, wollt leuchten.

Asche.
Asche, Asche.
Nacht.
Nacht-und-Nacht. – Zum
Aug geh, zum feuchten.

*

Zum
Aug geh,
zum feuchten –

Orkane.
Orkane, von je,
Partikelgestöber, das andre,
du
weißts ja, wir
lasens im Buche, war
Meinung.

seams, palpable, here
they gape wide open, here
it grew together again—who
covered it up?

*

Covered it
up—who?

Came, came.
Came a word, came,
came through the night,
wanted to shine, wanted to shine.

Ashes.
Ashes, ashes.
Night.
Night-and-night.—To
the eye, go, to the moist.

*

To
the eye go,
to the moist—

Hurricanes.
Hurricanes, from whenever,
particle flurries, the other,
you
know this, we
read it in the book, it was
opinion.

War, war
Meinung. Wie
faßten wir uns
an – an mit
diesen
Händen?

Es stand auch geschrieben, daß.
Wo? Wir
taten ein Schweigen darüber,
giftgestillt, groß,
ein
grünes
Schweigen, ein Kelchblatt, es
hing ein Gedanke an Pflanzliches dran –
grün, ja
hing, ja,
unter hämischem
Himmel.

An, ja,
Pflanzliches.

Ja.
Orkane, Par-
tikelgestöber, es blieb
Zeit, blieb,
es beim Stein zu versuchen – er
war gastlich, er
fiel nicht ins Wort. Wie
gut wir es hatten:

Was, was
opinion. How
did we grasp
each other—with
these
hands?

And it stood written that.
Where? We
put a silence over it,
poison-stilled, huge,
a
green
silence, a sepal, a
thought of plant life hung from it—
green, yes
hung, yes,
under spiteful
skies.

Of, yes,
plant life.

Yes.
Hurricanes, par-
ticle flurries, there remained
time, remained,
to try it with the stone—it
was hospitable, it
didn't interrupt. How
good we had it:

Körnig,
körnig und faserig. Stengelig,
dicht;
traubig und strahlig; nierig,
plattig und
klumpig; locker, ver-
ästelt –: er, es
fiel nicht ins Wort, es
sprach,
sprach gerne zu trockenen Augen, eh es sie schloß.

Sprach, sprach.
War, war.

Wir
ließen nicht locker, standen
inmitten, ein
Porenbau, und
es kam.

Kam auf uns zu, kam
hindurch, flickte
unsichtbar, flickte
an der letzten Membran,
und
die Welt, ein Tausendkristall,
schoß an, schoß an.

*

Schoß an, schoß an.
Dann –

gritty,
gritty and stringy. Stalky,
dense;
clustery and raying; knobbly,
level and
clumpy; loose, bran-
ching—: he, it
did not interrupt, it
spoke,
liked speaking to dry eyes, before it closed them.

Spoke, spoke.
Was, was.

We
did not let go, held tight
in the midst, a
pore-structure, and
it came.

Came up to us, came
right through, sewed
invisibly, sewed
at the last membrane,
and
the world, a thousandcrystal,
formed, formed.

*

Formed, formed

Then—

Nächte, entmischt. Kreise,
grün oder blau, rote
Quadrate: die
Welt setzt ihr Innerstes ein
im Spiel mit den neuen
Stunden. – Kreise
rot oder schwarz, helle
Quadrate, kein
Flugschatten,
kein
Meßtisch, keine
Rauchseele steigt und spielt mit.

*

Steigt und
spielt mit –

In der Eulenflucht, beim
versteinerten Aussatz,
bei
unsern geflohenen Händen, in
der jüngsten Verwerfung,
überm
Kugelfang an
der verschütteten Mauer:

sichtbar, aufs
neue: die
Rillen, die

Chöre, damals, die
Psalmen. Ho, ho-
sianna.

Nights, separated out. Circles,
green or blue, red
squares: the
world puts its innermost
into play with the new
hours.—Circles
red or black, bright
squares, no
flight shadows,
no
plane table, no
smokesoul rises and plays along.

*

Rises and
plays along

In owlflight, near
petrified leprosy,
near
our fled hands, in
the latest fault lines,
above the
bullet trap on
the ruined wall:

visible, a-
gain: the
furrows, the

choirs, back then, the
psalms. Ho, ho-
sanna.

Also
stehen noch Tempel. Ein
Stern
hat wohl noch Licht.
Nichts,
nichts ist verloren.

Ho-
sianna.

In der Eulenflucht, hier,
die Gespräche, taggrau,
der Grundwasserspuren.

*

(– – taggrau,
der
Grundwasserspuren –

Verbracht
ins Gelände
mit
der untrüglichen
Spur:

Gras.
Gras,
auseinandergeschrieben.)

The
temples still stand. A
star
still has its light.
Nothing,
nothing is lost.

Ho-
sanna.

In the owlflight, here,
the conversations, daygray,
of groundwater tracks.

*

(—daygray,
of
groundwater tracks—

Discarried
into the terrain
with
the unmistakable
track:

Grass.
Grass,
written asunder.)

Die Niemandsrose

Dem Andenken Ossip Mandelstamms

NoOnesRose

To the memory of Osip Mandelstam

Es war Erde in ihnen, und
sie gruben.

Sie gruben und gruben, so ging
ihr Tag dahin, ihre Nacht. Und sie lobten nicht Gott,
der, so hörten sie, alles dies wollte,
der, so hörten sie, alles dies wußte.

Sie gruben und hörten nichts mehr;
sie wurden nicht weise, erfanden kein Lied,
erdachten sich keinerlei Sprache.
Sie gruben.

Es kam eine Stille, es kam auch ein Sturm,
es kamen die Meere alle.
Ich grabe, du gräbst, und es gräbt auch der Wurm,
und das Singende dort sagt: Sie graben.

O einer, o keiner, o niemand, o du:
Wohin gings, da's nirgendhin ging?
O du gräbst und ich grab, und ich grab mich dir zu,
und am Finger erwacht uns der Ring.

Das Wort vom Zur-Tiefe-Gehn,
das wir gelesen haben.
Die Jahre, die Worte seither.
Wir sind es noch immer.

Weißt du, der Raum ist unendlich,
weißt du, du brauchst nicht zu fliegen,

There was earth inside them, and
they dug.

They dug and dug, thus did
their day go, their night. And they did not praise God,
who, so they heard, wanted all this,
who, so they heard, knew all this.

They dug and heard nothing more;
they didn't grow wise, invented no song,
thought up no language for themselves.
They dug.

A stillness came, a storm too came,
all the seas came.
I dig, you dig, and the worm too digs,
and what sings over there says: they dig.

O one, o no one, o noone, o you:
Where did it lead, as it led nowhere?
O you dig and I dig, and I dig myself toward you,
and on our finger the ring awakens.

The word about going-into-the-depth,
that we have read.
The years, the words since then.
It is still and always us.

You know, space is infinite,
you know, you don't need to fly,

weißt du, was sich in dein Aug schrieb,
vertieft uns die Tiefe.

Bei Wein und Verlorenheit, bei
beider Neige:

ich ritt durch den Schnee, hörst du,
ich ritt Gott in die Ferne – die Nähe, er sang,
es war
unser letzter Ritt über
die Menschen-Hürden.

Sie duckten sich, wenn
sie uns über sich hörten, sie
schrieben, sie
logen unser Gewieher
um in eine
ihrer bebilderten Sprachen.

ZÜRICH, ZUM STORCHEN

für Nelly Sachs

Vom Zuviel war die Rede, vom
Zuwenig. Von Du
und Aber-Du, von
der Trübung durch Helles, von
Jüdischem, von
deinem Gott.

you know, what wrote itself into your eye
deepens the depth for us.

WITH WINE AND LOSTNESS, with
both dwindling:

I rode through the snow, you hear?
I rode God into the far—the near, he sang,
'twas
our last ride over
the human-hurdles.

They ducked, when
they heard us overhead, they
wrote, they
lied our neighs
into one of
their pixilated lingos.

ZÜRICH, HOTEL ZUM STORCHEN

for Nelly Sachs

Our talk turned on the Too Much, on the
Too Little. On you
on and-yet-you, on
blurring through brightness, on
Jewishness, on
your God.

Da-
von.
Am Tag einer Himmelfahrt, das
Münster stand drüben, es kam
mit einigem Gold übers Wasser.

Von deinem Gott war die Rede, ich sprach
gegen ihn, ich
ließ das Herz, das ich hatte,
hoffen:
auf
sein höchstes, umröcheltes, sein
haderndes Wort –

Dein Aug sah mir zu, sah hinweg,
dein Mund
sprach sich dem Aug zu, ich hörte:

Wir
wissen ja nicht, weißt du,
wir
wissen ja nicht,
was
gilt.

SELBDRITT, SELBVIERT

Krauseminze, Minze, krause,
vor dem Haus hier, vor dem Hause.

On
that.
On the day of an ascension, the
Minster stood over there, it came
with some gold across the water.

There was talk of your God, I spoke
against him, I
let the heart I had
hope:
for
his highest, his death-rattled, his
contending word—

Your eye looked at me, looked away,
your mouth
spoke across to the eye, I heard:

We
just don't know, you know,
we
just don't know,
what
counts.

THREESOME, FOURSOME

Curly mint, mint, curly,
before the house here, before the hour.

Diese Stunde, deine Stunde,
ihr Gespräch mit meinem Munde.

Mit dem Mund, mit seinem Schweigen,
mit den Worten, die sich weigern.

Mit den Weiten, mit den Engen,
mit den nahen Untergängen.

Mit mir einem, mit uns dreien,
halb gebunden, halb im Freien.

Krauseminze, Minze, krause,
vor dem Haus hier, vor dem Hause.

Soviel Gestirne, die
man uns hinhält. Ich war,
als ich dich ansah – wann? –,
draußen bei
den andern Welten.

O diese Wege, galaktisch,
o diese Stunde, die uns
die Nächte herüberwog in
die Last unsrer Namen. Es ist,
ich weiß es, nicht wahr,
daß wir lebten, es ging
blind nur ein Atem zwischen
Dort und Nicht-da und Zuweilen,
kometenhaft schwirrte ein Aug

This hour, your house,
its conversation with my mouth.

With the mouth, with its silence,
with the words that refuse themselves.

With the wide, with the narrow stations,
with the nearby devastations.

With me alone, with us three,
half-bound, half-free.

Curly mint, mint, curly,
before the hour here, before the house.

So many constellations, dis-
played to us. I was,
when I looked at you—when?—
outside with
the other worlds.

O, these paths, galactic,
O this hour that billowed
the nights over to us into
the burden of our names. It is,
I know, not true,
that we lived, a mere
breath blindly moved between
there and not-there and sometimes,
comet-like an eye whizzed

auf Erloschenes zu, in den Schluchten,
da, wo's verglühte, stand
zitzenprächtig die Zeit,
an der schon empor- und hinab-
und hinwegwuchs, was
ist oder war oder sein wird –,

ich weiß,
ich weiß und du weißt, wir wußten,
wir wußten nicht, wir
waren ja da und nicht dort,
und zuweilen, wenn
nur das Nichts zwischen uns stand, fanden
wir ganz zueinander.

DEIN
HINÜBERSEIN heute Nacht.
Mit Worten holt ich dich wieder, da bist du,
alles ist wahr und ein Warten
auf Wahres.

Es klettert die Bohne vor
unserm Fenster: denk
wer neben uns aufwächst und
ihr zusieht.

Gott, das lasen wir, ist
ein Teil und ein zweiter, zerstreuter:
im Tod
all der Gemähten
wächst er sich zu.

toward extinguished matter, in the canyons,
there where it burned out, stood
tit-gorgeous time, along
which grew up and down
& away what
is or was or will be—,

I know,
I know and you know, we knew,
we didn't know, for we
were there and not there,
and sometimes, when
only Nothingness stood between us, we
found truly together.

YOUR
HAVING CROSSED over tonight.
With words I brought you back, here you are,
all is true and a waiting
for the true.

The bean climbs in front
of our window: think
of who grows up near us and
watches it.

God, we read it, is
a part and a second one, scattered:
in the death
of all the mowed ones
he grows toward himself.

Dorthin
führt uns der Blick,
mit dieser
Hälfte
haben wir Umgang.

Zu beiden Händen, da
wo die Sterne mir wuchsen, fern
allen Himmeln, nah
allen Himmeln:
Wie
wacht es sich da! Wie
tut sich die Welt uns auf, mitten
durch uns!

Du bist,
wo dein Aug ist, du bist
oben, bist
unten, ich
finde hinaus.

O diese wandernde leere
gastliche Mitte. Getrennt,
fall ich dir zu, fällst
du mir zu, einander
entfallen, sehn wir
hindurch:

Das
Selbe

That's where
our gaze leads us,
with this
half
we stay in touch.

TO BOTH HANDS, there
where the stars grew for me, far
from all skies, near
all skies:
How
it wakes there! How
the world opens for us, straight
through us!

You are
where your eye is, you are
above, are
below, I
find my way out.

O this wandering empty
hospitable Middle. Separated,
I accrue to you, you
accrue to me, we devolve
to each other, we see
through:

The
same

hat uns
verloren, das
Selbe
hat uns
vergessen, das
Selbe
hat uns – –

ZWÖLF JAHRE

Die wahr-
gebliebene, wahr-
gewordene Zeile: . . . *dein*
Haus in Paris – zur
Opferstatt deiner Hände.

Dreimal durchatmet,
dreimal durchglänzt.

. . . .

Es wird stumm, es wird taub
hinter den Augen.
Ich sehe das Gift blühn.
In jederlei Wort und Gestalt.

Geh. Komm.
Die Liebe löscht ihren Namen: sie
schreibt sich dir zu.

has
lost us, the
same
has forgotten
us, the same
has us—

TWELVE YEARS

The line that stayed
true, that became
true: . . . *your*
house in Paris—into the
sacrificial altar of your hands.

Three times breathed-through,
three times shone-through.

. . . .

It grows mute, it grows deaf
behind the eyes.
I see the poison bloom.
In whatever word or shape.

Go. Come,
Love erases its name: it
writes itself toward you.

Mit allen Gedanken ging ich
hinaus aus der Welt: da warst du,
du meine Leise, du meine Offne, und –
du empfingst uns.

Wer
sagt, daß uns alles erstarb,
da uns das Aug brach?
Alles erwachte, alles hob an.

Groß kam eine Sonne geschwommen, hell
standen ihr Seele und Seele entgegen, klar,
gebieterisch schwiegen sie ihr
ihre Bahn vor.

Leicht
tat sich dein Schoß auf, still
stieg ein Hauch in den Äther,
und was sich wölkte, wars nicht,
wars nicht Gestalt und von uns her,
wars nicht
so gut wie ein Name?

DIE SCHLEUSE

Über aller dieser deiner
Trauer: kein
zweiter Himmel.

WITH ALL MY THOUGHTS I
left the world: and there you were,
you my quiet, you my Open one, and—
you received us.

Who
says that everything died for us
when our eyes broke?
Everything awoke, everything began.

A large sun came swimming, brightly
did soul and soul stand toward it, clear,
commandingly their silence drew
its orbit.

Easily
your lap opened, calmly
a breath rose into the ether,
and what cloud-cambered, wasn't it,
wasn't it a shape we projected before us,
wasn't it
as good as a name?

THE SLUICE

Above all this grief
of yours: no
second heaven.

. . . .

An einen Mund,
dem es ein Tausendwort war,
verlor –
verlor ich ein Wort,
das mir verblieben war:
Schwester.

An
die Vielgötterei
verlor ich ein Wort, das mich suchte:
Kaddisch.

Durch
die Schleuse mußt ich,
das Wort in die Salzflut zurück-
und hinaus- und hinüberzuretten:
Jiskor.

STUMME HERBSTGERÜCHE. Die
Sternblume, ungeknickt, ging
zwischen Heimat und Abgrund durch
dein Gedächtnis.

Eine fremde Verlorenheit war
gestalthaft zugegen, du hättest
beinah
gelebt.

. . . .

To a mouth,
for which it was a thousandword,
I lost—
I lost a word
that had remained with me:
sister.

To
the many gods
I lost a word, that searched for me:
Kaddish.

Through
the sluice I had to go,
so as to save the word, back
to and across and over the saltflood:
Yizkor.

MUTE AUTUMN ODORS. The
aster, unbent, passed
between homeland and abyss through
your memory.

A strange lostness was
palpably present, you could
almost have
lived.

EIS, EDEN

Es ist ein Land Verloren,
da wächst ein Mond im Ried,
und das mit uns erfroren,
es glüht umher und sieht.

Es sieht, denn es hat Augen,
die helle Erden sind.
Die Nacht, die Nacht, die Laugen.
Es sieht, das Augenkind.

Es sieht, es sieht, wir sehen,
ich sehe dich, du siehst.
Das Eis wird auferstehen,
eh sich die Stunde schließt.

PSALM

Niemand knetet uns wieder aus Erde und Lehm,
niemand bespricht unsern Staub.
Niemand.

Gelobt seist du, Niemand.
Dir zulieb wollen
wir blühn.
Dir
entgegen.

ICE, EDEN

There is a land called Lost,
a moon grows in its reeds,
what with us died by frost
glows all around and sees.

It sees, for it has eyes,
earths each one, and bright.
The night, the night, the lyes.
This eye-child's gift is sight.

It sees, it sees, we see,
I see you, you see.
The ice will resurrect,
ere this hour can defect.

PSALM

NoOne kneads us again of earth and clay,
noOne conjures our dust.
Noone.

Praised be thou, NoOne.
For your sake we
want to flower.
Toward
you.

Ein Nichts
waren wir, sind wir, werden
wir bleiben, blühend:
die Nichts-, die
Niemandsrose.

Mit
dem Griffel seelenhell,
dem Staubfaden himmelswüst,
der Krone rot
vom Purpurwort, das wir sangen
über, o über
dem Dorn.

TÜBINGEN, JÄNNER

Zur Blindheit über-
redete Augen.
Ihre – »ein
Rätsel ist Rein-
entsprungenes« –, ihre
Erinnerung an
schwimmende Hölderlintürme, möwen-
umschwirrt.

Besuche ertrunkener Schreiner bei
diesen
tauchenden Worten:

A Nothing
we were, we are, we will
remain, flowering:
the Nothing-, the
NoOnesRose.

With
pistil soul-bright,
stamen heaven-desolate,
the corona red
from the scarlet-word, that we sang
above, O above
the thorn.

TÜBINGEN, JÄNNER

Eyes con-
vinced to go blind.
Their—“a
riddle is pure
source”—, their
remembrance of
swimming Hölderlin-towers, gull-
circled.

Visits of drowned carpenters by
these
diving words:

Käme,
käme ein Mensch,
käme ein Mensch zur Welt, heute, mit
dem Lichtbart der
Patriarchen: er dürfte,
spräch er von dieser
Zeit, er
dürfte
nur lallen und lallen,
immer-, immer-
zuzu.

(»Pallaksch. Pallaksch.«)

CHYMISCH

Schweigen, wie Gold gekocht, in
verkohlten
Händen.

Große, graue,
wie alles Verlorene nahe
Schwestergestalt:

Alle die Namen, alle die mit-
verbrannten
Namen. Soviel
zu segnende Asche. Soviel
gewonnenes Land

If,
if a man,
if a man was born, today, with
the lightbeard of
the patriarchs: he could,
speaking of these
days, he
could
but babble and babble,
all-all, way-ways
agagain.

("Pallaksch. Pallaksch.")

ALCHEMICAL

Silence, cooked like gold, in
charred
hands.

Great, gray,
close, like all that's lost,
sistershape:

All the names, all the al-
so burned
names. So much
ash to be blessed. So much
land won

über
den leichten, so leichten
Seelen-
ringen.

Große. Graue. Schlacken-
lose.

Du, damals.
Du mit der fahlen,
aufgebissenen Knospe.
Du in der Weinflut.

(Nicht wahr, auch uns
entließ diese Uhr?
Gut,
gut, wie dein Wort hier vorbeistarb.)

Schweigen, wie Gold gekocht, in
verkohlten, verkohlten
Händen.
Finger, rauchdünn. Wie Kronen, Luftkronen
um – –

Große. Graue. Fährte-
lose.
König-
liche.

above
the light, so weightless
soul-
rings.

Great. Gray. Cinder-
less.

You. Back then.
You with the livid
bit-open bud.
You in the wine-flood.

(Isn't it true, us too
this clock did release?
Good,
good, how your word died past here.)

Silence, cooked like gold, in
charred, charred
hands.
Finger, smoke-thin. Like crowns, aircrowns
around—

Great. Gray. Trace-
less.
Re-
gal.

EINE GAUNER- UND GANOVENWEISE GESUNGEN ZU PARIS EMPRÈS PONTOISE

Von Paul Celan
Aus Czernowirz Bei Sadagora

Manchmal nur, in dunkeln Zeiten,
Heinrich Heine, An Edom

Damals, als es noch Galgen gab,
da, nicht wahr, gab es
ein Oben.

Wo bleibt mein Bart, Wind, wo
mein Judenfleck, wo
mein Bart, den du raufst?

Krumm war der Weg, den ich ging,
krumm war er, ja,
denn, ja,
er war gerade.

Heia.

Krumm, so wird meine Nase.
Nase.

Und wir zogen auch nach *Friaul.*
Da hätten wir, da hätten wir.
Denn es blühte der Mandelbaum.
Mandelbaum, Bandelmaum.

Mandeltraum, Trandelmaum.
Und auch der Machandelbaum.
Chandelbaum.

A GONIF- AND GANGSTER-DITTY SUNG IN PARIS EMPRÈS PONTOISE

by Paul Celan

From Czernowitz near Sadagora

Only sometimes, in dark times,

Heinrich Heine, "An Edom"

Back then, when there still were gallows,
then too, isn't it true, there was
an Above.

Where's my beard, wind, where
my Jew's-patch, where
my beard, that you tussled?

Crooked was the path I took,
crooked it was, yes,
because, yes,
it was straight.

Hey-ho.

Crooked, like my nose becomes.
Nose.

And we made our way to *Friuli.*
There we'd have, there we'd have.
For it blossomed, the almond tree.
Almondtree, Talmundree.

Almondream, Traumandtree.
Also the Junipertree.
The Candletree.

Heia.
Aum.

Envoi

Aber,
aber er bäumt sich, der Baum. Er,
auch er
steht gegen
die Pest.

Heya-
Aum.

Envoi.

But,
but it rears up, the tree. It,
it too
stands against
the Plague.

II

II

FLIMMERBAUM

Ein Wort,
an das ich dich gerne verlor:
das Wort
Nimmer.

Es war,
und bisweilen wußtest auch du's,
es war
eine Freiheit.
Wir schwammen.

Weißt du noch, daß ich sang?
Mit dem Flimmerbaum sang ich, dem Steuer.
Wir schwammen.

Weißt du noch, daß du schwammst?
Offen lagst du mir vor,
lagst du mir, lagst
du mir vor
meiner vor-
springenden Seele.
Ich schwamm für uns beide. Ich schwamm nicht.
Der Flimmerbaum schwamm.

Schwamm er? Es war
ja ein Tümpel rings. Es war der unendliche Teich.
Schwarz und unendlich, so hing,
so hing er weltabwärts.

FLIMMERTREE

A word,
to which I lost you gladly:
the word
Never.

It was,
and at times you too knew it,
it was
a freedom.
We swam.

Do you remember that I sang?
With the flimmertree I sang, the rudder.
We swam.

Do you remember that you swam?
Open you lay before me,
lay for me, lay
before me be-
fore my for-
ward jumping soul.
I swam for both of us, I didn't swim.
The flimmertree swam.

Did it swim? There was
a pool around us, yes. It was the endless pond.
Black and endless, thus it hung,
thus it hung worlddownward.

Weißt du noch, daß ich sang?

Diese –
o diese Drift.

Nimmer. Weltabwärts. Ich sang nicht. Offen
lagst du mir vor
der fahrenden Seele.

ERRATISCH

Die Abende graben sich dir
unters Aug. Mit der Lippe auf-
gesammelte Silben – schönes,
lautloses Rund –
helfen dem Kriechstern
in ihre Mitte. Der Stein,
schläfennah einst, tut sich hier auf:

bei allen
versprengten
Sonnen, Seele,
warst du, im Äther.

EINIGES HAND-
ÄHNLICHE, finster,
kam mit den Gräsern:

Do you remember that I sang?

This—
o this drift.

Never. Worlddownward. I didn't sing. Open
you lay before
the traveling soul.

ERRATIC

The evenings dig themselves
under your eye. With the lip ga-
thered syllables—beautiful,
soundless round—
help the crawlstar
in their midst. The stone,
once temple-close, now opens here:

with all
the scattered
suns, soul,
you were, up in the ether.

SOMETHING HAND-
LIKE, dark,
came with the grasses:

Rasch – Verzweiflungen, ihr
Töpfer! –, rasch
gab die Stunde den Lehm her, rasch
war die Träne gewonnen –:

noch einmal, mit bläulicher Rispe,
umstand es uns, dieses
Heute.

. . . RAUSCHT DER BRUNNEN

Ihr gebet-, ihr lästerungs-, ihr
gebetscharfen Messer
meines
Schweigens.

Ihr meine mit mir ver-
krüppelnden Worte, ihr
meine geraden.

Und du:
du, du, du
mein täglich wahr- und wahrer-
geschundenes Später
der Rosen –:

Wieviel, o wieviel
Welt. Wieviel
Wege.

Quickly—despairs, you
potters!—, quickly
the hour offered the clay, quickly
the tear was won—:

once more, with bluish panicle,
it stood around us, this
Today.

. . . WHISPERS THE FOUNTAIN

You prayer-, you blasphemy-, you
prayersharp knives
of my
silence.

You my with me crip-
pling words, you
my straight ones,

And thou:
thou, thou, thou
my daily true- and truer-
flayed Later
of the Roses—:

How much, oh how much
world. How many
ways.

Krücke du, Schwinge. Wir – –

Wir werden das Kinderlied singen, das,
hörst du, das
mit den Men, mit den Schen, mit den Menschen, ja das
mit dem Gestrüpp und mit
dem Augenpaar, das dort bereitlag als
Träne-und-
Träne.

Es ist nicht mehr
diese
zuweilen mit dir
in die Stunde gesenkte
Schwere. Es ist
eine andre.

Es ist das Gewicht, das die Leere zurückhält,
die mit-
ginge mit dir.
Es hat, wie du, keinen Namen. Vielleicht
seid ihr dasselbe. Vielleicht
nennst auch du mich einst
so.

You crutch, you wing. We—

We will sing the children's song, the one,
listen, the one
with the hu, with the mans, with the humans, yes the
one with the brushwood and with
the pair of eyes that lay ready there as
tear-and-
tear.

IT IS NO LONGER
this
heaviness sunk
at times with you
into this hour. It is
another one.

It is the weight that holds back the emptiness,
that accom-
panies you.
Like you, it has no name. Maybe
you are the same. Maybe
some day you'll call me that
too.

RADIX, MATRIX

Wie man zum Stein spricht, wie
du,
mir vom Abgrund her, von
einer Heimat her Ver-
schwisterte, Zu-
geschleuderte, du,
du mir vorzeiten,
du mir im Nichts einer Nacht,
du in der Aber-Nacht Be-
gegnete, du
Aber-Du –:

Damals, da ich nicht da war,
damals, da du
den Acker abschrittst, allein:

Wer,
wer wars, jenes
Geschlecht, jenes gemordete, jenes
schwarz in den Himmel stehende:
Rute und Hode –?

(Wurzel.
Wurzel Abrahams. Wurzel Jesse. Niemandes
Wurzel – o
unser.)

Ja,
wie man zum Stein spricht, wie
du

RADIX, MATRIX

As one speaks to stone, as
you,
to me from the abyss, from
a homeland, en-
sistered. Here-
thrown, you,
you pretime for me,
you to me in a night's nothing,
you in the but-night en-
countered, you
But-You—:

Back when, when I wasn't there,
back when, when you
paced off the field, alone:

Who,
who was it, that
Geschlecht, the murdered one, the one standing
black into the sky:
Rod and testicle—?

(Root.
Abraham's root. Jesse's root. NoOne's
root—o
ours.)

Yes,
as one speaks to stone, as
you

mit meinen Händen dorthin
und ins Nichts greifst, so
ist, was hier ist:

auch dieser
Fruchtboden klafft,
dieses
Hinab
ist die eine der wild-
blühenden Kronen.

SCHWARZERDE, schwarze
Erde du, Stunden-
mutter
Verzweiflung:

Ein aus der Hand und ihrer
Wunde dir Zu-
geborenes schließt
deine Kelche.

EINEM, DER VOR DER TÜR STAND, eines
Abends:
ihm
tat ich mein Wort auf –: zum
Kielkropf sah ich ihn trotten, zum
halb-
schürigen, dem

with my hands grab
there and onto nothingness, so
is, what's here:

this fertile
floor too gapes,
this
Downward
is one of the wild-
blooming crowns.

BLACKEARTH, black
earth, you, hour-
mother
Despair:

Something born you-ward
from the hand and its
wounds, shuts
your calyces.

TO ONE WHO STOOD BEFORE THE DOOR, one
evening:
to him
I opened my word—: toward the
changeling I saw him trot, toward the
half-
sheared, the

im kotigen Stiefel des Kriegsknechts
geborenen Bruder, dem
mit dem blutigen
Gottes-
gemächt, dem
schilpenden Menschlein.

Rabbi, knirschte ich, Rabbi
Löw:

Diesem
beschneide das Wort,
diesem
schreib das lebendige
Nichts ins Gemüt,
diesem
spreize die zwei
Krüppelfinger zum heil-
bringenden Spruch.
Diesem.

. . . .

Wirf auch die Abendtür zu, Rabbi.

. . . .

Reiß die Morgentür auf, Ra- –

brother born
in the grunt's begrimed boot,
him with the bloodied
god-
member, the
chirping manikin.

Rabbi, I rasped, Rabbi
Löw:

This
one's word, circumcise it, for
this
one, write the living
Nothing on his spirit, spread
this
one's two
cripplefingers into the re-
demptive saying.
For this one.

. . . .

The evening door too, slam it shut, Rabbi.

. . . .

The morning door, throw it open, Ra- —

MANDORLA

In der Mandel – was steht in der Mandel?
Das Nichts.
Es steht das Nichts in der Mandel.
Da steht es und steht.

Im Nichts – wer steht da? Der König.
Da steht der König, der König.
Da steht er und steht.

    Judenlocke, wirst nicht grau.

Und dein Aug – wohin steht dein Auge?
Dein Aug steht der Mandel entgegen.
Dein Aug, dem Nichts stehts entgegen.
Es steht zum König.
So steht es und steht.

    Menschenlocke, wirst nicht grau.
    Leere Mandel, königsblau.

AN NIEMAND GESCHMIEGT mit der Wange –
an dich, Leben.
An dich, mit dem Handstumpf
gefundnes.

Ihr Finger.
Fern, unterwegs,
an den Kreuzungen, manchmal,

MANDORLA

In the almond—what stands in the almond?
Nothingness.
What stands in the almond is Nothingness.
There it stands and stands.

In Nothingness—what stands there? The King.
There the King stands, the King.
There he stands and stands.

    Jew's curl, you'll not turn gray.

And your eye—whereto stands your eye?
Your eye stands facing the almond.
Your eye, it stands facing Nothingness.
It stands by the King.
So it stands and stands.

    Human curl, you'll not turn gray.
    Empty almond, royal-blue.

CHEEK TO CHEEK with no one—
with you, life.
With you, found with the hand-
stump.

You fingers.
Far away, under way,
at the crossroads, sometimes,

die Rast
bei freigelassenen Gliedern,
auf
dem Staubkissen Einst.

Verholzter Herzvorrat: der
schwelende
Liebes- und Lichtknecht.

Ein Flämmchen halber
Lüge noch in
dieser, in jener
übernächtigen Pore,
die ihr berührt.

Schlüsselgeräusche oben,
im Atem-
Baum über euch:
das letzte
Wort, das euch ansah,
soll jetzt bei sich sein und bleiben.

. . . .

An dich geschmiegt, mit
dem Handstumpf gefundenes
Leben.

Zweihäusig, Ewiger, bist du, un-
bewohnbar. Darum

resting
by relaxed limbs
on
the dustpillow Once.

Lignified heartstock: the
smoldering
love- and light-servant.

A little half lie
flame still
in this, in that
tired-out pore,
that you touch.

Noise of keys overhead,
in the breath-
tree above you:
the last
word that looked at you
shall now be and stay with itself.

. . . .

Cheek to cheek with you, with
the handstump-found
life.

DIOECIOUS, ETERNAL, you are, un-
inhabitable. Therefore

baun wir und bauen. Darum
steht sie, diese
erbärmliche Bettstatt, – im Regen,
da steht sie.

Komm, Geliebte.
Daß wir hier liegen, das
ist die Zwischenwand –: Er
hat dann genug an sich selber, zweimal.

Laß ihn, er
habe sich ganz, als das Halbe
und abermals Halbe. Wir,
wir sind das Regenbett, er
komme und lege uns trocken.

. . . .

Er kommt nicht, er legt uns nicht trocken.

SIBIRISCH

Bogengebete – du
sprachst sie nicht mit, es waren,
du denkst es, die deinen.

Der Rabenschwan hing
vorm frühen Gestirn:

we build and build. Therefore
it stands, this
wretched bedstead,—in the rain,
is where it stands.

Come, beloved.
That we lie here, that
is the partition—: He
then has enough by himself, twice.

Let him be, let him
have all of himself, as one half
and then again as one half. We,
we are the rainbed, let him
come and bed us dry.

. . . .

He doesn't come, he doesn't bed us dry.

SIBERIAN

Bowprayers—you
didn't join in, they were,
you think so, yours.

The ravenswan hung
before the early asterism:

mit zerfressenem Lidspalt
stand ein Gesicht – auch unter diesem
Schatten.

Kleine, im Eiswind
liegengebliebene
Schelle
mit deinem
weißen Kiesel im Mund:

Auch mir
steht der tausendjahrfarbene
Stein in der Kehle, der Herzstein,
auch ich
setze Grünspan an
an der Lippe.

Über die Schuttflur hier,
durch das Seggenmeer heute
führt sie, unsre
Bronze-Straße.
Da lieg ich und rede zu dir
mit abgehäutetem
Finger.

with corroded eyelid-fissure
a face stood—even under this
shadow.

Little bell, left
lying in the
icewind
with your
white pebble in the mouth:

Stuck in my
throat too, the millennium-
colored stone, the heartstone,
I too
raise verdigris on
my lip.

Over the scree plain here,
through the sedgesea it
leads today, our
bronze-road.
There I lie and talk to you
with flayed
finger.

BENEDICTA

Zu ken men arojfgejn in himel arajn
Un fregn baj got zu's darf asoj sajn?
Jiddisches Lied

Ge-
trunken hast du,
was von den Vätern mir kam
und von jenseits der Väter:
– –, Pneuma.

Ge-
segnet seist du, von weit her, von
jenseits meiner
erloschenen Finger.

Gesegnet: Du, die ihn grüßte,
den Teneberleuchter.

Du, die du's hörtest, da ich die Augen schloß, wie
die Stimme nicht weitersang nach:
's mus asoj sajn,

Du, die du's sprachst in den augen-
losen, den Auen:
dasselbe, das andere
Wort:
Gebenedeiet.

Ge-
trunken.
Ge-

BENEDICTA

Tsu ken men aroyfgeyn im himl arayn
Un fregn bay got tsu s'darf azoy zayn?
Yiddish song

Dr-
ink you did,
what came to me from the fathers
and from beyond the fathers:
——, pneuma.

Bl-
essed be you, from afar, from
beyond my
extinguished finger.

Blessed: You, who greeted it,
the tenebrae lamp.

You, who heard it, as I closed my eyes, how
the voice stopped singing after:
s'mus azoy zayn.

You, you who said it in the eye-
less, the open fields:
the same, the other
word:
Beblessed.

Dr-
unk.
Bl-

segnet.
Ge-
bentscht.

À LA POINTE ACÉRÉE

Es liegen die Erze bloß, die Kristalle,
die Drusen.
Ungeschriebenes, zu
Sprache verhärtet, legt
einen Himmel frei.

(Nach oben verworfen, zutage,
überquer, so
liegen auch wir.

Tür du davor einst, Tafel
mit dem getöteten
Kreidestern drauf:
ihn
hat nun ein – lesendes? – Aug.)

Wege dorthin.
Waldstunde an
der blubbernden Radspur entlang.
Auf-
gelesene
kleine, klaffende
Buchecker: schwärzliches

essed.
Ge-
bentsht.

À LA POINTE ACÉRÉE

The ores are exposed, the crystals,
the druses.
Some unwritten, solidified
into language, lays
open a sky.

(Upward faulted, outcrop,
crosswise, thus
we too lie.

Door you stood before once, chalkboard,
with the slain
chalkstar on it:
it
now belongs to a—reading?—eye.)

Paths to get there.
Forest-hour a-
long the blubbering wheelspoor.
Ga-
thered
small, gaping
beechnuts: blackish

Offen, von
Fingergedanken befragt
nach – –
wonach?

Nach
dem Unwiederholbaren, nach
ihm, nach
allem.

Blubbernde Wege dorthin.

Etwas, das gehn kann, grußlos
wie Herzgewordenes,
kommt.

openness, queried
by fingerthoughts
about—
about what?

About
the unrepeatable, about
it, about
everything.

Blubbering paths to get there.

Something that can walk, without
a greeting, as if turned into a heart,
comes.

III

III

DIE HELLEN
STEINE gehn durch die Luft, die hell-
weißen, die Licht-
bringer.

Sie wollen
nicht niedergehen, nicht stürzen,
nicht treffen. Sie gehen
auf,
wie die geringen
Heckenrosen, so tun sie sich auf,
sie schweben
dir zu, du meine Leise,
du meine Wahre –:

ich seh dich, du pflückst sie mit meinen
neuen, meinen
Jedermannshänden, du tust sie
ins Abermals-Helle, das niemand
zu weinen braucht noch zu nennen.

ANABASIS

Dieses
schmal zwischen Mauern geschriebne
unwegsam-wahre
Hinauf und Zurück
in die herzhelle Zukunft.

THE BRIGHT
STONES pass through the air, the bright-
white, the light-
bringers

They don't
want to come down, nor fall,
nor hit. They open
up
like humble
dog roses, that's how they open,
they float
toward you, my quiet one,
you, my true one—:

I see you, you gather them with my
new, my
everyman's hands, you put them
into the Bright-Again no one
has to weep for or name.

ANABASIS

This
narrow, written-between-walls
impassably-true
Upward and Back
into the heartbright future.

Dort.

Silben-
mole, meer-
farben, weit
ins Unbefahrne hinaus.

Dann:
Bojen-,
Kummerbojen-Spalier
mit den
sekundenschön hüpfenden
Atemreflexen –: Leucht-
glockentöne (dum-,
dun-, un-,
unde suspirat
cor),
aus-
gelöst, ein-
gelöst, unser.

Sichtbares, Hörbares, das
frei-
werdende Zeltwort:

Mitsammen.

EIN WURFHOLZ, auf Atemwegen,
so wanderts, das Flügel-
mächtige, das
Wahre. Auf

There.

Syllable-
pier, sea-
colored, far
into the unchartered.

Then:
buoys-,
sorrowbuoys-cordon
with the
pretty-as-seconds caroming
breathreflexes—: lumi-
nous belltones (dum-,
dun-, un-,
unde suspirat
cor), un-
leashed, re-
deemed, our.

Visible, audible, the
free-
d tentword:

Gathered together.

A BOOMERANG, on breathroutes,
as it wanders, the wing-
mighty, the
True. On

Sternen-
bahnen, von Welten-
splittern geküßt, von Zeit-
körnern genarbt, von Zeitstaub, mit-
verwaisend mit euch,
Lapilli, ver-
zwergt, verwinzigt, ver-
nichtet,
verbracht und verworfen,
sich selber der Reim, –
so kommt es
geflogen, so kommts
wieder und heim,
einen Herzschlag, ein Tausendjahr lang
innezuhalten als
einziger Zeiger im Rund,
das eine Seele,
das seine
Seele
beschrieb,
das eine
Seele
beziffert.

HAWDALAH

An dem einen, dem
einzigen
Faden, an ihm

star-
orbits, kissed by
world-splinters, by time-
kernels scarred, by timedust, co-
orphaned with you,
Lapilli, dw-
arfed, diminished, de-
stroyed,
displaced and discarded,
by itself the rhyme,—
thus it comes
flying, thus it comes
again and home,
a heartbeat, a millennium long
to stop as the
only clockhand in the circle,
that a soul,
that his
soul
described,
that numbers
one
soul.

HAVDALAH

On the one, the
only
thread, on it

spinnst du – von ihm
Umsponnener, ins
Freie, dahin,
ins Gebundne.

Groß
stehn die Spindeln
ins Unland, die Bäume: es ist,
von unten her, ein
Licht geknüpft in die Luft-
matte, auf der du den Tisch deckst, den leeren
Stühlen und ihrem
Sabbatglanz zu – –

zu Ehren.

LE MENHIR

Wachsendes
Steingrau.

Graugestalt, augen-
loser du, Steinblick, mit dem uns
die Erde hervortrat, menschlich,
auf Dunkel-, auf Weißheidewegen,
abends, vor
dir, Himmelsschlucht.

you spin—you,
ensnared by it, into
the open, and on,
into the bound.

Large
the spindles stand
into unland, the trees: there comes,
from below, a
light knitted into the air-
mat, on which you set the table, for the empty
chairs and their
sabbath radiance in—

in honor.

LE MENHIR

Increasing
stone-gray.

Grayfigure, eye-
less you, stone-gaze, with which
earth brought us forth, human,
on dark-, on wild-rosemary-paths,
evenings, in front of
you, heaven's abyss.

Verkebstes, hierhergekarrt, sank
über den Herzrücken weg. Meer-
mühle mahlte.

Hellflüglig hingst du, früh,
zwischen Ginster und Stein,
kleine Phaläne.

Schwarz, phylakterien-
farben, so wart ihr,
ihr mit-
betenden Schoten.

NACHMITTAG MIT ZIRKUS UND ZITADELLE

In Brest, vor den Flammenringen,
im Zelt, wo der Tiger sprang,
da hört ich dich, Endlichkeit, singen,
da sah ich dich, Mandelstamm.

Der Himmel hing über der Reede,
die Möwe hing über dem Kran.
Das Endliche sang, das Stete, –
du, Kanonenboot, heißt »Baobab«.

Ich grüßte die Trikolore
mit einem russischen Wort –
Verloren war Unverloren,
das Herz ein befestigter Ort.

Concubined, carted over here, sunk
away over the heartback. Sea-
mill milled.

Bright-winged you hung, early,
between broom-bush and stone,
little night moth.

Black, phylactery-
color, thus you were,
you, also-
praying siliquae.

AFTERNOON, WITH CIRCUS AND CITADEL

In Brest, before the flaming rings,
in the tent, where the tiger sprung,
there I heard how you, Finitude, sung,
there I saw you, Mandelstam.

The sky hung over the roadstead,
the gull hung over the crane.
The Finite sung, the Steady,—
you, gunboat, are named "Baobab."

I greeted the tricolor
with a Russian word—
Lost was Unlost,
the heart an anchored place.

BEI TAG

Hasenfell-Himmel. Noch immer
schreibt eine deutliche Schwinge.

Auch ich, erinnere dich,
Staub-
farbene, kam
als ein Kranich.

KERMORVAN

Du Tausendgüldenkraut-Sternchen,
du Erle, du Buche, du Farn:
mit euch Nahen geh ich ins Ferne, –
Wir gehen dir, Heimat, ins Garn.

Schwarz hängt die Kirschlorbeertraube
beim bärtigen Palmenschaft.
Ich liebe, ich hoffe, ich glaube, –
die kleine Steindattel klafft.

Ein Spruch spricht – zu wem? Zu sich selber:
Servir Dieu est régner, – ich kann
ihn lesen, ich kann, es wird heller,
fort aus Kannitverstan.

BY DAY

Hare-pelt sky. Still and always
a clear wing writes.

I, too, remember,
dust-
colored one, came
as a crane.

KERMORVAN

You, little common-centaury-star,
you alder, you beech, you fern:
with you, near ones, I go far away,—
we fall into your, homeland's, snare.

Black the cherry laurel hangs
near the bearded date-palm trunk.
I love, I hope, I believe—
the little stone-date gapes.

A saying says—to whom? To itself:
Servir Dieu est régner,—I can
read it, I can, it is becoming brighter,
leaving Kannitverstan.

Ich habe Bambus geschnitten:
für dich, mein Sohn.
Ich habe gelebt.

Diese morgen fort-
getragene Hütte, sie
steht.

Ich habe nicht mitgebaut: du
weißt nicht, in was für
Gefäße ich den
Sand um mich her tat, vor Jahren, auf
Geheiß und Gebot. Der deine
kommt aus dem Freien – er bleibt
frei.

Das Rohr, das hier Fuß faßt, morgen
steht es noch immer, wohin dich
die Seele auch hinspielt im Un-
gebundnen.

KOLON

Keine im Licht der Wort-
Vigilie erwanderte
Hand.

Doch du, Erschlafene, immer
sprachwahr in jeder
der Pausen:

I HAVE CUT BAMBOO:
for you, my son.
I have lived.

This hut, to be carried-
away tomorrow, it
stands.

I did not help build it: you
don't know into what kind of
vessels I put the sand around me, years ago, on
behest and command. Yours
comes from the open—it remains
free.

The culm taking root here will still
stand, tomorrow, wherever your
soul may cast you in the bound-
less.

COLON

No in the light of the word-
vigil reconnoitered
hand.

Yet you, sleeping one, always
speechtrue in each of
the pauses:

für
wieviel Vonsammengeschiedenes
rüstest du's wieder zur Fahrt:
das Bett
Gedächtnis!

Fühlst du, wir liegen
weiß von Tausend-
farbenem, Tausend-
mündigem vor
Zeitwind, Hauchjahr, Herz-Nie.

for
how much Togetherseparated
do you ready once more for the journey:
the bed
Memory!

Do you sense it, we lie
white from thousandcolored,
thousand-
mouthed pre-
timewind, breathyear, heart-never.

IV

IV

WAS GESCHAH? Der Stein trat aus dem Berge.
Wer erwachte? Du und ich.
Sprache, Sprache. Mit-Stern. Neben-Erde.
Ärmer. Offen. Heimatlich.

Wohin gings? Gen Unverklungen.
Mit dem Stein gings, mit uns zwein.
Herz und Herz. Zu schwer befunden.
Schwerer werden. Leichter sein.

IN EINS

Dreizehnter Feber. Im Herzmund
erwachtes Schibboleth. Mit dir,
Peuple
de Paris. *No pasarán.*

Schäfchen zur Linken: er, Abadias,
der Greis aus Huesca, kam mit den Hunden
über das Feld, im Exil
stand weiß eine Wolke
menschlichen Adels, er sprach
uns das Wort in die Hand, das wir brauchten, es war
Hirten-Spanisch, darin,

im Eislicht des Kreuzers »Aurora«:
die Bruderhand, winkend mit der
von den wortgroßen Augen
genommenen Binde – Petropolis, der

WHAT HAPPENED? The stone stepped out of the mountain.
Who woke up? You and I.
Language, language. Co-star. By-earth.
Poorer. Open. At home.

Where did it lead? Toward unfaded.
With the stone it went, with us two.
Heart and heart. Judged too heavy.
Become heavier. Be lighter.

IN ONE

February 13. In heart's mouth
awakened shibboleth. With you,
Peuple
de Paris. *No pasarán.*

Lambs to the left: he, Abadias,
the old man from Huesca, came with his dogs
across the field, in exile
stood white cloud
of human nobility, spoke
the word into our hand, the one we needed, it was
shepherd's Spanish, in it,

in the icelight of the cruiser "Aurora":
the brotherhand, waving the
blinders pulled off the word-
wide eyes—Petropolis, the

Unvergessenen Wanderstadt lag
auch dir toskanisch zu Herzen.

Friede den Hütten!

HINAUSGEKRÖNT,
hinausgespien in die Nacht.

Bei welchen
Sternen! Lauter
graugeschlagenes Herzhammersilber. Und
Berenikes Haupthaar, auch hier, – ich flocht,
ich zerflocht,
ich flechte, zerflechte.
Ich flechte.

Blauschlucht, in dich
treib ich das Gold. Auch mit ihm, dem
bei Huren und Dirnen vertanen,
komm ich und komm ich. Zu dir,
Geliebte.

Auch mit Fluch und Gebet. Auch mit jeder
der über mich hin-
schwirrenden Keulen: auch sie in eins
geschmolzen, auch sie
phallisch gebündelt zu dir,
Garbe-und-Wort.

unforgotten wander-city lay
tuscanly on your heart too.

Peace to the huts!

CROWNED OUT,
spat out into the night.

Under what
stars! All
grayhammered hearthammersilver. And
Berenice's mane, here too,—I braided,
I unbraided,
I braid, unbraid,
I braid.

Blue ravine, into you
I drive the gold. With it too,
with what's spent on whores and wenches,
I come and I come. To you,
loved one.

With curses and prayer too. And too with each
of the bludgeons whizzing
above me: they too fused
into one, they too
phallically bundled for you,
sheaf-and-word.

Mit Namen, getränkt
von jedem Exil.
Mit Namen und Samen,
mit Namen, getaucht
in alle
Kelche, die vollstehn mit deinem
Königsblut, Mensch, – in alle
Kelche der großen
Ghetto-Rose, aus der
du uns ansiehst, unsterblich von soviel
auf Morgenwegen gestorbenen Toden.

(Und wir sangen die Warschowjanka.
Mit verschilften Lippen, Petrarca.
In Tundra-Ohren, Petrarca.)

Und es steigt eine Erde herauf, die unsre,
diese.
Und wir schicken
keinen der Unsern hinunter
zu dir,
Babel.

WOHIN MIR das Wort, das unsterblich war, fiel:
in die Himmelsschlucht hinter der Stirn,
dahin geht, geleitet von Speichel und Müll,
der Siebenstern, der mit mir lebt.

Im Nachthaus die Reime, der Atem im Kot,
das Auge ein Bilderknecht –

With names, steeped
in every exile.
With names and seeds,
with names, dipped
in all the
chalices, brimful with
your king's blood, Human,—in all
chalices of the great
ghetto-rose, from which
you look at us, immortal from so many
dead who died on dawnpaths.

(And we sang the Warszawianka.
With reedy lips, Petrarch.
Into tundra-ears, Petrarch.)

And an earth rises up, ours,
this one.
And we'll send
not a single one of ours down
to you,
Babel.

WHERE the word, that was immortal, fell for me:
into the heaven's ravine behind the forehead,
that is where goes, led by spittle and litter,
the sevensisters' starflower that lives with me.

In the binnacle, the rhymes, the breath, in mud,
the eye an imageknave—

Und dennoch: ein aufrechtes Schweigen, ein Stein,
der die Teufelsstiege umgeht.

LES GLOBES

In den verfahrenen Augen – lies da:

die Sonnen-, die Herzbahnen, das
sausend-schöne Umsonst.
Die Tode und alles
aus ihnen Geborene. Die
Geschlechterkette,
die hier bestattet liegt und
die hier noch hängt, im Äther,
Abgründe säumend. Aller
Gesichter Schrift, in die sich
schwirrender Wortsand gebohrt – Kleinewiges,
Silben.

Alles,
das Schwerste noch, war
flügge, nichts
hielt zurück.

And yet: an upstanding silence, a stone,
that skirts the devil's stairway.

LES GLOBES

In the muddled eyes—read there:

the sun's, the heart's ecliptics, the
gorgeously whizzing Fornothing.
The deaths and everything
they gave birth to. The
generation-chain,
that lies buried here and
that still hangs here, in the ether,
edging the abysses. All
the faces' writing, into which
whirring wordsand drilled—Mini-eternal,
syllables.

Everything,
even the heaviest, was
fledged, nothing
held back.

HUHEDIBLU

Schwer-, Schwer-, Schwer-
fälliges auf
Wortwegen und -schneisen.

Und – ja –
die Bälge der Feme-Poeten
lurchen und vespern und wispern und vipern,
episteln.
Geunktes, aus
Hand- und Fingergekröse, darüber
schriftfern eines
Propheten Name spurt, als
An- und Bei- und Afterschrift, unterm
Datum des Nimmermenschtags im September –:

Wann,
wann blühen, wann,
wann blühen die, hühendiblüh,
huhediblu, ja sie, die September-
rosen?

Hüh – on tue . . . Ja wann?

Wann, wannwann,
Wahnwann, ja Wahn, –
Bruder
Geblendet, Bruder
Erloschen, du liest,
du liest und du,
dies hier, dies:

HUHEDIBLU

Clum-, clum-, clum-
siness on
wordpaths and -swaths.

And—yes—
the Vehmic poets' bastard offspring
lurch and vesper and viper,
epistle.
Toadied stuff, out of
hand- and fingertripe, above it
scripture-distant a
prophet's name spoors, as
ad- and by- and afterwrit, under
the date of the nolongerhumanday in September—:

When,
when do they bloom, when,
will they bloom, the, hühendibloom,
hudediblue, yes them, the September-
roses?

Hüh – on tue . . . Yes, when?

When, whenwhen,
Delusionwhen, yes, delusion,—
Brother
Blinded, brother
Extinguished, you read,
you read and you,
this here, this:

Dis-
parates –: Wann
blüht es, das Wann,
das Woher, das Wohin und was
und wer
sich aus- und an- und dahin- und zu sich lebt, den
Achsenton, Tellus, in seinem
vor Hell-
hörigkeit schwirrenden
Seelenohr, den
Achsenton tief
im Innern unsrer
sternrunden Wohnstatt Zerknirschung? Denn
sie bewegt sich, dennoch, im Herzsinn.

Den Ton, oh,
den Oh-Ton, ah,
das A und das O,
das Oh-diese-Galgen-schon-wieder, das Ah-es-gedeiht,

auf den alten
Alraunenfluren gedeiht es,
als schmucklos-schmückendes Beikraut,
als Beikraut, als Beiwort, als Beilwort,
ad-
jektivisch, so gehn
sie dem Menschen zuleibe, Schatten,
vernimmt man, war
alles Dagegen –
Feiertagsnachtisch, nicht mehr, –:

Frugal,
kontemporan und gesetzlich

Dis-
parateness-: When
will it bloom, the When,
the Wherefrom, the Whereto and What,
and who
lives out of- and to- and toward-oneself, the axis-
tone, Tellus, in its soul-
ear whirring from keen
hearing, the
axistone deep
in the inside of our
starround dwelling Contrition? For
it moves, nevertheless, with heartsense.

The tone, oh,
the Oh-tone, ah,
the *A* and the *O*
the Oh-these-gallows-already-again, the Ah-it-thrives,

on the old
mandrake-acres it prospers,
as unadorned-adorning added weed,
as adjected-weed, as adjective-word, as axeword,
ad-
jectival, thus do they
attack the human, shadows,
one perceives, all
was against—
holidaydessert, no longer,—:

Frugal,
up-to-date and in all legality

geht Schinderhannes zu Werk,
sozial und alibi-elbisch, und
das Julchen, das Julchen:
daseinsfeist rülpst,
rülpst es das Fallbeil los, – call it (hott!)
love.

Oh quand refleuriront, oh roses, vos septembres?

HÜTTENFENSTER

Das Aug, dunkel:
als Hüttenfenster. Es sammelt,
was Welt war, Welt bleibt: den Wander-
Osten, die
Schwebenden, die
Menschen-und-Juden,
das Volk-vom-Gewölk, magnetisch
ziehts, mit Herzfingern, an
dir, Erde:
du kommst, du kommst,
wohnen werden wir, wohnen, etwas

– ein Atem? ein Name? –

geht im Verwaisten umher,
tänzerisch, klobig,
die Engels-
schwinge, schwer von Unsichtbarem, am

Schinderhannes goes to work,
sociable and alibi-elfish, and
lil' Julia, lil' Julia,
daseinsfat belches,
a belch releases the guillotine,—call it (hott!)
love.

Oh quand refleuriront, oh roses, vos septembres?

HUTWINDOW

The eye, dark:
as hut window. It gathers
what was world, remains world: the Wander-
East, the
floating ones the
humans-and-Jews,
the people-of-the-clouds, magnetically
it pulls, with heartfingers, at
you, earth:
you come, you come,
dwell we will, dwell, something

—a breath? a name?—

wanders around in the orphaned,
dancingly, klunkily,
the angels-
wing, heavy from invisibles, at

wundgeschundenen Fuß, kopf-
lastig getrimmt
vom Schwarzhagel, der
auch dort fiel, in Witebsk,

– und sie, die ihn säten, sie
schreiben ihn weg
mit mimetischer Panzerfaustklaue! –,

geht, geht umher,
sucht,
sucht unten,
sucht droben, fern, sucht
mit dem Auge, holt
Alpha Centauri herunter, Arktur, holt
den Strahl hinzu, aus den Gräbern,

geht zu Ghetto und Eden, pflückt
das Sternbild zusammen, das er,
der Mensch, zum Wohnen braucht, hier,
unter Menschen,

schreitet
die Buchstaben ab und der Buchstaben sterblich-
unsterbliche Seele,
geht zu Aleph und Jud und geht weiter,

baut ihn, den Davidsschild, läßt ihn
aufflammen, einmal,

läßt ihn erlöschen – da steht er,
unsichtbar, steht

the mauled foot, top-
heavily trimmed
by blackhail, that
fell also there, in Vitebsk,

—and they, who sowed it, they
wrote it away
with mimetic bazooka fist!—,

goes, goes around,
seeks,
seeks below,
seeks above, far away, seeks
with the eye, takes
down Alpha Centauri, Arcturus, takes
the beam too, from the graves,

goes to ghetto and Eden, gathers
the constellation, that he,
a human, needs for dwelling, here,
among humans,

paces
off the letters and the letters' mortal-
immortal soul,
goes to aleph and yod and goes further,

builds it, the Davidshield, lets it
flare up once

lets it flame out—there it stands,
invisible, stands

bei Alpha und Aleph, bei Jud,
bei den andern, bei
allen: in
dir,

Beth, – das ist
das Haus, wo der Tisch steht mit

dem Licht und dem Licht.

DIE SILBE SCHMERZ

Es gab sich Dir in die Hand:
ein Du, todlos,
an dem alles Ich zu sich kam. Es fuhren
wortfreie Stimmen rings, Leerformen, alles
ging in sie ein, gemischt
und entmischt
und wieder
gemischt.

Und Zahlen waren
mitverwoben in das
Unzählbare. Eins und Tausend und was
davor und dahinter
größer war als es selbst, kleiner, aus-
gereift und
rück- und fort-
verwandelt in
keimendes Niemals.

with alpha and aleph, with yod,
with the others, with
them all: in
you,

Beth,—which is
the house, where the table stands with

the light and the light.

THE SYLLABLE PAIN

It gave itself into Your hand:
a You, deathless,
on which all that was I came to itself. Wordfree
voices drove around, empty-forms, all
went into them, mixed
and unmixed
and again
mixed.

And numbers were
interwoven with the
uncountable. One and a thousand and what
before and after
was larger than itself, smaller, ma-
tured and
back- and forth-
transformed into a
germinating Never.

Vergessenes griff
nach Zu-Vergessendem, Erdteile, Herzteile
schwammen,
sanken und schwammen. Kolumbus,
die Zeit-
lose im Aug, die Mutter-
Blume,
mordete Masten und Segel. Alles fuhr aus,

frei,
entdeckerisch,
blühte die Windrose ab, blätterte
ab, ein Weltmeer
blühte zuhauf und zutag, im Schwarzlicht
der Wildsteuerstriche. In Särgen,
Urnen, Kanopen
erwachten die Kindlein
Jaspis, Achat, Amethyst – Völker,
Stämme und Sippen, ein blindes

E s s e i

knüpfte sich in
die schlangenköpfigen Frei-
Taue –: ein
Knoten
(und Wider- und Gegen- und Aber- und Zwillings- und Tau-
sendknoten), an dem
die fastnachtsäugige Brut
der Mardersterne im Abgrund
buch-, buch-, buch-
stabierte, stabierte.

Forgotten grabbed
for the To-be-forgotten, continents, heartinents
swam,
sank and swam. Columbus,
eyeing the autumn-
colchis, the mother-
flower,
murdered masts and sails. Everything set forth,

free,
discovery-eager
the windrose wilted, ex-
foliated, an ocean
bloomed by scores and by days, in the blacklight
of the wildrhumbslines. In coffins,
urns, canopic jars
little babes awoke:
jasper, agate, amethyst—peoples,
tribes and clans, a blind

Let there be

knotted itself in-
to the serpentheaded free-
hawsers—: a
knot
(and contra- and counter- and yet- and twin- and thou-
sand-knot), on which
the carnivalsuckling brood
of the polecatstars in the abyss
book-, book-, book-
staved, staved.

LA CONTRESCARPE

Brich dir die Atemmünze heraus
aus der Luft um dich und den Baum:

so
viel
wird gefordert von dem,
den die Hoffnung herauf- und herabkarrt
den Herzbuckelweg – so
viel

an der Kehre,
wo er dem Brotpfeil begegnet,
der den Wein seiner Nacht trank, den Wein
der Elends-, der Königs-
vigilie.

Kamen die Hände nicht mit, die wachten,
kam nicht das tief
in ihr Kelchaug gebettete Glück?
Kam nicht, bewimpert,
das menschlich tönende Märzrohr, das Licht gab,
damals, weithin?

Scherte die Brieftaube aus, war ihr Ring
zu entziffern? (All das
Gewölk um sie her – es war lesbar.) Litt es
der Schwarm? Und verstand,
und flog wie sie fortblieb?

Dachschiefer Helling, – auf Tauben-
kiel gelegt ist, was schwimmt. Durch die Schotten

LA CONTRESCARPE

Break the breathcoin out
of the air around you and the tree:

that
much
is asked of him
whom hope carts up and down
along the hearthumpway—that
much

at the curve
where he meets the breadarrow,
that drunk the wine of his night, the wine
of the misery-, the kings-
vigil.

Didn't they come along, the hands that guarded,
didn't it come along, the deep
in the calix-eye embedded happiness?
Didn't it, eyelashed, come,
the human-sounding march-ear, that shed light,
back then, all around?

Did the carrier pigeon sheer off, was her ring
decipherable? (The cloud
-mass around her—it was readable.) Did the
flock permit it? And understood,
and flew as she stayed away?

Rooftile slipway,—on pigeon-
keel lies what swims. Through the bulkheads

blutet die Botschaft, Verjährtes
geht jung über Bord:

Über Krakau
bist du gekommen, am Anhalter
Bahnhof
floß deinen Blicken ein Rauch zu,
der war schon von morgen. Unter
Paulownien
sahst du die Messer stehn, wieder,
scharf von Entfernung. Es wurde
getanzt. (Quatorze
juillets. Et plus de neuf autres.)
Überzwerch, Affenvers, Schrägmaul
mimten Gelebtes. Der Herr
trat, in ein Spruchband gehüllt,
zu der Schar. Er knipste
sich ein
Souvenirchen. Der Selbst-
auslöser, das warst
du.

O diese Ver-
freundung. Doch wieder,
da, wo du hinmußt, der eine
genaue
Kristall.

Es ist alles anders, als du es dir denkst, als ich es mir denke,
die Fahne weht noch,

the message bleeds, what's beyond expiration
date goes early overboard.

Via Kraków
you came, at the Anhalter
railway station
smoke flowed towards your gaze,
it already belonged to tomorrow. Under
paulownias
you saw the knives stand, again,
sharpened by distance. There was
dancing. (Quatorze
juillets. Et plus de neuf autres.)
Überdwarf, apeverse, slant mouth
mimed life stuff. The lord,
wrapped in a banner, stepped
among the assembled. He snapped
a little
souvenir. The self-
timer, that was
you.

Oh this dis-
friending. Yet again,
there where you must go, the one
accurate
crystal.

EVERYTHING IS DIFFERENT from what you think, from what I think,
the flag still flutters,

die kleinen Geheimnisse sind noch bei sich,
sie werfen noch Schatten, davon
lebst du, leb ich, leben wir.

Die Silbermünze auf deiner Zunge schmilzt,
sie schmeckt nach Morgen, nach Immer, ein Weg
nach Rußland steigt dir ins Herz,
die karelische Birke
hat
gewartet,
der Name Ossip kommt auf dich zu, du erzählst ihm,
was er schon weiß, er nimmt es, er nimmt es dir ab, mit Händen,
du löst ihm den Arm von der Schulter, den rechten, den linken,
du heftest die deinen an ihre Stelle, mit Händen, mit Fingern, mit
Linien,

– was abriß, wächst wieder zusammen –
da hast du sie, da nimm sie dir, da hast du alle beide,
den Namen, den Namen, die Hand, die Hand,
da nimm sie dir zum Unterpfand,
er nimmt auch das, und du hast
wieder, was dein ist, was sein war,

Windmühlen

stoßen dir Luft in die Lunge, du ruderst
durch die Kanäle, Lagunen und Grachten,
bei Wortschein,
am Heck kein Warum, am Bug kein Wohin, ein Widderhorn hebt dich
– *Tekiah!* –
wie ein Posaunenschall über die Nächte hinweg in den Tag, die
Auguren

the little secrets are still secret,
they still throw shadows, on this
you live, I live, we live.

The silver coin on your tongue melts,
it tastes of tomorrow, of forever, a road
to Russia rises into your heart,
the Karelian birch
has
waited,
the name Osip comes toward you, you tell him
what he already knows, he takes it, he takes it off you with hands,
you detach his arms from their shoulder, the right, the left,
you fasten yours in their stead, with hands, with fingers, with lines,

—what tore off, grows back together again—
you have them now, so take them now, you have them both,
the name, the name, the hand, the hand,
there, take them as your pledge,
he takes that too, and you have
again what's yours, what was his,

windmills

push air into your lungs, you row
through the canals, lagoons, and grachten,
in wordlight,
no Why at the stern, no Where-to at the bow, a ram's horn lifts you
—*Tekiah!*—
like a trumpet blast above nights into day, the augurs

zerfleischen einander, der Mensch
hat seinen Frieden, der Gott
hat den seinen, die Liebe
kehrt in die Betten zurück, das Haar
der Frauen wächst wieder,
die nach innen gestülpte
Knospe an ihrer Brust
tritt wieder zutag, lebens-,
herzlinienhin erwacht sie
dir in der Hand, die den Lendenweg hochklomm, –

wie heißt es, dein Land
hinterm Berg, hinterm Jahr?
Ich weiß, wie es heißt.
Wie das Wintermärchen, so heißt es,
es heißt wie das Sommermärchen,
das Dreijahreland deiner Mutter, das war es,
das ists,
es wandert überallhin, wie die Sprache,
wirf sie weg, wirf sie weg,
dann hast du sie wieder, wie ihn,
den Kieselstein aus
der Mährischen Senke,
den dein Gedanke nach Prag trug,
aufs Grab, auf die Gräber, ins Leben,

längst
ist er fort, wie die Briefe, wie alle
Laternen, wieder
mußt du ihn suchen, da ist er,
klein ist er, weiß,
um die Ecke, da liegt er,

maul each other, man
has his peace, god
has his, love
returns to the beds, the hair
of the women grows back,
the inturned bud
on their breasts
rises to day again, toward life-,
toward heart-lines it wakens
in your hand, that rose along the loinpath,—

what is it called, you country
behind the mountain, behind the year?
I know what it's called.
Like the Winter's Tale, it is called,
it is called like the Summer's Tale,
your mother's Three-Year-Land, that's what it was,
what it is,
it wanders everywhere, like language,
throw it away, throw it away,
then you'll have it again, like
that pebble from
the Moravian swale
your thought carried to Prague,
to the grave, all the graves, into life,

it's long
gone, like the letters, like all
the lanterns, you must
search for it again, there it is,
it's small, it lies there,
[um die Ecke, da liegt er]

bei Normandie-Njemen – in Böhmen,
da, da, da,
hinterm Haus, vor dem Haus,
weiß ist er, weiß, er sagt:
Heute – es gilt.
Weiß ist er, weiß, ein Wasser-
strahl findet hindurch, ein Herzstrahl,
ein Fluß,
du kennst seinen Namen, die Ufer
hängen voll Tag, wie der Name,
du tastest ihn ab, mit der Hand:
Alba.

UND MIT DEM BUCH AUS TARUSSA

Все поэты жиды
Marina Tsvetaeva

Vom
Sternbild des Hundes, vom
Hellstern darin und der Zwerg-
leuchte, die mitwebt
an erdwärts gespiegelten Wegen,

von
Pilgerstäben, auch dort, von Südlichem, fremd
und nachtfasernah
wie unbestattete Worte,
streunend
im Bannkreis erreichter
Ziele und Stelen und Wiegen.

near Normandy-Niemen—in Bohemia,
there, there, there,
behind the house, in front of the house,
white it is, white, it says:
Today—counts.
White it is, white, a water-
surge rushes through it, a heartsurge,
a river,
you know its name, the banks
hang heavy with day, like the name,
you scan it, with your hand:
Alba.

AND WITH THE BOOK FROM TARUSSA

Все поэты жиды

Marina Tsvetaeva

About
the constellation of the Dog, of
the brightstar in it and the dwarf-
light, that also weaves
at the earthward mirrored paths,

about
pilgrim staffs, there too, about southern matters, foreign
and nightfibernear
like unburied words,
roving
in the fixed circle of realized
goals and stelae and cradles.

Von
Wahr- und Voraus- und Vorüber-zu-dir-,
von
Hinaufgesagtem,
das dort bereitliegt, einem
der eigenen Herzsteine gleich, die man ausspie
mitsamt ihrem un-
verwüstlichen Uhrwerk, hinaus
in Unland und Unzeit. Von solchem
Ticken und Ticken inmitten
der Kies-Kuben mit
der auf Hyänenspur rückwärts,
aufwärts verfolgbaren
Ahnen-
reihe Derer-
vom-Namen-und-Seiner-
Rundschlucht.

Von
einem Baum, von einem.
Ja, auch von ihm. Und vom Wald um ihn her. Vom Wald
Unbetreten, vom
Gedanken, dem er entwuchs, als Laut
und Halblaut und Ablaut und Auslaut, skythisch
zusammengereimt
im Takt
der Verschlagenen-Schläfe,
mit
geatmeten Steppen-
halmen geschrieben ins Herz
der Stundenzäsur – in das Reich,
in der Reiche

About
True- and Ahead- and Over-to-you-,
about
the upward-said
that lies ready there, resembling one
of one's own heartstones, that one spat out
together with their un-
destructible clockwork, out
into Unland and Untime. Of such
ticking and tocking amidst
the gravel-cubes with
the on Hyena-spoors backward,
upward trackable
ancestor-
row of Those-
of-the-names-&-his-
roundravine.

About
a tree, about one.
Yes, about it too. And about the forest around it. About the forest
Untread, about
the thought from which he grew, as sound
and halfsound and ablaut and auslaut, scythianly
rhymed together
in the cadence
of the marooned foreheads,
with
breathed-in steppe-
stalks written into the heart
of the hour-caesura—in the realm,
in the vastest of

weitestes, in
den Großbinnenreim
jenseits
der Stummvölker-Zone, in dich
Sprachwaage, Wortwaage, Heimat-
waage Exil.

Von diesem Baum, diesem Wald.

Von der Brücken-
quader, von der
er ins Leben hinüber-
prallte, flügge
von Wunden, – vom
Pont Mirabeau.
Wo die Oka nicht mitfließt. Et quels
amours! (Kyrillisches, Freunde, auch das
ritt ich über die Seine,
ritts übern Rhein.)

Von einem Brief, von ihm.
Vom Ein-Brief, vom Ost-Brief. Vom harten,
winzigen Worthaufen, vom
unbewaffneten Auge, das er
den drei
Gürtelsternen Orions – Jakobs-
stab, du,
abermals kommst du gegangen! –
zuführt auf der
Himmelskarte, die sich ihm aufschlug.

the realms, in
the great internal rhyme
beyond
the mute-peoples' zone, into you,
language-scale, word-scale, home-
scale: exile.

About this tree, this forest.

About the bridge-
ashlar, from which
he ricocheted into
life, fully-
fledged from wounds,—from
Pont Mirabeau.
Where the Oka doesn't flow along. Et quels
amours! (Cyrillic, friends, that too
I rode over the Seine,
rode it across the Rhine.)

About a letter, about that.
About the One-Letter, the East-letter. About the hard,
the tiny wordpile, about
the unarmed eye, that he
brings to Orion's three
belt-stars—Jacob's
staff, you,
here you come again!—
on the
star map that opened for him.

Vom Tisch, wo das geschah.

Von einem Wort, aus dem Haufen,
an dem er, der Tisch,
zur Ruderbank wurde, vom Oka-Fluß her
und den Wassern.

Vom Nebenwort, das
ein Ruderknecht nachknirscht, ins Spätsommerohr
seiner hell-
hörigen Dolle:

Kolchis.

IN DER LUFT, da bleibt deine Wurzel, da,
in der Luft.
Wo sich das Irdische ballt, erdig,
Atem-und-Lehm.

Groß
geht der Verbannte dort oben, der
Verbrannte: ein Pommer, zuhause
im Maikäferlied, das mütterlich blieb, sommerlich, hell-
blütig am Rand
aller schroffen,
winterhart-kalten
Silben.

Mit ihm
wandern die Meridiane:

About the table, where this happened.

About a word, from the pile,
on which it, the table,
became rowing bench, from the river Oka
and its waters.

About the adverb
a galley slave gnashes, into the latesummerear
of his keen-
eared oarlock:

Colchis.

IN THE AIR, there your root remains, there,
in the air.
Where Earthliness clots, terrestrially,
breath-and-clay.

Tall
he walks up there, the banned, the
burned one: a Pomeranian, at home
in the Cockchafersong, that remained motherly, summerly, bright-
blooded at the edge
of all harsh
hardwintercold
syllables.

With him
the meridians wander:

an-
gesogen von seinem
sonnengesteuerten Schmerz, der die Länder verbrüdert nach
dem Mittagsspruch einer
liebenden
Ferne. Aller-
orten ist Hier und ist Heute, ist, von Verzweiflungen her,
der Glanz,
in den die Entzweiten treten mit ihren
geblendeten Mündern:

der Kuß, nächtlich,
brennt einer Sprache den Sinn ein, zu der sie erwachen, sie –:

heimgekehrt in
den unheimlichen Bannstrahl,
der die Verstreuten versammelt, die
durch die Sternwüste Seele Geführten, die
Zeltmacher droben im Raum
ihrer Blicke und Schiffe,
die winzigen Garben Hoffnung,
darin es von Erzengelfittichen rauscht, von Verhängnis,
die Brüder, die Schwestern, die
zu leicht, die zu schwer, die zu leicht
Befundenen mit
der Weltenwaage im blut-
schändrischen, im
fruchtbaren Schoß, die lebenslang Fremden,
spermatisch bekränzt von Gestirnen, schwer
in den Untiefen lagernd, die Leiber
zu Schwellen getürmt, zu Dämmen, – die

sucked
in by his
sun-steered pain, that partners the countries after
the noonday spell of
a loving
distance. Every-
where is Here and is Today, is, made of despairs,
radiance,
into which the Sundered step with their
blinded mouths:

the kiss, at night,
burns the meaning into a language they waken to, they—:

come home into
the uncanny ban-beam,
that gathers the dispersed, those
led through the stardesert soul, the
tentmakers up above in the space
of their gazings and ships,
the tiny sheaves of hope,
wherein there's a rustle of archangelwings, of fate,
the brothers, the sisters, those found
too light, too heavy, too light
with the
world scales in the blood-
defiled, in
the fertile womb, the lifelong strangers,
spermatically crowned by constellations, heavily
camped out in the shallows, the bodies
piled up into thresholds, dams,—the

Furtenwesen, darüber
der Klumpfuß der Götter herüber-
gestolpert kommt – um
wessen
Sternzeit zu spät?

ford-creatures, over which
the clubfoot of the gods comes
stumbling—by
whose
star-time too late?

Commentary

NOTE ON THE COMMENTARIES

I would like first to acknowledge my debt to—and humbly thank—Barbara Wiedemann, whose untiring and unstinting efforts have given us not only the definitive edition of Paul Celan's poems, but also these extremely useful commentaries. Beyond reading and rereading the poems themselves, consulting these commentaries is, to my mind, the best way into the contexts and the multilayered geologies and karstic land- and language-scapes of Paul Celan's work. This is due to Wiedemann's deeply learned, nonpartisan, non-interpretive, literary-historical, and scientific manner of presenting the facts of and about the poems. In her 2018 *Neue kommentierte Gesamtausgabe* of Paul Celan's poems—a revision of her 2003 *Gesamtausgabe*—the poems take up roughly 570 pages; the commentaries and bibliographies, slightly more than 600 pages. It is primarily this edition that I have used to create my own, much reduced, commentary section. If in the first volume, *Breathturn into Timestead*, the commentaries, although also already based on her 2003 edition, do contain a large part of materials I myself gathered over the forty years I worked on those translations, for the present volume—translated over the last three years—the commentaries rely nearly totally on Wiedemann's work and are essentially a condensation and translation of these augmented with my own additions.

Pierre Joris

Brooklyn, NY, April 26, 2020

MOHN UND GEDÄCHTNIS / POPPY AND MEMORY

Celan organized the fifty-six poems that make up this volume, composed between 1944 and spring 1952, into four cycles not in strict chronological order. Twenty-six of the poems were first published in *Der Sand aus den Urnen / The Sand from the Urns* (referred to from here on as *SU*) in Vienna in 1948. The period of composition thus includes the last stay in Czernowitz (February

1944 to April 1945), the move to Bucharest (April 1945), the flight to Vienna (December 1947), and the move to Paris (July 1948). The poems can be dated mainly through indirect sources. The registration of first publication and composition dates in the author's copy of the third edition date probably from the early sixties, when Claire Goll's accusations of plagiarism, which concerned primarily the early poems, had reached a wide public. (See the introductory notes for *NoOnesRose.*)

Title: *Mohn und Gedächtnis / Poppy and Memory*: See the cycle of that same name in *SU*. See also verse 10 of "Corona."

DER SAND AUS DEN URNEN / THE SAND FROM THE URNS

See the volume of poems of the same title, Celan's first book, published in Vienna in 1948. Because of his move to Paris, he could not personally oversee the publication; given the number of—at times meaning-distorting—typos, he had the book withdrawn. See also the poem of that title in this section.

"Ein Lied in der Wüste" / "A Song in the Desert"
1945, Bucharest. First published in *Der Sand aus den Urnen / The Sand from the Urns*.

1, 3, 5, 7, 9, 11 Acra: Name of a fortified compound in Jerusalem built by Antiochus Epiphanes, ruler of the Seleucid Empire, following his sack of the city in 168 BCE. The fortress played a significant role in the events surrounding the Maccabean Revolt and the formation of the Hasmonean kingdom. It was destroyed by Simon Thassi during this struggle. See 1 Maccabees, 1:32ff.

11 Cherub / cherub: Hebrew for an unearthly, angel-like being that often fulfills the function of guardianship, thus of Paradise; see Gen. 3:24 and of the ark, and 1 Kings 8:6.

12 und fühl noch den Brand auf den Wangen / and still feel the burn on the cheeks: See verse 2 of the next poem.

"Nachts ist dein Leib" / "At night your body's"
1944, Czernowitz; probably after July 1944, as the poem is not in *Poems 1938–1944*.

"Umsonst malst du Herzen" / "For naught you draw hearts"

1945, Bucharest.

1, 7 Herzen / hearts, 5 Halme der Schwermut / stalks of melancholy, 5 Blumen der Zeit / flowers of time, 11 O Halm / O stalk, 11 o Blume der Zeit / O flower of time: See verses 7 and 10 of "Die feste Burg" / "The Mighty Fortress."

8 gehüllt in den Mantel, der einst von den Schultern dir sank / wrapped in the coat that once sank from your shoulders: See Rilke's *Cornet*: "'Frierst Du?—Hast Du Heimweh?' / Die Gräfin lächelt. / Nein. Aber das ist nur, weil das Kindsein ihm von den Schultern gefallen ist" ("'Are you cold?—Are you homesick?' / The countess smiles. / No. But that is so only because childhood fell from his shoulders") (my translation). Celan's poem makes use of other elements from the *Cornet* (courtyard, fall, banner, etc.).

10 und folgt jenem Blatt, das vorausschwebt / and follows the leaf that floats ahead: See verse 7 of "Auf hoher See" / "On the High Seas" and verse 17 of "Ein Körnchen Sands" / "A Grainlet of Sand."

"Marianne" / "Marianne"

1945, or more likely 1946; Bucharest.

T Marianne: Personification of the French Republic; see Celan's Romanian poem "Poem pentru umbra Marianei."

2 Sodom: See Gen. 19, 24ff.

2 Babel, 3 tower See Gen 11:4–7: See also the early (not included or translated poem) "An den Wassern Babels" / "At the Waters of Babylon."

7 zu zehnt / ten: This may be a reference to the minyan, the quorum of ten Jewish adults required for certain religious obligations, such as a prayer service.

9 ein Krüglein Bläue / a little jug of blueness: In March 1954, Celan dedicated a copy of *Poppy and Memory* to Ingeborg Bachmann with this fragment of the verse (see letter #37).

"Talglicht" / "Tallowlight"

1945, or more likely 1946; Bucharest. First published in *SU*.

1 Die Mönche mit haarigen Fingern / The monks with hairy fingers: See

verse 2f. of "Schwarze Flocken" / "Black Flakes," published in *SU* but not included here: "A moon / it is or two, since fall under monkish cowl / brought a message to me too, a leaf from Ukrainian slopes." Barbara Wiedemann suggests a possible connection of that month with the fact that September 15, 1935, was the date of the Nazi Nuremberg Laws, which stripped the German Jews of their civil rights.

1 schlugen das Buch auf / laid open the book, 6 Ein kleiner Hengst jagt über die blätternden Finger / A little stallion gallops over the leaf-turning fingers: See verses 4 and 9f. of "Königswut" / "King's Rage" (*Breathturn into Timestead*, pp. 74, 75).

2 Jason: In the Greek myth, Jason is the leader of the Argonauts on their journey to Colchis on the Black Sea, where, among other things, he has to sow dragon teeth and fight with the warriors that grow from these. See the altered reference to this in verse 2 of "Das Gastmahl" / "The Banquet." Ancient Colchis, also Ovid's place of exile, is not too far from Celan's homeland, the Bukovina. In a later letter Celan will establish the connection between this toponym and the Latin and French name for the flower known in German as *Herbstzeitlose*, the autumn crocus (see PC/GCL #145, "Die Silbe Schmerz" / "The Syllable Pain," and verse 80 of "Und mit dem Buch aus Tarussa" / "And with the Book from Tarussa").

"Die Hand voller Stunden" / "The hand full of hours"
1945, or more likely 1946; Bucharest.

One fragment has come down together with the translation of Paul Éluard's poem "Pablo Picasso" (cf. FN 120f.). First published in *SU*.

3 So hobst du es leicht auf die Waage des Leids, da war es schwerer als ich / So you lifted it easily onto the scales of grief; there it lay, heavier than I: See verse 8 of "Was geschah?" / "What happened?" and verse 5 of "Und schwer" / "And Heavy."

"Halbe Nacht" / "Half Night"
1945 possibly, but before October 24, 1946; Bucharest. First published in *SU*.

3 daß getanzt sei von Dunkel zu Dunkel / so that there be dancing from darkness to darkness: See "Von Dunkel zu Dunkel" / "From Darkness to Darkness."

"Dein Haar überm Meer" / "Your Hair over the Sea"

1945 possibly, but before October 24, 1946; Bucharest. First published in *SU*.

5 und spieen mich an / and spat upon me: See Matt. 27:30: "And they spit upon him, and took the reed, and smote him on the head."

6 "O komm übers Meer!" / "O come over the sea!": See Jesus' command to Peter: "And he said, Come. And when Peter was come down out of the ship, he walked on the water, to go to Jesus" (Matt. 14:29).

7 Ich aber malt als ein Kahn die Schwingen / But I as a pinnace paint the wings purple: Unverified possible reference to Shelley's "The Witch of Atlas," given the following lines in stanza 45, in Julius Seybt's translation: "Ein Stern, hinschießend auf der Fluch der Nacht, / Ein schneller Aar im Morgenlicht, zerteilend / Den Wirbelsturm mit seiner Schwingen Macht— / **Getrieben von den Schwingen, strebt der Kahn** / Aus wildem Strom zu seinem Quell hinan." / "Like a star up the torrent of the night, / Or a swift eagle in the morning glare / Breasting the whirlwind with impetuous flight, / **The pinnace, pared by those enchanted wings,** / Clove the fierce streams towards their upper springs."

"Espenbaum" / "Aspen tree"

1945 possibly, but before October 24, 1946, Bucharest. First published in *SU*.

1f. Espenbaum, dein Laub blickt weiß ins Dunkel. / Meiner Mutter Haar ward nimmer weiß / Aspen tree, your leaves gaze white into the dark. / My mother's hair ne'er turned white: The leaves of the aspen tree (*Populus tremula*) are lighter on top than below. See verses 5 and 6 ("Can none of the aspen, none of the willows / take away your sorrow, bring you comfort") of "Nähe der Gräber" / "Nearness of the Graves" (from *SU*, not included here). The form, a two-line stanza with nature opening, takes off from a popular Romanian folk song form, often with elegiac content (doina); see also "We three, we four."

2 Meiner Mutter Haar ward nimmer weiß / My mother's hair ne'er turned white, 3 so grün ist die Ukraine / so green is the Ukraine: Celan's mother, Friederike Antschel, was murdered in the German concentration camp in Mikhaylovka near Haisyn in the Ukraine in winter 1942–1943, at the age of forty-six or forty-seven. This motif of snow in the Ukraine is repeated in a

number of poems. See verse 3 of "Schwarze Flocken" / "Black Flakes," published in *SU* but not included here: "brought a message to me too, a leaf from Ukrainian slopes." In relation to hair, see also verse 8 of "Mandorla."

7 Runder Stern / Round star: See verse 5 of "Sleepmorsels," *Breathturn into Timestead*, p. 136. The word "round star" was also used for the yellow badge, or Judenstern.

8 wund von Blei / seared by lead: See verse 31 of "Deathfugue."

"Aschenkraut" / "Cineraria"

Exact date unknown, but before December 4, 1946; Bucharest. First published in *SU*.

T Cineraria: The German title is "Aschenkraut" (literally "ash-weed"). In a note of July 1960, in the context of Claire Goll's accusations of plagiarism, Celan explained the title as "the name of the Cineraria as it is known to every German speaker" (GA, p. 439), and in a letter to Walter Jens: "'Aschenkraut' is not a metaphor, it is the name of the Cineraria, and thus of something extremely concrete" (May 9, 1961; GA, p. 373).

"Das Geheimnis der Farne" / "The Secret of the Ferns"

Before December 4, 1946, Bucharest. First published in *SU*.

1 der Schatten laubgrünes Herz / the shadows' leafgreen heart: The expression is picked up again in verse 3 of "What's required as stars" (*Breathturn into Timestead*, pp. 268–69).

5 ein Tausendschön hier, das befragt wird nach dunklerer Liebe / a daisy here, queried for a darker love: The *Tausendschön* or *Gänseblümchen*, our daisy (*Bellis perennis*), is used to determine if "s/he loves me / loves me not" by pulling off the petals of the flower. Celan noted this in his copy of *Das kleine Blumenbuch* (The Little Flower Book), a gift to Ruth Kraft (FN, p. 44).

"Der Sand aus den Urnen" / "The Sand from the Urns"

Before October 24, 1946, Bucharest.

T Der Sand aus den Urnen / The Sand from the Urns: This title is used as the title for Celan's first book of poems, then again as a section head in *Poppy and Memory*.

T Der Sand aus den Urnen / The Sand from the Urns, 6 Du füllst hier die Urnen / You fill up the urns here: See verses 8–11 of "Ich habe Bambus geschnitten" / "I have cut bamboo."

3 und bitterem Schamhaar / and bitter pubic hair: A letter to the German literary critic Walter Jens is quoted in the commentary to the poem "In der Gestalt eines Ebers" / "In the Shape of a Boar."

"Die letzte Fahne" / "The Last Flag"

Before December 4, 1946, Bucharest; the poem has come down to us in the 1946 typescript via Petre Solomon's papers.

Dedicated on an early manuscript to the Estonian poet (see "Erinnerung an Frankreich" / "Remembrance of France") Ilmar Laaban, who lived in Sweden and whom Celan had probably met in the surrealist circles in Paris, and with whom he was still in touch in the sixties. Laaban translated poems by Celan into Swedish and Estonian. When the volume *Mohn und Gedächtnis* was in preparation, Celan had all dedications removed, explaining to his editor that otherwise "the poems appear as too fixed to me, and in some cases linked to persons close to whom I no longer want them to be."

6 dein irrender Bart / your erring beard: Following Lev. 19:27, the shaving of the corners of the beard is forbidden to pious Jews, though not the trimming with scissors. To differentiate Jewish from Christian populations, even that was prohibited in some countries; it was thus in fact an imposed marking like the yellow star. In connection to "erring" one may also think of the figure of the "wandering Jew" as it evolved in France in the Middle Ages.

"Ein Knirschen" / "A crunching"

Before October 24, 1946, Bucharest. After the first magazine publication in *Der Plan*, the poem was gathered in *SU*. Wiedemann refers the reader to a scene in *Don Quixote*, where the hero encounters a barber carrying a brass basin on his head to protect his hat from the rain.

"Das Gastmahl" / "The Banquet"

Before December 4, 1946, Bucharest. The poem (see "Remembrance of France") had been dedicated provisionally to Otto Basil. Celan would meet

Basil, the recipient of the 1946 manuscript and the editor of the magazine *Der Plan*, in Vienna.

2 die Schwelle mit Zähnen geflügt, vor Morgen der Jähzorn gesät / the threshold be ploughed with teeth, before dawn choler be sowed: See the commentary to verse 2 of "Talglicht" / "Tallowlight" re the story of Jason.

4, 13 langsamen Rad / slow wheel: See verse 11 of "Engführung."

11f. steiget mit mir auf die Tische: / wie anders sei noch geschlafen als stehend // climb on the tables with me: / how else to sleep now except standing up: See the closing line of the first letter to Margul-Sperber, his Bucharest mentor: "But I want to climb on the table, as if to sleep, and embrace you" (February 11, 1948, PC/AMS, p. 244).

"Dunkles Aug im September" / "Dark Eye in September"
1946, Bucharest. First printed in *Der Sand aus den Urnen.*

T September: See "September Crown" and the commentary to "Huhediblu."

1 Steinhaube / Stonehood: The word seems to have been considered at some point as a possible title for *Lightduress.*

7 Zum zweitenmal blüht die Kastanie / A second time the chestnut blooms: As the annotation in the manuscript shows, Celan refers to the occasional additional fall blossom of the horse chestnut. See his letter to Gisèle of September 27, 1955: "the chestnut trees, redbrown and stern, made young with blooms, as we love them" (PC/GCL, p. 68). Ilana Shmueli, Celan's last lover, remembers in connection with this poem a warning of Celan's from January 1970: "this blooming of the chestnuts in the fall is a lethal malady, watch out" (Shmueli, p. 58).

9 Orion: A giant and hunter in Greek myth, who had been blinded and given sight again. The constellation named after him is visible in Central Europe in fall and winter. See also verse 66ff. of "And with the Book from Tarussa," verse 2 of "Lilac air" (*Breathturn into Timestead*, pp. 322–23), and verse 1 of "The Hunter" (an early poem).

13 an den Toren / at the gates: Also the title of the first cycle of *SU.*

"Der Stein aus dem Meer" / "The Stone from the Sea"
Probably after October 24, 1946, Bucharest. First printed in *SU.*

T Der Stein aus dem Meer / The Stone from the Sea, 3 So blieb uns zu spinnen / What remains for us is to spin, 4 des Steins aus der Tiefe / the stone from the depth: See the title and verse 3f. of "Out of the Sea": "from which one spins eternity's foam."

8 die Schwärze des Meers / the blackness of the sea: Celan had spent time at the Black Sea during his Bucharest years. See also verse 2 of "Talglicht" / "Tallowlight" and verse 4 from "Aschenglorie" / "Ashglory" in *Breathturn into Timestead*, pp. 62–65.

9 Sie tragen ihm Lanzen voran, so trugen wir Traum / They carry lances ahead, as we carried dream: *Lanze* (lance) is a near anagram of Celan's birth name in its Romanian spelling, Ancel (and a complete one in English). See also the text called "Eine Lanze" ("A Lance") written with Edgar Jené (who appears there as "Eine"—with Celan being "Lanze") in Vienna (MFV, #297).

"Erinnerung an Frankreich" / "Remembrance of France"

Exact date of composition unknown, but before October 9, 1947. The poem belongs among those dedicated to Ingeborg Bachmann with "f.D." ("for you") (see PC/IB, p. 103). First printed in *SU* with a dedication to Edgar Jené, probably on January 25, 1948. Jené was a friend from the Vienna period, who had also overseen the unsuccessful printing of *SU* and had contributed two etchings. In August 1948 Celan published his essay "Edgar Jené and the Dream about the Dream" to accompany thirty lithographs by Jené. In early November 1952 Celan asked his publisher to cut all dedications, as these bound the poems too closely to people in whose proximity he no longer wanted to see himself. He did not—as he did with the dedication to Klaus Demus for "The Jars"—reinstate the dedication to Jené in the second edition.

T Frankreich / France, 1 der Himmel von Paris / the sky of Paris: Celan had spent the 1938–1939 academic year studying medicine in Tours, France. On that occasion, especially during his visits to Paris, he had come in contact with the literature of surrealism.

2 die große Herbstzeitlose / the great autumn crocus: See the commentary to the poem "Die Silbe Schmerz" / "The Syllable Pain" re Apollinaire's poem "Les Colchiques," and further references.

5 Monsieur Le Songe: French for "Mister Dream"; see a comparable

process in Rilke's Fifth Duino Elegy, also closely tied to the naming of Paris: "the milliner, Madame Lamort" (verse 88, Rainer Maria Rilke, *Duino Elegies: The Sonnets to Orpheus*, vol. 1, edited and translated by Stephen Mitchell [Vintage International: 1982], pp. 32-33).

"Chanson einer Dame im Schatten" / "Chanson of a Lady in the Shadows"
1947–1948. Not in the *SU* manuscript or volume. The manuscript and typescript were added probably beginning August 1949 to a letter to the Dutch music student Diet Kloos, whom he had just met (PC/DKB, pp. 24–27, 65–67).

1, 32 Tulpen / tulips: See verse 8 of "Der Stein aus dem Meer" / "The Stone from the Sea."

27 Er trägt es von Schwelle zu Schwelle / He wears it from threshold to threshold: See the title of the volume of poems after *Poppy and Memory*.

"Nachtstrahl" / "Nightbeam"
Date of composition unknown. The manuscript is dated 1948, Vienna. First printed in *SU*. This is one of the poems dedicated "f.D." to Ingeborg Bachmann, who refers to it in her poem "Herbstmanöver" (Autumn maneuver).

1 Am lichtesten brannte das Haar meiner Abendgeliebten / The hair of my evening beloved burned most brightly: There is a similar image in the early (possibly late 1930s) poem "Du siehst es" ("You light your hair like kindling").

3 Rome: Celan was in the Italian capital for the first time only in 1964; see the commentary to verse 7 of "Mittages" / "Midday" (*Breathturn into Timestead*).

7 als ich weilte auf Reisen in Spätland und Briefe schrieb an den Morgen / when I tarried on journeys in Lateland and wrote letters to morning: Celan studied in France in 1938–1939—thus in Western Europe—and sent letters from there to his eastern homeland.

7f. Briefe schrieb an den Morgen. // Ein schöner Kahn ist der Sarg / wrote letters to morning. // A gorgeous skiff is that coffin: See verse 5 of "Hinterm kohlgezinkten" / "Behind coalmarked" (*Breathturn into Timestead*, pp. 50–51).

"Die Jahre von dir zu mir" / "The Years from You to Me"

Date of composition unknown. *SU* ms. 1948. First printed in *SU*.

One of the poems dedicated "f.D." to Ingeborg Bachmann.

5 in den Spiegeln der Tiefsee / in the mirrors of the deepsea: See the beginning of Celan's essay "Edgar Jené and the Dream of the Dream": "I am supposed to say a few words I heard in the deepsea, where so much is passed over in silence and so much happens. I breached objects and objections of reality and stood before the sea's mirror surface" (Waldrop's translation, adapted; GW III, p. 155).

"Lob der Ferne" / "In Praise of Distance"

1948, Vienna. First printed in *Der Sand aus den Urnen*. This is one of the poems dedicated "f.D." to Ingeborg Bachmann.

1, 3, 11, 15 Im Quell deiner Augen / In the springs of your eyes: See Celan's short Romanian poem: "Iarba ochilor tăi, iarbă amară. / Flutură vant peste ea, pleoapă de ceară. // Apa ochilor tăi, apă iertată" (PCFW, p. 161), translated by Andrei Codrescu as: "Your eyes' field of grass, bitter grass. / The wind, wax eyelid, ruffles it. // Your eyes' water, forgiven water." Codrescu further comments: "The 'eyes' are dispersed in the grass and in the water. The water is, oddly, 'forgiven'—we don't know by whom, not by the poet; the phrasing of 'your eyes' water' has an echo of the 'water of life and death' in a Romanian fairy tale about two springs, one of 'life,' one of 'death,' which the hero must choose between. In the fairy tale, the 'authentic' hero chooses the spring of the 'water of life.' Two previous contenders drink the 'water of death'—they are pretenders. The fairy tale is called 'Life Without Death, Youth Without Age.'"

"Das ganze Leben" / "The Whole Life"

December 28, 1946, Bucharest. This is one of the poems dedicated "f.D." to Ingeborg Bachmann, who refers to it in her poem "Reigen."

11 Es zückte das Messer des Glücks über uns mit erloschenen Augen / It wielded the knife of happiness above us with extinguished eyes: See verse 8 of "Aus dem Meer" / "Out of the Sea": "O messerumfunkelte Augen" / "O eyes, knives flashing around you."

"Spät und Tief" / "Late and Deep"

April 20, 1948, Vienna. On the manuscript, the date is followed by the note: "(spring, Mariahilfer Str.)"; in Mariahilferstraße Celan used to frequent the Café Casa Piccola. The poem had been dedicated temporarily to Isac Chiva, the Romanian ethnologist who had fled from Budapest to Vienna with Celan and had later prepared Celan's arrival in Paris.

First printed in *SU* with the title "Deucalion and Pyrrha."

6 Wir schwören bei Christus dem Neuen, den Staub zu vermählen dem Staube / We swear upon Christ the New to marry dust to dust, 24 Umkehr / a turning, 27 Es komme ein Mensch aus dem Grabe / Let a man come forth from the grave: The son of God in the New Testament states: "I promise you this. If you don't change and become like a child, you will never get into the kingdom of heaven" (Matt. 18:3); see also, in the drafts for the Meridian speech: "Das Gedicht ist eine Umkehr" / "The poem is a turning" (TCA/MFV, #419, p. 131); and Gen. 3:19: "for you are dust, and to dust shall return." Further reading traces (marks in the margin) in Ernst Bloch's *The Principle of Hope*: "Ja noch wirksamer als die persischen Messianismen sind im Parakleten die weiterlebend jüdischen: der Glaube an den erschienenen Messias enthielt wiederum den Glauben an den noch nicht erschienenen in sich" ("Even more effective than those in Presian messianism are according to the Paraclete, those of the still living Jewish messianism: faith in the Messiah who has appeared prolonged in turn faith in the Messiah who has not yet appeared") (my translation), with the marginal note by Celan: "compare 'Wir schwören bei Christus / dem Neuen . . .' [we swear by Christ the New . . .] / Vienna 1948" (further marginal note in vol. 2, p. 1502).

16 Mühlen des Todes das weiße Mehl der Verheißung / mills of death the white meal of the Promise: See verse 3f. of "Das Gastmahl" / "The Banquet," as well as the commentary on "Todesfugue" / "Deathfugue" re the "Knochen-Mühle" / "bone-mill." On May 9, 1961, Celan wrote to Walter Jens: "Here too something (oh so concrete) is evoked: the—the word could be read in all newspapers after the end of the war—death-mills Auschwitz, Treblinka etc. Here I was reminded by the poem and through the poem—anamnesis!—of something: it arises not just from the context, but also from the two titles, 'Deucalion and Pyrrha' [the original, later discarded title] and 'Late and

Deep'" (GA, p. 372f.). The verse plays a special role from the beginning on in the Goll affair. In January 1946 the documentary film *Death Mills* (German title *Todesmühlen*) by Billy Wilder and Hamus Burger was shown in the parts of Germany and Austria under U.S. occupation. Celan was appalled by the poet and literary critic Hans Egon Holthusen's 1954 (and later several times repeated) assertion that he "found the 'deathmills' trivial and the 'white flower of the promise' that is supposedly ground in them, an artificial and therefore completely dead metaphor" (*Fünf junge Lyriker / Five Young Poets*, p. 386). Holthusen had been an SS officer during the war.

23f. es komme das gurgelnde Meer, / der geharnischte Windstoß der Umkehr / let the gurgling sea come, / the armored gust of the wind of a turning: See verse 11f. of "Es war Erde in ihnen" / "There was earth inside them."

27 Es komme ein Mensch aus dem Grabe / Let a man come forth from the grave: See verse 12f. of "Tübingen, Jänner" and verse 8 of "Give the Word."

"Corona" / "Corona"

1948, Vienna. First published in *SU*.

T Corona: Latin and Italian for "wreath," "crown"; Italian also for "fermata," a pause in music of unspecified length on a note or rest. See verse 3f. of "Cleared" (*Breathturn into Timestead*, pp. 246–47): "Freigegeben, auch dieser / Start. // Bugradgesang mit / Corona" / "Cleared, this start / also. // Bow-wheelchant with / fermata."

7 Geschlecht / sex: The German word *Geschlecht* refers both to the sex qua organ, and to lineage, descendance, or race. See, for example, Jacques Derrida's essays on the use of the word by Heidegger.

"Todesfuge" / "Deathfugue"

Possibly May 1945, in Bucharest. First published in the magazine *Contemporanul*, Bucharest, May 2, 1947, under the title "Tangoul mortii" / "Death tango," in a Romanian translation by Celan's friend Petre Solomon. Solomon suggests in his memoir that "Paul was still reworking the poem in 1947—as proof I give the title" (which did change that year after publication in Romanian). Reprinted in *SU*. The composition of the poem before Celan's move to Bucharest in April 1945 is, according to Wiedemann, at least probable. The poem is not included in the 1946 typescript, but is part of the bundle of poems sent to Otto Basil slightly later.

Concerning the origin of the poem Celan wrote in 1960: "the Jewish—when in May 1945 I wrote *Deathfugue*, back then, I seem to remember, I had just read the accounts of the Lwów Ghetto in Izvestia" (PN, p. 170). This report had appeared in fact already on December 23, 1944, in both *Izvestia* and *Pravda*, when Celan was still living in Czernowitz. Beyond the specifics of the Lwów Ghetto events, the article reported on the fate of Jews in concentration camps on Ukrainian soil, thus also on the fate of Celan's parents, while being simultaneously a document of Soviet anti-Semitism. One of the illustrations of the *Izvestia* article shows a picture of, according to the Russian caption, "the German machine used for the crushing of the bones of the burned corpses."

After the poem had been mentioned in relation to Claire Goll's plagiarism accusations in the early sixties (see the introductory commentaries to *NoOnes-Rose*, and the general introduction to this volume), Celan stopped reading what is his most famous poem publicly; see his note following a request for a recording of the poem on January 22, 1970: "This poem has now, and for a long time yet, to stay with itself. I myself no longer read it in public." Barbara Wiedemann says that there is no proof that the poem "Er" (published first shortly before Celan's death) by the Bukovinian poet Immanuel Weißglas, a school friend of Celan's, which shows clear parallels to "Deathfugue," predates Celan's poem. Weißglas himself wrote that he saw both poems as "deeply anchored in the lyric consciousness of our time. Parallelisms in no way show claims for any kind of priority." He called the suggestions of plagiarism on the part of Celan "jackal-like snooping . . . with the deceitful aim to question a poetic creation of Hölderlinesque facture." The French critic Jean Bollack, who had been a friend of Celan's, claims that "Deathfugue" was "an answer to Weißglas's poem, whose existence he knew of. He reorganized its component parts, without adding extra ones: it is the same elements though he creates something completely different with them" (Jean Bollack, *Poésie contre poésie: Celan et la littérature*, Presses universitaires de France: 2001, p. 28).

Celan wrote to his publisher, saying that "Todesfuge" is a stand-alone poem, thus to be considered as a stand-alone cycle: "I'm therefore asking you to give the title a page by itself (similarly as for [the cycles] 'The Sand from the Urns,' 'Counterlight' and 'Night Blades')" (November 5, 1952, Bertrand Badiou's reference).

See also the letter to Walter Jens of May 5, 1961, which elucidates a number of elements in the poem: "The 'grave in the air'—dear Walter Jens, that is in this poem, God knows, neither a borrowing nor a metaphor . . . The snake (Ophis, Nahash etc.)—: this has doubtlessly to do with the archetypical. (Among the ancients—how often have they played with snakes . . .) / You see, dear Walter Jens, in 'Deathfuge' it is not 'death' that plays with the snakes—it is 'the man in the house' who plays with the snakes, the same one who writes 'your golden hair, Margarete.' And here, Walter Jens, besides the archetypal, there is . . . archetypal transformation: hair (and here, given the Gretchen figure, one also thinks of braids) often transforms (in fairy tales as in myths) into snakes" (GA, p. 533; notes for this, GA, p. 462).

T Todesfuge / Deathfugue: In a letter to the publisher Herbert Greiner-Mai, Celan wrote on February 23, 1961: "My poem Deathfugue (not: *The* Deathfugue) is not composed 'according to musical principles'; rather, once this poem was there, I took it as not unjustified to name it 'Deathfugue': from that death which it—with its own—tries to bring into language. In other words: 'Deathfugue,' is a single word in no way discerptible into its 'constituent parts.'" Celan reminded Ingeborg Bachmann: "Deathfugue is also this for me: a tombstone epigraph and a tombstone [. . .] My mother too has only this grave" (November 12, 1959; Bertrand Badiou's suggestion).

1 Schwarze Milch / Black milk: See Celan's note 588 for the Meridian speech: "Black milk of morning: that's not one of those genitive metaphors, as they are presented to us by our so-called critics, to keep us from approaching the poem; it is no longer a figure of speech or an oxymoron, it is reality. / Genitive metaphor = No, a being-born-to-each-other of the words under heart's distress."

4 wir schaufeln / we dig: Ilana Schmueli remembers in 2004 in connection to Celan's work in the Tabaresti labor camp: "When asked about the camp, he would answer monosyllabically: 'I dig; I shovel'" (PC/Ishm, p. 136).

5 Ein Mann wohnt im Haus der spielt mit den Schlangen / A man lives in the house he plays with the snakes: See reading traces in the Georg Trakl poem "Psalm": "In seinem Grab spielt der weiße Magier mit seinen Schlangen" (In

his grave the white magician plays with his snakes); and Celan's note: "Strange! / cf. Deathfugue" (p. 65). To Jens, who cited the Trakl line in his defense of Celan against Claire Goll's plagiarism accusation (*Die Zeit*, June 9, 1961; GA, p. 368), Celan wrote about the archetypical meaning of playing with snakes: "I mention this note to suppress the closeness to the Trakl line; I just think that something decisive becomes visible here: that only a second encounter makes an encounter . . . into an encounter [daß erst Wiederbegegnung Begegnung zur . . . Begegnung macht]" (GA, p. 533).

6, 14, 24, 28, 30, 34 Deutschland: These are the only times the word *Deutschland* is used—six times—in the work authorized for publication by Celan (it also appears in the poem "Wolfsbohne," not published during his lifetime). The first English translation of this poem I encountered was by Jerome Rothenberg in his *New Young German Poets* (tr. Jerome Rothenberg [San Francisco: City Lights Books, 1959], p. 16). It was the only word left in German, and, I believe, to good effect. To honor that first groundbreaking Celan translation, I have retained Rothenberg's "Deutschland,"—as, by the way, John Felstiner also did in his version (*Selected Poems and Prose of Paul Celan*, tr. John Felstiner, 2001, pp. 31–33).

6, 14, 22, 32, 35 Margarete, 15, 23, 36 Shulamit: The two women's names represent major works of the German and the Jewish cultural tradition: Johann Wolfgang's *Faust*, and the Old Testament's *Song of Solomon*. Here is Celan in *The Meridian*: "In a well intended discussion of the 'Death Fugue' the German middle school kids are told that Shulamit is a name from the Balkans etc. / Shulamit, that is a name from the Song of Songs" (#589). Bertrand Badiou notes that the Hebrew name Shulamit shares three consonants with the word for peace, "shalom," similar in that to Celan's mother's name, Friederike, which contains the noun *Friede* (peace).

25 er ruft streicht dunkler die Geigen dann steigt ihr als Rauch in die Luft / he calls scrape those fiddles more darkly then as smoke you'll rise in the air: See Celan's comment on this line in lines 139 and 140 of "Engführung": ". . . no / smokesoul rises and plays along."

31 er trifft dich mit bleierner Kugel / he strikes you with lead bullets: See verse 8 of "Espenbaum" / "Aspen tree."

GEGENLICHT / COUNTERLIGHT

See the title of a collection of aphoristic texts first published in the magazine *Die Tat* (Zurich, March 12, 1949; also GW III, pp. 163–65, and in my translation throughout *Microliths*). See further the prose essay "Edgar Jené and the Dream about the Dream": "Oft haben wir als Wache geschworen: im heißen Schatten ungeduldiger Fahnen, im Gegenlicht des fremden Todes, am Hochaltar unserer heiliggesprochenen Vernunft" / "Many oaths have we sworn in our waking lives, in the hot shadow of impatient flags in the counterlight of alien death, at the high altar of our sanctified reason" (GW III, p. 160; Waldrop translation, altered, p. 9).

"Auf Reisen" / "Traveling"

Probably 1948, in Vienna. Celan was in Paris as of July 14, 1948. On the manuscript for *SU* it says: "(before departure)." On September 10, 1948, Celan sent the poem to Alfred Margul-Sperber in Bucharest with the date "Innsbruck, 28. June 1948." First printed in *SU*.

2 dein Haus in Paris zur Opferstatt deiner Hände / your house in Paris your hands' sacrificial altar: Celan lived in Paris from July 14, 1948, until his death there. See the citation of this line in "Zwölf Jahre" / "Twelve Years," verses 3 to 5.

4 Gehöft / homestead: See the later poem "Hollow Lifehomestead" in *Breathturn into Timestead*, p. 29.

4 Gespann für dein Herz / a team for your heart: Untranslatable pun: Celan, very well versed in botany, here probably deconstructed the word *Herzgespann*, the name of a plant, *Leonurus cardiaca*, native to western Asia, also called motherwort, throw-wort, or lion's-tail. The plant grows on waysides, dumping grounds, and the like. See the commentary to verse 2 of "Embankments, Roadsides, Vacant Lots, Rubble." See also Celan's readings in Jean Paul (Richter)'s work, where the word occurs on a number of occasions.

5 Dein Haar möchte wehn, wenn du fährst—das ist ihm verboten. / Your hair wants to waft when you ride—but that's forbidden: See verse 1 of "Lock" (*Threshold to Threshold*): "Lock, that I didn't braid, that I let waft."

"In Ägypten" / "In Egypt"

April 23, 1948. The manuscript gives "Paris" as the place of composition; the poem was temporarily dedicated to Ingeborg Bachmann, to whom Celan sent it as a birthday present that year.

3, 6, 9 Ruth: Hebrew רוּת, the title character of the Book of Ruth. In the narrative, she is not an Israelite but rather is from Moab; she marries an Israelite. Both her husband and her father-in-law die, and she helps her mother-in-law, Naomi, find protection. Although not a Jew, she is presented to the Jews as the model of absolute marital fidelity. In Czernowitz and Bucharest, Celan had a very close friend whose name was Ruth Kraft.

3, 6, 9 Naomi: Hebrew נָעֳמִי, Ruth's mother-in-law in the Old Testament's Book of Ruth. The etymology of her name is not certain, but it is possible that it means "good," "pleasant," "lovely," or "winsome." Ruth Kraft's full name was Noëmi Ruth Kraft.

3, 6, 9 Miriam: Hebrew מִרְיָם, sister to Moses and Aaron; described in the Old Testament as a prophetess and singer of a song of praise after the Israelites crossed the Red Sea (Exod. 15:20).

"Ins Nebelhorn" / "Into the Foghorn"

Predates October 1950. Paris, Jardin des Tuileries.

"Vom Blau" / "Of the blue"

Predates October 1950. Paris.

On February 17, 1958, Celan answered questions about the poem posed by a Bremen school class, insisting that "a poem is an attempt to grapple with reality, an attempt to gain reality, to make reality visible. Thus reality for the poem is in no way something fixed, predetermined, but something that is at issue, something to be questioned. In the poem something real *happens* . . . 'We compared the rolling pearl with a parting tear!'—No: the rolling pearl is the rolling pearl, it 'rolls' at this (and at no other) place of the poem, it stands—at least in its intention—in connection with the poem" (PN, *Microliths* #299).

3 Perle, und du wächst / pearl, and you grow: 5f. Du rollst: das schwarze Hagelkorn der Schwermut / You roll: melancholia's black hailstone: See

verses 5 and 8 of "Ruhe aus in deinen Wunden" / "Rest in your wounds" (*Breathturn into Timestead*, pp. 104–105).

5 schwarze Hagelkorn / black hailstone: See verse 19 of "Hüttenfenster" / "Hutwindow."

"Wer wie du" / "Who like you"

Before August 19, 1948, Paris (according to a letter, and could thus be the first poem written in Paris).

2 pickt den Stern aus meinen Augen, eh er funkelt / picks the star from my eyes before it twinkles: See verses 7 to 9 of "In Time's Corner," *Breathturn into Timestead*, pp. 297–98.

"Brandmal" / "Stigma"

Before March 8, 1949, Paris.

T Brandmal: Celan marked the following lines in Petronius' *Cena Trimalchionis* (which he knew already in Bucharest, as his Romanian prose poem "Erau nopt" / "Those were nights" [RP 73] shows): "itaque quamdiu vixerit, habebit stigmam, nec illam nisi Orcus delebit" ("for as long as he lives, he will carry a stigma, and that only Orcus will extinguish").

1–3 denn wir lagen im Uhrwerk der Schwermut / und bogen die Zeiger wie Ruten, / und sie schnellten zurück / for we lay in melancholia's clockwork / and bent the hands like rods, / and they sprang back: See "Down melancholy's rapids," verse 13 of "Twenty Forever," and verse 7 of "Behind coalmarked" (*Breathturn into Timestead*, pp. 7, 23, and 51, respectively).

2 und bogen die Zeiger wie Ruten / and bent the hands like rods, 5f. und zwölfmal sagte ich du zur Nacht deiner Worte, / und sie tat sich auf und blieb offen / and twelve times I said you to the night of your words, / and it opened and stayed ajar: Cf. v 1, 5f. and 8 of "Abend der Worte" / "Evening of the Words."

8 Zündschnur / fuse, 9 Blitz / lightning bolt: Sudden spark discharges belong to the program of the French surrealists, with whom Celan was in contact again during his early days in Paris. (See "Erau nopt" / "Those were nights.") From André Breton's 1924 *Manifesto of Surrealism*: "It is, as it were, from the

fortuitous juxtaposition of the two terms that a particular light has sprung, *the light of the image*, to which we are infinitely sensitive. The value of the image depends upon the beauty of the spark obtained: it is, consequently, a function of the difference of potential between the two conductors" (André Breton, *Manifestoes of Surrealism*, tr. Richard Seaver and Helen R. Lane, Ann Arbor Paperback, 1972, p. 37).

"Wer sein Herz" / "He who rips"

Before May 26, 1949, Paris. One of the poems dedicated "f.D." to Ingeborg Bachmann.

1 Wer sein Herz aus der Brust reißt / He who rips his heart from his breast: See Celan's note: "compare 'He who rips his heart . . .'" in his copy of Musil's *The Man Without Qualities*, next to "the hearts seemed to stand still, to be taken out of the breast, to join the silent train in the air. 'Then the heart was torn from my breast,' a mystic said: Agathe remembered this" (my translation; in the original on p. 1170).

"Kristall" / "Crystal"

Beginning of 1950 at the latest, Paris. One of the poems dedicated "f.D." to Ingeborg Bachmann.

The poem integrates, while estranging them, some elements of old folk-motifs and poems, such as Hans Carosso's "Der Alte Brunnen" ("The old fountain") or Clemens Brentano's "Hörst du wie die Brunnen rauschen" ("Do you hear the fountains roar?"). Wiedemann suggests that it has "a special significance for Celan's opus, and is quoted literally or alluded to all the way to the late work. The motif of the 'crystal' also belongs to this context. It plays a special role from the very start of Claire Goll's plagiarism accusations" (GA, p. 187).

4 Sieben Nächte höher wandert Rot zu Rot / Seven nights higher, red wanders to red: See "In Late-red" (p. 87), title and verse 5 of "With Time-Red Lips" (p. 151), verse 19 of "The Vintagers" (p. 157), and verse 17f. of "Unwashed, unpainted," (*Snowpart*, *Breathturn into Timestead*, p. 321).

6 sieben Rosen später rauscht der Brunnen / seven roses later, rustles the fountain: See the cycle title *Seven Roses Later* from *Threshold to Threshold*, and the title and verse 11 of "... whispers the Fountain."

6 rauscht der Brunnen / rustles the fountain: See the well-known poem by Clemens Brentano "Hörst du wie die Brunnen rauschen?" (Do you hear the fountains roar?). The German *rauschen*, in the song and elsewhere, has been translated variously as "murmur," "roar," "rustle," and "gush."

"Totenhemd" / "Shroud"

Before 1950, Paris.

1 Was du aus Leichtem wobst / What you of gossamer wove: A reference to verse 19 of "Schwarze Flocken" / "Black Flakes," a poem published in *SU* but not included here: "Kam mir die Träne. Webt ich das Tüchlein" / "A tear came to me. I wove the little cloth."

9 Haldengott / attleheapgod: Consider what Jean Boase-Beier has to say about the etymologies of this image-complex: "The image of a god of rubble-heaps, recalling the 'Trummerhaufen' of Germany in the aftermath of war and Allied bombing, and the 'Trummerfrauen' who worked at clearing them up, suggests, with its reference to a drum, the repetitive sounds or feelings of traumatic memory. But beyond this image, the language itself is full of significance. 'Halde' is another word for 'Trummerhaufen' and 'Trimmer' derives from 'Trumm' ('piece'), which is originally from Old High German 'drum,' a word which, like the Old English 'thrum,' means a 'small fragment.' 'Trummer,' a word that is only present in the synonymity of 'Trummerhaufen' to 'Halde' thus recalls the English word 'drum' for 'Trommel,' via its homophony with the Old High German word. And the Old High German 'drum' and the Old English 'thrum' have given us the modern technical word 'thrum' in English: the end of a warp thread. 'Warp' derives from the Old English 'weorpan,' which led to 'werferi' in German, a word that appears in the second stanza, and 'weapon' in English, and is related to the Indo-Germanic 'ueri,' which gave the German 'Wunde' and the English 'wound.' Furthermore, because the first line (in its English translation) is 'That which you wove,' the warp-end 'thrum' that echoes through 'Trommef' and 'Trummer'

ties together the images of weaving and drumming. For more discussion of the dense web of words in this poem, see . . . also Box 5, where some of these connections are represented" (Jean Boase-Beier, *Translating the Poetry of the Holocaust: Translation, Style and the Reader*, pp. 110, 111).

Box 5 One thread in '*Totenhemd*'

Was Du aus Leichtem **wobst**
...
Aber der **Haldengott**
rührt seine dumpfeste **Trommel**

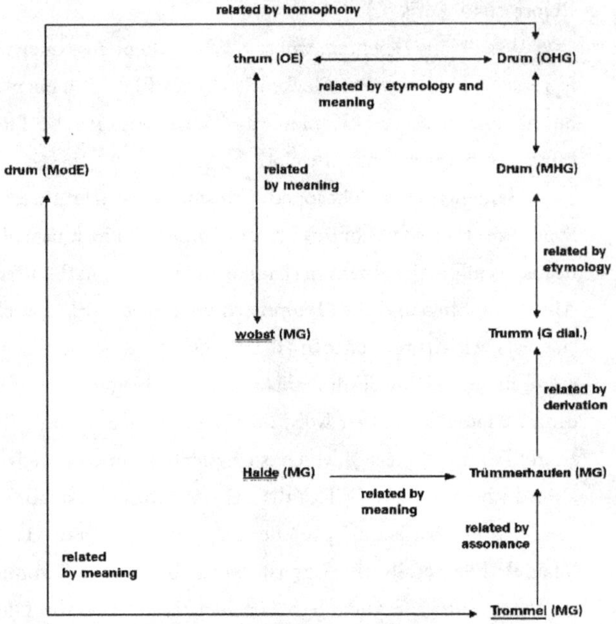

OE – Old English; ModE – Modern English; OHG – Old High German; MHG – Middle High German; MG – Modern German; G dial. – German dialect

Direction of arrows does not signal historical or other linguistic process but one possible way the translator might trace meanings and forms.

"Auf hoher See" / "On the High Seas"

1949, Paris.

Celan sent the poem on October 7, 1949, in a letter to Diet Kloos-Barendregt with the title "Rauchtopas" (Smoky quartz). Celan added: "I think it is a beautiful poem, Diet, no, I'm sure it is a beautiful poem. A good sign" (PC/DKB, pp. 38–40, 75f.). Diet Kloos-Barendregt wore a smoky quartz ring, given her by Jan Kloos, her husband, who had been tortured and murdered by the Nazis in her presence.

1, 4 Paris: In the official town seal of Paris, Celan's hometown since July 1948, there is a ship with the motto "Fluctuat nec mergitur" (It floats but doesn't sink).

"Ich bin allein" / "I am alone"

1950 (before October), Paris.

1 Aschenblume / ashflower: See the commentary to "Aschenkraut" / "Cineraria."

"Die Krüge" / "The Jars"

June 1949, Paris. In a letter to Erica Lillegg, started on June 15, 1949, around midnight, Celan writes concerning this poem: "And here is an embarrassed and shy, a gone astray and uncertain one. I will offer it as a gift to little Klaus, but before him, only you know it, it belongs to you, with all the earlier and the ones to come."

Dedication: Klaus Demus, an art historian, had been a friend of Celan's since their first meeting in Vienna in 1948. See the fascinating and enlightening volume of (as yet untranslated) correspondence between Celan, Demus, and the latter's wife, Nani. It is the only dedication that Celan kept in the book, removing several others.

"Nachts" / "At night"

1949 (according to a letter of August 1, 1957, to Christine Brückner, ref. Badiou). This is one of the poems dedicated "f.D." to Ingeborg Bachmann.

"So schlafe" / "So sleep"

1950 (before October), Paris. One of the poems dedicated "f.D." to Ingeborg Bachmann.

"So bist du denn geworden" / "So you have become"

1950 (before October), Paris.

"Die feste Burg" / "The Mighty Fortress"

1950, Paris. On September 23, 1950, Celan wrote to Erica Lillegg: "Do you recognize the house? It is the house in Kärnten, in which you live, the one in front of which your mother sits and knits. That there was a gable with a (green!) sorrow-flag may not be accurate, but still it is Your house in Kärnten and therefore the house I long for."

T The Mighty Fortress: See Martin Luther's hymn "A Mighty Fortress Is Our God."

7 Halm und Herz und Blume / stalk and heart and flower, 10 flower, heart and stalk: See verses 1, 5, 7, and 11 of "Umsonst malst du Herzen" / "For naught you draw hearts."

"Der Tauben weißeste" / "The whitest of doves"

1950 (before October), Paris. One of the poems dedicated "f.D." to Ingeborg Bachmann. In an earlier edition Wiedemann had suggested that it was connected to the arrival "on 10. 14. 1950 of Ingeborg Bachmann in Paris for a long visit (from mid-October until December), to reconnect with the love affair of their Vienna days."

5f. From my hand you take the great flower: / It's neither white nor red nor blue: Cf. title & v. 1 of "Errinerung an Frankreich" / "Remembrance of France"; blue, white, and red are the French national colors, although not in the order the poem gives them.

8 Wir waren nie / We never were: See marginal note "we never were" in Edmond Jabès's *Le Livre de Yukel* next to: "'Ce lieu est amour. Il est absence de lieu.' Reb Zack" / "'This place is love. It is the absence of place.' Rabbi Zack."

HALME DER NACHT / NIGHT STALKS

Title of Cycle: *Halme der Nacht / Night Stalks:* See the poem "Aus Herzen und Hirnen" / "From hearts and brains" in this cycle.

"Schlaf und Speise" / "Sleep and Nourishment"

March 19, 1951, Paris. The poem had provisionally been dedicated to Max Hölzer, the editor of *Surrealist Publications.*

"Der Reisekamerad" / "The Traveling Companion"

Date of composition unknown. The manuscript is dated "Paris, 1951?"

T Der Reisekamerad / The Traveling Companion: See interview with Karl Schwedhelm for Süddeutsches Radio of April 7, 1954 (broadcast on June 15, 1954), for which he also read this poem: "Looking for a title for this poem specifically, I realized that it was once again a matter of a childhood memory, in fact a tale by Andersen that I didn't remember at all, while I was writing the lines of this poem, but . . . that declared itself afterwards. So then I used the title of the Andersen tale as the title of the poem, although the content of the poem in no way coincides with that of the tale. Permit me to add that it—that the poem itself takes off from the tale but then travels along its own path." He told the German critic Walter Jens on May 16, 1961 concerning Andersen: "We read much Andersen to our boy, and . . . I see how much all that can be heard in my poems, even if not always as visibly as in the title of 'Traveling Companion.'" The hero of the fairy tale in question is an innocent young boy who is sent out into the world by his dying father; because he thwarts the desecration of a coffin in a chapel, he is accompanied on his travels by a stranger (who turns out to be the dead man he helped) until he finds happiness (Hans Christian Andersen, *Fairy Tales of Hans Christian Andersen*, http://www.gutenberg.org/files/27200/27200-h/27200-h.htm#travelng.). Celan had heard these fairy tales from his mother.

6 Deiner Mutter Mündel bückt sich nach der Krume Lichts / Your mother's ward bends down toward the crumb of light: See verse 9 of "Ich hörte sagen" / "I Heard It Said."

"Augen" / "Eyes"

Date of composition unknown. The manuscript is dated "Paris, 1951?"

5 Nacht / night, 6 als ich Nesseln pflückt' / as I gathered nettles: Possibly here is also a memory of an Andersen tale: in "The Wild Swans" a young girl gathers nettles at night, which she will spin into shirts for her brothers in order to free them from a spell. http://www.gutenberg.org/files/27200/27200-h/27200-h.htm#wild_swa.

11 Ewigkeit / eternity: See the title of the next poem.

"Die Ewigkeit" / "Eternity"

Paris, Levallois-Perret. In the summer of 1951 Celan lived for a few weeks in the Paris suburb of Levallois-Perret in a friend's house (at 14 Villa Chaptal, which is today the Hauts-de-Seine Département).

T Eternity: See verse 11 of the preceding poem and the two poems with the same or similar titles in *Breathturn into Timestead*, on pp. 177, 399, 273, 163, and 141.

"Brandung" / "Breakers"

September 16, 1951, Paris. Celan had probably returned on September 12, 1951, by land and sea from a visit to London.

1 Du, Stunde, flügelst in den Dünen / You, hour, you flutter in the dunes: Cf. v. 8 of "Im Zeitwinkel schwört / "In Time's Corner" (BiT, 299).

"Aus Herzen" / "From hearts"

1951, Paris. One of the poems dedicated "f.D." to Ingeborg Bachmann. In late 1953, Bachmann dedicated a copy of her volume *Die Gestundete Zeit* to Celan, with verse 8 of this poem: "getauscht, um getröstet zu sein" / "exchanged, to be consoled."

2, 24 stalks of night: cf. title of cycle.

"Unstetes Herz" / "Unsteady heart"

August 29, 1951, London, Golders Green. In London Celan regularly visited his aunt Berta Antschel, his father's sister, who had emigrated from Vienna to London in 1938. In the mainly Jewish London quarter of Golders Green there is a large crematorium and cemetery, where, among others, the urn with the ashes of Sigmund Freud is kept.

3f. you step / with the poplars down to the ponds: See verse 4 of "Landscape," verse 5 of "I Heard It Said," and verses 2–4 of "Notturno."

"Sie kämmt ihr Haar" / "She combs her hair"

February 22, 1951, Paris. Consider this reference in a letter to Erica Lilegg: "I believe it to be one of my most beautiful ones, if only because it came to me out of thin air. The air that we breathe, naturally" (March 9, 1951).

1 Sie kämmt ihr Haar wie mans den Toten kämmt / She combs her hair as one combs that of the dead: See verses 22 and 24 of "Nächtlich geschürzt" / "Pursed at Night."

"Da du geblendet von Worten" / "As you blinded by words"

November 19, 1951, Paris.

"Landschaft" / "Landscape"

Date of composition uncertain. On November 14, 1951, Celan sent the poem to Klaus and Nani Demus, saying that it was "a few days old" (PC/KND, p. 84). This is one of the poems dedicated "f.D." to Ingeborg Bachmann.

T Landscape: See the poems with the same title in *Breathturn into Timestead*.

1 Pappeln – Menschen / poplars—humans: See double meaning of the Latin word *populus*: as masculine noun it means "people" or "folk," and as feminine noun, "poplar tree."

f. Ihr hohen Pappeln – Menschen dieser Erde! / You tall poplars—humans of this earth! / You black ponds of happiness—you mirror them to death!: See verse 3f. of "Unstetes Herz" / "Unsteady heart."

"Stille!" / "Silence!"

Christmas 1951, Paris. Probably one of the first poems written after the beginning of Celan's relationship with his wife-to-be, Gisèle Lestrange. One of the poems dedicated "f.D." to Ingeborg Bachmann.

T Stille! / Silence!: The German *Stille* (both an adjective and a noun), made emphatic with the added exclamation mark, given the poem's date is possibly an allusion to the Christmas song "Stille Nacht"—"Silent Night."

4 als wir mischten das Ja und das Nein / when we mixed the Yes and the No, 12f. und die Zunge lallte uns Süße . . . / (So lallt sie, so lallt sie noch immer.) / and the tongue babbled something sweet . . . / (So it babbles, so it still and always babbles.): See verse 20 and the commentary to verse 23 of "Tübingen, Jänner," as well as verse 5 of "Sprich auch du" / "Speak, You Too."

"Wasser und Feuer" / "Water and Fire"

September 1951, Paris. One of the poems dedicated "f.D." to Ingeborg Bachmann. In the manuscript the source is given: "M/iss Julie—a Strindberg film—." The film *Fröken Julie* (Miss Julie) (1951) by the Swedish director Alf Sjöberg, named after a one-act play by August Strindberg, was awarded the Palme d'Or at the 1951 Cannes film festival during the first part of September, and then opened in French movie houses. It is a psychological drama that ends with the heroine in desperation taking her own life.

1, 25 Eiben / yews: *Taxus baccata*—both the red arils and the needles of this evergreen tree are poisonous.

18 around St. John's: That is, around June 24, the name day of St. John the Baptist.

"Zähle die Mandeln" / "Count the almonds"

April 30, 1952. In the late sixties this would be the only poem from *Poppy and Memory* that Celan would read at public readings (1968 in Bonn, Kiel, Hannover, Frankfurt, and Tübingen). This is one of the poems dedicated "f.D." to Ingeborg Bachmann.

1f. Zähle die Mandeln, / zähle, was bitter war und dich wachhielt / Count the almonds, / count what was bitter and kept you awake: See Jer. 1:11f.: "Jeremiah, what seest thou? And I said, I see a rod of an almond tree. Then said the LORD unto me, Thou hast well seen: for I will hasten my word to perform it."

Luther's German translation, literally englished, gives: "'I see an awakening branch' . . . And the Lord said: 'You hast well seen: for I will watch over my word, so that I may do it.'" Luther reproduced a wordplay with the Hebrew שקד, which, depending on the voweling, can mean "almond" or "I will watch." "Bitter," Wiedemann suggests, though also linked to the concept of the "bitter almond," links here to the bitter herbs of the Seder meal, in memory of the bitterness of the fate the Israelites were subjected to in their Egyptian exile. In 1952, Passover began on April 10.

4 dein Aug, als du's aufschlugst / your eye, when you opened it: See verse 11 of "Wo Eis ist" / "Where There's Ice," and verse 1 of "Von Dunkel zu Dunkel" / "From Darkness to Darkness."

4 dein Aug, als du's aufschlugst / your eye, when you opened it, 5 ich spann jenen heimlichen Faden / I spun that secret thread: See verses 9 and 11 of "Ich weiß" / "I know."

11 schwangen die Hämmer frei im Glockenstuhl deines Schweigens / the hammers swing free in the belfry of your silence: See verse 8ff. of "Heute und morgen" / "Today and Tomorrow" and verse 16 of "Blume" / "Flower."

14 selbdritt / all three: See the title "Selbdritt, selbviert" / "Threesome, Foursome." Traditionally this collective number refers to a generational constellation, before all that of St. Anne, Mary, and the Jesus child ("Anna Selbdritt").

VON SCHWELLE ZU SCHWELLE / THRESHOLD TO THRESHOLD

The volume consists of forty-seven poems written between the middle of 1952 and late 1954, and organized nonchronologically in three cycles. Only a few poems of that period were not included in *Threshold to Threshold*. Dates of composition, first printings, and variations were noted by Celan on his copy of the second (1960) printing. Those notations happened at the moment of the public phase of the Goll affair, in which one of the poems from *Threshold to Threshold* played a major role (see "In the Shape of a Boar" and the commentary).

The manuscript of *Threshold to Threshold* is dated February 1, 1955. Publication on June 23, 1955, by Deutsche Verlags-Anstalt, Stuttgart.

T Von Schwelle zu Schwelle / Threshold to Threshold: A citation from verse 27 of "Chanson of a Lady in the Shadow," in *Poppy and Memory*.

Concerning the title, Celan wrote on February 22, 1954, to Jürgen Rausch at DVA: "It suggests, I believe or at least hope, besides a certainly not inessential trait of the poetic, namely its liminal character, also the never-coming-to-rest of the poetic as well as any statement's—plainly unrealizable—infinity-claim. / Added to this is perhaps also, though at another level, that the same 'Hauptwort' [literally: "main word"] / noun comes twice before the reader's (more or less alert) eye." Badiou, however, also points to the following comment Celan made to Karl-Eberhardt Felten at DVA: "Originally this volume was supposed to be called 'Argumentum e silentio'; too bad that I let myself be persuaded to rebaptize it. But: water signs: they also exist."

Dedication: For Gisèle: the volume is dedicated to his wife, the painter and graphic artist Gisèle Celan-Lestrange. All the poems in the volume were written after their meeting in November 1951. It is the only one of Celan's books dedicated to a single living person.

SIEBEN ROSEN SPÄTER / SEVEN ROSES LATER

See verse 6 of "Crystal."

"Ich hörte sagen" / *"I Heard It Said"*

Prior to summer 1953.

4 das den Kreis um den Stein legt / that lays the circle around the stone: See the affirmative note "that lays the circle around the stone . . ." from 1967 in Edmond Jabès' *Le livre des questions* on page 192 at the following lines: "Reb Jacob also believed in emphasis, which he compared to the gash, with its fake rings in the water, made by the stone fallen into the pond. The wound closes

instantly. It is the rings that reproduce themselves while growing larger and that witness—oh derision—of the scope of the evil" (my translation).

5 Ich sah meine Pappel hinabgehn zum Wasser / I saw my poplar go down to the water: See verse 3 of "Unsteady heart."

7 ich sah ihre Wurzeln gen Himmel / I saw its roots beg skyward for night: See Celan's affirmative note (and marginal notation) "see 'I heard it said'" in connection with Gershom Scholem's line in his *On the Mystical Shape of the Godhead: Basic Concepts in the Kabbalah*: "The tree grows upside down—an image familiar to us from many myths" (p. 42 of English translation). See verse 1 of "In the air."

9 ich las nur vom Boden auf jene Krume / I picked up from the ground only the crumb: See verse 6 of "The Traveling Companion." The word "crumb" / *Krume* (as the French "miette") would gather a specific meaning in relation to this poem and to her artistic work for Celan and his wife; see the letter from GCL of December 29, 1966: "An etching that one likes, that makes one reflect a little or that disquiets. Whose secret tries to go through one somehow. That's truly major. That, Paul, is more than a crumb, Paul, and all we wanted was 'only a crumb'" (PC/GCL, p. 471).

10 die deines Auges Gestalt hat und Adel / that has your eye's shape and nobility: See the letter to GCL of July 29, 1965, in remembrance of this poem: "I see your eyes: your eye's shape and nobility" (PC/GCL, p. 252).

"Im Spätrot" / "In Late-red"

1953, Vallauris. Celan and GCL spent their honeymoon from the end of December 1952 to the beginning of January 1953 in Provence, first in Avignon, Saint-Rémy, and Les Baux, and then in Vallauris (Alpes Maritimes), a center for ceramics promoted by Picasso.

T Im Spätrot / In Late-red: See, also in connection with the cycle's title, verse 4 of "Crystal": "Seven nights higher, red wanders to red."

"Leuchten" / "To Shine"

May 25, 1954.

This is the first poem in which Celan uses a line of dots, possibly, Wiedemann suggests, to indicate text hidden or left out. Less than ten poems in the whole oeuvre use this device.

"Gemeinsam" / "Together"

August 21, 1952.

2 so auf den Schwellen nennt / naming on the thresholds: See the title of the volume.

"Mit Äxten spielend" / "Playing with Axes"

1953 (after May 16, 1953, and before April 5, 1954, according to letters).

T Mit Äxten spielend / Playing with Axes: The poem's title had at some point been considered as the title for a cycle.

6 den Bettel der Worte / the word trash at their feet: See Ingeborg Bachmann's response in her poem "Scherbenhügel": "Be silent! Keep safe your trash, / the words, dismayed by tears, / below the hill of shards, / that always puckers the furrows" (my translation).

"Das Schwere" / "The Load"

January 20, 1953. This date is recorded only in the author's copy, thus maybe added only from memory and having symbolic value: Wiedemann suggests that the date is inscribed "in full consciousness of the importance of '20. Jänner' [January 20], as Celan uses it in the Meridian speech." See "I hear, the axe has blossomed" [*Breathturn into Timestead*, p. 331]. The poem is composed before April 5, 1954, as correspondence shows.

8, 9 Blei / lead: See verse 8 of "Aspen tree": "My mother's heart was seared by lead."

11 das Brot bricht / breaks the bread: See Matt. 26:26: "And as they were eating, Jesus took bread, and blessed it, and broke it, and gave it to the disciples, and said, Take, eat; this is my body."

12 Tränke / trough [watering place]: The word appears only one other time in Celan's work, in verse 13 of "Tenebrae."

"Ein Körnchen Sands" / "A Grainlet of Sand"

Before October 27, 1952 (according to correspondence).

10 Sandkorn / sandgrain: The only other use is in verse 9 of "Bahndämme, Wegränder, Ödplätze, Schutt" / "Embankments, Roadsides, Vacant Lots, Rubble."

17 und ich schweb dir voraus als ein Blatt / and I float ahead of you as a leaf: See verse 10 of "For naught you draw hearts."

"Strähne" / "Lock"

October 18, 1952.

T Strähne / Lock: Celan uses the French word *mèche* as an endearment for Gisèle Celan-Lestrange (see PC/GCL, p. 28).

1 Strähne, die ich nicht flocht / Lock, that I didn't braid: See verse 6 of "Crowned out."

1 die ich wehn ließ / that I let blow: See verse 5 of "Traveling": "Your hair wants to waft when you ride—but that's forbidden."

1 die ich wehn ließ / that I let blow, 14 umbuscht von Singrün und Kummer / ambushed by evergreen and sorrow: See Rilke's Tenth Duino Elegy: "Why didn't I kneel more deeply to accept you, / inconsolable sisters, and, surrendering, lose myself / in your loosened hair," and "Though they are really our winter-enduring foliage, our dark evergreen" (translated by Stephen Mitchell). *Sin(n)grün*, evergreen, is the oleander evergreen plant *Vinca minor*, often found in cemeteries and used in funeral wreaths.

17 flockiger / flaky: See Celan's reading notes probably for Hans Henny Jahnn's novel *Das Holzschiff.*

17 Haarstern / comet's tail: See Georg Büchner's *Danton*: " . . . über dem Ort steht ein Haarstern, unter dessen versengenden Strahlen dein Rückenmark ganz ausgedörrt wird?" / "above the place there stands a comet's tail, under whose singeing beams your spinal cord dessicates." Jean Paul Richter also uses the word. Grimm gives this meaning, but not the homonym for feather-star or crinoid.

"Aus dem Meer" / "Out of the Sea"

1953, before March 25, 1954 (PC/GCL, Letter 32, footnote 11).

On November 30, 1953, Celan wrote to Rolf Schroers in connection with the death of his newborn son, François (see "Epitaph for François"): "during the last weeks before the delivery I couldn't get the last stanza of *The Whole Life* out of my mind: 'The suns of death are white like the hair of our child: /

it stepped forth from the flood when you pitched a tent on the dune. / It wielded the knife of happiness above us with extinguished eyes.' I don't know what to think."

T Aus dem Meer / Out of the Sea: See the title and verses 3 and 13 of "Der Stein aus dem Meer" / "The Stone from the Sea."

9 wir fingen den Schattenfisch / we caught the shadowfish: *Schattenfisch* is the name of a fish species also called *Schatten* or *Meerschatten* in German; the fish family is Sciaenidae, in English usually called croaker or drumfish. I prefer to keep the literal word "shadowfish."

"Zwiegestalt" / "Biform"

Before April 5, 1954.

See Pajari Räsänen's perceptive reading of this poem in his 2007 Ph.D. dissertation:

> The poetic image is "by no means visual," as Celan maintains. The non-visual poetic image, turning into a word, wakes up to another reality *as* another dream, another's dream; the transmission of an image must be "blind enough," lose itself in order to ignite the other's eye and sight as a candle and a wick, as in the poem "Zwiegestalt" . . . The figure (*Gestalt*) is double (*Zwiegestalt*) not only due to the (blind?) fumbling that opts for another image in the middle of the poem . . . and not only because of the distinction between eye and sight, candle and wick, but also because the figure of *you* or "your house" and / or "my soul" are perhaps *one* figure, one double figure; "the roof ridge of my soul" seems to be the one of "your house," your *house of being* perhaps, which is at the same time "my soul," the occupiable, hospitable space offered by the poem—and yet, an abode to be abandoned now, as it seems, inasmuch as it is still a question of "my soul" from whose "roof ridge" you have now blown away the snow. Blown away, that is: breathed. An abode, a confidence (*Mitwisserschaft*), a complicity to be inhabited and abandoned, first by "me" and then, after "your" having liberated the soul of its cover of snow, after having exorcized the haunted house, by "you." Inhabited and abandoned, both at once—perhaps. So it would not be a question of carrying over a content, a message, but rather the form, the figure to be occupied and to be abandoned, both at once; a figure to be

liberated by harnessing one's dream and letting its hoofs speak to the snow. Harnessing one's dream means, perhaps, to affirm that it is indeed *my* dream, the other's address having become blind in the darkness of *my* interiority—it is not the same or the similar, but another figure, and yet one that we share now, one through which we communicate across the irreducible duplicity, in the exchange between I and you: *Zwiegestalt.*

The chiasmatic inversion amounts also to saying that it is not the poematic encounter which bears reference to a real-life encounter, but that every true, authentic encounter (*wirkliche Begegnwig*) happens in remembrance of the poem's secret—the irreducible blindfold or veil between us, through which we approach each other. Celan may well be designated as a "transcendentalist" inasmuch as his poems speak "of the conditions of their own possibility." And, at the same time, they speak of how any true encounter bears witness to the immemorial, archaic imprint of what is called poetry (*Counter-figures: An Essay on Antimetaphoric Resistance: Paul Celan's Poetry and Poetics at the Limits of Figurality*, Pajari Räsänen, pp. 233–34, https://helda.helsinki.fi/bitstream/handle/10138/19366/counterf.pdf?sequence=2).

"Fernen" / "Distances"

November 9, 1954.

See Adrian del Caro's reading of this poem:

> This veil of concealment is a product of the evening; when evening goes about the task of measuring the distance from the shapes it assumes to the shape that it has imparted to the poet and his counterpart, then a veil forms that the two will breathe. In breathing this veil they take it in and dispel it, breaking down the concealment. The only distance alluded to in this poem is the one contemplated by the evening, which is capable of taking many shapes, apparently. The shape that is the evening is therefore one point, while the shape that the evening gives to the two is another point. Lying between these two points is distance, which the evening would measure (which the evening is fixing to measure: "wenn der Abend sich anschickt zu messen, wie weit . . ."). If the poet and his counterpart breathe the veil that is caused by the evening's effort to measure this distance, then the two are, in effect, breathing the distance and breaking down the difference between them. The evening that assumes shapes, and the shapes imparted by

the evening, would become one and the same in the act of breathing the veil together.

When the ability of the evening to assume shapes and impart shapes is breathed by the poet and his counterpart, then matters are as they should be. Taking and giving are now properties of the poet, and the evening no longer possesses the power to conceal by creating distance. There is a suggestion of a metavision here, whereby the poet in speaking directly to his counterpart is endowed with heightened seeing—paradoxically by means of having breathed the veil out of existence. We know that the shapes of evening are unclear, and there is capriciousness in the evening's shape-taking and shape-giving. We could therefore agree with Firges' reading of this poem as one in which Celan's self or ego is no longer enmeshed in the counterpart (*The Early Poetry of Paul Celan*, p. 83).

"Wo Eis ist" / "Where There's Ice"

Before May 15, 1954 (according to diary).

6f. Du nanntest ihn mir, jenen Namen: / ein Schein wie von Asche lag drauf— / You told it to me, that name: / a glare as of ashes coated it—, 10 ich gab dir den Doppelnamen. / I gave you the double name: The Lestrange family received its title of nobility at the time of the crusades, a time also of a swell of anti-Semitic persecutions throughout Europe. Their marriage linked that name with that of a Jew.

11 Du schlugst dein Aug auf darunter— / You opened your eye beneath it—: See verse 4 of "Count the almonds" and verse 1 of the next poem, "From Darkness to Darkness."

12 Wuhne / the hole in the ice: See the reading trace in Kluge/Götze: "Wu(h)ne F. 'hole in the ice,'" as well as reading notes from the fifties: "WUHNE, WUNE: ins Eis gehauenes Loch [a hole made in the ice]."

18 dein Aug—halt es offen / your eye—keep it open: See the reference in "Ein Auge, offen" / "One Eye, Open."

"Von Dunkel zu Dunkel" / "From Darkness to Darkness"

December 5, 1954.

T Von Dunkel zu Dunkel / From Darkness to Darkness: See verse 3 of "Half Night."

1 Du schlugst die Augen auf / You opened your eyes: See verse 4 of "Count the almonds" and verse 11 of the previous poem, "Where There's Ice."

4 Setzt solches über? / Does this carry across?, 6 ferryman: See Celan's letter to the publisher Schiffers in connection with his Picasso translation: "Picasso's text doesn't just want to be translated but also—if I may misuse a Heidegerrian term—*übergesetzt* [carried across]. You see: I consider this as—among other things—something like a ferryman's job. Can I hope that in relation to payment for my work you not only count the words but also the oar strokes" (May 1, 1954, FN, p. 145f.).

"In Gestalt eines Ebers" / *"In the Shape of a Boar"*

November 5, 1952. Possibly a poem for the first anniversary of meeting Gisèle Lestrange; see the references to this in poems from the *Breathcrystal* cycle of *Breathturn into Timestead* (see, in *Breathturn into Timestead*, "Paths in the shadow-breakage" and "You Dream"). GCL mentions this poem in her letter of November 7, 1952: "I am so happy that you wrote this new poem" (PC/GCL, p. 24).

1f. In Gestalt eines Ebers / stampft dein Traum / In the shape of a boar / your dream stomps: The beginning of the poem plays a special role in Claire Goll's plagiarism accusations (see the introductory commentary to *NoOnes-Rose*). In this context Celan wrote on May 19, 1961, to Jens: "so I asked myself from where I may have gotten my 'boar.' / Boars, dear Walter Jens,—they do exist, that's all. / [. . .] (If poems came only—and directly—from other poems, then it would be obvious to search for my—no doubt mythic—boar in other poems, poems with which I was acquainted from very early on; it did do that—although I believe it to be a literary-historical rejuvenated perspective—I am anticipating here, I know. There is such a poet, and I know that I owe him a lot; I mean W.B. Yeats [. . .] And—with my poems, but not only with them—I am returned to my childhood, to the books of my childhood, and to . . . Gustav Schwab. Who knows if my boar isn't the Caledonian one)" (GA, p. 531f.). In 1962 Celan translated W. B. Yeats's poem "He mourns for the Change that has come upon him and his Beloved, and longs for the End of the World," which starts with the lines "I would that the Boar without bristles had come from the West / And had rooted the sun and moon and stars out of the sky

/And lay in the darkness, grunting, and turning to his rest" (GA, p. 811f.). See references in "Your dream."

6f. Eine bittere Nuß / wühlt er hervor unterm Laub / A bitter nut / it rooted up from beneath the foliage: See the already cited letter to Jens: " the rooting up of the bitter nut is doubtlessly an erotic action [. . .]. (And this comes to me right now, here is further confirmation: for me—in *The Sand from the Urns*—the pubic hair is bitter" (GA, p. 532), as well as the confirming reading traces in Hans Henny Jahnn's *Perrudja*: "A boar mounted her; human shape" (p. 510, with a note at the end of the volume). See also verses 1 and 4 of "Paths in the shadow-breakage."

"Bretonischer Strand" / "Breton Beach"

Fall 1954. A first version was written after September 23, 1954, in a notebook with jottings on his reading of Heidegger's *Introduction to Metaphysics*; the poem was probably written in La Ciotat, also before October 30, 1954 (see "Tonight Too"). From August 29 to September 9, 1954, Celan traveled in Brittany. An earlier title names the beach as "Plage du Toulinguet," that is, the beach of the peninsula of Pen-Hat on the Pointe du Toulinguet on the Crozon (Finistère-Sud). GCL's calendar records a stay at Pointe du Toulinguet on September 1, 1954. See also the word list and the French interlinear translation in the version for GCL (PC/GCL, p. 43). Also written in Brittany were "Matière de Bretagne" and the poems of the Breton cycle in *Die Niemandsrose / NoOnesRose* (see especially "The bright stones").

"Gut" / "Good"

Paris, March 8, 1954.

"Zu zweien" / "By Twos"

Before March 25, 1954 (PC/GCL, letter 32, footnote 11).

1 schwimmen die Toten / The dead swim: See verse 10 of "Inselhin" / "Islandward."

Der Gast / The Guest

Paris, October 27, 1952.

MIT WECHSELNDEM SCHLÜSSEL / WITH A CHANGING KEY

See the poem with this title in the cycle. The title had been considered at some point as a possible volume title.

"Grabschrift für François" / "Epitaph for François"

October 1953. The only poem in Celan's work published with a date. According to the French poet Yves Bonnefoy, the poem was written a few days before the birth of François, Celan's first child; after the child's death on October 8, 1953, Celan wrote to Klaus Demus: "The child is dead. / It survived the very complicated birth, three attempts with forceps, finally cesarean cut, by only thirty hours. / He was my son, our son, our François" (PC/KND, p. 130). See also the poem "Schläfenzang" / "Temple Clamps" in *Breathturn into Timestead*, p. 10.

T François: "François," simultaneously a name and the word for "Frenchman," for Celan and Gisèle from the beginning on functioned as a code name for a future child. See also the commentaries to the poem "Assisi."

5 Wir hören sie schlagen und schlagen / We hear them slam and slam: See the letter to GCL of January 7, 1952: "You see, when I come to you I have the impression of leaving a world, of hearing the doors slam behind me, doors and more doors, for there are many, the doors of this world, made of misunderstandings, false clarities, vexations. Maybe there remain other doors for me, maybe I have not yet parsed the whole space across which this net of signs that lead one astray is stretched.—" (PC/GCL, letter #5).

"Aufs Auge gepfropft" / "Grafted on Your Eye"

1954. Celan read the poem on April 7, 1954, as "one of the last ones I have written" in the context of a radio interview for Süddeutscher Rundfunk.

"Der uns die Stunden zählte" / "He Who Counted the Hours for Us"

July 3, 1954.

"Assisi" / "Assisi"

Paris, early 1954.

Celan visited Assisi on November 20, 1953, while on a trip to Italy. The poem was composed before March 25, 1954 (PC/GCL, letter #32, footnote

11), and he read it in public in Frankfurt on March 28, 1954. His source for the life of Saint Francis was G. K. Chesterton's *St. Francis of Assisi*.

T Assisi, 1–4 Umbrische Nacht / Umbrian night, 18 sie betteln noch, Franz / they're still begging, Francis: The Umbrian city of Assisi is the birthplace and workplace of San Francesco d'Assisi, founder of the Franciscan mendicant order. Francis's poem "Cantico del frate sole" / "Canticle of Brother Sun," using end and internal rhymes and repetitions, as does Celan's, in which he expresses his pleasure over the closeness of all of God's creatures, is one of the first major poems in the Italian language. Concerning the name Franz / Francis, see also the poem "Epitaph for François." The name Umbria comes from Latin *umbra* (shadow).

3 mit dem Stein, den du hertrugst / with the stone you carried: Francis collected and begged for stones to reconstruct two churches that lay in ruins near Assisi. See Chesterton: "He went about by himself collecting stones. He begged all the people he met to give him stones. In fact he became a new sort of beggar, reversing the parable; a beggar who asks not for bread but a stone" (Chesterton, Gilbert K.: St. Francis of Assisi, London 1951, p. 67f.). With regard to the Jewish tradition of putting stones or pebbles on graves, see verses 49–52 of "Everything is different."

9 Irdener Krug, den die Hand eines Schattens für immer verschloß / Earthen jug, which a shadow's hand plugged up forever, 15 das ins Schloß fiel / that clicked shut: Chesterton draws parallels between the story of Jesus and the life of Francis, and concludes: "It shows that the casket that was locked in Palestine can be unlocked in Umbria; for the Church is the keeper of the keys," where "casket" means both a small ornamental box for jewels and a grave and urn (p. 140).

12 Grautier [literally: gray animal] / donkey: Francis understood his body as a "brother donkey," seeing in it only a mount for the soul.

14 im Schnee, den die nackteste Hand streut / in the snow the most naked hand spreads: See Chesterton: "Apparently it was literally a cold world at the moment, and snow was on the ground. [. . .] He went out half-naked in his hair-shirt into the winter woods, walking the frozen ground between the frosty trees: a man without a father" (p. 65f.).

17f. Glanz, der nicht trösten will, Glanz / Die Toten—sie betteln noch,

Franz / Splendor, that will not console, splendor. / The dead—they're still begging, Francis: See verse 8 of Francis's "Cantico": "Et ellu è bellu e radiante cum grande splendore" (And he, the sun, is beautiful and shines with great splendor), which Chesterton does *not* cite. The trip to Italy took place a few weeks after François's death; the name of the saint, like that of the deceased son, is connected with France: "according to this version, his name was not Francis at all but John; and his companions called him 'Francesco' or 'The little Frenchman' because of his passion for the French poetry of the Troubadours. The more probable story is that his mother had named him John when he was born in the absence of his father, who shortly returned from a visit to France where his commercial success had filled him with so much enthusiasm for French taste and social usage that he gave his son the new name signifying the Frank of Frenchman" (p. 43).

18 Die Toten / The dead: Tommaso da Celano, Francis's first biographer, was also the author of the "Dies irae" in the liturgy of the Catholic mass for the dead.

"Auch heute abend" / "Tonight Too"

La Ciotat, October 19, 1954. From September 19 to October 30, 1954, Celan was a guest at La Rustique Olivette, a writers' and artists' foundation in the Mediterranean harbor town La Ciotat (Département des Bouches-du-Rhône). A draft was noted in Karl Löwith's *Heidegger: Denker in dürftiger Zeit*.

"Vor einer Kerze" / "In Front of a Candle"

1953. The poem is mentioned in a March 19, 1954, letter to Joachim Moras, probably in relation to the interview with Schwedhelm (PN, #298). Its forty-five verses make it the longest poem of *Threshold to Threshold*, where it is the twenty-fourth of forty-seven poems, and thus the center of the volume.

1–3 Aus getriebenem Golde, so / wie du's mir anbefahlst, Mutter, / formt ich den Leuchter / Of chased gold, just / as you bade me, mother, / I shaped the candlestick: See God's commandments for the candlestick in the tabernacle: "And thou shalt make a candlestick of pure gold: of beaten work shall the candlestick be made" (Exod. 25:31). Note that the two first stanzas have seven lines each.

6f. deines / Totseins Tochter / your / deadness's daughter: See Celan's note for the Euripides motto in Lev Shestov's *In Job's Balances*: " . . . ein Totsein / a being dead [a deadness] (cf. 'In front of a candle' . . .) / 9. 17. 61." (p. 27, RB, p. 152). The motto in Celan's German Shestov edition reads: "Wer weiß wohl, ob das Leben nicht ein Totsein ist, das Totsein aber Leben?" (p. 39), which the English Shestov translation gives as: "Who knows if life is not death, and death life?" The German *Totsein* as used by Celan is stronger and more active (i.e., "a being-dead") than the simple noun "death."

17 sprech ich den Segen / I speak the blessing: On the eve of the Sabbath, according to Jewish Virtual Library, the woman of the household lights at least two candles, representing the dual commandments to remember and to keep the sabbath. "After lighting, she waves her hands over the candles, welcoming in the sabbath. Then she covers her eyes, so as not to see the candles before reciting the blessing, and recites the blessing below. The hands are then removed from the eyes, and she looks at the candles, completing the mitzvah of lighting the candles. 'Blessed are you, Lord, our God, sovereign of the universe, Who has sanctified us with His commandments and commanded us, to light the lights of Shabbat. Amen'" (Jewish Virtual Library, "Shabbat: Shabbat Evening Home Rituals," https://www.jewishvirtuallibrary.org/shabbat-evening-home-ritual). See also the reading note of July 14, 1957, in Jean Paul's *The Valley of Campan*: "Sabbathlight / sabbathlight / for 'Before a Candle'" (Badiou's reference), for: "Wahrlich, ein solches Thal ist es werth, daß man in die Stickluft des Grabes das Gruben-und Sabbathslicht der Wahrheit statt seines Ichs hinunterläßt, um zu sehen, ob das Ich in einer solchen Tiefe noch athme" ("In truth, such a valley is worth it to lower the miners-and sabbath-light of truth rather than one's I-light, to see if at such a depth the I still breathes") (Jean Paul, *Werke*, Berlin n.d. vols. 39–44, p. 14; my translation).

"Mit wechselndem Schlüssel" / "With a Changing Key"

Probably 1953; before March 25, 1954 (PC/GCL, letter #32, footnote 11).

T Mit wechselndem Schlüssel / With a Changing Key: See the title of the cycle that includes the poem. The title had also been considered as a possible title for the volume itself. See the reading notes in Wilhelm Capelle, *Die Vorsokratiker*, quoting Parmenides (p. 163): "Dort ist das Tor, durch das die Pfade von Tag und Nacht gehen. Türsturz und steinerne Schwelle umfassen es. Es selber—in Äthers Höhen—ist von mächtigen Türflügeln ausgefüllt. Zu ihnen hat Dike, die Göttin der Vergeltung, die wechselnden Schlüssel" ("There are the gates of the tracks of day and night / fitted above with a lintel / and below with a threshold of stone / and the openings themselves, high up in the air, / are closed by mighty doors. / Dikê holds the keys to them.") (Charles Stein's excellent English translation does not, however, give, as does the German, the sense that Dikê holds one key that is changing/variable, which is what intrigued Celan.)

"Hier" / "Here"
1953, Paris, rue des Écoles; it is only on May 15, 1960, that Celan pencils the place and date of the poem's composition into his copy of the printed book. He lived in the rue des Écoles (in the fifth arrondissement) until the beginning of July 1953.

Beda Allemann remembered: "As Celan told me one day, it was first planned as a Hiroshima-poem. Of the name of that major Japanese city, which will forever be inscribed in the history of humanity, there remained in the process of the poem's composition only the adverb of place 'hier / here'—and as allusion, the naming of the cherry blossom, that wants to be blacker here than there" (*Argumentum e silentio*, p. 15). Wiedemann adds: "Through the reinterpretation of the initial syllable the event is transposed into the present; eight years after the atom bomb was dropped by the U.S.A. (8. 6. 1945) the events were part of public discussions: through the declaration of peace by the citizens of Hiroshima (8. 6. 1953) and the film *Hiroshima* by Hideo Sekigawa (10. 7. 1953) on the one side, and the date-conscious declaration of its rise to the status of a nuclear power by the U.S.S.R. (8. 8. 1953) on the other."

4 vertäut / towroped: See Celan's note to the word *vertäuen* in the novel *Das Holzschiff* by Hans Henny Jahnn, p. 7: "vertäuen: zwei kleine Schleppdampfer, hinten und vorn dem Schiff vertäut / : / Schiff durch Taue 'festmachen'" ("to moor: to moor two little tugboats one at the forward and one aft of the ship / : / secure a ship with [tow] ropes") (my translation).

"Stilleben" / "Still Life"
July 19, 1953, Evry-Petit-Bourg (Tournebride). That month Celan spent his holidays at the Lestrange family property near Evry-Petit-Bourg (Seine-

et-Oise), what is today Evry (Essonne); *tournebride* refers to the servants' quarters (near a castle or country house).

9 aus der Ferne / from afar: See the justification for the final comma, which the publisher's editor had deemed unnecessary: "For me, the 'afar' seems to gain space that way" (May 24, 1954, TCA/VS, p. 69).

"Und das schöne" / "And the Beautiful"

Exact date unknown, but before April 5, 1954.

7 die Steine, die du häuftest / the stones you heaped up: Regarding the Jewish tradition of putting stones or pebbles on graves, see "Assisi" and "Everything is different" (verses 49–52).

"Waldig" / "Forested"

Before November 13, 1954, Rochefort-en-Yvelines. Celan occasionally spent time in this property (an old watermill) owned by the Lestrange family in Rochefort-en-Yvelines (Seine-et-Oise).

13 Eisvogel / kingfisher: See verse 3 of "Voices." The German word for kingfisher, *Eisvogel*, translates, literally, as "icebird."

"Abend der Worte" / "Evening of the Words"

1953, before March 25, 1954 (see PC/GCL, letter # 32, footnote 11). Celan read the poem on March 28, 1954, at a public reading in Frankfurt.

1 Abend der Worte—Rutengänger im Stillen! / Evening of the words—dowser in stillness!, 5f. die Narbe der Zeit / tut sich auf / time's scar / opens, 8 Wortnacht / Wordnight: See verses 2 and 5ff. of "Stigma."

"Die Halde" / "The Slope"

September–October 1954, La Ciotat.

4–6 O diese Halde, Geliebte, / wo wir pausenlos rollen, / wir Steine / Oh this slope, beloved, / down which we ceaselessly roll, / we stones: See verse 4 of "Wingnight": "Gravel, rolling abyssward."

13 staunend in eins schaut / stares us into one: See the poem "In One" and the commentary re reading traces in Helmuth v. Glasenapp's *Die Philosophie der Inder*: "Die Tendenz zur Reduktion geht aber noch weiter: auch für

unser Empfinden ganz verschiedene Dinge glaubte man ineinssetzen zu können." ("But the tendency toward reduction goes even further: even things that for our understanding are very different, were believed to be able to be gathered into one") (Helmuth v. Glasenapp. *Die Philosophie der Inder. Alfred Kröner, Stuttgart (1949)*; further marginal notes, p. 26f.; my translation). See also verses 11 and 14 of Celan's translation of William Shakespeare's sonnet CV: "Fair, kind, and true, have often lived alone, Which three till now, never kept seat in one." / "Ich find, erfind—um sie in eins zu bringen" and "In Einem will ich drei zusammenschmieden" (January 11, 1963, GW V, p. 345).

"Ich weiß" / "I Know"

July 29, 1954, Rochefort-en-Yvelines.

8 verpuppt / pupated, 12 ein Faden mehr, der dich umspinnt / one thread more that spins you in, 14 die Fäden glänzen / the threads shine: The original title of the poem was "Cocoon."

9 Und Augen, die dich suchen / And eyes that search for you, 11f. Ein Blick: / ein Faden mehr, der dich umspinnt / A gaze: / one thread more that spins you in: See verse 4f. of "Count the almonds."

"Die Felder" / "The Fields"

August 15, 1954, Rochefort-en-Yvelines.

1, 15 Immer die eine, die Pappel / Always the one, the poplar: For the importance of the tree, see the poems "Landscape" and "Aspen tree."

"Andenken" / "Remembrance"

September 27, 1954, La Ciotat. The poem is transmitted together with a reading note referencing Rudolf Borchardt's translation of the old ionic Homeric "Demeterlieds" / "Demeter's Song," in *Altionische Götterlieder unter dem Namen Homers* (Munich, 1924; LPC).

T Andenken / Remembrance, 1, 4 Feigengenährt / fig-nourished, 5 im Anhauch des Meers / in sea's breath: See Hölderlin's poem "Andenken" / "Remembrance," especially verse 16, "Im Hofe aber wächset ein Feigenbaum" ("but a figtree is growing in the courtyard") and verse 56, "Es nehmet aber / Und gibt Gedächtnis die See" ("But memory / is taken and given by the Ocean") (in Richard Sieburth's translation; verse 56 is marked up by Celan in his copy, vol. 2, pp. 196 and 198). Note that these lines are followed (after one penultimate line) by maybe the most famous Hölderlinian verse: "Was bleibet aber, stiften die Dichter" ("But poets establish what remains").

3 das Mandelauge des Toten / the dead one's almond-eye, 9 Weißhaar / white hair: Wiedemann: "The placement of the poem as the last one of a cycle that began with 'Epitaph for François' makes one think of a poem of remembrance dating nearly exactly to a year after the birth and death of his son . . . Concerning the almond in the context of Jewish identity, see 'Count the almonds.'"

INSELHIN / ISLANDWARD

T Inselhin / Islandward: See the final poem of the cycle with the same title. It had also been considered as a possible title for the volume itself. See report to Gisèle about discussions with the publisher: "They like 'Islandward' but are afraid that this title is not catchy enough" (PC/GCL, letter # 48; see also "Argumentum e silentio").

"Nächtlich geschürzt" / "Pursed at Night"

September 9, 1952, Paris. Celan read this poem at readings until the end of his life, last in October 1969 in Jerusalem.

Dedication: Celan had met the art historian Hanne Lenz and the writer Hermann Lenz in April 1954 in Stuttgart and on that occasion had given them a manuscript copy of the poem, on which he dated the dedication as April 4, 1954 (PC/HHL, p. 13); at the beginning Celan uses the Jewish form (Hannah) of Lenz's first name (Hanne). He let this stand in the print version, although he had known her real first name since January 1955. Concerning the biblical Hannah (in Hebrew the name means "the graceful," "the favored (by God with a child)"), see 1 Sam. 2:1–10.

4 die Schäfte der Fichten / the spruces' trunks: Remembrance of a visit in late July 1952 to Millstatt in Kärnten (see Celan's correspondence with Klaus and Nani Demus, PC/KND, p. 223).

22 eine Leiche / a corpse, 24 laß uns sie kämmen / let us comb it: See the earlier poem "She combs her hair."

"Auge der Zeit" / *"Eye of Time"*

No exact date known; the poem was written before April 5, 1954, as letters show.

"Flügelnacht" / *"Wingnight"*

No exact date known; the poem was written before September 30, 1954.

4 Kiesel, abgrundhin rollend / Gravel, rolling abysswards: See verses 3–6 of "The Slope."

10–12 Kalk ist und Kreide. / Und Kiesel. / Schnee / Limestone is, and chalk / And gravel. / Snow: Responding to his publisher's copy editor who questioned the comma in "Limestone is, and chalk" Celan wrote: "You correctly chalk up my misuse of a comma, which I used there because through it I wanted to indicate the staccato of the following verses. But you are of course correct, the comma is used incorrectly here" (May 24, 1955, TCA/VS, p. 91).

"Welchen der Steine du hebst" / *"Whichever Stone You Lift"*

1953/1954 (before November 3, 1954).

12/10 Äon / eon: from the Greek word ὁ αἰών (ho aion), from the archaic αἰϝών (aiwon). In Homer it typically refers to life or lifespan. "Age" in the sense of "ages," "forever," "timeless," or "for eternity." Rarely if ever used by Celan; see, however, the introductory note for his volume of Mandelstam translations, where he writes: "as for nearly none of his contemporaries and companions sharing his fate, for Osip Mandelstam, born in the year 1891, the poem was the place where what language can recognize and reach was assembled around that middle from which it gathers shape and truth: around the Being of the one who questions the hour, his own and the world's, the heartbeat and the Eon. This speaks to the measure in which the Mandelstamian poem, the poem of someone who suffered perdition and which arises anew from its perdition, concerns us today" (1959; BA 15. I, p. 59).

"In Memoriam Paul Éluard" / *"In Memoriam Paul Éluard"*

November 21, 1952, Paris. First draft in Celan's copy of Gerard Manley Hopkins's *Poems*. For the next reworkings, Celan used letterhead from the Paris Hotel Lutetia, where the Gestapo was quartered during the occupation, and which after the liberation of Paris served as a reception center for freed detention camp inmates. The poem was written the day before Paul Éluard's funeral and after Celan had viewed the publicly exhibited corpse, on November 20, 1952. On March 29, 1962, Celan wrote to Karl-Eberhardt Felten (of the DVA publishing house): "This poem ["Shibboleth"] does not stand without reason next to "In Memoriam Paul Éluard," a poem that does remember, along with Éluard, the Czech poet who was condemned to death during the Prague trials and for whose pardon his friend Éluard had refused to intervene. But then, from the second, the stranger blueness, yet again: We.—I will, if time and circumstances allow it, also name that—Czech—name in the next edition" (Badiou's reference). Celan does not, however, include the name of Záviš Kalandra, the poet and historian condemned (as a "Trotskyist") and executed in 1950, in the later editions. Éluard's most famous poem is "Liberté" / "Freedom," from the 1942 volume *Poésie et vérité*.

"Schibboleth" / "Shibboleth"

Fall 1954 (before September 30, 1954), La Ciotat. Celan had thought for a while to dedicate the poem to Michael Guttenbrunner, a poet who had been part of the 1934 Vienna uprising, and who was arrested for his membership in the illegal social-democratic party after the Anschluss of Austria by Nazi Germany and, though this has been questioned, condemned to death, a sentence commuted to military service on the front lines. Celan probably knew him from his stay in postwar Vienna.

Concerning the poem, Celan wrote on October 3, 1954, to the Romanian-born anthropologist Isac Chiva: "I would love to know what you think of . . . 'Shibboleth' (a word of Hebrew origin, found in the Old Testament; in German it means something close to 'Erkennungszeichen' [identifier, distinguishing mark]), and here I included the memory of the workers' Vienna uprising and that of revolutionary Madrid. Strangely enough, the unicorn wanted to be led to the goats of Estremadura: reminiscence, here, of a flamenco we listened to at your place" (PC/Chiva, p. 135). And in a letter from January 15, 1964, to Gerhard Kirchhoff: "Estremadura: that is the Spanish Estremadura; the voices are—original: back then I had heard a Spanish song sung by Germaine Montero—shepherds' voices. That they are very far away, nearly unreachable, is true. Nearly unreachable, not totally unreachable. / The unicorn is—also—poetry." Celan is probably referring to Montero's song "Ya Se Van los Pastores."

See also Jacques Derrida's study of Celan's work with the title *Shibboleth.*

On the placement of the poem after "In Memoriam Paul Éluard," see previous commentary.

T, 21 Schibboleth / Shibboleth: The correct pronunciation of the initial sound "sh" served as a distinguishing mark; see Judges 12:6: "Then said they unto him, Say now Shibboleth: and he said Sibboleth: for he could not frame to pronounce it right. Then they took him, and slew him at the passages of Jordan: and there fell at that time of the Ephraimites forty and two thousand." See also verse 1 of "In One," verse 20 of "Crowned out," and the reading trace in Celan's copy of Joyce's *Ulysses*: "(Behind his hand.) She's drunk. The woman is inebriated. (He murmurs vaguely the past of Ephraim.) Shitbroleeth." (The word is circled and the lines marked in the margins).

10 Doppelflöte / double flute: Simone Martini's fresco in the basilica of Assisi, visited by Celan a few years earlier, includes a double flute player (see the poem "Assisi").

12f. Zwillingsröte / in Wien und Madrid / twin redness / in Vienna and Madrid, 23 February: The Vienna workers' uprising against the Austrofascist regime of Bundeskanzler Dollfuß took place on February 13–14, 1934. See verse 1 of "In One" and verse 16 of "We become." On February 16, 1936, the People's Front won the elections for the legislature in Madrid, while all surrounding electoral districts went over to the right. See also verse 4 of "Skull-thinking."

23 *No pasarán*: Spanish for "they will not pass," the motto of the International Brigades during the Spanish Civil War. See also verse 3 of "In One."

24 Einhorn / Unicorn: As the above cited letter to Chiva shows, Celan didn't here think only of his childhood friend Erich Einhorn, with whom he had no contact in 1954. See Celan's remark to Gerhard Kirchhoff: "The unicorn is—also—poetry" (January 15, 1964; Badiou).

30 Estremadura: Part of Spain, along the southern border with Portugal, which in 1936 was one of the principal seats of the Popular Front government (Badajoz). See the citation of Kirchhoff letter above, in the commentary to "Shibboleth."

"Wir sehen dich" / "We See You"

December 7, 1954. This is the latest poem in the volume. On December 14, 1954, Celan wrote to his publisher: "The new volume of poems is now as good as finished. What is not yet determined is the order of the poems in the three cycles that make up the book—& the title" (TCA/VS VIII).

"Kenotaph" / "Cenotaph"

May 19, 1954, Paris. The poem is one of the first poems written after Celan had received the proofs of Hans Egon Holthusen's review "Fünf Junge Lyriker II" (*Merkur* 74, Jahrgang 8; sent to him on March 16, 1954) and after having been made aware on March 25, 1954, of Claire Goll's open letter (GA, pp. 187–89) through the copy received by his publisher, S. Fischer Verlag (PC/GCL, letter # 32). This letter, with its accusations that Celan had stolen from her husband Ivan Goll, had been sent by Claire Goll starting in August 1953 to various West German cultural institutions and individuals in order to harm Celan. The effect becomes visible in Holthusen's review in connection with anti-Semitic elements: he ostracizes Celan by claiming that the images in his poetry—such as "the mills of death"—have no concrete referent in reality.

T Cenotaph: From Greek κενός, kenos, meaning "empty," and τάφος, taphos, or "tomb." Thus a tomb for someone whose remains are elsewhere or couldn't be secured (see verse 4f.). Celan always called his "Deathfugue" his mother's only tomb. In Holthusen's review, closing with praise for the "Deathfugue," the poem is, however, downgraded to being not an actual human experience but merely a (literary) "theme": "With very few simple paradoxes Celan was able to master a theme that exceeds all human composure and all artistic imagination: by making it very 'light' and transcending it through a dreamy surrealism already beyond language, it could escape the bloody chamber of horrors of history and rise up into the ether of pure poetry" (p. 390).

1 Fremdling / stranger: See Holthusen: "In Paul Celan, who was born at the eastern edge of the German speaking area, in Czernowitz, and who has lived for many years in Paris, we encounter a stranger and outsider of poetic speech" (p. 285).

4f. Der hier liegen sollte, er liegt / nirgends / He who was supposed to lie here, / lies / nowhere: See Holthusen: "Language is a sovereign inner reality and its response to the outside world of objects is a subjective momentary mythology of beings that 'do not exist'" (p. 385).

6f. The world that opened its eye / on all sorts of arrays: See the reading notes in Nietzsche's *Human, All Too Human*: "Die Kunst macht den Anblick des Lebens erträglich, dadurch, dass sie den Flor des unreinen Denkens über dasselbe legt." / "Art makes looking at life bearable in that it lays arrays of unclean thinking over it" (BPPC, p. 208, entry 1283; my translation). The German word *Flor* has two meanings: (1) an array or abundance of flowers; (2) (as in *Trauerflor*) a mourning band, crêpe, gauze.

"Sprich auch du" / "Speak, You Too"

Exact date of composition unknown, but before July 23, 1954.

5 But do not split the No from the Yes: See verse 4 of "Silence!"

"Mit zeitroten Lippen" / "With Time-Red Lips"

September–October 1954, La Ciotat; before October 3, 1954 (see letter to Isac Chiva re "Shibboleth").

T Mit zeitroten Lippen / With Time-Red Lips, 5f. mit zeitroten Lippen. // Mund, gezeitigt vom Meer / with time-red lips. // Mouth, time-tamed by the sea: See the resumption of the close connections between language and time in the radio essay *The Poetry of Osip Mandelstam*: "Osip Mandelstam's poem wants to develop what can be perceived and reached with the help of language and make it actual/timely [*aktuell*] in its truth. In this sense we are permitted to understand this poet's 'Acmeism' as a language that has borne fruit in time [*gezeitigte Sprache*]" (my translation, adapted from the Stanford University Press edition). See also "In Late-red," with its allusions to "Crystal," and verse 19 of "The Vintagers."

13 Glorie / glory: Latin *gloria*, for "fame," "radiance," "splendor," also "gloriole," "halo," "aura," and various light occurrences.

"Argumentum e silentio" / "Argumentum e Silentio"

1954, before September 30.

T Argumentum e silentio: Latin for an "argument from silence," used to express a conclusion that is based on the absence of statements in historical documents, rather than their presence. Celan underlined it (and added a marginal mark "-i-") in his reading of Helmuth v. Glasenapp: "The fact that neither Alexander's campaign nor the travels of Indians into the Roman empire are mentioned in any Indian text, teaches that the 'argumentum e silentio' cannot be taken as proof against a possible influence." The use of this legal formula is no doubt linked to the context of Claire Goll's accusations that Celan had plagiarized her husband's work. The title had also been considered by the poet as a possible title for the whole volume, but his publisher rejected it. Celan reused the term in 1959 in a prose fragment, #246.6 in *Microliths*: "There exists . . . a language-taboo specific to the poem and only to it, which not only pertains to its vocabulary, but also to categories such as syntax, rhythm or articulation; some matters become understandable through the unspoken; the poem knows the argumentum e silentio."

Dedication: Celan met René Char for the first time on July 26, 1954; the dedication was added only when the poem was printed in book form. As Celan knew, Char was acquainted with Claire Goll. Celan would receive Char's volume *Le poème pulvérisé* with its theoretical text entitled "Argument" (translated as "Argumentum" in a note by Celan) only in December 1954.

1 An die Kette gelegt / Shackled: See the reading traces (underlining) in Albert Vigoleis Thelen's novel *Die Insel des Zweiten Gesichts / The Island of Second Sight*: "A few days later he [the ape Beppo] was shackled [*an die Kette gelegt*], which did however permit him to keep the tree dust-free. He too had stolen," and "It was, however, impossible to explain to her husband that Beppo needed to be shackled [*an die Kette gelegt*] before it was too late" (also marked in the margins, pp. 183 and 186 in the German edition; my translation).

3 die Nacht / Night, 4 nach ihr / for her, 5 ließ sie / she let: The word *Nacht* is feminine in German (as it is in French, *la nuit*). In the context of this poem I have preferred to use "she" as the English pronoun, rather than the normal "it." Which I did, before coming across this: "Night here must be seen as the Romantics, especially Novalis, often view it: 'She' personifies the passive, but creative world-principle, the 'Mother of being'" (Rainulf A. Stelzmann, "Paul Celan's 'Argumentum e Silentio': An Interpretation," *Monatshefte* 67, no. 1 [Spring 1975], pp. 16–20).

31 Stromgebiet / river basin: See Celan's underlinings in Helmuth v. Glasenapp's *Die Philosophie der Inder*: "While the major part of the Rigvedas seem to still belong to the era in which the Aryans who had immigrated over

the northwestern mountain passes, still lived in the river basin [*Stromgebiet*] of the Indus, the hymns of the last ten books of the Rigveda, the majority of the magic songs of the Atharvaveda and the sacrifical spells of the Yajurveda already lead into an era when the Aryans were extending their dominance toward the east and were settling as a ruling class among an enslaved population of a different race" (p. 31, BPPC section E entries 137–38; my translation).

"Die Winzer" / "The Vintagers"

September 16, 1953.

Dedication: The literary scholar Nani (Anna) Demus and the art historian and poet Klaus Demus were friends of Celan's since his Vienna days. A copy of the poem is dated "London, Willesden Green / March 1, 1955"; i.e., on Nani Demus's birthday. Celan had met up with the couple in London between February 27 and March 3, 1955.

4 die Nacht, an die sie gelehnt sind / the night they lean on: On August 1, 1953, Nani Demus, Klaus Demus, and Ingeborg Bachmann sent a postcard to Celan just before Bachmann left Vienna; it said in part: "We are drinking to the next meeting, some day in Paris, in a darkly beautiful location known only to the initiated" (ND) and "The wall is wholly black now, but may it be light when you come. The glasses are empty, but they will be full when you come" (IB) (PC/IG, p. 69, English edition).

6 der Stein, über den ihr Krückstock dahinspricht / the stone, across which their walking cane speaks: See the prose text "Conversation in the Mountains," which Celan composed in August 1959: "and my stick it spoke, it spoke to the stone" (my translation) (GW III, p. 172), and verses 1 and 25 of "Radix, Matrix," as well as Celan's title for one of GCL's etchings: "Dialogue avec une pierre—Conversation with a stone" (1958).

19 latemouth: Considered as a possible title for the last cycle of the book; see also "With Time-Red Lips" and verse 4 of "Crystal."

"Inselhin" / "Islandward"

June 22, 1954.

T Inselhin / Islandward: See the title of the cycle; the word was also considered as a title for the collection.

10 Ihr Toten, ihr Schwimmer / You the dead, you the swimmers: See verse 1 of "By Twos," and Rimbaud's "Le Bateau Ivre" / "The Drunken Boat," which Celan would translate in July 1957: "ich schwamm und ward durchschwommen: / ein Leichnam um den andern, der rücklings schlafwärts zog" / "I swam and was swum through: / a corpse around the other who / drew toward sleep" (GW IV, p. 107; my translation of Celan's German translation). Rimbaud's original lines are: "Et je voguais, lorsqu'à travers mes liens frêles / Des noyés descendaient dormir, à reculons! . . ." / "and so I scudded, while through my frayed / Cordage drowned sailors sank sleepwards, back first!" (Clayton Eshleman's translation, in Clayton Eshleman, *Conductors of the Pit*, Soft Skull Press, 2005, p. 5).

SPRACHGITTER / SPEECHGRILLE

The thirty-three poems (divided into six cycles) that make up this volume were written between March 6, 1955, and November 3, 1958. It is the first volume of Celan's for which we have exact dates of composition for all individual poems; this may in some part be a consequence of Claire Goll's plagiarism accusations, which had had some resonance in the West German press since 1954 (see "Cenotaph" and the introductory commentary for the volume *NoOnesRose*). The dates of composition are recorded in a copy of the book Celan dedicated to GCL in December 1960 (see PC/GCL, letter #129). *Speechgrille* is the smallest of Celan's collections; the period in question—from which there exist only three poems, not included in the volume—seems to be the one in which he wrote the least. Concerning this writer's block, see also his letter to Hermann Lenz of June 24, 1956: "But believe me, I would have written a long time ago, if—I still could write. For I have such a wordless year behind me—behind me?—, that I have to doubt if this state will ever end" (PC/HHL, p. 49). *Speechgrille* is the first volume without titles for the cycles, though there are some drafts of such.

The book was published in March 1959 as Celan's first volume of poems with S. Fischer Verlag, in Frankfurt am Main. Only nine of the poems had not previously been published in magazines.

Concerning the title *Sprachgitter / Speechgrille*, see the poem of that name in the third cycle, the comments on it, and the letter to his editor, Rudolf Hirsch: "At the same time I tell myself that what speaks along with me in 'Speechgrille' is also the existential, the difficulty of all speaking (-to-each-other) and simultaneously its structure (cf. 'Raumgitter' [spacegrille]), with which the at first seemingly amphibian is pushed back again—You see I'm still hesitating." (July 26, 1958; see *Paul Celan Rudolf Hirsch, Briefwechsel*, ed. by Joachim Seng, Suhrkamp, 2004, pp. 44–45; my translation). See also the note from the drafts for the Büchner Prize speech: "The pictorial is by no means something visual; it is, like everything else connected with language, a mental phenomenon. [. . .] It is, here too, a manifestation of language, a speech-art that has to be heard in the written, i.e. the silent (the language-grille, which is also the speechgrille, makes this visible" (MFV, #256, p. 107).

I

"Stimmen" / "Voices"

Origination: Parts I–IV: July 21–22, 1956, Rochefort-en-Yvelines; Part V: July 3 (Verbier)–November 2, 1957, Paris; Part VI: beginning of June to November 2, 1957, Paris; Part VII: July 21, 1956 (Rochefort-en-Yvelines)–July 21, 1957; Part VIII: November 26, 1957–November 2, 1958. From June 7 to the beginning of July 1957 Celan was on holiday in Austria and Switzerland; on June 23, 1957, he was in Zürich; later that month for a few days in Verbier (Wallis). Elements of Part V are sketched (in close connection with notes for "Snowbed") in Arno Schmidt's book *Leviathan*, which Celan finished reading on July 4, 1957, in Verbier.

T, 1, 9, 13, 18, 20, 23, 38 *Stimmen / Voices*, 31 Jakobsstimme / Jacobsvoice, 44f. *Keine / Stimme / No / voice*: In relation to "Engführung" / "Stretto," see the note for that title.

3 Wenn der Eisvogel taucht / When the kingfisher dives: See Christoph Schwerin's remembrance of a visit to Rochefort: "On one occasion we were walking along a stream when we saw a little bird, emerald green, turquoise blue, diving headfirst into the water. Celan knew the French name, *martin-pêcheur*, I didn't know the German one. We found the bird in 'Brehms Tierleben' [. . .]. It was the kingfisher, described as follows by Brehm: 'In the

sunshine the kingfisher is a blue and red and green simultaneously flashing, simultaneously diving sudden jet-flame, that lights up in a dazzle and suddenly dies out'" (*Als sei nichts gewesen* [As if nothing had happened], [Berlin: Edition Ost, 1997], p. 203; my translation. "Brehms Tierleben" is a classic German scientific reference book, first published in the 1860s by Alfred Edmund Brehm). See also verse 13 of "Forested."

The German name for the kingfisher, *Eisvogel*, translates literally as "ice-bird," and as such has resonance in Celan's elemental universe (snow, ice, etc.), something the English name does not conjure.

4 sirrt die Sekunde / the second saws: The great Celan scholar Werner Hamacher's essay on inversion bears on this line and is worth quoting at some length here:

> The figure of inversion, imaged explicitly in the text that follows sequentially, is also latent in this one. The objective world of the embankment, its image helpfully turned toward the "you" who is addressed, enters the water-mirror's image—like the voices, which are nicked ["scratched," in my translation], averted and untrusted, in the watery reach—upended and stood on its head. This transformation—a metamorphosis like the one Alcyone undergoes when she is changed into a "kingfisher" as she dives after her drowned husband—is occasioned by a cutting. What is trusted and familiar steps "mowed" into another image: mowed, that is, by the cut of Sekunde, here understood in its etymological sense—by the secare of time. Time changes the voices into the writing of the water-mirror, changes the familiar images of the objective world into the averted, upended, and afflicted images of the literary text. The text offers them no ground beyond that of an *unda* in which they sink away and, following a later paronomasia, sing away. The same displacement underlies the language in which the poem articulates this transformation of a stable image into one that is upended. Not only is the metaphor of reaping drawn from the metaphor sleeping in a foreign word (in the secare of Sekunde)—a practice Celan follows to abundance; this word, die Sekunde ["the second" or "the moment"], is itself to be cut and read as diese Kunde ["this message," "information," "impartment"]. This possibility is suggested in the phonetic combination of s and i in sirrt, which provokes a corresponding contamination of the ie and Se that follow; it is also suggested by the colon after

Sekunde, which allows the second quatrain to appear as the content of this message. Die Sekunde—diese Kunde, the second—this impartment: it is time, as something which cuts, that informs the inversion of the imaged world. But this temporal information effects the inversion only by also subjecting the second, the temporal atom, to its own principle of fission, by splitting the unity of its impartment. What stands on separate banks—"on each of the banks"—is brought together by the very principle of sundering which begets an "other image." DieSeKunde is not just a metamorphosis but also metaphor in its strict sense; it is the motion of metaphorizing itself: stepping across and carrying over. Every image and turn in Celan's text follows this alteration, dictated by its excentric center, dieSeKunde. They are not metaphors for representation but rather metaphors of metaphorizing; not images of a world, but images of the production of images; not the transcription of voices, but the writing of the nicked voices of poetry itself. They inscribe themselves as the script of alteration, by themselves exposed to this very alteration. They write—they are dieSekunde: the incisive changing of words in which the phenomenal and linguistic world is opened onto a caesura which none of the shapes of this world can conjure because these first arise only through it" (Werner Hamacher and William D. Jewett, "The Second of Inversion: Movements of a Figure through Celan's Poetry," *Yale French Studies* 69, *The Lesson of Paul de Man* [1985], pp. 276–311).

In my translation I decided to forgo the literal "the second buzzes," which in English feels as bad as it sounds, and after trying out "the second sings" which gets some of the "i" and "e" sounds to rhyme, but maybe a little too lyrically soft-bellied, I finally went for the more adventurous "saws"—which had a sound maybe harsher than "sir" but also brings in a sense of cutting and of a language, a saw as proverb, etc.

5–8 Was zu dir stand / an jedem der Ufer, / es tritt / gemäht in ein anderes Bild / What stood toward you / on each of the banks / steps / mown into another image: In his last letter to Ilana Shmueli, Celan wrote of his "gratitude for you thinking of me, your feeling toward me, your standing by me. You know I wrote the lines: 'What stood toward you / on each of the banks, / steps / mown into another image.'—Make the lines untrue, Ilana" (December 4, 1970, Shmueli, p. 86, English edition, p. 125). See in this context also the various comments on the concept of standing, and on verse 27 of "A Gonif- and Gangster-Ditty."

10–12 Komm auf den Händen zu uns. / Wer mit der Lampe allein ist, / hat nur die Hand, draus zu lesen / Come to us on your hands. / Whoever is alone with the lamp, / has only the hand to read from: See the reference to this toward the end of the Büchner Prize speech (GW III, p. 201), and the note in the sketches for that speech, together with the lament of the protagonist to be unable to walk on the head, at the beginning of Büchner's tale *Lenz* and Isaac Babel's story collection *Red Cavalry*: "except sometimes it annoyed him that . . . / Cavalry Babel, the Jewish boy who walks on his hands . . ." (MFV, p. 192). See also verses 13–15 of "Ricercar."

21 wo Spätholz und Frühholz / where latewood and earlywood: See also the poem "Latewoodday," *Breathturn into Timestead*, p. 33.

23 Stimmen, kehlig, / Voices, throaty, 29 mittschiffs / midships: See the fragment in Arno Schmidt's *Leviathan*: "Worte, mitschiffs geborsten, / Kehliges, augenumsegelt / lauf— (Words, cracked up midships / throatyness, sailed around by eyes / run—)" (my translation).

23 im Grus / in the debris: Celan marked the word *Grus* in the title story of Schmidt's *Leviathan* (p. 47) and in his *Scenes from the Life of a Faun* (p. 152 of German edition, read on July 5, 1957).

31 Jakobsstimme / Jakobsvoice, 33 Die Tränen im Bruderaug / The tears in the brothereye: See the biblical story of Jacob and Esau (Gen. 27:34) and the commentary to verse 6 of "Schwarze Flocken" / "Black Flakes," ("Jakobs himmliches Blut, benedeiet von Äxten / Jacob's heavenly blood, blessed by axes"), a poem published in *SU* but not included here. Wiedemann's commentary also mentions the noun "Hetman" from line 8: "for the single other occurrence of the verb 'benedeien / bless' originating in the German text of the Ave Maria, see the poem 'Benedicta.' The Cossack Hetmanate founded in 1668 after an uprising accompanied by anti-Semitic pogroms was closely connected with the Orthodox Church."

II

"Zuversicht" / "Confidence"

March 24, 1955–October 8, 1957.

T Zuversicht / Confidence, 11 noch Brüder / still brothers: On April 9, 1959, Celan wrote to Peter Jokostra: "Confidence, as title, as beginning—and, the 'end word,': 'brothers—,'" and concluded: "What confidence? Via Kafka, thinking along with you: 'The fact that nothing exists except a spiritual world takes away hope and gives us certainty!' I've always read that as if it was a basis for being, for living, for breathing." Celan is citing from Kafka's Third Octavo Notebook.

5 Stollen / mineshaft: See the reading note from Hans Henny Jahnn's *Das Holzschiff*: "Stollen—der Mensch tastet sich durch einen finsteren Stollen" ("Mine shafts—Man gropes through a dark mineshaft") (p. 87; my translation).

"Mit Brief und Uhr" / "With Letter and Clock"

Beginning of 1956 (Geneva) to November 3, 1958, the date on which Celan found the title. From January 1 to April 30, 1956, Celan worked as a translator at the International Employment Exchange in Geneva.

T Mit Brief und Uhr / With Letter and Clock: *Letter and Clock* had been considered as a possible title for the cycle.

"Unter ein Bild" / "Below a Painting"

July 29, 1955 (the sixty-fifth anniversary of Vincent van Gogh's death)–November 3, 1958 (title).

This title, according to Barbara Wiedemann, can be seen as "contrasting with an essay by Meyer Shapiro in the first issue of the magazine *Perspektiven* (which included Marianne Moore poems in Celan's translation): *Über ein Bild van Goghs. Der Zusammenbruch eines grossen schöpferischen Geistes* . . . in which Shapiro writes about this painting." The "über" of the German title of Shapiro's essay translates as "on" or "above" a painting. That essay also cites the painter speaking about an early drawing: "The lines of the roofs and the gutters shoot like arrows from a bow into the distance; they are shot without any hesitation."

T Unter ein Bild / Below a Painting: the poem was first published in the magazine *Akzente* below a picture of Vincent van Gogh's last painting *Wheatfield with Crows* (1890).

3 Später Pfeil, der von der Seele schnellte. / Late arrow, shot from the soul: See commentary to title above, but note also the connection with Celan's astrological sign, Sagittarius; thus see the poem "Next to the hailstone" (*Breath-*

turn into Timestead, p. 11), where he writes: "a bowstring, from which / your arrow script whirrs, / archer."

4 Beide Welten / Both worlds: See Celan's note "Both worlds!" in the margins of Walter Benjamin's essay "Two Poems by Hölderlin," further underlining the sentence "Subsequently the duality of the worlds disappears; with death the quality of courage falls away; and in the unfolding nothing is given except the existence of the poet" (English edition of *Selected Writings*, edited by Marcus Bullock and Michael W. Jennings. Harvard University Press: 1996, vol. I, 1913–1926, p. 33).

"Heimkehr" / "Homecoming"

Probably December 1955.

T Heimkehr / Homecoming: Celan wrote two other poems with the same title.

T Heimkehr / Homecoming, 18f. das sein tauben-, sein schnee- / farbenes Fahnentuch festmacht / fastening its dove-, its snow-colored flagcloth: See the opening of Kafka's story "Heimkehr" / "Homecoming": "I have returned, I have passed under the arch and am looking around. It's my father's old yard . . . A torn piece of cloth, once wound around a stick in a game, flutters in the breeze. I have arrived" (translated by Tania and James Stern, *The Complete Stories*, p. 492, https://www.vanderbilt.edu/olli/class-materials/Franz_Kafka.pdf).

13 heimgeholt in sein Heute / brought home into its today: See verse 1 of the following poem (on facing pages in the original volume).

"Unten" / "Below"

October 21, 1955–February 12, 1959.

1 Heimgeführt ins Vergessen / Brought home into forgetting: See the title and verse 13 of the previous poem, "Homecoming." (The two poems were on facing pages in the original volume.)

4f. Heimgeführt Silbe um Silbe, verteilt / auf die tagblinden Würfel / Brought home syllable by syllable, distributed / over the dayblind dice: See verse 8f. of "Die Gauklertrommel" / "The jugglerdrum": "which casts us home into / the dice-cup . . ." (*Breathturn into Timestead*, pp. 48–49).

10 Tracht / tracht: A term from mineralogy: "The rough shape in which a crystal occurs is known as habit. By contrast, the entirety of the crystal shapes of a crystal is referred to as tracht . . . Thus, tracht describes the quantity of surfaces (hkl) or surface shapes (crystal shapes) (hkl) present on a polyhedral crystal" (Foundry Lexicon). Esther Cameron remembered in 1986 that Celan was extremely pleased that she had recognized this word as a term from mineralogy (Cameron, p. 339).

"Heute und morgen" / "Today and Tomorrow"
March 6, 1955–November 3, 1958.

One of four poems Celan dedicated and sent to Ingeborg Bachmann in a copy of the magazine (*Jahresring* 57/58) it was first published in.

1 So steh ich / So I stand: An early version used the verb *ragt* ("loom," "stand above")." Celan replaces it with "stand" on August 4, 1956. At that time Celan was trying to get counsel from various friends concerning the Goll affair, which had reached a first climax about then (see "Voices"). In a letter to Klaus Demus he wrote that day in the context of his detailed letter to Alfred Andersch (see my translation of this letter on pages 150–159 of *Microliths*): "You see from my letter to A., that I have to fight on many fronts—I will, if it comes to it, wage war on *all* fronts, even if only a handful of people stand with me!" (PC/KND, p. 210). He wrote in a notebook on July 30, 1957: "steht / nicht mehr ragt" (stands / no longer looms). As already noted, the word *stehen* (to stand) is a core term in Celan's oeuvre, all the way from the meaning of "withstanding" and Jewish resistance, through, for example, writing, to its sexual connotations. (See my essay "Where is Olson Now?" http://writing.upenn.edu/epc/authors/olson/blog/joris.pdf, where I compare it to Charles Olson's use of the verb "to stand" and the noun "stance.")

8f. Durchpocht / von schweigsam geschwungenen Hämmern / Beaten through / by silently swung hammers: See verse 11 of "Count the almonds": "did the hammers swing free in the belfry of your silence"; and verse 16f. of "Blume" / "Flower": "the hammers / will swing free."

11 Flügelaug / wing'eye: See verses 9–11 of "The free-blown lightcrop" (*Breathturn into Timestead*, p. 197): "as if there fluttered / any still-to-be- / fertilized eye."

"Schliere" / "Streak"

August 30, 1955–August 4, 1956.

T Schliere / Streak, 1 Schliere im Aug / Streak in the eye, 8 Glasspur / glasspoor: In the eye's vitreous body, filled with a jelly-like substance, there can be places that, because of a different density, refract the light differently and thus may alter sight. See the note in *The Meridian*, p. 138: "streak in the eye—blindspots." The German word *Schliere* can, however, also be found in geology (thus in a Celan-owned geological dictionary by Günther), where *Schliere* refers to lens-shaped formations that arise when lava cools down. The Günther entry continues: "[formations] that can be porous, dense or glassy, though this last one (the hyalene structure) is rarer, because lava is never as completely free of water as, for ex., artificial glass-flows are" (Siegmund Günther, *Physische Geographie*, Sammlung Göschen 26, Stuttgart 1895 LPC, p. 37). *Glasspoor* had temporarily been used as the title for the cycle.

15–16 ein durchs Dunkel getragenes Zeichen / a sign / carried through darkness: In the *Jahresring* magazine publication, this line read: "ein vorerinnertes Zeichen" (a pre-remembered sign), and in an interview with the radio station Süddeutscher Rundfunk (see the commentary to "The Traveling Companion") Celan said: "Poems are also somehow a re-remembering and sometimes even a pre-remembering."

19f. als stumm / vibrierender Mitlaut / as / a mutely vibrating consonant: See the Mandelstam radio play in *The Meridian*, p. 216: "It is this tension of the times, between its own and the foreign which lends that pained-mute vibrato to a Mandelstam poem by which we recognize it. (This vibrato is everywhere in the intervals between the words and the stanza, in the 'courtyards' where rhymes and assonances stand, in the punctuation . . .)."

III

"Tenebrae" / "Tenebrae"

March 10–October 8, 1957.

T Tenebrae: Latin for "darkness"; see in the Vulgate Matt. 27:45: "A sexta autem hora tenebrae factae sunt super universam terram usque ad horam nonam" ("Now from the sixth hour there was darkness over all the land unto the ninth hour"). Tenebrae or Officium tenebrarum is the name of a religious service of Western Christianity held during the three days preceding Easter, and characterized by gradual extinguishing of candles, and by a "strepitus," or loud noise, taking place in total darkness near the end of the service. It is a Catholic liturgy but one with marked Jewish features. In the Hebrew original four of the five lamentations (of twenty-two verses each) begin an alphabetic order with a consonant of the Hebrew alphabet (alphabetic acrostic); in the Latin (Catholic) version the Hebrew consonant is set as the letter name at the head of the verse and gives rise to specific coloratura in the musical settings. See verses 10–11 of "Benedicta" ("You, who greeted it, / the tenebrae lamp") and Celan's title for one of GCL's etchings: *Ténèbres* (Tenebrae). In 1957, Easter fell on April 21.

In *Spur des Wortes*, Otto Pöggeler recounts that when he visited Celan in April 1957, the poet told him that "Tenebrae" was "one of his favorite poems: that it had come to him on the street and that he was able to write it down complete when he got home—this hadn't happened to him much recently. He himself was not a believer, but the poem was like a negro spiritual. Because of the hieratic character of the Latin language he had not chosen the French title 'Leçons de ténèbres' [Couperin's Oratorium, a recording of which Celan owned and which Jean Bollack suggested as core inspiration for the poem]." See also Felstiner's discussion of the poem in *Paul Celan: Poet, Survivor, Jew*, pp. 101–105.

T Tenebrae, 1f. Nah sind wir, Herr, / nahe und greifbar / We are near, Lord, / near and graspable: See Hölderlin's "Patmos": "Near and / hard to grasp, the god. / Yet where danger lies, / grows that which saves. / Eagles dwell / in darkness, and without fear" (Richard Sieburth's translation, *Hymns and Fragments* [Princeton University Press, 1984], p. 89).

4 ineinander verkrallt / clawed into each other: Barbara Wiedemann points to *The Theory and Practice of Hell*, where Eugen Kokon cites Oscar Berger's account of Treblinka: "Sometimes there were shipments that held only corpses. I believe these people must have been gassed in the cars, for I never noticed any wounds. The bodies were convulsively intertwined, the skin blue" (p. 184), and the corroborative note by Celan of July 18, 1965, in Richard Beer-Hofmann's *Jaácob's Traum* (*Jacob's Dream*): "Ineinander verkrallt!" /

"clawed into each other" next to Jacob's acknowledgement to God: "Doch aneinander hangen, ewig—Du und ich!" / "But eternally hanging on each other—you & I" (p. 148 in the original: Berlin: Ein Vorspiel, 1925).

6 dein Leib, Herr / your body, Lord, 14 Es war Blut, es war / was du vergossen, Herr / It was blood, it was / what you spilled, Lord: See Matt. 26:28: "For this is my blood of the new covenant, which is shed for many for the remission of sins"; and verse 11 of "The Load": "Curry my horse, when the hand here breaks the bread."

12 Mulde und Maar / crater and maar: Various reading notes and word lists in the Tübingen philological edition of *Sprachgitter* cite *Mulde*, "crater," in connection with glacier formations (TA/SG, p. 114), and *Maar*, "maar," in relation to volcanic formations as given in the Kluge-Götze etymological dictionary of the German language (TA/SG, p. 120, reference to p. 254 in Kluge-Götze).

13 Zur Tränke / To the trough: The word *Tränke* / "trough" (watering place) appears only one other time in Celan's work, in verse 12 of "The Load."

18 Augen und Mund stehn so offen und leer / Eyes and mouths gape, so open and empty: See Celan's translation of Jean Cayrol's text for Alain Resnais's Auschwitz film, *Nacht und Nebel* (*Night and Fog*): "Zuletzt haben alle das gleiche Gesicht. Es sind alterslose Wesen, die mit offenen Augen sterben" ("At the end, they all have the same face. They are ageless creatures that die with their eyes open") (GW IV, p. 89).

"Blume" / "Flower"

Late February–October 7, 1957.

T Blume / Flower: Celan's son Eric turned two in June 1957; it is his word *fleur* (*Blume*, flower) that Celan translates here.

7f. das Wort, das den Sommer heraufkam: / Blume / the word that came up the summer: / flower, 10–12 Dein Aug und mein Aug: / sie sorgen / für Wasser / Your eye and my eye: / they ensure / water: See verses 50 and 56ff. of "Engführung" / "Stretto."

14–16 Herzwand um Herzwand / blättert hinzu. // Ein Wort noch, wie dies / Heartwall by heartwall / refoliates. // One more word, like this one: See verse 5 of "Lowwater" and verse 374ff. of Celan's translation of *The Young*

Fate by Paul Valéry: "und sie lauscht / voll Zuversicht der Herzwand, die fromm sich regt und regt" ("and she listens / to the heartwall that, pious, moves and moves") (Celan, in his translation, creates that "Herzwand" / "heartwall." In the French original the line is: "Ecoute, avec espoir, frapper au mur pieux / Ce coeur"—literally "listen, with hope, to this heart beating against the pious wall" [GW IV, p. 151].)

16f. Ein Wort noch, wie dies, und die Hämmer / schwingen im Freien / One more word, like this one, and the hammers / will swing free: See verse 11 of "Count the almonds" and verse 8f. of "Today and Tomorrow."

"Weiß und Leicht" / "White and Light"

October 23, 1956–October 8, 1957.

On October 17, 1957, Celan sent this poem, together with "Night," "With Letter and Clock," "Snowbed," and "Matière de Bretagne," to Ingeborg Bachmann with the following explanation: "I am sending you a few poems, Ingeborg, read them. / There is barely a poem in which I didn't leave room for you. That space is the truth of the poems. / When I wrote 'White and Light'—it took days and days—, there came, at the very last, the word 'Verlorne' [lost one]. I knew immediately that that was you, I tried to defend myself—but you had to stay, for truth's sake" (first publication in *Die Zeit*, April 28, 2016, p. 48; PC/IB, letter #55, p. 73).

2 Im Windschatten / In the windshadow: In a reading note of September 21, 1954, Celan had marked this sentence in Heidegger's *What Is Called Thinking?*: ". . . Sokrates sei der reinste der Denker des Abendlandes, die Nachfolger hätten sich in den Windschatten stellen müssen." The English translation by J. Glenn Gray renders the phrase that uses the word "Windschatten" as ". . . those who followed had to run for shelter" (Martin Heidegger, *What is Called Thinking?*, New York: Harper & Row, 1968).

6 Die Strahlen. Sie wehn uns zuhauf / The rays. They blow us into a heap: See Celan's confirming note, "The rays. They blow us into a heap," in relation to Gershom Scholem writing in *Die Geheimnisse der Schöpfung* ("The secrets of creation") (not translated as far as I could discover): "Das Strahlen—das ist das geheime Licht, in dem die Tora erstrahlt und das die Häupter der [von Jecheskel erschauten Tiergestalt] erleuchtet. Diese ›Häupter‹ aber sind nichts

anderes als die ›Einsichtigen‹ [im Buche Daniel], die immerdar leuchten und jenes ›Gewölbe‹ und das Leuchten, das von dort ausgeht, einsichtig betrachten. Dies aber ist das Licht der Tora, das immerdar und unaufhörlich leuchtet" ("The radiating—that is the secret light the Torah radiates and that lights the heads [seen by Ezekiel as animal-shapes]. These 'heads,' however, are nothing else than the wise men [in the Book of Daniel] . . . This, however, is the light of the Torah which radiates always and endlessly"), p. 50. See also verse 2 of "Weggebeizt" / "Eroded": "the beamwind" (*Breathturn into Timestead*, p. 19).

23f. die Stirnen, die man uns lieh, / um der Spiegelung willen / the foreheads that were lent to us, / for the sake of the mirrorings: See Celan's note in Scholem's *Die Geheimnisse der Schöpfung*, "the forehead that were lent us, / for the sake of the mirrorings / (White and light)," in connection with Scholem's phrase "The Shekinah has nothing of its own. But she receives and safekeeps everything and rules with her, as it is often called, 'lent' strength in the below." (In German, "Die Schechina hat nichts aus sich selbst. Sie empfängt und bewahrt aber alles und waltet mit dieser ihr, wie es oft heißt, 'geliehenen' Kraft im Unteren.") (Further marginal marks, p. 36f., and the note on p. 37.)

30 Meermühle geht / Seamill turns: See the unidentified reading note: "Auskolkung, Kolk, Vertief[un]g in der Sohle eines Flusses (Strudellöcher) an Meeresküsten (Meermühlen) oder im Untergrund von Gletschern" (my translation: "scouring, scour, hollow in a riverbed (scour holes) on seacoasts (sea-mill) or in the underground of glaciers") (TA/SG, p. 114). Clemens Podewils (as recalled by Pajari Räsänen in his *Counter-figures: An Essay on Antimetaphoric Resistance: Paul Celan's Poetry*) reported the following comment by Celan concerning the word *Meermühle*: "These compound nouns have been held against me, for example Meermühle / seamill. But aren't pebbles, rocks, cliffs ground by the sea into what they are? . . . Basically my word formations are not inventions. They belong to the oldest layers of language. What matters for me? To get away from words as simple descriptions. I would like to again hear the name of things in the words. The description isolates the presented object. In the name, however, each thing speaks to us in its connection [*Zusammenhang*: coherence] with the world."

"Sprachgitter" / "Speechgrille"

June 14, 1957, Vienna, Rennweg–October 8, 1957 (dated corrections). Celan's friends Klaus and Nani Demus, whom he visited during his holidays in Austria (see also "Voices"), lived in the Rennweg, the third district of Vienna.

T Sprachgitter / Speechgrille: Also the title of the volume. In Vienna Celan received a postcard dated "Whitsuntide 1957" (June 9, 1957) from Günther Neske with the image of the confessional screen (the *Sprechgitter*) of the former Saint Clare convent in Pfullingen (Württemberg); the text spoke to Celan's intention of publishing his next book with Neske. See the marginal note in Jean Paul's *Kampaner Thal*: "unter dem tiefer einsinkenden Gewitter schlugen die Nachtigallen lauter, gleichsam als lebendige Gewitterstürmer, hinter blühenden Sprachgittern" / "under the fast approaching storm the nightingales raised their voices, as if they were living lightning stormers, behind blooming speech-grilles" (Bd. 42/43, S. 20; my translation, as the available English translation avoids *Sprachgittern* and translates it as "hedges"). Celan told Demus that those were the two inspirations for the title. He wrote his friend Joachim Seng, "I tell myself that in 'Sprachgitter' the existential, the difficulty of all speaking (to one another) and at the same time the structure of that speaking is what counts" (*Gedichte*, p. 643).

1–4 Augenrund zwischen den Stäben. // Flimmertier Lid / rudert nach oben, / gibt einen Blick frei. / Eyeround between the bars. // Flitterbug lid / rows upward, / frees a gaze: See Rilke's famous poem "The Panther," in *New Poems*: "His gaze against the sweeping of the bars / has grown so weary, it can hold no more. / To him, there seem to be a thousand bars / and back behind those thousand bars no world." And farther on: "An image enters then, / goes through the tensioned stillness of the limbs— / and in the heart ceases to be" (Rainer Maria Rilke, *Selected poems / Ausgewählte Gedichte*, translated by Stanley Appelbaum, Mineola, NY: Dover Publications, 2011, poem #56).

6 der Himmel, herzgrau, muß nah sein / the heavens, heartgray, must be near: See the note to the Büchner Prize speech: "Artistry and word-art—that may have the feeling of something occidental, evening-filling, Poetry is something else; poetry, heartgray, sublunar, heavens- and heart-gray, heart and heavens-gray breath-marbled language in time" (MFV, p.110).

7 Tülle / socket: Celan had many notes from various dictionaries, plus

French translations, concerning this word essentially referencing the metal holder into which one sticks a light, also called *Lichthalter* (lightholder).

13 unter einem Passat / under one trade wind: Celan's Kluge-Götze etymological dictionary defines *Passat*, a trade wind, thus: "These easterly winds blowing regularly in the lower latitudes are beneficent for crossings."

17 Lachen / pools: Marjorie Perloff writes, in "'Sound Scraps, Vision Scraps': Paul Celan's Poetic Practice," her analysis of the poem: "*Lachen*, in this context, has the primary meaning of puddles or pools: two gray pools of water blot the flagstones. But *Lachen* also means 'notches'—the stones are notched with the sign of the two unknown strangers—and in the singular, the noun 'Lachen' is the common word 'laughter'—in this case, a mirthless, hollow chuckle of sorts. In all three cases, the flagstones reflect the 'heartgray' condition of the lovers: the desire for communion—with hidden priest? God? and especially the 'you' who is his beloved—has failed."

18, 19 zwei / Mundvoll Schweigen / two / mouthfuls of silence: As Dennis J. Schmidt puts it, Celan's "'Two mouthfuls of silence' (*zwei / Mundvoll Schweigen*) . . . mark the place of the poem for Celan . . . such silence is not to be confused with mere quiet but needs to be heard as the unvocalized voice of the poem. . . . a voice estranged from language, rendering the effort to listen to language in the poem rare, demanding, and painful at once" (Dennis J. Schmidt, "Black Milk and Blue: Celan and Heidegger on Pain and Language," in: *Word Traces: Readings of Paul Celan*, ed. Aris Fioretis, Johns Hopkins, 1994, pp. 110–29).

"Schneebett" / "Snowbed"

June 23, Zürich–October 8, 1957. First fragments as notes in Arno Schmidt's *Leviathan* (Hamburg, Rowohlt 1949), where further fragments point to "Voice IV" and "Embankments, Roadsides, Vacant Lots, Rubble."

1, 9 Sterbegeklüft / deathcliffs, 4 Steilwand / rockwall: See the reading traces in Arno Schmidt's story "Enthymesis" in the volume *Leviathan*, with a marginal arrow mark by Celan: "Als er durch Felsengewirr sich bis an ihren Fuß gearbeitet hatte, sah er bestürzt die wilden Mauern unabsehbar nach beiden Seiten laufen; Geröllhalden körnten blockig vor; lange Schatten hingen verrenkt im schweigenden Geklüft; himmelhoch neigte sich die Wand über den Zurücktaumelnden" / "He finally worked his way on foot to its base through a rock jumble, but to his dismay he saw no end to the wild wall on either side; before him pebbled slopes bouldered away in kernels; long, wrenched shadows hung in silent fissures; the sky-wall bent low over his reeling figure" (p. 17 in the English edition of *Collected Novellas: Collected Early Fiction 1949–1964*, translated by John E. Woods, Dalkey Archive Press, 1994). See also the note from Celan's June 1957 stay in Vienna: "Seelengeklüft" / with the addition: "Vienna: Sterbehaus" / "Deathhouse" (TA/SG, p. 116). Re "Steilwand" / "cliff" see "Enthymesis": "Der Führer deutete auf eine etwa 1 Stadion hohe rötliche Steilwand und wisperte schüchtern: 'Da soll es sein . . .'" / "The guide pointed out a reddish cliff about 1 stadion high and whispered timidly: 'That's it, they say . . .'" (p. 6 in the English edition).

1, 3 Ich komm / I come: Temporarily considered as a title for the poem.

2 Hartwuchs im Herzen / hardgrowth in the heart, 18 In den Gängen / In the passageways: See the reading traces in the story "Gadir" in *Leviathan*: "Now there running down the halls.—And I bounded up the mountains through the crouching, frozen tree shapes. ('Give us good going, ye, gravel, granite and hard stuff . . .')," p. 60 in English translation. I prefer to translate *Gänge* with "passageways" rather than "the hall," and *Hartwuchs* as "hard growth" rather than "hard stuff." Celan had a note in the back of the book: "Hartwuchs im Herzen" / "hardgrowth in the heart."

5 Atemgeflecktes Geleucht. Strichweise Blut / Breathflecked lightglow. Blood streaks: See "Gadir" (with marginal mark): "*Herbstnebel dampft auf* / am hellen Mittag; warm und dicht, grünlich vom verwischten Pflanzengeleucht: nun findet ihr mich nicht mehr" / "*Autumn fog billows up* / in the bright afternoon: warm and thick, greenish from the gloss wiped off plants: you won't find me now," and the note in the book: "Atemgeflecktes Geleucht. / Strichweise Blut / Breathflecked lightglow. Blood streaks" and "—Hinab durchs Geleucht" / "—down through the lightglow."

6f. Wölkende Seele, noch einmal gestaltnah. / Zehnfingerschatten—verklammert. / Clouding soul, once more near-shapely. / Tenfingershadow—gripclasped: See notes in *Leviathan*: "Wölkende Seele, gestaltmüd / Wölkende Seele, noch einmal gestaltnah. / Zehnfingerschatten—verklammert." / "Clouding soul, shape-tired / Clouding soul, once more near-shapely / Tenfinger-shadow—gripclasped."

12f. Kristall um Kristall, / zeittief gegittert, / Crystal after crystal, / meshed timedeep: See the note in *Leviathan*: "Crystal after crystal, / meshed timedeep," and Lotze's term *Raumgitter* (spacegrille) for the inner structure of crystals (Franz Lotze, *Geologie*, Sammlung Göschen Band 13, Berlin 1955, p. 17).

"Windgerecht" / *"Windtrue"*

August 13–October 8, 1957; the last date corresponds to a title change.

1 Tafelwand / Tablewall: See "Steinwand" / "rockwall" in line 4 of the previous poem.

1 Nachtfries / nightfrieze: See the note "Fries: der Nachtfries" / "frieze: the nightfrieze," in Celan's reading notes from summer 1957 from Moritz Hoernes and Friedrich Behn, *Kultur der Urzeit* (1921), and his word list "Zahnfries, Rautenfries, Schuppenfries, Blattfries, Laubfries, Würfelfries" ("tooth frieze, rhombus frieze, scale frieze, leaffrieze, foliagefrieze, dicefrieze") of August 13, 1957 (TCA/SG, p. 113).

4 Leuchtassel / Lightipede: See Celan's word note "*Leuchtassel*" in connection with the elucidation in Jean Paul's *Kampaner Thal* of the word *Skolopender*: "Skolopender oder Feuerasseln leuchten Nachts; man muß sich hüten, sie nicht aus den Blumenkelchen mit den Düften ins Gehirn zu ziehen" / "Scolopendra or fire-assels [*Scolopendra electrica*] glow at night; one has to be careful not to draw them into the brain with the scents from the flower calices" (see also Celan's marginal mark in Jean-Paul, vols. 39–44, p. 45; also reading notes of July 14, 1957; via Badiou).

6 Augenstimmen / Eyevoices, 14, 15 Die Stimmen / The voices: See the cycle of poems *Voices*.

16 herznah / heartnear: See Celan's marginal note "heartnear! / speechgrille" in connection with Hans Kohn's *Martin Buber*: "Immer innerlicher, immer herznäher wird das Bild, immer tiefer senkt es sich in das Leben selber ein, und der es vor fünftausend Jahren in den Sternen schaute, erblickt es heute im Auge des Freundes" (Always more innerly, more heartnear comes the image, it sinks always deeper into life itself, and he who saw it five thousand years ago in the stars, sees it today in the eye of a friend) (p. 151f., note p. 151).

17 brandbestattet / cremation-buried: See the reading traces in Behn referring to the second half of the Bronze Age in western Europe: "Erstes

Auftreten der Brandbestattung" (First appearance of cremation burial) and "Fast ausschließliche Herrschaft der Brandbestattung" (Near exclusive dominance of cremation burials) (*Kultur der Urzeit*, vol. 2, pp. 83, 85), and the corresponding reading notes (TCA/SG, p. 112).

"Nacht" / "Night"

September 19–October 17, 1957. First fragments connected with Celan's reading in Behn, Heidegger (*Der Satz vom Grund* [*The Principle of Reason*] read in May that year), and possibly E. Strasburger's *Lehrbuch der Botanik* (*Textbook of Botany*) (TCA/SG, p. 114).

2 Zuspruch / exhortation: A Heidegger word from the lecture mentioned above where it comes in thus: "Im Satz vom Grund spricht der Anspruch des Grundsatzes. Im Satz vom Grund spricht der Zuspruch des Wortes vom Sein. Der Zuspruch bleibt jedoch um vieles älter als der Anspruch" (Martin Heidegger, *Der Satz Vom Grund*, in *Gesamtausgabe*, Band 10, S. 171ff.). See also Johannes Fritsche's footnote re *Zuspruch* in his *Historical Destiny and National Socialism in Heidegger's* Being and Time:

> Note that "zusprechen" is different from the compound verb 'sprechen zu (jemandem)," to talk to (someone). "Zuspruch" means speaking, admonition, consolation, exhortation, claim, and it is often used precisely to convey all these meanings at the same time. According to Heidegger, Plato "entspricht dem, was sich ihm zusprach." "Ent-sprechen" consists of "sprechen," to talk, and the prefix "ent-." It can mean 'to correspond, to be in accordance with, to be equivalent to" and also—as in Heidegger's sentence—"to meet, answer, fulfill, a request or expectation"; thus, the "entsprochen" in Heidegger's text entspricht the verb "erwidert" in *Being and Time* in my interpretation in chapter I; note that this verb, too, does not require an accusative object. There is a sentence in which Heidegger regards even a widersprechen in the sense of erwidern ihm etwas (to contradict someone) as entsprechen: "When man, in his way, from within unconcealment reveals that which presences, he merely responds [entspricht er nur] to the call [dem Zuspruch] of unconcealment even when he contradicts it [wo er ihm widerspricht]" (note 14 to chapter 5, n.p.).

"Matière de Bretagne" / "Matière de Bretagne"

August 9–10, 1957, Paris; from fragments dated August 1956 and corrections dated May 17, 1957. Celan himself indicated August 13, 1957, as the date of composition. Probably the first poem began (May 17, 1957, according to earlier notes) after Celan acquired his first major Mandelstam edition (*Cobranie covinenij* [Collected Works]) in May 1957. The draft also stands in close connection with Celan's translation of Rimbaud's "Drunken Boat." See also the commentary on "White and Light," re Ingeborg Bachmann.

T Matière: The French word *matière* means "material," "matter," "theme," with possible additions of "pus," "excrements," "brainmass." See Celan's remarks to Walter Jens: "Where there are such re-encounters, they affirm themselves also language-wise . . . : semantically—as in the case of the synonymity of 'matière' and 'pus' which was detected by you (and, tellingly, not by me), or, but that is rarer, in the etymological" (May 16, 1961, GA, p. 532).

T Bretagne: From April 26 to May 1, 1957, Celan was in the Celtic landscape of Brittany on the French Atlantic coast; a range of further poems and the Breton cycle in *NoOnesRose* were written there (see "Die hellen Steine" / "The bright stones" and commentary).

T Matière de Bretagne: On January 23, 1961, Celan told Norbert Koch that there was a connection with the Breton King Arthur cycle of tales, pointing also back to the use of "Avalun" / "Avalon" from an early poem ("Flügelrauschen," not reproduced here) in *SU*. In connection with that poem, Celan explained to Beda Alleman: " I am including with these lines an old poem, that was doubtlessly a precursor of the later poem—in memory of Crozon and—among other things also—of the red sails of the Breton fishermen ('Matière'). Back then—Avalon . . .—it was still called: 'Flügelrauschen'" (March 27, 1962; Badiou's reference).

1, 23 Ginsterlicht / Gorselight, 2 Dorn / thorn: Gorse (*Ulex europaeus*), the only Fabaceae species with thorns, flowers golden yellow from April to July.

10 beim Stern, die milchigen / next to the star, the milky: See, in Celan's translation of Rimbaud's "Drunken Boat": "Grünhimmel trank ich, Sterne, taucht ein in milchigen Strahl" (Greenskies I drank, stars, infused in milky beam), where the original is: ". . . je me suis baigné dans le Poème / De la mer, infusé d'astres, et lactescent, / dévorant les azurs verts; . . ." (on July 30, 1957; verse 22, GW IV, p. 103).

11f. Steindattel, / unten, gebuscht, klafft / stone-mussel / below, tufted, gapes: Celan noted the expression *Steindattel klafft* several times (TCA/SG,

p. 118), also in his Brehm (*Brehms Tierleben in 4 Bänden*, 1956) the description of the Mytilidae (vol. 1, p. 135). The reference here is to the date mussel (*Steindattel* [stone-date] in German), a mollusk of the genus *Lithophaga* (literally "stone-eaters," as these mussels bore into stone and coral). When the valves of a mussel are open, or they "gape," the animal is dead. See also verse 8 of "Kermovan."

16 Hände / hands: See, in Celan's letter to Norbert Koch: "'The hands'—: it is . . . the hands, both hands, the left and the right, it is—I quote Osip Mandelstam—our (everyone's!) 'Twohandedness.'"

"Schuttkahn" / "Rubble Scow"

May 10–June 10, 1957. A later copy made specifically for Ingeborg Bachmann on October 18, 1957, is entitled "Rheinufer" / "Rhine-shore" (BA 5, 2, 227); re Celan's stay in Cologne, see the poem "Köln, Am Hof" / "Cologne, Am Hof."

3f. ein totes / Warum steht am Heck / a dead / Why stands at the stern: 6, Geleichtert. Die Lunge / Lightened. The lung: See the reference in verses 23 and 26 of "Es ist alles anders" / "Everything is different."

6f. Die Lunge, die Qualle / bläht sich zur Glocke / The lung, the jellyfish / swells into a bell: Celan probably read this in his Brehm: "Another type of jellyfish is the Lungenqualle [lung-jellyfish] (*Rhizostoma pulmo*), which inhabits the Mediterranean. Its tender yellow bell can reach a diameter of 60 to 80 centimeters" (vol. 1, p. 51).

IV

"Köln, Am Hof" / "Cologne, Am Hof"

Sunday, October 20, 1957, 2:30 p.m., Paris, quai de Bourbon. Compare this specific time indication with the time-theme of the poem. The quai de Bourbon runs along the shore of the Île Saint-Louis with a view of the right bank of the Seine; the Paris "Dome" / "cathedrals," referring to Notre-Dame, is close by and visible, though not from every location.

T Köln, Am Hof / Cologne, Am Hof, 8, 9 Dome / cathedrals, 10 Ströme / streams: After a conference in Wuppertal, where he had seen Ingeborg Bachmann again, Celan was in Cologne on October 14, 1957, lodging in a hotel on

Am Hof street close by the cathedral and the shore of the Rhine. The street leads from the archbishop's palace (*Hof*) to the Rathausplatz (City Hall Square); in the Middle Ages this area had been allotted to the Jews. See Bachmann's dedication in the second printing of her book of poems *Die gestundete Zeit* (Time deferred): "München, Am Hof / Ingeborg."

T Köln, Am Hof / Cologne, Am Hof, 6 Verbannt und Verloren / Exiled and Lost: Celan wrote to the translator Adolph Hofmann concerning the capitalization of "Am": "For here one has to be able to read that in other (residential) cities there are squares that have the same name. It is only from there that the—not by chance—capitalized Verbannt / Exiled and Verloren / Lost can be experienced. That's also valid for everything else that comes into language in this poem" (May 18, 1960; Badiou's reference).

3 die Mitternachtsziffer / the midnight cipher: This compound appeared already in drafts for the poem "Windgerecht" / "Windtrue" (TCA/SG, p. 44).

11 ihr Uhren tief in uns / you clocks, deep in us: On November 7, 1957, Celan wrote to Ingeborg Bachmann in remembrance of her stay in Paris in 1950: "I stumbled on a pocket calendar of 1950. Under October 14 I had written: Ingeborg. It was the day you came to Paris. On 14 October 1957 we were in Cologne, Ingeborg. / You clocks deep in us" (PC/IB #56, p. 94).

"In die Ferne" / "Into the Distance"

October 24–December 2, 1957, i.e., before and after moving into his first apartment, on rue de Longchamp, on November 19, 1957; on December 2, 1957, Celan left for a trip to Germany.

4 die Freistatt / the sanctuary: Place of refuge, safe haven, asylum: *Die Freistatt / The sanctuary* was considered at some point as the title for the volume *Threadsuns*.

5 Schärfer als je die verbliebene Luft: du sollst atmen / Sharper than ever the remaining air: you shall breathe: See his comments on the poem "Sie kämmt ihr Haar" / "She combs her hair" in a letter to E. Lilles, and this pointer in the Meridian speech: "That I worry these [reference to the "old and even ancient forms of uncanniness" he just mentioned] with such stubbornness today, probably is in the air—the air we have to breathe today" (MFV, p. 5).

"Ein Tag und noch einer" / "One Day and One More"

December 13–26, 1957, Paris. On December 11, 1957, Celan had returned from a trip to Germany during which he had also visited Ingeborg Bachmann in Munich.

4 Ich gewann, ich verlor / I won, I lost: See verse 6f. of "Erinnerung an Frankreich" / "Remembrance of France." The poem belongs to those marked "for you" in Bachmann's copy of the second printing of *Poppy and Memory*. On November 23, 1957, Celan wrote to Ingeborg Bachmann: "But now I am coming soon, not for long, for one day, for another—if you want and allow me to. / Let us then go in search of the lamp, Ingeborg, you and I, use" (PC/IB #63, p. 101). After the visit she wrote: "Here in the hotel I only have this crumpled-up piece of paper, everything else is in the Franz Josephstrasse with the candlestick" (December 11, 1957; PC/IB #70, p. 107).

"In Mundhöhe" / "At Mouth Level"

October 26–27, 1957.

2 Finstergewächs / darkgrowth: Barbara Wiedemann connects this compound word with verse 4 of "Das Geheimnis der Farne" / "The Secret of the Ferns": "flowery it darkens upward before they drink, as if it were not water."

4 Schneegarn / snowsnare: See Celan's reading notes to this explanation of woodcuts under the ten commandments of Jean Paul Richter's catechism: "There, next to the column he has fixed the only human being in the world . . . the contralto Taubert. He takes him for a hunter, who had set the Tyras or the snowsnare [*Schneegarn*], and thanks God that the hen is intelligent and escapes the adultery-net" (Jean Paul, vol. 39, p. 77). One part of Jean Paul's volume *Kampaner Tal* is a "whimsical" (Dixit Carlyle in his review in the British Quarterly of August/September 1847) commentary on the woodcuts accompanying the Ten Commandments in the little Lutheran Catechism used in the dominions of Bayreuth and Anspach. The term *Schneegarn* appears several times in Celan's notes. I here use David Young's translation of the term.

10 Blattnarben, Knospen / Leafscars, buds: See the reading traces in a caption for the reproduction of an elm tree shoot in Lothar Geitler's *Morphologie der Pflanzen* (Sammlung Göschen 141, Berlin 1953; with marginal marks, p. 33).

12 Schelfe / Involucre: This word list appears in a folder marked "September 1958" by Celan: "Schelfe; (Fruchthülse, Schale) / schelfen, schilfen, inkl. / Teile abblättern" / "involucre; (involucrum, covering) / to peel, to pare incl. to strip off parts" (TCA/SG, p. 117).

"Eine Hand" / "A Hand"

January 7, 1958, Paris.

Celan mailed a manuscript copy of the poem on the day of composition to Ingeborg Bachmann.

"Aber" / "But"

December 30, 1957–November 3, 1958.

4 Strahlengang / Beampath: See Celan's reading of Karl Stumpff's *Astronomie* and Strumpff's commentary on a caption that reads: "Aufstellung und Strahlengang in Reflektoren" (Setup and optical path in reflectors): "None of these arrangements permit to avoid that the central part of the optical path is interrupted by the additional mirror" (Karl Stumpff, *Astronomie*, Das Fischer Lexicon 4, Frankfurt a.m., December 1957, p. 80). See also the allusion in verses 1–3 of "Weißgeräusche" / "Whitesounds" in *Threadsuns* (*Breathturn into Timestead*, pp. 146–47), where I translated *Strahlengänge* as "ray- / passages": "Whitesounds, bundled, / ray- / passages / over the table / with the bottle post hither." This poem was originally dedicated to Hans Mayer, who had been witness to Celan and Ingeborg Bachmann's reunion in Wuppertal. The word had also been considered as a possible title for the volume that would be called *Lichtzwang / Lightduress*.

14f. die Schwäne, / in Genf, / the swans / in Geneva, 17 ins Ziel einer Seele / targeting a soul: See the reading traces—with the corroborating note "the swans in Geneva / 5.17. 59"—in his copy of Plato's *Der Staat* (*The Republic*): "There he saw the soul which had once been Orpheus choosing the life of a swan out of enmity to the race of women, hating to be born of a woman because they had been his murderers" (translated by Benjamin Jowett; p. 405 in Celan's German edition: Platon, *Sämtliche Werke*, Bd. 2. Hg. v. Ericj Loewenthal, Heidelberg 1950).

16 als schwirrte, vom Nichts her, ein Wurfholz / as if there whirred, out

of the Nothing, a boomerang: See my commentary to the poem "Schwirrhölzer" / "Bullroarers" (*Breathturn into Timestead*, p. 486), and "Ein Wurfholz" / "A boomerang," as well as verse 1 ("I gave, I gave—it returns as a stone") of the poem "Judenwelsch, nachts" (not included).

"Allerseelen" / "All Souls"

November 1–4, 1957. A sheet dated "Paris, 2. November 1957"; the title refers to the Catholic remembrance day for the souls of the departed celebrated on that day (though not in France). Notes for the beginning of the poem come down to us together with drafts for the poem "Voices" and the translation of Antonin Artaud's poem "Prayer."

3 besamt / Inseminated: See Celan's reading note in Hans Henny Jahnn's *Das Holzschiff* (The wooden boat): "Didn't the just inseminated queen bee rip out the intestines of the drone that has just been reeling from pleasure?" (p. 92, in part underlined by Celan; my translation).

14 Findlinge / Erratics: See *Findling* in Celan's unidentified reading notes (TCA/SG, p. 113), and the description in his Günther geology book, p. 132, of *Erratische*. *Findlinge* are drift or glacial or erratic boulders. See also verse 7 of "By the great": "the six- \ edged, denialwhite \ erratic" (*Breathturn into Timestead*, p. 21). The word had momentarily been considered as a possible title for the volume *Threadsuns*. See also the poem "Erratic."

"Entwurf einer Landschaft" / "Sketch for a Landscape"

January 2, 1958.

1 Rundgräber / Roundgraves: In relation to Stonehenge and the burial site at the fortress of Mycenae, Behn speaks of a *Gräberrund*, a graves-round, or circle of graves (*Kultur der Urzeit*, vol. 2, p. 93). The only other use of the word is in "Mittags" / "Midday" (*Breathturn into Timestead*, pp. 36–37).

3 Steilstufen / steep scarps, 6 Quelltuff / Calc-tufa: See Franz Lotze, *Geologie*, p. 33, on *Quelltuff* (calc-tufa) and *Sintermassen* (travertine), and see Celan's notes to the Lotze entries in TCA/SG, pp. 110 and 112. (The *Oxford Dictionary of Geology & Earth Sciences* defines calc-tufa as "sedimentary rock formed by the deposition or precipitation of calcium carbonate, or more rarely

silica as a thin layer around saline springs," and travertine as calcium carbonate deposited by "precipitation from carbonate-saturated waters, particularly from hot springs.")

4 Laven, Basalte / Lavas, basalts: Further reading traces in Lotze, p. 77: "Dieser 'initiale Vulkanismus' ist also gekennzeichnet durch submeerische Laven vom Typus der Diabase, Ophiolithe, Basalte (grüne Gesteine)" ("This 'initial vulcanism' is also characterized by subsea lavas of diabasic, ophiolite, and basaltic [green rock formations] types.")

12f. ein Steinsattel, drauf, / gebeult / a stonesaddle, on it, / warped: Lotze, p. 40: "Mannigfach können Gesteine 'verkrümmt' sein, knieförmig (Flexuren), in nach oben gespannten Bögen (Sättel, Beulen), in nach unten konvexen Bögen (Mulden)" ("Often rocks can be 'warped,' knee-shaped [flexures], in upward tensed arches [saddles, buckles], in downward convex arches [troughs]").

V

"Ein Auge, offen" / "One Eye, Open"

May 28–July 21, 1958, Paris. Not only the month of composition—May—but also the place—Paris—was originally part of the first line. On the late afternoon of the day (May 28, 1958) of the resignation of the French prime minister Pierre Pflimlin—a time of acute danger of war, due to the Algeria crisis—a massive demonstration of the left took place in Paris in defense of the democratic system, which seemed endangered by the demands for extraordinary executive powers by Charles de Gaulle, Pflimlin's designated political successor. It is certain that Celan took part in this demonstration. (See also the next poem, "Oben, geräuschlos" / "Above, noiseless.") Nelly Sachs received an earlier version around May 30, 1958, with the words: "All the unanswerable questions in these dark days. This ghostly, mute not-yet, this even more ghostly and mute no-longer and once-again, and in-between the unforeseeable, even tomorrow, even today" (PC/NS, letter #10, p. 10).

T Ein Auge, offen / One Eye, Open: Consider this sentence from Jean Cayrol's text for Alain Resnais's Auschwitz film *Night and Fog*: "La guerre s'est assoupie, un œil toujours ouvert" (War fell asleep, one eye always open), the second half of which Celan leaves out in his translation: "Der Krieg schlummert nur" / "War only slumbers" (GW IV, pp. 96–97).

2 Das nicht mehr zu Nennende, heiß / The no longer to be named, hot: In the first draft, this line was followed by: "das vor kurzem Erlernte: / Sprengköpfe, Strontium-/ spiegel / what was learned recently: / warheads, strontium- / mirror" (TCA/SG, p. 72). These were fragments from current discussions about arming the Bundeswehr (West German army) with tactical nuclear weapons. Cf. also "Engführung" / "Stretto."

4 Niemandes Stimme, wieder / No one's voice, again: See verse 51f. of "Stimmen" / "Voices."

9f. Die Träne, halb, / die schärfere Linse / The tear, half, / the sharper lens: See verses 15–19 of "Pau, später" / "Pau, later" (*Breathturn into Timestead*, pp. 126–27).

"Oben, geräuschlos" / "Above, noiseless"

May 19–June 30, 1958. Following the putsch by the army on May 13, 1958, in Algiers and the ensuing disturbances in France (where a state of emergency was declared on May 17), De Gaulle held a press conference on May 19 in a Paris heavily patrolled by the CRS (the general reserve of the French National Police), in which he offered himself as savior for the country, on the condition of being given extraordinary powers (see also the previous poem).

1f. Oben, geräuschlos, die / Fahrenden: Geier und Stern, / Above, noiseless, the / travelers: vulture and star 28–31 Oben, die / Fahrenden / bleiben / unhörbar / Above, the / travelers / remain / inaudible: See verse 3f. of "Inselhin" / "Islandward" and the references in verses 20–22 of "Frihed." We do not know if Celan knew that the French bomber called Vautour (Vulture) had been used in training flights in Israel since the spring of 1958.

4 zehn an der Zahl, das Sandvolk, / tallying ten, the sandpeople, 26 bis zehn / to ten: See verse 7 of "Marianne."

"Die Welt" / "The world"

June 10, 1958. On that day the German paper *Frankfurter Allgemeine Zeitung* (FAZ) reported on De Gaulle's intention to reinforce the executive powers of the president in the new constitution in imitation of the U.S. constitution and to ensure France's independence by making it a nuclear power. The poem shows Celan's use of Lothar Geitler's book *Morphologie der Pflanzen.*

T Die Welt / The world: See also the later poem with the same title (*Breathturn into Timestead*, pp. 452–53).

6 Knoten / nodes: Reading traces and marginal marks in Geitler show that *Knoten* here are "nodes" in plants, i.e., the place on a plant stem where a leaf is attached.

7 Düsenspur / contrail: In a letter to Heinz Schöffler, Celan, refusing the evaluation of his vocabulary as romantic, points specifically to this word (June 24, 1965, Badiou's reference). A photo with caption appeared in the FAZ on June 10, 1958, in connection with noise-reducing measures for British Vulcan jet planes.

9 Hochblatt / spathe: In botany, a spathe is "a large sheathing bract enclosing the flower cluster of certain plants, especially the spadix of arums and palms" ("Spathe," Lexico, https://www.lexico.com/definition/spathe).

Esther Cameron's reading of this poem is useful here:

> Like many of Celan's poems, this one seems based on a sensory impression, yet the impression is conveyed in such a way that we have difficulty making out exactly what he saw. The one leaf outlined against the jet-trail (or perhaps perceived in the jet-trail, like a shape in a cloud?) is not easy to account for. But it is clear from the first two lines that this picture, whatever it was, seemed to the poet to summarize our whole existence. What we get is something halfway between the scene as it might ordinarily be described, and the inner meaning it has revealed to him. In this picture, freedom seems to be associated with a total and unnatural detachment. Yet this detachment is also a solidarity, for in the last two lines the image of the 'free-standing' leaf is metamorphosed into the statement 'We [. . .] stand by the banners.' In passing, we may note that this metamorphosis goes by way of the *word*—"free"—by which the image of the leaf has already been described. Suppose, on seeing the leaf, he had translated his impression with the word *abgelöst* (detached)? But of course the word-choice was dictated by a wish to arrive at the final statement, by a wish for solidarity that causes him to see things in the light of its hone (Cameron, p. 33).

"Ein Holzstern" / "A woodstar"

August 30–31, 1958. This is the poem with the latest composition date in the volume.

Celan's dedication of a copy of this volume to his son refers to this poem: "A Eric, dont j'ai mis les / étoiles dans la nuit, / avec mon cœur qui l'en remercie / To Eric, whose stars I put in the night, / with my heart which thanks him for it" (PC/GCL, letter # 108). See also verse 14ff of "Engführung" / "Stretto."

5 Salz aus der Nacht fällst / salt, fell from the night: See the reading trace "Ausfällung" / "precipitation" (TCA/SG, p. 119) in Roland Brinkmann, *Abriß der Geologie*: "Angesichts der Beständigkeit übersättigter Kalklösungen findet auf offener See keine Ausfällung statt" (Given the constancy of oversaturated lime solutions, no precipitation happens on the open sea) (p. 71), and in Lotze: "Erwärmung des Wassers, Verdunstung, auch starke Durchbewegung und Kohlensäureentzug durch Organismen kann zur Verminderung der Kohlensäurekonzentration und damit zur Ausfällung von CaCO3 führen" (Warming of the water, evaporation, also strong movement and carbon dioxide extraction by organisms can lead to the diminution of carbon dioxide concentration and thus to the precipitation of CaCO3) (p. 32 and the corresponding reading note; TCA/SG, p. 110). See also the note from the drafts of the Meridian speech: "Der Akt des Ausfällens von Sprache aus der Sprache ist ein Akt der Willkür; an der einmaligen Richtung dieser Willkür—sie ist an der unmerklichen, aber folgestrengen Abweichung von den morphologischen, syntaktischen, semantischen Kategorien zu erkennen—;" (The action of the precipitation of language from language is an arbitrary action—it can be recognized by the unnoticeable, but consequent deviation from the morphological, syntactic and semantic categories—;) (TCA/MFV, p. 107).

6 wieder die Windgalle sucht / again seeks the rainbow's lightfoot: Grimm cites Adelung's definition of *Windgalle*: "heller schein am himmel der sonne gegenüber, ein anzeichen von sturmwind" / "bright light in the sky opposite the sun, a sign of storm-wind." Adelung's definition also says: "[*Windgalle*] often described as in the shape of the foot of a rainbow, as the latter is also a sign for a coming storm." The English "windgall" refers to "a small painless swelling just above the fetlock of a horse, caused by inflammation of the tendon sheath," which I do not think Celan means here.

"Sommerbericht" / "Summer Report"
August 18, 1958.

4 Glockenheide / cross-leaved heath: *Erica tetralix*: found in bogs, wetlands, and heaths (thus its name), this evergreen plant with red flowers is native to Western Europe.

5 Windbruch / windbreak: See the reading traces in Adalbert Stifter's *Der Waldgänger*: "Nachforschung über gerissene Stämme, Windbrüche, eingestürzte Stellen" (Research concerning torn trunks, windbreaks, collapsed places) (also marginal marks, p. 417), as well as the reading note from circa 1957: "als endlich der Wald zum fahlen Windbruch verdorben war" (when the forest had finally rotted down to a pallid windbreak) (Adalbert Stifter, *Bunte Steine, Erzählungen* [Gesammelte Werke in sieben Bänden, Bd. 3], Hg. v. Max Stefl. Leipzig 1942.LPC).

"Niedrigwasser" / "Lowwater"
Paris, August 26, 1958. The poem is based to a good extent on information gathered from Roland Brinkmann's book *Abriß der Geologie*, which Celan had bought on August 22, 1958. See also Celan's reading notes in TCA/SG, p. 121.

5 Niemand schnitt uns das Wort von der Herzwand / No one cut the word from our heart wall: See Jer. 4:4: "Circumcise yourselves to the LORD, and take away the foreskins of your heart, ye men of Judah and inhabitants of Jerusalem: lest my fury come forth like fire, and burn that none can quench it, because of the evil of your doings," and verses 14–16 of "Blume" / "Flower."

"Bahndämme, Wegränder, Ödplätze, Schutt" /
"Embankments, Roadsides, Vacant Lots, Rubble"
August 4–5, 1958, Paris. On August 4, 1958, Celan translated Osip Mandelstam's "Der Sterne Einerlei" (GW V, p. 71) and "Die Städte, die da blühn" (GW V, p. 85; the latter ended with the word "Schutt" / "Rubble." Fragments of the poem come down to us connected to "Stimmen VI" / "Voices VI" and "Schneebett" / "Snowbed," as well as to "Sommerbericht" / "Summer Report."

T Bahndämme, Wegränder, Ödplätze, Schutt / Embankments, Roadsides, Vacant Lots, Rubble: See the description in Alois Kosch's book *Was blüht denn da?* in the sequence "Wegränder, Ödplätze, Schutt, Bahndämme" of the *Nick-*

ende Distel (musk thistle) (*Carduus nutans*, p. 118), as well as Celan's notes to his Meridian speech "Hinweis auf ›Bahndämme, Wegränder, Ödplätze etc. = / Secret routes = Franzos = Roadsides, Vacant Lots, Rubble etc.! / das später im Woyzeck Gelesene = : (Krolow als Zeuge: Rochefort: Bahndamm— / Reference to 'Embankments, Roadsides, Vacant Lots etc.' ! read later in Woyzeck = : (Krolow as witness: Rochefort: Embankment—" (TCA/MFV, p. 182), "Das Substantivische / . (Benveniste) / Schutt, Ödplätze = Büchner Danton / . / Partizip, infinite Zeitform" / "The substantive (Benveniste) Rubble, Vacant Lots = Büchner Danton / . / The participle, infinite time-form" (TCA/MFV, p. 198), and "als Regieangabe: Ödplätze—Schutt etc. / . / nur als Sprache möglich / as stage direction: vacant lots rubble etc.—possible only as language" (TCA/MFV, p. 107).

2–4 Distelähnlichems: / einiges / Rot / thistle-likeness: / some / red: See the reddishly blooming motherwort, in German *Herzgespann* (*Leonurus cardiaca*), a labiate plant with sharp, pricking bits on the bloom; the plant also appears (in an untranslatable punning form) in the poem "Traveling," written in Vienna just before Celan left for Paris. According to his botany book (Kosch, p. 120), the plant is found "on waysides, rubble, hedges."

6f. Die Luftschleier vor / deinem verzweifelten Aug / The airveils before / your despairing eye: See, in *Gespräch im Gebirg* / *Conversation in the Mountains*: "Genauer: sie [die Juden] haben, auch sie, Augen, aber da hängt ein Schleier davor, nicht davor, nein, dahinter, ein beweglicher Schleier; kaum tritt ein Bild ein, so bleibts hängen im Geweb" / "Or, more exactly: they have, even they have eyes, but with a veil hanging in front of them, no, not in front, behind them, a moveable veil; no sooner does an image enter than it gets caught in the web" (GW III, p. 170; English translation, Rosmarie Waldrop, PCCP, p. 18).

11 Augärten, damals / Augarten, back then: Celan knew the Augarten—a large public park situated in Leopoldstadt, the second district at the eastern edge of Vienna's Praterinsel—from his stay in that city in 1948; in the summer of 1957 he returned for the first time to Vienna.

13f. vom Marchfeld, vom / Steppengras dort / about Marchfeld, the / steppe grass there: This landscape in the eastern part of Vienna, framed by the Danube to the south and the Marchfeld plain spreading to the Slovakian border in the east, was the site of many historical battles; it has a salt steppe (today the nature preserve Sandberg) near the village of Baumgarten. The Marchfeld represents the western edge of distribution for a number of Asiatic plants. See also Celan's notes from his June 1957 stay in Austria, when he visited the Prater with his friend Klaus Demus: "Riesenrad. Klaus: auf dem Marchfeld wächst Steppengras, Paul! / Giant [Ferris] wheel. Klaus: steppe grass grows on the Marchfeld" (TCA/SG, p. 116). See also Celan's marginal marks in his German edition of Leo Shestov's *In Job's Balances*: "Früher war weder an dem Steppengras, noch an dem Beifußkraut irgend etwas Feindseliges, Erschreckendes oder Geheimnisvolles" ("Until now there had been nothing hostile or terrible or mysterious in that tussock or in those dried grasses") (p. 211 in both the German and the English editions).

15 Das tote Ringelspiel / The dead merry-go-round: Austrian for "carousel." A number of such carousels were destroyed in a fire at the Prater on April 8, 1945; only in 1949, after Celan had left Vienna, did new merry-go-rounds start up again.

"Engführung" / "Stretto"

July 21, 1957–November 3, 1958. First fragments together with his draft for a translation of Robert Desnos's "Epitaph" (GW IV, p. 801). The main composition work began on February 17, 1958, right after Celan finished writing the Bremen speech (January 25–26, 1958, GW III, p. 185f.; see CP, pp. 33–36). Celan himself indicated May 3, 1958, as the date of completion, though we lack specific proof concerning this. Maybe it is a mistake and he meant to write May 30, 1958—on that day Celan presented the poem to the participants of a German-French writers' conference in Poigny-la-Forêt, where he also gave an explication of the poem's background, specifically the current debate on arming of the German Bundeswehr with atomic weapons. In a letter to Paul Schallück he called it the "atom-poem," and writing to Walter Höllerer about "Engführung," he says, "You know of course that it is about atomic-death / Atomtod" (PC/SSB, p. 612). He started the poem right after completing the translation of Alexander Blok's poem "The Twelve," (GW V, pp. 11–45). That year he also translated a range of Yesenin's poems and work by other Russian poets. Verses 129 to 140 were written on May 12, 1958; on that day the German newspaper *Die Welt* reported on China's claim to be building atomic weapons.

Celan noted on the proofs: "Stretto is a single poem. The separate parts have to follow each other directly" (TCA/SG, p. 89). He insisted that the poem start, after a separating asterisk, only on the lower half of the page. It thus picks up the asterisks of the "Voices" cycle that opens the volume.

T Engführung / Stretto: "close, narrow, drawn together, (1) the bringing in of overlapping entries of the subject in a fugue 'closer', i.e., after shorter intervals of time, than those at which they originally came (Ger. Engführung). The objects of stretto are to show the contrapuntal possibilities of the subject and to increase the cumulative effect of successive sets, or of a final set, of entries . . . (2) the word is also used of a quickening of tempo towards the end of a piece" (*Collins Encyclopedia of Music* [London: Chancellor Press, 1984], p. 526). On March 21, 1958, Celan wrote to Walter Jens in relation to the two multisectional poems in *Sprachgitter*: "I have truly led the words, the voices, into the narrows / enggeführt / (have let myself be led by them into the narrows / mich von ihnen engführen lassen)—into the inexorability of the last poem (time-wise it wasn't the last, but I knew it was the last one)" (see Seng, p. 283). Celan himself chose *Strette* as the title for the French translation, which was published only after his death (*Strette: Poèmes, suivis du Méridien et d'Entretien dans la montagne*. Translations by André du Bouchet, Jean-Pierre Burgart, Jean Daive, and John E. Jackson [Paris: Mercure de France, 1971]; Badiou's reference). Note that *Stretto*, true to its musical meaning, is the final section of the book *Speechgrille*, the only section provided with a name (the others have Roman numerals as titles).

1 Verbracht / Displaced: Euphemism for "moved away," "deported"; see verse 13 of "Ein Wurfholz" / "A boomerang." The sound of the German word also immediately brings to mind the word *verbrechen*, a crime, or a crime committed.

3 mit der untrüglichen Spur / with the unmistakable track, 161f. taggrau, / der Grundwasserspuren / daygray, / of groundwater tracks, 167f. der untrüglichen / Spur / the unmistakable / track: See—also in relation to the preceding poem, "Bahndämme" / "Embankments"—Celan's translation of Jean Cayrol's text for Alain Resnais's film *Night and Fog*: "Dieselbe Bahnstrecke heute: Taglicht und Sonne. Langsam schreitet man sie ab—auf der Suche

wonach? / Nach einer Spur der Leichen?" / "The same railroad track today: daylight and sun. Slowly one paces it off—searching for what? / for the corpses' track" (GW IV, pp. 79–81; my translation of Celan's German).

5 Halme / stalks, 10 Ein Rad, langsam / A wheel, slowly, 11 Speichen / spokes: See Celan's translation of Yesenin's poem "Keine Halme mehr, kein Blatt" / "No more stalks, no leaf" (GW V, p. 187; my translation of Celan's German).

9 du bist— / bist zuhause / you are— / are at home: See the marginal note "4. 17. 59 / cf. / Engführung!!" to verse 186 of Hölderlin's "The Rhine": "Die Liebenden aber / Sind, was sie waren, sie sind / Zu Hause, wo die Blume sich freuet" / "But lovers remain / As before, at home / Wherever flowers exult" (Sieburth, *Hymns and Fragments*, p. 78).

10 Ein Rad, langsam / a wheel, slowly: See verses 4 and 13 of "Das Gastmahl" / "The Banquet."

10–13 Ein Rad, langsam, / rollt aus sich selber, die Speichen / klettern, / klettern auf schwärzlichem Feld / A wheel, slowly, / rolls out of itself, the spokes / climb, / climb on a blackish field: See verse 20f. of "À la pointe acérée."

34 ich tickte euch zu / I ticked toward you: According to Dietlind Meinecke, referring to a conversation in July 1965, Celan wanted "it to be understood that bombs were ticking in this poem, that something of that order is announcing itself" (*Wort und Name bei Paul Celan* [Bad Homburg, 1970], S. 177).

43 Nahtstellen / seams: See the prose fragments, probably from 1957, #133: "Life's seams: the finger, always the same one, feels its way toward them, cannot find them," and #134: "And yet, it seems to me, when thought, poorly enough, puzzles over the seams, that a certain straight line cannot be excluded" (*Microliths*, p. 71).

61–63 Orkane. / Orkane, von je, / Partikelgestöber / Hurricanes. / Hurricanes, from whenever, 95f. Orkane, Par- / tikelgestöber / Hurricanes, par- / ticle flurries: Wiedemann refers to Dante's *Inferno*, where in Canto V, stanza 73, Dante tells Virgil, "Poeta, volentieri / parlerei a que' duo, che insieme vanno, / e paion sì al vento essor leggieri." That "vento," "wind"/"air" in most English translations, is given in the German translation as "Orkan" (hurricane). Note: Celan associated Dante's characters Paolo and Francesca with himself (Paul) and his wife (Gisèle Lestrange, who was French, *française*). See also Jean Paul Richter's "Rede des toten Christus vom Weltgebäude herab," in *Siebenkäs*: "Zufall, weißt, du selber, wenn du mit Orkanen durch das Sternen-Schneegestöber schreitest . . ." (Chance, you know it yourself, when with hurricanes you step through star-snow flurries . . .) (my translation). To Heinz Schöffler Celan wrote on June 24, 1965: "in 'Stretto' I have tried (cf. 'particle flurries') to speak of atoms and of atomic bombs—to speak of that too, and not only implicitly."

65–67 wir / lasens im Buche, war / Meinung / we / read it in the book, it was / opinion: On August 10, 1962, Celan wrote to Erich Einhorn: "In my latest book of poems ('Speechgrille') you'll find the poem 'Stretto,' which evokes the ravages of the atomic bomb. Centrally, fragmentarily, stands this word by Democritus: 'Nothing exists except atoms and empty space, everything else is opinion.' I don't have to emphasize that the poem is written for the sake of this opinion—of the humans, and thus against all emptiness and atomization" (PC/EE, p. 7).

118f. ein Tausendkristall, / schoß an / a thousandcrystal formed: In its intransitive use, the word *anschießen* is a synonym for "crystallize." Ernst Robert Curtius uses "anschießen" (between quotation marks) translated as "forms": "Forms are configurations and systems of configurations in which the incorporeal things of the mind can manifest themselves and become apprehensible. Dante orders the blessed in circles of light and crosses of light. A crystal consists in a space lattice of electrons and molecules. Mathematics and optics employ the concept of the lattice (Concept? metaphor? Does natural science use metaphors?). Literary forms perform the function of such lattices. As diffused light is concentrated in the lens, as crystals form [*anschiessen*], so the matter of poetry is crystallized into a configurational schema. (*European Literature and the Latin Middle Ages*, translated by Willard R. Trask [Princeton University Press, 1952], p. 390).

122 entmischt / separated out: In Celan's library Friedrich Ueberwegs's *Philosophie des Altertums* (vol. 1, Hg. v. Karl Praechter, Berlin 1926; cited in BPPC, section A, entry 186, footnote 68), has a mark and underlining at the following paragraph: "Anaxagoras [. . .] like Empedokles, leads all coming-to-be and passing-away back to mixing [*Mischung*] and separating out [*Ent-*

mischung], but as final mixing elements claims an *unlimited multiplicity of qualitatively determined* but different from each other ur-materials, that he calls *the seeds of things* [. . .]."

140 Verwerfung / fault lines: Esther Cameron remembers a conversation of August 4, 1969: "Then we talked about the poems from Speechgrille. He said what interested him were the language 'fault lines' / sprachlichen 'Verwerfungen' /—he identified this as a term from geology" (Cameron, p. 338). In English this geological term gives a range of words with the particle "fault": fault-line, -scarp, -plane, -spring, -zone, etc. On October 10, 1960, Celan used the term in a draft for the Meridian speech: "Thickness: to be understood from the geological, and thus from the slow catastrophes and the dreadful fault lines / Verwerfungen / of language—" (MFV, #186).

141–143 überm / Kugelfang an / der verschütteten Mauer / above the / bullet trap on / the ruined wall: See the translation of Cayrol's text for *Night and Fog*: "Der den Blicken verborgene, für Erschießungen eingerichtete Hof von Block elf; die Mauer mit Kugelfang" / "the court of Block eleven, hidden to the eyes, set up for executions by shooting; the wall with bullet trap" (GW IV, p. 87).

144–149 sichtbar, aufs / neue: die / Rillen, die // Chöre, damals, die / Psalmen. Ho, ho- / sianna / visible, a- / gain: the / furrows, the / choirs, back then, the / psalms. Ho, ho- / sanna: See "In die Rillen" / "Into the furrows" (*Breathturn into Timestead*, pp. 2–5) for the only other occurrence of the word "Rillen" / "furrows." See, in his translation of Cayrol's text: "Man schließt die Türen./ Man beobachtet./ Das einzige Zeichen — aber das muß man ja wissen — ist die von Fingernägel gepflügte Decke. Beton läßt such erweichen. / They close the doors. / They watch. / The only sign—but one has to know that—is the roof ploughed by fingernails. Concrete lets itself be moved" (GW IV, p. 95; my translation). On July 18, 1960, Celan wrote approvingly, "die Rillen, die Psalmen" / "the furrows, the psalms," next to the following sentence, in Scholem's *Major Trends of Jewish Mysticism*: "Employing every device of that mystical precision with which the Kabbalists read the Bible, he infused extraordinary apocalyptical meanings into the words of the Psalms, and held up the Psalter as a textbook of the millennium and the Messianic catastrophe" (p. 248 of the English edition, Schocken, 1995).

DIE NIEMANDSROSE / NOONESROSE

The fifty-three poems that make up this volume—organized into four not completely chronologically arranged cycles—were composed between March 5, 1959, and the beginning of 1963. Paul Celan had considered the book to be finished in the main as early as May 1962, and publication for later that year had been foreseen. Then, on September 22, 1962, Celan, himself surprised by the emergence of the first longer poems that would make up the fourth cycle, told Klaus Wagenbach: "Furthermore, the *NoOnesRose* shows a tendency to want to enlarge itself somewhat."

The years of composition were marked by the reemergence of an aggressive strain of anti-Semitism in Germany. See this little poem, not retained by Celan for the volume at hand, dated Paris, November 27, 1959: "Much human unland this year. / Things written / by my own hand, return, a boomerang, / from afar: Put me now, it says, / into your poison-cabinet.—But I don't have one. You, you too, have to enter / my heart. / O Abram, Abram." Extremely deleterious for Celan's life will be the public phase of the Goll affair: in early April 1960 Claire Goll for the first time publishes a text in the Munich magazine *Baubudenpoet*, in which she accuses Celan of having plagiarized her dead husband Ivan Goll's work, further claiming that the murder of Celan's parents is a "legend," while simultaneously using the cliché of the avaricious uncreative Jew (GA, #59). These accusations are indeed total lies: resemblances between poems by Celan and some posthumous late poems by Yvan Goll were created by fraudulent tampering by Claire Goll, who knew Celan's volume *SU*. The West German press picked up these accusations and spread them further without fact-checking. Because of the doubts thrown on the authenticity of his poems, poems he knew to be anchored in his life, Celan felt himself existentially questioned and threatened. The years of composition are therefore marked by major psychic crises. While Celan never publicly spoke out about the Goll affair (see, however, the very detailed unsent letter to Alfred Andersch in *Microliths*, pp. 150–159), indirect references can be seen both in the major prose-essay of those years, the Meridian essay, written as an acceptance speech for the Büchner Prize (the major German literary award), which he was awarded in 1960, and in a range of these poems that also integrate some of the thinking of the *Meridian* speech. As Celan put it in a letter to Ingeborg Bachmann on September 21, 1963: "I have a new volume of poems coming out in the next few weeks—a variety of things have been woven into it, and in some of them I have taken a rather 'inartistic' path, as was essentially bound to happen. The document of a crisis, if you like—but what would poetry be if it were not that too, and radically so?" (PC/IB, English edition, #195, p. 249).

T *Die Niemandsrose / NoOnesRose*: See verse 12f. of "Psalm," and Rilke's epigraph, also used by Celan in drafts of the "Walliser Elegie" (not reproduced here) in 1962: "Rose, oh reiner Widerspruch, Lust, / Niemandes Schlaf zu sein unter soviel / Lidern" ("Rose, oh pure contradiction, desire / to be no one's sleep under so many / lids") (Bd. 2, S. 185; my translation). To his son Eric, Celan called the book *La Rose de Personne* or *La Rose Nulle*, as French title variations (April 12, 1966; PC/GCL, letter # 406); on a sheet added to a notebook of reading notes of April 1966, stands: "LA ROSE NULLE" / "THE NULL [THE NOTHING] ROSE."

Osip Mandelstam, the Russian poet of Jewish descent to whom this volume is dedicated, was born in Warsaw in 1891. He did not die, as Celan had assumed until he learned differently in 1961, in a German concentration camp, but in one of Stalin's transit camps near Vladivostok in 1938. In 1959 S. Fischer Verlag published a selection of Mandelstam's poems in Celan's translation, and in 1961 a further poem in translation was published in the same publisher's *Almanach* magazine. The publication of six poems from *NoOnesRose* in the first 1963 issue of *Neue Rundschau* magazine is also preceded by two Mandelstam poems in translation, and is dedicated to Osip Mandelstam. Celan not only thinks of him as the greatest Russian poet, but considers Mandelstam his brother (see "Brother Osip," a poem fragment, published in the notes to GN, p. 371):

Brother Osip
Pain plays with words
he plays at giving it names
he searches for the Noone's Places,

and there, there you wait.
You are the Russianjew,
the Jewrussian, and

See also various poems with Mandelstamian resonances throughout the work and the radio play "The Poetry of Osip Mandelstam" in *The Meridian*, p. 215.

I

"Es war Erde in ihnen" / "There was earth inside them"
July 27, 1959, Paris.

4 Und sie lobten nicht Gott / And they did not praise God: Felstiner suggests that "These diggers who 'did not praise God' stem from a Psalm: 'The dead praise not the Lord. Neither they that go down into silence'" (in *Paul Celan: Poet, Survivor, Jew*. New Haven: Yale UP, 1995, p. 151).

11f. es kam auch ein Sturm, / es kamen die Meere alle / a storm too came, / all the seas came: Reference to the Flood; see also verse 23f. of "Late and Deep."

14 und das Singende dort sagt: Sie graben / what sings over there says: they dig: A reference to the juxtaposition-confrontation of making music and digging in the "Deathfugue."

15 niemand / no one: See the reference to verse 4 of "Psalm."

16 Wohin gings, da's nirgendhin ging? / Where did it lead, as it led nowhere?: See verse 5 of "What Happened?"

"Das Wort vom Zur-Tiefe-Gehn" / "The word about going-into-the-depth"
On the evening of March 5, 1959. The poem is a birthday present for Gisèle Celan-Lestrange with the dedication "For your birthday, my love, for the nineteenth of March, today, march 5th" (see PC/GCL, letter #106). The draft title, "La leçon d'allemand" (TA/NR, p. 11) and its first line of March 27, 1959, refers to a shared reading of a poem by Georg Heym. See the first stanza of Heym's poem: "Deine Wimpern, die langen, / Deiner Augen dunkele Wasser, / Laß mich tauchen darein, / Laß mich zur Tiefe gehn" / "Your eyelids, so long, / Your eyes' dark waters, / Let me dive therein, / Let

me go into the depth" (p. 133). There is a copy of Heym's verses by Gisèle Celan-Lestrange with a translation, possibly by Paul Celan, of December 25, 1965, in PC/GCL, letter #106 and commentary in vol. 2.

See also verse 11ff. of his translation of Mandelstam's poem "Die Freiheit, die da dämmert" / "The freedom that dawns there": "Wer, Zeit, ein Herz hat, hört damit, versteht: / er hört dein Schiff, Zeit, das zur Tiefe geht" / "He who, Time, has a heart, hears with it, understands: / he hears your ship, Time, that goes into the depth" (February 18, 1959, GWV, p. 103; my English translation of Celan's German translation).

4 Wir sind es noch immer / It is still and always us: In the first edition copy dedicated to GCL, this verse is repeated/handwritten below the poem (see PC/GCL, p. 176); it was often used in the sense of conjuring togetherness (see PC/GCL, pp. 215, 218). See also the final verse of "Schaufäden, Sinnfäden" / "Sight Threads, Sense Threads": "Wir sind es noch immer"—which I translated there as "It is still us" (*Breathturn into Timestead*, pp. 86–87), as well as verses 38f. and 42 of "Engführung" / "Stretto" and verse 1 of "Du sei wie du" / "You be like you" (*Breathturn into Timestead*, pp. 314–15).

8 vertieft uns die Tiefe / deepens the depth for us: See the triply underlined note "vertiefen!" / "deepen!" in the context of drafts for the poem "Bretonischer Strand" / "Breton Beach."

"Bei Wein und Verlorenheit" / "With wine and lostness"

March 15, 1959. A review of *Speechgrille* by Oliver Storz had appeared the day before in the *Stuttgarter Zeitung* under the title "Die schimmernden Gitter der Sprache Paul Celans" (The shimmering lattice of Paul Celan's language). In it, Celan is called, among other things, "Master of the trendy technique of the associative concatenation of dream images"; quotations from "Tenebrae" and "Stretto" are disfigured because of omissions and stanza break mistakes.

T Bei Wein und Verlorenheit / With wine and lostness: See also the poem "Bei Glüh-und Mühwein" / "Over mulled and toiled wine" (*Breathturn into Timestead*, pp. 172–73).

1 Verlorenheit / lostness, 10–12 sie / logen unser Gewieher / um / they / lied our neighs / into: On March 12, 1959, Celan wrote to Ingeborg Bachmann: "I have little to report. I experience a few slights every day, plentifully

served, on every street corner. The last 'friend' to honor me (and Gisèle) with his mendacity was René Char. And why not? I translated him, after all (alas!), and so his gratitude, which I had been able to experience in the past, albeit in smaller doses, could not fail to be expressed. / Lies and baseness, almost everywhere. / We are alone and helpless" (PC/IB, English edition, #123, p. 162).

"Zürich, Zum Storchen" / *"Zürich, Hotel Zum Storchen"*
May 30, 1960, Paris.

T Zürich, Hotel Zum Storchen, Dedication, *For Nelly Sachs*, 9 On the day of an ascension: The poem refers to Celan's first encounter, on May 26, 1960, Ascension Day, at that hotel in Zurich, with the German-Jewish poet Nelly Sachs, who lived in Sweden. A dated and signed manuscript copy is kept in Sachs's literary estate (PC/NS, pp. 41–43).

1f. Vom Zuviel war die Rede, / vom / Zuwenig / Our talk turned on the Too Much, on the / Too Little: See Felstiner's suggestion that "Celan's opening sentence gives a nod to Margarete Susman, who lived in Zurich and whose 1946 book *Job and the Fate of the Jewish People* says that vis-à-vis the catastrophe, 'every word is a Too Little and a Too Much'" (PSJ, p. 158).

9f. das / Münster stand drüben / the / Minster stood over there: From the hotel one sees the Großmünster on the other shore of the Limmat.

10f. es kam / mit einigem Gold übers Wasser / it came / with some gold across the water: A reference to the Book of Job: "Von Mitternacht kommt Gold, um Gott her ist schrecklicher Glanz" (Job 37:22). The King James Version has this as: "Fair weather cometh out of the north: with God is terrible majesty," missing the "gold," though other English versions have it as "golden splendor." See also verse 10 of "Nah, im Aortenbogen" / "Near, in the aortic arch," which reads: "Ziv, that light" in *Breathturn into Timestead* (pp. 200–201). I comment (p. 535) on the mystical meaning of "Ziv" and quote the following letters to Sachs:

> It would seem that Celan himself had a mystical light experience in the company of Nelly Sachs, first in Zurich and then in Paris. The following letters make reference to and would seem to corroborate this experience (PC/NS, #105 and #108):

December 8, 1967

My dear Nelly,

it was so good to hold your letter in my hands and to be reminded by you yourself of that light that shone over the water in Zurich and then in Paris. Once, in a poem, a name for it even came to me through hebrew.

And with my warmest congratulations upon your birthday!

Your Paul

Paris, March 22, 1968

My dear Nelly,

thank you for your lines, for the reminder of that light.

Yes, that light. You will find it named in my next book of poetry, which is to appear in autumn—called by a Hebrew name.

Warmest!

Paul.

22–27 Wir / wissen ja nicht, weißt du, / wir / wissen ja nicht, / was / gilt / We / just don't know, you know, / we / just don't know, / what / counts: See Celan's note in his agenda (May 26, 1960): "Hotel Zum Storchen / 4 pm Nelly Sachs, alone. 'I am a believer.'" Celan wrote to Hermann Kasack on May 30, 1960: "May I tell you what she said to me a few days ago—we were speaking about her faith—when I told her about my hope to be able to blaspheme and quarrel to the end? Nelly Sachs nodded and commented: 'Wir wissen ja nicht was gilt [We just don't know what counts] . . .'" (PC/NS, p. 41). In her Meersburger prize acceptance speech, Sachs said explicitly: "Everything counts. Everything is ferment, that works. And we—smoking from error—try, well or badly—we try again and again" (Nelly Sachs, *Werke, kommentierte Ausgabe in vier Bänden*, hg. v. Aris Fioretos, Matthias Weichelt, and Ariane Huml, vol. 4, 2010, p. 80).

"Selbdritt, selbviert" / "Threesome, Foursome"

June 11, 1960, Paris. The poem was written between Celan's meeting with Sachs in Zurich (he was accompanied by his wife, Gisèle, and their son Eric), and Sachs's visit to Paris.

T Selbdritt / Threesome: The note in his diary recording his arrival in

Zurich with Gisèle and Eric reads: "7 p.m. Zurich (Selbstdritt [Threesome])." The only other use of the term is in verse 14 of "Count the almonds."

1 Krauseminze, Minze, krause / Curly mint, mint, curly: For the two-line stanza form and nature theme, see the commentary to "Espenbaum" / "Aspen tree." The plant appears as "Blut-Krause-Minze" / "blood-curly-mint" in Nelly Sachs's poem "The Hour at Endor": "Aus der Fruchtschale der Welt / griffst du die Tollkirsche, / die alle Himmel falsch anfärbt / Blut-Krause-Minze sät. / From the world's fruitbowl / you pick the nightshade berry / that stains all skies as fake / and sows blood-curly-mint" (Nelly Sachs, *Und niemand weiss weiter.* Ellermann; Auflage: 2 (1957), v. 59–62, p. 71; my translation).

8 mit den nahen Untergängen / with the nearby devastations: See the poem cycle entitled "Untergänge" / "Devastations," which follows closely in Sachs's volume.

10 halb gebunden, halb im Freien / half-bound, half-free: See the reference in verses 5–7 of "Havdalah" and verses 12f. and 16f. of "I have cut bamboo."

"Soviel Gestirne" / "So many constellations"

June 19, 1960.

6f. galaktisch, / o diese Stunde, / galactic, / O this hour: The whole of this passage makes reference to Jean Paul's novel *Der Komet* (JPL).

6f. galaktisch / o diese Stunde / galactic, / O this hour, 17 zitzenprächtig die Zeit / tit-gorgeous time: PC plays on the etymology of "galaxy," the *Milky* Way.

7 o diese Stunde / O this hour: Most likely an allusion to Nelly Sachs's poem "Die Stunde zu Endor." From June 13 to 17, Sachs had visited the Celans in Paris (JPL).

14 kometenhaft schwirrte ein Aug / comet-like an eye whizzed: Allusion to verses 19–21 of "Aber" / "But."

21–23 ich weiß, / ich weiß und du weißt, wir wußten, / wir wußten nicht / I know, / I know and you know, we knew, / we didn't know: See also the play with conjugations in verses 13f. and 17 of "Es war Erde in ihnen" / "There was earth inside them."

"Dein Hinübersein" / "Your having crossed"

June 20, 1960.

The first poem to show traces of Celan's reading of Gershom Scholem's *On the Kabbalah and Its Symbolism.*

T A provisional title had been "Shekinah."

1f. Dein Hinübersein / Your having crossed: The origin of the poem, according to GCL, was her fainting caused by circulatory problems.

6 Es klettert die Bohne / The bean climbs: See "Wir warden" / "We become," an uncollected poem published posthumously:

We will
live: you,
my son, and you,
beloved, you
his mother, and with you two
I—in this
your
hospitable country:
in France. With
its people, with
all people.

The bean climbs, the
white one and the
light red one—but
think also on the
workers' flag in Vienna—
in front of our house
in Moisville.

According to GCL Celan sowed beans on the windowsill to observe the growth stages of plants with his son.

10f. Gott, das lasen wir, ist / ein Teil und ein zweiter, zerstreuter / God, we read it, is / a part and a second one, scattered: See the kabbalistic-Hasidic conception of the Shechinah (thus the poem's provisional title) as the designation for the aspects of God poured out into the world, and the reading traces in Scholem's *On the Kabbalah and Its Symbolism*: "However, this conception of the 'ambivalence,' the alternating phases of the Shekhinah, is related to that of its exile (galuth). The exile of the Shekhinah goes back to the Talmud. 'In every exile into which the children of Israel went, the Shekhinah was with them.' In the Talmud this means only that God's presence was always with Israel in its exiles. In the Kabbalah, however, it is taken to mean that a part of God Himself is exiled from God" (p. 107 of English edition; with marginal marks by Celan in his edition).

"Zu beiden Händen" / "To both hands"
July 1, 1960.

See Celan's letter to Nelly Sachs of that same day: "A book, *Die Judenbuche* [*The Jew's Beech*, a novella by Annette von Droste-Hülshoff], is on its way to you; it was suddenly there a few days ago at the booksellers; I had picked it up while searching for something different—something that, once again as always, remains the same—the Flechtheims who had it published are presumably Jews" (PC/Sachs 45, p. 29).

14f. O diese wandernde leere / gastliche Mitte / O this wandering empty / hospitable Middle: The numeric middle of the poem lies between those two verses. See the uncollected poem "Die leere Mitte" / "The Empty Middle," written on April 17–18, 1966, in a psychiatric hospital in Paris (thus written a week after Passover, a feast where unleavened bread is used; the "red" could be a reference to the biblical use of the lamb's blood to mark the door of every Jewish home in Egypt):

> The Empty Middle that we helped sing,
> as it stood upward, bright,
>
> as it let the breads pass, leavened and unleavened,
>
> darkened around by the red, by otherness,
> from questions, following you,
>
> a long time already.

20f. Das / Selbe / The / same: See the letter to Sachs and a marginal mark in Heidegger's *What Is Called Thinking?* in connection with Parmenides:

"The variation of Parmenides' statement runs: / 'The conditions of the *possibility of experience* in general are at the same time conditions of the *possibility of the objects of experience*' (*Critique of Pure Reason* A 158, B 197). The 'at the same time' is Kant's interpretation of το αύτό, the same" (p. 243 of the English edition).

"Zwölf Jahre" / "Twelve Years"

July 14, 1960, Kermorvan, Trébabu. Celan spent most of July in the family's little property named Kermorvan in Trébabu near Le Conquet in Brittany.

T Zwölf Jahre / Twelve Years, 3–5 . . . *dein / Haus in Paris — zur / Opferstatt deiner Hände. / your / house in Paris — into the / sacrificial altar of your hands*: On July 14, 1948, exactly twelve years earlier, Celan had arrived in Paris coming from Vienna; the "Third Reich" also lasted twelve years. The first title draft ("Traveling II") references the title "Traveling," the second verse of which is cited here.

6 durchatmet / breathed-through: While working on the *Meridian* speech, Celan noted: "Zeithöfe, durchatmet, umatmet / Timesteads, breathed through, breathed around" (TAM, #280).

13 Geh. Komm / Go. Come: Compare in Büchner's *Dantons Tod* the figure of Lucile, who foresees Camille's death: "So schnell, mein Freund? Geh! Komm! Nur das sie küßt ihn und das! Geh! Geh! / So fast, my friend? Go! Come! Only that *she kisses him* and that! Go! Go!" (Georg Büchner, *Werke und Briefe*, Münchner Ausgabe, Carl Hanser Verlag, 1988, p. 97; my translation).

"Mit allen Gedanken" / "With all my thoughts"

August 14, 1960. In the copy of the first edition dedicated to GCL, Celan on April 26, 1965, copied the poem once more below the printed text, with the following dedication: "For you, mon Amour, this poem, once more, it will, this one too, help us resist" (PC/GCL, letter # 176). In connection with an unauthorized use of the second stanza, Celan calls the poem specifically a love poem (to Jean Starobinski, PC/GCL, commentary on letter #219 in vol. 2).

3 du meine Leise, du meine Offne / you my quiet, you my Open one: See verse 12f. of "Die hellen Steine" / "The bright stones."

17–19 wars nicht Gestalt und von uns her, / wars nicht / so gut wie ein Name? / wasn't it a shape we projected before us, / wasn't it / as good as a name?: Possible reading traces from a book bought in 1954, Helmuth v. Glasenapp's *Philosophie der Inder*: "The appropriate formula for the distinction between the visible and the invisible . . . can be found in the expressions *Rûpa* (shape) and *Nâma* (name); under 'name' one understood originally the naming of the individual as inseparable [from the name] according to old magic beliefs, and later more generally what of the individual was not perceptible through the senses" (partly with double marginal marks, p. 33 of the German edition).

"Die Schleuse" / "The Sluice"

September 13, 1960 (Paris)–May 20, 1961 (the evening before the harvest festival Shavuot). Celan had returned home a few days before September 13, 1960, from a difficult visit to a very ill Nelly Sachs in Stockholm. The original title, "Stockholm, Linnégatan tolv" (TCA/NR, p. 28) wrongly indicates Celan's address in Stockholm: he didn't live in number 12 [tolv] but in number 2, "två" in Swedish.

T Die Schleuse / The Sluice, 15f. Durch / die Schleuse mußt ich, / Through / the sluice I had to go, 17 Salzflut / saltflood: A sluice separates the inland waterways and the Baltic Sea in Stockholm.

8–10 verlor ich ein Wort, / das mir verblieben war: / Schwester / I lost a word / that had remained with me: / sister: See verse 5 of "Chymisch" / "Alchemical."

12 Vielgötterei / the many gods: See the second commandment: "Thou shalt have no other gods before me" (Exod. 20:2).

14 Kaddisch / Kaddish: Aramaic for "holy." The Kaddish (Aramaic: קדישׁ, qaddiš, "holy") is a hymn of praises to God found in Jewish prayer services. The central theme of the Kaddish is the magnification and sanctification of God's name. It is the prayer traditionally recited in memory of the dead, although it makes no mention of death. It is included in all three daily prayer services. The term "Kaddish" is often used to refer specifically to "The Mourner's Kaddish," said as part of the mourning rituals in Judaism in all prayer services, as well as at funerals (other than at the gravesite) and memorials, and for eleven months after the death of a close relative. When mention is made of "saying Kaddish," this unambiguously refers to the rituals of

mourning. Mourners say Kaddish to show that despite the loss they still praise God.

17 in die Salzflut / the saltflood: See the reading traces in Homer's *Odyssey*, which Celan had in W. Schadewald's German translation; in Robert Fagle's English version: "Telemachus, walking the beach now, far from others, washed his hands in the foaming surf and prayed to Pallas: 'Dear god, hear me! Yesterday you came to my house, you told me to ship out on the misty sea and learn if father, gone so long, is ever coming home.'" Double marginal note and an arrow from "god" to "Athena." The German "Salzflut" is here translated as "foaming surf," in Charles Stein's version as "gray salt water," and by other English translators as "gray sea," "churning waters," "hoary sea," etc. See also verse 2 of "Füll die Ödnis" / "Shovel the void" (*Breathturn into Timestead*, pp. 230–31). See further the reference in verse 6 of "Nah, im Aortenbogen" / "Near, in the aortic arch" (*Breathturn into Timestead*, pp. 200–201), also a poem that references Sachs.

19 *Jiskor / Yizkor*: ("Remembrance") prayers are recited by those that have lost either one or both of their parents. These may additionally say Yizkor for other relatives. Some might also say Yizkor for a deceased close friend. The Yizkor prayers are recited four times a year, on Yom Kippur, Shemini Atzeret, the last day of Passover, and Shavuot. The word already appears with this meaning in Celan's diary of October 25, 1959, in connection with the review by Blöcker (see below), and there too Sachs is named: "The—only—solution: to go to Stockholm, and together with Nelly Sachs write a Yiskor-poem: / We commemorate / our dead in . . . / our graves in, . . . in the air . . . / we know one of the many, / who has desecrated them: / with his words. / 'He plays with the snakes, / he writes . . . ' / We name his name: it is / Günter Blöcker, / he lives / in Berlin. / He is not alone, / he has friends. / Who shakes his hand, / shakes his hand" (Celan's literary estate in Paris).

On October 11, 1959, Günter Blöcker had reviewed *Sprachgitter* in the Berlin newspaper *Der Tagesspiegel*, suggesting that Celan's poems about the Holocaust were "exercises on music paper" and thus not "sinngebend / meaningful," as Celan was functioning "im Leeren / in emptiness," which, Blöcker insinuates, with a classically anti-Semitic trope, may be due to the poet's origins ("an der Herkunft"). In his letter to Max Frisch of October 12, 1959, Celan wrote: "Dear Max Frisch, / Hitlerism, Hitlerism, Hitlerism, The peaked caps. / Please take a look at what Herr Blöcker, the leading figure in the new generation of critics.... and author — alas — of essays on Kafka and Bachmann, has written" (PC/IB, pp. 258–59).

"Stumme Herbstgerüche" / "Mute autumn odors"
Paris, October 5, 1960, on the eve of Succoth.

On the same day Celan noted in the context of his work on the Meridian speech: "The tendency to fall silent cannot not be heard; here no ultrashort can help.— / In the gruffness of the language there manifests itself, it cannot not be heard, the tendency to fall silent" (TCA/MFV, #601). And in the essay itself, the line: "the poem shows, unmistakably, a strong tendency to fall silent" (TCA/MFV, p. 8, section 32a).

2 Sternblume / aster: The German word literally means "star-flower," though the "star" is of course discernible in the name "aster."

3f. zwischen Heimat und Abgrund durch / dein Gedächtnis / between homeland and abyss through / your memory: See verse 3f. of "Radix, Matrix" and its Hölderlin reminiscence. See also the allusions in verse 3f. of "Radix, Matrix," verse 26 of "Hafen" / "Harbor" (*Breathturn into Timestead*, pp. 40–41) re "Heimat" / "homeland," and verse 22 of "Shibboleth."

"Eis, Eden" / "Ice, Eden"
November 8, 1960. The poem shows the first trace of Celan's reading of Ernst Bloch's *The Principle of Hope* (see also "Chymisch" / "Alchemical"). It is the first published poem with meter and rhyme since "Zu zweien" / "By twos" in *Threshold to Threshold.*

T Eis / Ice, 11 auferstehen / resurrect: See Bloch's chapter "Andreae's 'Chemical Wedding of Christian Rosenkreutz Anno 1459'": "So, in alchemy of this kind, this was supposed to be the solemn significance announced above: that of an Easter Day to be fantastically created against ice and barriers." And: "A reveille was intended which was to resound through the whole earthly layer, an 'Awake, frozen Christ,' through lead, creation, society and the remaining Alteritas" and "all this was to be levelled precisely at the 'frozen heavens'" (Celan's underlinings), with "stand up you Christ" and "frozen heavens" as marginal notes (pp. 635 and 636 of the English edition).

T Eden, 1 Es ist ein Land Verloren / There is a land called Lost: Concerning the loss of Paradise, see Gen. 3:23–24, King James Version: "Therefore the Lord God sent him forth from the garden of Eden, to till the ground from whence he was taken. / So he drove out the man; and he placed at the east of the garden of Eden Cherubims, and a flaming sword which turned every way, to keep the way of the tree of life."

8 das Augenkind / This eye-child: Nelly Sachs, from whom Celan received shortly before the writing of the poem the news that she had been released from the hospital, called Eric soon after their meeting in Zurich "the wide-eyed enchanted child" (in Christopher Clark's translation, PC/Sachs, p. 40).

9f. Es sieht, es sieht, wir sehen, / ich sehe dich, du siehst / It sees, it sees, we see, / I see you, you see: For the use of this conjugation-figure see also verses 13f. and 17 of "Es war Erde in ihnen" / "There was earth inside them."

"Psalm" / "Psalm"

January 5, 1961.

T Psalm / Psalm 6 wir blühn / we / want to flower: See Psalm 103:15: "As for man, his days are as grass: as a flower of the field, so he flourisheth."

1 Niemand knetet uns wieder aus Erde und Lehm / NoOne kneads us again of earth and clay, 2 unsern Staub / our dust, 16 Staubfaden / stamen: See Gen. 2:7: "And the Lord God formed man of the dust of the ground, and breathed into his nostrils the breath of life; and man became a living soul"; "All go unto one place; all are of the dust, and all turn to dust again" (Eccles. 3:20) and "And I will make thy seed as the dust of the earth: so that if a man can number the dust of the earth, then shall thy seed also be numbered" (Gen. 13:16). In Bloch: "The Golem was to be found there too, not just in the pre-mechanical region in which Rabbi Löb as a cabbalist wanted to attempt the business of creation, with a lump of clay and a magic slip of paper" (p. 631). On February 5, 1961, Celan translated Shakespeare's sonnet LXXI: "O! if, I say, you look upon this verse, / When I perhaps compounded am with clay, / Do not so much as my poor name rehearse;" / "Du laß, ruh einst dein Blick auf diesen Worten, derweil ich Staub bin, Staub bin und nicht mehr" (verse 9f., GW V, p. 339).

4 Gelobt seist du, Niemand / Praised be thou, NoOne: Allusion to verse 15 of "Es war Erde in ihnen" / "There was earth inside them": "O one, o no

one, o noone, o you." See also Psalm 119:12: "Gelobt seist du, Herr," which the King James Version translates as "Blessed art thou, O Lord." (*Gelobt*, from *loben*, means "praised," more than "blessed," and the literal translation of the German version would be: "Praised be thou, O Lord.")

Concerning the change of the pronoun "niemand" / "no one" into a name, see Odysseus' ruse to overcome the giant Polyphemus in Homer. Also Kafka's story "Der Ausflug ins Gebirge / Excursion into the Mountains," translated into Romanian by Paul Celan, here in English by Michael Hofmann: "'I don't know,' I cried in a toneless voice, 'I really don't know. If nobody comes, then nobody comes. I've done nobody any harm, nobody ever did me any harm, yet nobody wants to come to my aid. Nobody upon nobody. But that's not it either. Only nobody comes to help me—nobody upon nobody would be fine. I would quite like—and why wouldn't I?—to go on an excursion with a crowd of nobodies. Into the mountains, of course, where else? The way those nobodies would crowd together, all their crossed and linked arms, their many feet, separated by minute steps!'" See also Celan's "Conversation in the Mountains": "They do not talk, they speak, and who speaks does not talk to anyone, cousin, he speaks because nobody hears him, nobody and Nobody" (translated by Rosmarie Waldrop; originally in GW III, p. 171). See also verse 21 of "Radix, Matrix." And in *Microliths*, this, from the fragmentary dialogue #148: "Karl: Understood. So, I hear no one. (After a pause, with irony) Den Herrn Niemand. *Mister Nobody,* thus."

12f. die / Niemandsrose / the / NoOnesRose: See the title of this volume. Concerning the rose in the context of Judaism, see also verse 8 of the poem from *SU*, not retained in *Poppy and Memory*: "Dein Haus ritt die finstere Welle, doch barg es ein Rosengeschlecht;" / "Your house rode the wave of darkness, though saved by a rose-descendance/house/family." See also the comparison of Israel to a rose in Hosea 14:6, though in English versions of the Bible, the rose is replaced by the lily.

17 Krone / the corona, 18 Purpurwort / scarlet-word, 20 Dorn / thorn: See the Passion of Christ: "And they stripped him, and put on him a scarlet robe. And when they had platted a crown of thorns, they put it upon his head, . . . and mocked him, saying, Hail, King of the Jews!" (Matt. 27:28f.). Regarding the connection between the rose and the cross in the alchemical secret so-

ciety of the Rosicrucians, see Bloch: "Cross and rose, the first the symbol of pain and dissolution, the second the symbol of love and life, thus united allegorically in the 'work of perfection'" (p. 637).

See also "The flower of joy has also symbolized sorrow. Fading quickly, it has been identified with death and with the evanescence of earthly beauties. Surrounded by thorns, it has been identified with pain and with the ambivalence involved in mortal love and in most mortal values. Even as a religious symbol of eternal promise, it has often been related to the thorns of anguish that surround its glory and the blood of martyrs shed for its sake" (Barbara Seward, *The Symbolic Rose* [New York: Columbia University Press, 1960]), p. 6; quoted by Shimon Sandbank in: "The Sign of the Rose: Vaughan, Rilke, Celan," *Comparative Literature*, vol. 49, no. 3 [Summer, 1997], pp. 195–208.

"Tübingen, Jänner" / "Tübingen, Jänner"

Paris, January 29, 1961. On that day Celan returned to Paris from a short visit to Walter Jens in Tübingen meant to ensure Jens's support in the Goll affair. In relation to Claire Goll and her enablers' defamatory accusations of plagiarism, Celan's reactions were seen by many as oversensitive or even as symptoms of a clinical paranoia, while a number of his friends asked him not to take those accusations seriously. The poem quotes "Der Rhein" / "The Rhine," a poem by Friedrich Hölderlin, who had studied in Tübingen and spent nearly half his life as "mentally deranged" in the care of Ernst Friedrich Zimmer at the latter's house—in the *Turmzimmer*, the tower room—on the Neckar. In the first draft Celan noted a reference to Wilhelm Waiblinger's book *Der kranke Hölderlin* (*The sick Hölderlin*); the poem quotes Christopher Schwab's report on the inhabitant of the "Hölderlin Tower" from vol. 6 of the Hellingrathschen Hölderlin edition. The tower and its reflections in the Neckar are visible on the way from the railway station to Jens's then residence in Haußerstrasse.

T Tübingen, Jänner: "Jänner" is an Austrian form of "Januar" / "January," though it also means to recall Büchner's *Lenz* ("Den 20. Jänner ging Lenz durch's Gebirg" / "On the 20th of January Lenz walked through the mountains," is the opening line) while also referencing Celan's poetics of dates as developed in the *Meridian* essay.

1f. Zur Blindheit über- / redete Augen / Eyes con- / vinced to go blind: See the reading traces in Hölderlin's hymn "Der Rhein" / "The Rhine": "Die Blindesten aber / sind Göttersöhne" /("Yet the blindest / are sons of gods") (verse 40f., Bd. 2, S. 150; Richard Sieburth's translation, in *Hymns and Fragments*, p. 71), and see also verse 1f. of "Frankfurt, September": "Blind, light- / bearded partition" (*Breathturn into Timestead*, pp. 110–11).

3–5 ein / Rätsel ist Rein- / entsprungenes / a / riddle is pure / source: See Hölderlin's "Der Rhein" / "The Rhine": "Ein Rätsel ist Reinentsprungenes. Auch / Der Gesang kaum darf es enthüllen. Denn / Wie du anfingst, wirst du bleiben / So viel auch wirket die Not" ("A riddle, the pure of source. Which / Even song may scarce disclose. For / As you began, so shall you remain / And though need / and nurture leave their mark") (verses 46–49, Bd. 2, S. 150; Richard Sieburth's translation in *Hymns and Fragments*, p. 71); place also marked and underlined by Celan in the Hellingrath edition (Bd. 4, S. 173).

9 Besuche ertrunkener Schreiner / Visits of drowned carpenters: His later host, the carpenter Zimmer, had already visited Hölderlin during the latter's stay in the mental asylum. The artist and lithographer Johann Georg Schreiner, whose last name literally means "carpenter," visited Hölderlin in his tower room in 1823, 1825, and 1826 and drew his portrait.

14 käme ein Mensch zur Welt, heute / if a man was born, today: See verse 5 of "Give the Word" (*Breathturn into Timestead*, pp. 92–93) and in this context verse 27 of "Spät und Tief" / "Late and Deep," as well as a marginal mark in Alexander Ulars's postface to his *Lao-Tse*, next to: "The newborn had snow-white hair and snow-white eyebrows and was of course as wise as other mortals at eighty. That's why he was named Lao-Tse, Old-Child" (BPPC section E, entry 61; my translation).

14–16 mit / dem Lichtbart der / Patriarchen / with / the lightbeard of / the patriarchs, 20 lallen und lallen / babble and babble: See Exod. 34:29: "And it came to pass, when Moses came down from mount Sinai with the two tables of testimony in Moses' hand, when he came down from the mount, that Moses wist not that the skin of his face shone while he talked with him." And Exod. 4:10: "And Moses said unto the Lord, O my Lord, I am not eloquent, neither heretofore, nor since thou hast spoken unto thy servant: but I am slow of speech, and of a slow tongue." See also verse 1f. of "Frankfurt, September" (*Breathturn into Timestead*, pp. 110–11).

20 nur lallen und lallen / but babble and babble: See verse 12f. of "Stille!" / "Silence!"

21f. immer-, immer- / zuzu / all-all, way-ways / agagain: Büchner's Woyzeck says in his delirium: "Immer zu! Immer zu! [. . .] Hör ich's immer, immer zu: stich tot, tot?" ("Again! Again! [. . .] I hear it again, again: stab dead, dead?") (p. 166; my translation).

23 "Pallaksch. Pallaksch.": Christoph Theodor Schwab, in his biography of Hölderlin, reports that this was a favorite word of the poet's, which he used to mean yes or no, or simply as an exclamation (Hölderlin, Hellingrath edition, vol. 6, p. 444).

"Chymisch" / "Alchemical"

January 31, 1961.

In 1955 the German poet and critic Hans Egon Holthusen (1913–1997)—who had been a member of the SS since 1933—in his contribution to Hans Bender's anthology *Mein Gedicht ist mein Messer: Lyriker zu ihren Gedichten* (*My Poem Is My Knife: Poets on their Poems*) (Munich, 1961) used alchemical vocabulary in writing about Celan's poems: "Gifted authors reach too high [*versteigen sich*] with metaphors like . . . 'the white meal of promise' or 'the whitehair of time.' Those are certainly not successful metaphors, but poetic changelings raised artificially as if in an alembic" (p. 49). Holthusen, like some other critics, saw in Celan a descendant of Yvan Goll and saying so indirectly negated the links to reality of his poems. The poem reinterprets alchemy in the context of the burning of corpses as an eradication of the traces of genocide.

T Chymisch / Alchemical, 1 Schweigen, wie Gold gekocht / Silence, cooked like gold: See Bloch, p. 635: "On the whole the alchemical meaning of Andreae's allegory is clear, but not as one which refers exclusively to metallurgy. If it is confined to the latter, then the 'Chemical Wedding' bears no or only very little relation to goldcooking," as well as other Bloch citations from the chapter on Andreae's "Chemical Wedding." Re Celan's interest in alchemy, see also "Ice, Eden," "In Prague," "Solve," and "Coagula."

1 Schweigen / Silence: In the Goll affair, friends as well as opponents blamed Celan for not speaking out himself about the matter. See also "Wohin mir das Wort" / "Where the Word," and the poem "Mit meinem Schweigen" / "With my silence," from the time of this volume but unpublished in his lifetime:

With my silence, long,
and before my word held me
out into its autumn, I
stood and stand:

I mirrored murder
back into the mouths

5f. wie alles Verlorene nahe / Schwestergestalt / like all that's lost, / sistershape: See verses 8–10 of "Die Schleuse" / "The Sluice." See also verse 5 of "Köln, Am Hof" / "Cologne, Am Hof" and the letter to Ingeborg Bachmann quoted in the commentary on the poem "Weiß und Leicht" / "White and Light."

"Eine Gauner- und Ganovenweise . . ." /
"A Gonif- and Gangster-Ditty . . ."
February 16, 1961–November 7, 1962.

On March 19, 1962, in a draft for a letter to Petre Solomon, Celan called the poem "ce poème anti-nazi, ce cri" / "this anti-nazi poem, this scream." Even before it was published, Celan handed copies of the poem out to a number of friends.

T Paris emprès Pontoise: Quote from François Villon's "Quatrain": "Je suis Françoys, dont il me poise, / Né de Paris emprès Pontoise, / Et de la corde d'une toise / Sçaura mon col que mon cul poise" (I am François/French, it weighs heavy on me, born in Paris near Pontoise, and from the six-foot cord, my neck will know what my ass weighs). Pontoise is a small town near Paris (Département Val d'Oise).

T Czernowitz: City of Celan's birth, at which moment it was part of the kingdom of Romania, while pre-1918 it had been the capital of the Austro-Hungarian crownland Bukovina.

T Sadagora: A small town near Celan's birth town; a center of Hasidism until World War II, in local legends also the hiding place for a range of what he here calls "gonifs and gangsters," and, also important, it was also the birthplace of the poet's mother, Friederike Antschel.

Epigraph: Beginning of the second stanza of "An Edom," a poem by the German Jewish poet Heinrich Heine (who died in Paris in 1886): "Manchmal nur, in dunkeln Zeiten, / Ward dir wunderlich zu Mut, / Und die liebefrommen Tätzchen / Färbtest du mit meinem Blut!" /("Only sometimes, in dark times / You'd behave strangely / And the piously loving paws / You'd color with my blood!") (p. 439 in Celan's edition, title marked in the table of contents). In the early history of Israel, Edom (a name derived from Esau, meaning "red" in Hebrew) was an enemical neighbor of Israel, and in Heine, "Edom" is a general term for a Jew hater.

4 Wo bleibt mein Bart, / Where's my beard, 5f. wo / mein Bart / where / my beard: Concerning the beard as symbol of Jewishness, see verse 6 of and commentary to "Die letzte Fahne" / "The Last Flag."

5 Judenfleck / Jew's-patch: A yellow ring-shaped badge or patch called the "Judenfleck" (literally "Jew's stain") to be worn by all Jews had been prescribed by the police in Germany as far back as 1530. In 1274 already, Edward I of England enacted the "Statute of Jewry," which included a requirement for every Jew older than seven to "wear a distinguishing mark on his outer garment . . . in the form of two Tables joined, of yellow felt of the length of six inches and of the breadth of three inches." In Nazi Germany, the yellow Star of David badge (the "Judenstern") was made the law in 1941. See also the use of the word "Gelbstern" / "Yellowstar" in verse 2 of the posthumously published poem "Dehngrenze."

8–10 krumm war er, ja, / denn, ja, / er war gerade / crooked it was, yes, / because, yes, / it was straight: See verses 5–7 of ". . . rauscht der Brunnen" / ". . . whispers the Fountain," and the unsent letter to Kurt Hirschfeld: "The crooked is the crooked, it knows how to evade straightening. Only the straight, which stands completely and as a person against it, keeps truth alive" (January 8, 1961; Badiou's reference). See also reading-notes in Burnet from Heraklitus: "Le sentier droit et le sentier courbe que suit le peigne du foulon est un et le même.—" / "The straight and the crooked path of the Fuller comb is one and the same" (p. 153 in Celan's French edition; John Burnet, *L'aurore de la philosophie grecque*, Paris, 1952: p. 101 in the English edition).

12 Krumm, so wird meine Nase / Crooked, like my nose becomes: See Celan's notes for the Büchner Prize speech: "that's why the poem, in its being and not through its subject matter first—is a school of true humanity: it teaches to understand the other as the other, i.e., in its otherness, it demands brotherliness with respect before this other, in the turning toward this other, even there where the other appears as the hooked-nosed and misshapen—in no way almond-eyed—accused by the 'straightnosed'" (TCA, #240). "Respect for the secret of the hooknosed creature—that is one way to the poem" (TCA, #411). "The hooknosed. Hook-languaged. Goitery—" (TCA, #412). "Long live the crooked-nose creature!" (TCA, #680). See also the commentary on verse 5 of "Einem, der vor der Tür stand" / "To one who stood before the door," and the letter to Franz Wurm of June 8, 1963: "the 'crooked-nosedness' stands, you have seen this accurately, for that particular, personal and—lifelong!—individual that also remains inscribed in all poetry, and that one tries to give the lie to again and again in these, only seemingly so 'lyrical' times" (August 6, 1963, PC/FW, p. 13).

14f. Und wir zogen auch nach *Friaul. / Da hätten wir, da hätten wir* / And we made our way to *Friuli. / There we'd have, there we'd have,* 28 *die Pest / the Plague*: Quotation from an old lansquenet song first recovered by Georg Forster: "Wir kamen in friaul, / do het wir alle sambt vol maul" ("We came to Friuli / where we all stuffed our faces fully") (*Frische Teutsche Liedlein*, #20, stanza 3 [Neudruck Halle, 1903], p. 89). A popular tradition also gives the following stanza: "Wir kamen für Triest, / do hätt'n wir allesamt die Pest" ("We came for Triest, / there we all had the pest"). The plague was a common pretext for anti-Jewish pogroms; see also Heine's *The Rabbi of Bacherach*. See also Celan's fragmentary translation of Shakespeare's sonnet #LXVI, where line 7, "And right perfection wrongfully disgraced," becomes "und das gerade schief und krumm gemacht" / "and the straight is canted and made crooked" (GA, p. 807).

16 Denn es blühte der Mandelbaum / For it blossomed, the almond tree: See verse 7 of "Nähe der Gräber" / "Nearness of the Graves," a poem from *SU*, not collected here: "Und steigt nicht der Gott mit dem knospenden

Stab . . ." ("And doesn't the god with the budding staff arise . . ."). See also the name of Celan's "brother" in poetry, Osip Mandelstam.

19 Machandelbaum / Junipertree: In the Brothers Grimm collection of German fairy tales, see the Platt German tale "Von dem Machandelboom"; there the bones of the son killed by the mother and eaten by the father are buried under the "Machandelbaum." Also, suggested by Brigitta Eisenreich (BE, p. 112): "the wood of the juniper tree was used in early times when the plague struck to fumigate the houses."

27 steht gegen / stands against: Regarding the concept of "stehen" / "to stand" (in an early version the poem ends "Er / steht" / "He / stands"; TCA/NR, p. 41) in the sense of resistance and standing against/defying (verse 25), see also the letter to Hirschfeld quoted above. See a range of further commentaries on "stehen" / "to stand" in this volume and in *Breathturn into Timestead*. Also note his translation of verses 13–15 of Emily Dickinson's poem "Four trees upon a solitary acre": "What Plan / They severally—promote—or hinder— / Unknown—" / "Ein jeder: wem bahnt er den Weg und wem / steht er entgegen?" in which "to hinder" is translated as "to stand against" (GW V, p. 399).

II

"Flimmerbaum" / "Flimmertree"

March 16, 1961.

T Flimmerbaum / Flimmertree: See the variations played on trees in the previous poem's verses 16–20. See also, in Gottfried Benn's talk "Problems of Poetry": "Flimmerhaare, sie tasten etwas heran, nämlich Worte, und diese herangetasteten Worte rinnen sofort zu einer Chiffre, einer stilistischen Figur" ("Flimmerhairs/Cilia, they grope something, namely words, and these groped words immediately coagulate into a cypher, a figure of style") (*Gesammelte Werke in vier Bänden*, hrsg. von Dieter Wellershoff, Wiesbaden/ München, 1959, Bd. 1, S. 511); "Flimmerbaum" / "Flimmertree" replaced a "Flimmerhaar" / "Flimmerhair" in early versions of the poem (TCA/NR, p. 48).

4, 28 Nimmer / Never, 7f. es war / eine Freiheit / it was / a freedom, 10,

25 Weißt du noch, daß ich sang? / Do you remember that I sang?: Brigitta Eisenreich remembers: "When after our separation I held the volume of poems in my hands, it seemed to me that both the twice repeated, thus important question and also the 'Never' in this poem very clearly pertained to me, all the more so as the verse 'it was / a freedom' connoted this 'Never'; 'You my freedom' had been one of the rare direct addresses to me that I had noted down; a freedom the loss of which toward the end of our relationship, as one of my letters makes clear, I regretted more than other things" (BE, p. 53).

"Erratisch" / "Erratic"

April 15, 1961. Title added on May 19, 1961. Marked as the first poem of that day; see also the next poem.

The poem shows traces of Celan's reading in Siegmund Günther's *Physicher Geographie*.

On April 14, 1961, a reader's letter, "Yvan Goll and Paul Celan," by Dietrich Schaefer, a Ph.D. candidate, was published in *Christ und Welt*, and widened Claire Goll's plagiarism allegations beyond *Poppy and Memory*, further demanding a public reaction from Celan, which should include a thank-you to Yvan Goll for the latter's supposed suggestions (newspaper cutting in Celan's literary estate). The same day *Die Zeit* published the article "Drei deutsche Dramatiker—drei Moralisten" ("Three German dramatists—three moralists") by Johannes Jacobi, in which Eugene Ionesco is accused of plagiarizing Yvan Goll. On May 19, 1961, *Die Zeit* published an editorial note under the title "Ruling for Celan," reporting on Reinhard Döhl's investigations of Claire Goll's allegations in the 1960 *Jahrbuch* of the German Academy for Language and Poetry, which had just been published, and on the article by Karl Dedecius, "Qual und Genuß des Übersetzens" ("Pain and delight of translation"), which does not critically evaluate Celan's just published Yesenin translations but plays them against his own (newspaper cutting in Celan's literary estate).

T Erratisch / Erratic, 6 Der Stein / The stone: See the notes to the drafts of the Büchner Prize speech: "The already tight/compact . . . fills itself . . . compacts itself around the Dark,—with the sense of that which stands against it; an erratic language-block, come from your own, a for you too available depth and height and distance, faces you with silence; even there it still gives you a chance . . ." (TCA/MFV, #185); and "thickness: to be understood from the geological, and thus from the slow catastrophes and the dreadful fault lines of language—" (TCA/MFV, #187); and "the sole hope: that the poem be there, once more, erratic—" (TCA/MFV, #188).

See also the commentary to verse 14 of "Allerseelen" / "All Souls."

6f. Der Stein, / schläfennah einst / The stone, / once temple-close: Jacob dreams the dream of the heaven's ladder after "he took of the stones of that place, and put them for his pillows, and lay down in that place to sleep" (Gen. 28:11), and in the morning he "took the stone that he had put for his pillows, and set it up for a pillar, and poured oil upon the top of it" (Gen. 28:18).

6f. Der Stein, / [. . .] tut sich hier auf / The stone, / [. . .] opens here: See verse 10 of "Die hellen Steine" / "The bright stones."

"Einiges Handähnliche" / "Something handlike"

April 15, 1961. Concerning the date and circumstances, see the previous poem and commentary.

1f. Einiges Hand- / ähnliche / Something hand- / like: See Celan's "Ein Brief" / "A Letter," which was published that April in the new edition of Hans Bender's anthology *Mein Gedicht ist mein Messer* (*My Poem Is My Knife*): "Craft means handiwork, a matter of hands. And these hands must belong to *one* person, i.e. a unique, mortal soul searching for its way with its voice and its dumbness. Only truthful hands write true poems. I cannot see any basic difference between a handshake and a poem" (Rosmarie Waldrop's translation, PCCP, p. 26).

". . . rauscht der Brunnen" / ". . . whispers the Fountain"

April 30, 1961.

T . . . rauscht der Brunnen / . . . whispers the Fountain, 11f. Später / der Rosen / Later / of the Roses: See verse 6 of "Kristall" / "Crystal." That poem plays a role in Claire Goll's plagiarism accusations and is treated in detail in the then just published analysis by Reinhard Döhl (GA, #83) (see the commentary to "Erratic").

2 Messer / knives: See Hans Bender's anthology *Mein Gedicht ist mein*

Messer (*My Poem Is My Knife*), in which Celan is represented with his letter to Bender (see the commentary to the previous poem).

2 Messer / knives, 16 Krücke / crutch, 17–19 Wir werden das Kinderlied singen, das, / hörst du, das / mit den Men, mit den Schen, mit den Menschen / We will sing the children's song, the one, / listen, the one / with the hu, with the mans, with the humans: See verses 5f. and 13 of "Gezinkt der Zufall" / "Chance, Marked" (*Breathturn into Timestead*, pp. 112–13).

5–7 Ihr meine mit mir ver- / krüppelnden Worte, ihr / meine geraden / You my with me crip- / pling words, you / my straight ones: See verses 8–10 of "Eine Gauner- und Ganovenweise" / "A Gonif- and Gangster-Ditty."

10f. mein täglich wahr- und wahrer- / geschundenes / my daily true- and truer / flayed: See verses 1–3 of "Zwölf Jahre" / "Twelve Years," and verse 6f. of "Hohles Lebensgehöft" / "Hollow Lifehomestead" (*Breathturn into Timestead*, pp. 28, 29).

17 das Kinderlied, / the children's song, 19 mit den Men, mit den Schen, / with the hu, with the mans: See the children's song "Meine Mu, meine Mu, meine Mutter schickt mich her" (My mo, my mo, my mother sent me here). Early versions of the poem have the corresponding "mit den Men-, / den Men, den Men- / schen" ("with the man-, / the man, the man-, / kind") (TCA/NR, p. 54).

"Es ist nicht mehr" / "It is no longer"
April 8–May 7, 1961.

"Radix, Matrix" / "Radix, Matrix"
May 11, 1961–March 13, 1963. An early title was "Hinterm Licht" / "Behind the light." The poem stands in close relation to Brigitta Eisenreich's telling Celan about her encounter in April 1945 in her hometown Enns in Lower Austria with a column of exhausted concentration camp inmates driven past her by Nazi soldiers, and their corpses along the road (BE, pp. 117–20). Celan gave her a typed copy of the poem (see BE, illustration #15, and p. 115f.).

T Radix, Matrix: The title concentrates a complex of images: *Radix* is Latin for "root" (see verse 21f.), or "origin," and *Geschlecht* (a word with no English or French equivalent, as Derrida noted) is difficult or impossible to translate, whose meanings encompass the physical male (see verse 19) or female sex, gender as such, and lineage/descendance (see verse 17). *Matrix* is Latin for "topsoil," "germinal layer," and in connection with radix (as male member), "uterus" or "womb." See verse 31, as well as the commentary to verse 1 of the following poem, "Schwarzerde" / "Blackearth."

1, 25 Wie man zum Stein spricht / as one speaks to stone: See the commentary to verse 6 of "Die Winzer" / "The Vintagers."

3f. vom Abgrund her, von / einer Heimat her / from the abyss, from / a homeland: See the opening lines of Hölderlin's fragmentary hymn "Vom Abgrund nämlich / haben wir angefangen" ("We set out from the abyss") (vol. 2, p. 259; Sieburth's translation, p. 199), and verse 3f. of "Stumme Herbstgerüche" / "Mute autumn odors."

14 Acker / field: Eisenreich pointed out the Austrian compounds *Totenacker* and *Gottesacker* for "cemetery." She was bicycling when she encountered the column: "I saw them stagger under the blows from the rifle butts of their guards, who, when they couldn't advance anymore, beat them to the ground [. . .] And then, in the evening, heaps of partly naked corpses lay in the local cemetery" (BE, p. 118).

18 stehende / standing: Concerning this word, accented here by its position at the end of the verse, see other occurrences and commentaries of the verb "stehen" / "to stand," including its sexual connotations. See also verse 1 of "Heute und morgen" / "Today and Tomorrow."

19 Rute / Rod, 21 Wurzel Abrahams. Wurzel Jesse / Abraham's root. Jesse's root, 31 Fruchtboden / fertile / floor, 35 Kronen / crowns: Jesse, also spelled Isai, was the father of King David in the Old Testament, and according to Isa. 11:1: "And there shall come forth a shoot from the stump of Jesse, and a branch shall grow out of his roots." Paul, in Rom. 15, transfers this prophecy to Jesus.

19 Rute / Rod, 30f. auch dieser / Fruchtboden klafft / this fertile / floor too gapes: In botany "Fruchtboden / receptacle" refers to the thickened part of a stem from which the flower organs (and, in some plants, the edible fruit itself) grow. Here I prefer to literally translate the German compound "Frucht-boden" as "fertile ground." See Bloch: "Or of Hassan the Basorite, the master of the magic rod, he strikes the ground with it: 'Then the earth

gaped open, and out came ten Ifrits, whose legs still stuck in the bowels of the earth while their heads towered far above the clouds' ('The Arabian Nights')" (vol. 2, p. 628; the origin for the fairy tale, *One Thousand and One Nights*, is underlined by Celan). For Celan's recommendation for readings in the Kabbalah, and on its erotic mysticism, see the commentary to "Mandorla" about Brigitta Eisenreich.

21f. Niemandes / Wurzel / NoOne's / root: A reference to verse 13 of "Psalm" and thus to the title of the volume.

27 Händen / hands: Jean-Pierre Lefebvre (in his translations of *Paul Celan, Choix de poèmes*, Poésie/Gallimard, 1998, p. 349) refers to Nelly Sachs's letter of 19 August 1960: "You have your hands, you have the hands of your poems . . . —take, please take ours as well! And take whatever is a hand and wants to be helpful and remain helpful through you, through your being . . ." (PC/NS, p. 36).

30f. auch dieser Fruchtboden klafft / this fertile / floor too gapes: In Emily Dickinson's "To my quick ear the Leaves," Celan translates the line "Creation seemed a mighty Crack" as "Ein Klaffen . . . / das muß die Schöpfung sein" (verses 5–8, GW V, p. 387), though here in English, Dickinson's "crack" does not work.

"Schwarzerde" / "Blackearth"

May 18, 1961. On that day Celan also wrote "A Letter," his contribution to Hans Bender's anthology *Mein Gedicht ist mein Messer* (*My Poem Is My Knife*) (GW III, p. 177f.; CP, pp. 25–26).

In his radio essay, "The Poetry of Osip Mandelstam," Celan wrote: "The question about the wherefrom becomes more urgent, more desperate—the poetry—in one of his essays he calls it a plough—tears open the abyssal strata of time, the 'black earth of time' appears on the surface. The eye, talking with the perceived, and pained, develops a new ability: it becomes visionary: it accompanies the poem into its underground. The poem writes itself toward an other, a 'strangest' time" (MFV, p. 219). See also the lines from Mandelstam's poem "The horseshoe-finder": "Влажный чернозем Нееры, каждую ночь распаханный заново / Вилами, трезубцами, мотыгами, плугами" ("Neaira's damp earth, tilled each night anew / by pitchforks, tridents, hoes, plows"), translated by Celan as "die feuchte Schwarzerde Neairas, neu umgebrochen jede Nacht / mit Forke, Dreizack, Karst und Pflug" (verse 63f.; GW V, p. 135).

1–3 Schwarzerde / Blackearth: In his dissertation, Richard Lee Pierre writes: "'Black earth,' sometimes transliterated as *chernozem*, refers to a band of rich soil covering parts of southern Russia, Siberia, Ukraine, southeastern Germany, and eastern Europe, including Celan's hometown of Chernovitz, Bukovina . . . the name of which reveals the root chern- ('black'), common to many Slavic and East European languages. Celan may have also drawn on the discourse of chernozem from his geological sources that discuss it (including Günther, 124 and Brinkmann, 44–45; see Schellengerger-Diederich, 309–310). At any rate, I argue that chernozem provides another kind of 'meridian' in Celan's poetics, a way of connecting poets and places through geological considerations, rather than state or national boundaries" ("Lyric Petrologies: Languages of Stone in Rilke, Trakl, Mandelstam, Celan, and Sachs," The University of Michigan, 2015; footnote 37, p. 105).

Chernozem is a black-colored soil containing a high percentage of humus and high percentages of phosphoric acids, phosphorus, and ammonia. It is very fertile and can produce high agricultural yields with its high-moisture storage capacity.

"Einem, der vor der Tür stand" / "To one who stood before the door"

Paris, May 20, 1961; dated corrections on May 23, 1961 (the day he wrote "Mandorla"), and September 20, 1961 (Yom Kippur). On May 20, 1961, he also wrote the poem "Judenwelsch, nachts," not included in any volume Celan himself published. On May 20, 1961, a negative review of Celan's Yessenin translations by Horst Bienek (claiming Celan "falsified" Yessenin by substituting a Celanesque "tone" for Yessenin's) came out in the FAZ, as did Ingeborg Bachmann's short story "Undine geht." See also various references in the commentaries to Celan's reading of Gershom Scholem's writings on the Kabbalah.

5 Kielkropf / changeling: In Germanic mythology, a *Kielkropf* refers to malformed offspring fathered by chthonic creatures of myth, or even the Devil replacing a stolen human child, somewhat similar to a changeling. See the

notes toward the Meridian speech: "Ricercar— / what is that? Is it the word from the almond-eyed beauty, that I hear you repeat, varied most opportunistically? Only when, with your most own pain, you'll have been with the crooked-nosed and yiddy and goitery dead of Auschwitz and Treblinka and elsewhere, will you also meet the eye and the almond" (MFP, #394, p. 127), and: "Das Krummnasige. Krumm-sprachige. Kielkröpfige—" / "The hooknosed. Hook-languages, Goitery—" (#412, p. 130). In that book I mistranslated *Kielkröpfige* as "Goitery," basing it on the German term *Kropf*, which means "goiter." "Changeling" is better for the noun, though "goitery" may work as an adjective.

5 Kielkropf / changeling, 10–12 mit dem blutigen / Gottes- / gemächt / with the bloodied / god- / member: The reference to the circumcision shows the "changeling" to be a Jew. See John Felstiner's essay on this poem in *Translating Poetry: The Double Labyrinth* (edited by Daniel Weissbort), where he writes: "Derrida called circumcision 'une blessure lisible.' Virtually every poem of Celan's bears a legible wound."

6f. halb- / schürigen / half- / sheared: Quality of the wool from sheep that are shorn twice a year, as against the better quality of sheep shorn only once a year. A general sense of imperfect, flawed, or unfinished.

14–17 Rabbi / Löw: // Diesem / beschneide das Wort / This / one's word, circumcise: See Scholem: "They call him golem and use him as a servant to do all sorts of housework. But he must never leave the house. On his forehead is written *'emeth* [truth]; every day he gains weight and becomes somewhat larger and stronger than all the others in the house, regardless of how little he was to begin with. For fear of him, they therefore erase the first letter, so that nothing remains but *meth* [he is dead], whereupon he collapses and turns to clay again" (*On the Kabbalah and Its Symbolism*, p. 159).

"Mandorla" / "Mandorla"

May 23, 1961 (see the previous poem and commentary). Celan made a typescript of the poem for Brigitta Eisenreich from memory (including a range of changes, notably in verse 14, where he replaced "Menschenlocke" / "human curl" with "Judenlocke" / "Jew's curl"). In relation to the poem he also insisted she read Georg Langer's *Die Liebesmystik der Kabbala* (BE, p. 122).

T Mandorla: Celan explained the meaning of "Mandorla" and "Mandel" / "almond" to Eisenreich as a reference to the vulva in many religious traditions (BE, p. 122). Celan had marked the word in a range of his books on the history of art. In this context, the *Encyclopaedia Britannica* sums up:

> Mandorla, (Italian: 'almond'), in religious art, almond-shaped aureole of light surrounding the entire figure of a holy person; it was used in Christian art usually for the figure of Christ and is also found in the art of Buddhism. Its origins are uncertain. The Western mandorla first appears in 5th-century mosaics decorating the Church of Santa Maria Maggiore in Rome, where it surrounds certain Old Testament figures. By the 6th century the mandorla had become a standard attribute of Christ in scenes of the Transfiguration (in which Christ shows himself to his Apostles transformed into his celestial appearance) and the Ascension (in which the resurrected Christ ascends to heaven) and, later, in other scenes involving the resurrected or celestial Christ, the death of the Virgin (in which, having descended from heaven, Christ stands by the deathbed of his mother), the descent into limbo, the Last Judgment, and the nonhistorical theme of Christ in majesty. In the late Middle Ages the mandorla also occasionally enclosed the Virgin in scenes of the Last Judgment and of her Assumption into heaven, reflecting her increased popularity. In the 15th century, however, with the growth of naturalism in art, the mandorla became less popular, being incongruous in a naturalistic context, and it was abandoned by the painters of the Renaissance.

For the meaning of the almond in a Jewish context, see verse 7 of "Nähe der Gräber" / "Nearness of the Graves," "Und steigt nicht der Gott mit dem knospenden Stab / And doesn't the God with the budding rod" (from *SU*, not included here), and verse 1f. of "Zähle die Mandeln" / "Count the almonds." Concerning the cliché of the beautiful almond-eyed Jewess, see the commentary to verse 5 of "Einem, der vor der Tür stand" / "To one who stood before the door."

"An niemand geschmiegt" / "Cheek to cheek"

May 25, 1961. Same day as "Zweihäusig, Ewiger" / "Dioecious, eternal."

3 Handstumpf / hand- / stump: for reflections on hands, see "Einiges Handähnliche" / "Something handlike."

14 Lichtknecht / light-servant: See Brigitta Eisenreich's poem "Eisstoss" ("Icepush"), which Celan had known since February 18, 1958: "Systols that hurt, but also / something white, dripping like wax, around the light-servant [Lichtknecht]" (my translation). There is a special ninth candle with which to light the eight candles of the Hanukkah menora, called the shammash, in German *Lichtknecht*, "light servant" or "-attendant."

"Zweihäusig, Ewiger" / "Dioecious, eternal"

May 25, 1961. Same day as "An niemand geschmiegt" / "Cheek to cheek."

1 Zweihäusig / Dioecious: Literally "two houses," "doubly housed"; a botanical term. Dioecy (Greek: διοικία, "two households") characterizes plant species that have distinct male and female individual organisms. Dioecious reproduction is biparental reproduction. See also Celan's title for an etching by Gisèle Celan-Lestrange, *Dioïque—Zweihäusig* (1966).

1f. Zweihäusig, Ewiger, bist du, un- / bewohnbar / Dioecious, eternal, you are, un-/ inhabitable: See verse 10f. of "Dein Hinübersein" / "Your having crossed" ("Gott, das lasen wir, ist / ein Teil und ein zweiter, zerstreuter: / "God, we read it, is / a part and a second one, scattered"), and in this context the origin of the word "shekinah," as meaning "to inhabit," "to live in." See also the Scholem quote in the commentary to that poem.

7 Komm, Geliebte / Come, beloved: See the end of Bachmann's story "Undine geht": "Komm. Nur einmal. / Komm." / "Come. Just once. / Come."

"Sibirisch" / "Siberian"

May 22–31, 1961.

T Siberian: See Celan's remark on Mandelstam in his radio play: "In the thirties Osip Mandelstam is caught in the 'purges.' The road leads to Siberia, where we lose his trace" (MFP, p. 221).

The first title of the poem—"Musée Cernuschi" (TCA/NR, p. 72)—refers to a museum of East Asian art in Paris.

1 Bogengebete / Bowprayers: See the reading traces in Eveline Lot-Falck's *Les rites de chasse chez les peuples sibériens* (Hunting rites among the Siberian peoples): "Entre les mains du chaman, l'arc devient une arme dirigée contre ses adversaires spirituels" (In the hands of a shaman, the bow becomes a

weapon directed against his spiritual adversaries"), and Celan's note at the bottom of that page (p. 98): "Confirmation of the poem *Bowprayers* written two hours ago." See also the final stanza of "Beim Hagelkorn" / "Next to the hailstone" (*Breathturn into Timestead*, pp. 10–11): "a bowstring, from which / your arrowscript whirrs, / archer," and the commentary: "Celan was born on November 23, under the sign of Sagittarius, the archer" (*Breathturn into Timestead*, p. 467).

13f. weißen Kiesel im Mund / white pebble in the mouth: The Greek rhetorician Demosthenes is supposed to have tried to overcome a speech defect by exercising his speech faculties with a pebble in his mouth. Note also the Jewish tradition of placing stones on graves (see verse 49 of "Es ist alles anders" / "Everything is different").

16 Herzstein / heartstone: The heart-shaped echinoid (*Calculus cordis*), i.e., a fossilized sea urchin. See also verse 18 of "Und mit dem Buch aus Tarussa" / "And with the Book from Tarussa." In German, stone and heart are often associated, as in the expression: "Mir viel ein Stein vom Herzen," literally, "a stone fell from/off my heart," indicating relief, as in the English expression "that took a weight off my mind."

20 Schuttflur / scree plain: A Celan-made composite geological term. See Celan's reading in Franz Lotze's *Geologie*, and his notes (TCA/SG, p. 110).

21 Seggenmeer / sedgesea: Wiedemann suggests this could refer to the crossing of the Red Sea by the children of Israel and points to Exod. 14:19ff.

25–26 mit abgehäutetem / Finger / with flayed / finger: Jean-Pierre Lefebvre (JPL, p. 351) suggests that "abhäuten designates exclusively the skinning of animals"—thus my "flayed"—"but may suggest here also, beyond the live wound, circumcision."

"Benedicta" / "Benedicta"

June 6, 1961. Written on Celan's son Eric's sixth birthday. See Celan's reading of Gershom Scholem's *On the Kabbala and Its Symbols*; see also "Dein Hinübersein" / "Your having crossed" and "Einem, der vor der Tür stand" / "To one who stood before the door."

T Benedicta / Benedicta, 6f. Ge- / segnet / Bl- / essed, 10 Gesegnet / Blessed, 19 Gebenedeiet / Beblessed , 24f. Ge- / *bentscht* / Ge- / *bentsht*: It is difficult, or rather impossible, to translate these grammatically based terms directly. The title thus has the form of a (female singular or neutral plural) past participle and comes from the Latin *bene dicere*, i.e., "to say or speak well," "to wish well," "to praise," "to bless." In this form it is a citation from the Vulgate's version of the second part of the Ave Maria: "Benedicta tu in mulieribus et benedictus fructus ventris tui, Jesus." The latinized German form is referenced: "Gegrüßet seist du, Maria, voll der Gnade, der Herr ist mit dir. Du bist gebenedeit unter den Frauen und gebenedeit sei die Frucht deines Leibes, Jesus" / "Blessed are you among women, and blessed is the fruit of your womb, Jesus." The last word, "Ge- / bentscht" / "Ge- / bentsht," transfers the Latin and German participles into Yiddish, where "gebentscht" arose like the German "gebenedeiet" from Latin *bene dicere*. Celan may have taken the word "benschen" from S. Wolf's *Wörterbuch des Rotwelschen* (p. 49). See also Celan's note: "Niemandsrose / zu Benedicta / damals, bei Mühlau, / (die Prozession)" / "NoOne's Rose / re Benedicta / back then, near Mühlau, / (the procession)" (TCA/NR, p. 74), as a recollection of Celan's visit on July 5, 1948, to the cemetery in Mühlau am Inn, where the poet Georg Trakl lies buried.

Epigraph: quotation from a popular Yiddish song (late sixteenth-century; Prague), which in an earlier version of the poem had been quoted in its totality: "Zu ken men aroif gejn in himel arajn / Un fregn baj got zu's darf asoj sajn? / 's darf asoj sajn. / 's mus asoj sajn. / 's ken of der welt doch gor andersch nit sajn" ("May one go up to heaven and ask God if it's allowed to be this way? It may be this way. It must be this way. The world can't be any other way") (TCA/NR, p. 75). These quotations come from the LP "Chansons populaires yiddisch," which Brigitta Eisenreich played for Celan. She recalls: "We listened to the songs together, but as I had only a very simple, already aged record-player at that time, the record suddenly stopped and kept repeating the same sentence: ' 's mus asoj sajn / It must be this way' [. . .] For Celan, a mechanical incident of that order had the value of a secret sign, independent of all common logic, as he told me immediately. I remember the incident exactly—he was stretched out on a bed, meditating on the odd interruption, and had closed his eyes—, this is not a matter of a poetic turn of phrase, but lived reality" (BE, p. 113f. and illustration #16).

5 Pneuma / pneuma: πνεῦμα in ancient Greek means "breath," and in a religious context "spirit" or "soul." The biblical Hebrew term *ruach* רוח—"breath," "wind," or "spirit"—is usually rendered with the word "pneuma" in the Greek New Testament. See also Celan's note for the Meridian speech: "'What's on the lung, put on the tongue' my mother used to say—. . . on breathroutes it comes, the poem, it is there, pneumatic: for everyone." And "Breath: The poem remains, if you allow me a little critical jargon, pneumatically touchable" (MFP, #263 and #266).

"—, Pneuma" / "—, pneume" replaces only in the printer's proofs the original line: "Pneuma–:" / "Sperma." See the reading traces (marks in the margin) of a Philon citation in Bloch: "Only the pure man, transformed by his own conversion, possesses the resurrecting power to dissolve, to renew and to wake the substances sunk like lead into the chaos. By means of the holy water, the logos spermatikos, he returns them to existence and leads them in purified form upwards, until all things below are transformed on high" (p. 644). See also Scholem, *The Kabbalah and Its Symbolism*: "The light of the Sabbath endures into the ensuing week, growing gradually dimmer, to be relieved in the middle of the week by the rising light of the next Sabbath. It is the day on which a special pneuma, the 'Sabbath soul,' enters into the believer, enabling him to participate in the right way in this day which shares more than any other day in the secrets of the pneumatic world. Consequently it was also regarded as a day specially consecrated to the study of the Kabbalah" (p. 139).

11 Teneberleuchter / tenebrae lamp: See the commentary to "Tenebrae."

12 die Augen schloß / closed my eyes, 15f. augen- / losen / eye- / less: See Scholem: "A number of our sources tell us that the Sabbath Psalms were sung with closed eyes, for as the Kabbalists explained, the Shekhinah is designated in the Zohar as 'the beautiful virgin who has no eyes,' that is to say, who has lost her eyes from weeping in exile" (p. 141).

16 den Auen / the open fields: Also from Scholem: "On Friday afternoon, some time before the onset of the Sabbath, the Kabbalists of Safed and Jerusalem, usually clad in white—in any case neither in black nor red, which would have evoked the powers of stern judgment and limitation—went out of the city into an open field, which the advent of the Shekhinah transformed into the 'holy apple orchard.' They 'went to meet the Bride'" (p. 141).

"À la pointe acérée" / "À la pointe acérée"

June 10–16, 1961. From the tenth to the thirteenth of that month, Rolf Schoers was in Paris to speak with Celan about possible responses to the Goll affair. The poem shows Celan's reading of Hofmannsthal and knowledge of Roland Brinkmann's *Abriß de Geologie*. Jacques Derrida's *Shibboleth* opens with a close look at or meditation on this poem, specifically the verses "some unwritten, solidified / into language." Writes Martin Stern in his abstract: "This title was borrowed from Baudelaire, but Baudelaire's formula 'la pointe acérée de l'infini' was longer. Celan gave his shortened version the function of a dedication, which means he dedicated his poem to the 'steely head' of a tool. With this in mind we can perhaps find a new understanding of the main field of metaphors in Celan's poem. They deal with the breaking open of rocks and crystals, the uncovering of ore and metals, but also of memories, that is memories of the fate of Judaism, of concentration camps and death. As Baudelaire's 'steely head' helps the miner to excavate minerals and metals, the sharpened words of the poem may help to dig up and preserve the memory of the millions of people who died in the Shoa" (abstract of *"Wege dorthin": Intertextualität und Sinnkonstitution in* Paul Celans Gedicht À la Pointe Acérée, Germanisch-Romanische Monatsschriften Jahrgang 66 [2016], pp. 459–65).

T À la pointe acérée: French for "On the sharp point." Celan underlined the quotation in Hugo von Hofmannsthal's *Andreas oder die Vereinigten*: "at that moment Andreas had the foreboding that here the infinite had hit him with a sharper arrow than any specific pain; he has three or four remembrances that all have this pointe acérée de l'infini (in the meeting with the old woman and the child on the first morning),—feels this unfelt pain, without knowing that at that moment he *loves*" (Hugo von Hofmannsthal's *Andreas oder die Vereinigten. Fragmente eines Romans.* Nachwort von Jakob Wassermann. Berlin 1932, pp. 120–21). The phrase comes from (and is also referenced as such by Hofmannsthal) Baudelaire's "Le confiteor de l'artiste," in *Le Spleen de Paris* (1862): "Que les fins de journées d'automne sont pénétrantes! Ah! pénétrantes jusqu'à la douleur! car il est de certaines sensations délicieuses dont le vague n'exclut pas l'intensité; et il n'est pas de pointe plus acérée que celle de l'Infini." In Keith Waldrop's translation: "The Artist's Confiteor: How the close of an autumn day pierces! Pierces to the point of pain, for delightful sensations, though vague, may be intense, and there is no sharper pang than that of Infinity" (Charles Baudelaire, *Paris Spleen: Little Poems in Prose*, tr. Keith Waldrop [Middletown, Conn.: Wesleyan University Press, 2009]). In a note to "The Poetry of Osip Mandelstam," Celan wrote: "In the finite-making / Verendlichung / we feel the infinitiveness / Infinitivische, / we feel that—so often invoked by Hofmannsthal—'sharp point of the infinite' of Baudelaire" (MFP, #389).

2 Drusen / druses: "A cavity (vugh) in an igneous rock or a mineral vein into which euhedral (well-formed) crystals of the rock or mineral vein project, or the crystals themselves. The cavity represents a volume of late-stage, vapour-rich magma trapped by the rock crystallizing around it. Crystals can grow freely into this medium and hence crystallize in perfect forms (e.g., smokey quartz in granite) to give well-shaped crystal faces. The word is German, *Druse* meaning decayed or weathered ore" (Michael Allaby, *Oxford Dictionary of Geology & Earth Sciences*, p. 181). See the poem by Eisenreich, "Bittgang," which Celan had known since February 18, 1958: "The lightshaft, / it breaks from the rooms in the haze-circle, / druses in the darkness-slopes [Finster Gefälle], / I quarrel about windows [Fenster] with you." He had told her: "Your writing strips me of everything. I shouldn't read your poems. All that happens in me already stands there. Druses—I won't dare use that word again" (BE, pp. 230, 68).

6 verworfen / faulted: Geologically, the noun formation *Verwerfung* means: "rock fault; fault; faulting; dip-slip fault; throw; shift; shifting; dislocation (of strata); displacement; upslide." In common parlance the word has the meanings of "condemnation," "rejection," "dismissal."

9–11 Tür du davor einst, Tafel / mit dem getöteten / Kreidestern drauf / Door you stood before once, chalkboard, / with the slain / chalkstar on it: By drawing a small star with chalk on a board fixed to her door, Celan signaled to Eisenreich that he had come by in her absence. She would then wipe out the star (BE, pp. 56, 201).

15f. an / der blubbernden Radspur entlang / a- / long the blubbering wheelspoor, 20f. schwärzliches / Offen / blackish / openness: See verses 11–14 of "Engführung" / "Stretto."

III

"Die hellen Steine" / "The bright stones"

July 10, 1961, 11:00 p.m. Kermorvan/Trébabu. Celan spent most of July and August 1961 holidaying in Trébabu near Le Conquet in Brittany in the same house as the previous year. This is the first of some fourteen poems written there that year, nine of which would be included in *Die Niemandsrose*. The manuscript of the poem has the following dedication: "Für Dich, Gisèle, für Dich / mon aimée— / For you, Gisèle, for you / my beloved—" (TCA/NR, p. 82). In the copy of the second edition (1964) he signed to his wife he added the following verses: "And our son Eric / lives with us, / happy, / grows up, / while we work / and are present for him" (PC/GCL, p. 221).

3f. die Licht- / bringer / the light- / bringers: The word is German for the Latin *luzifer*, and is simultaneously the name for the morning star and for Satan as the fallen angel, who, when coming to earth, tore open hell (see verse 6f.).

10 so tun sie sich auf / that's how they open: See verse 6f. of "Erratisch" / "Erratic."

12f. du meine Leise, / du meine Wahre / you, my quiet one, / you, my true one: See verse 3 of "Mit allen Gedanken" / "With all my thoughts."

"Anabasis" / "Anabasis"

Kermorvan, July 27–28, 1961. The poem shows the first traces of Celan's reading of Mandelstam's posthumous poems in R. N. Grinberg's almanac "возъушные иумц" / "Luftwege" / "Air Ways/Paths."

T Anabasis: In an older reading note, Celan translated the title word as "Hinaufmarsch" / "upward march" (the literal translation of the Greek word ἀνάβασις: ana = "upward" or "upcountry," bainein = "to step or march"), an expedition from a coastline up into the interior of a country (see also "Weiß" / "White" (*Breathturn into Timestead*, pp. 210–11). Celan had known Xenephon's work with this title (describing the retreat of the ten thousand Greek mercenary soldiers from the inland to the coast of the Black Sea) since 1955. For the biographical importance of the Black Sea coast, see "Talglicht"

/ "Tallowlight." Note also Mandelstam's connection with the Black Sea as refuge and exile and the place where he wrote the poems gathered in *Tristia*.

4f. Zurück / in die herzhelle Zukunft / Back / into the heartbright future: See Celan's note of September 16, 1961, in his French edition of Lev Shestov's *Kierkegaard and the Existential Philosophy*: "compare 'back into the future' (NoOnesRose)!" re Shestov's line: "Faith does not question, it does not turn around to look back" (BPPC, section F, entry 42, p. 378).

19f. *unde suspirat / cor*: Final verse of the text of Mozart's Latin solo motet "Exsultate, jubilate" (K.165/158a): "Tu virginum corona, / tu nobis pacem dona, / tu consolare affectus, / unde suspirat cor" ("You, o crown of virgins, grant us peace, console our feelings, from which our hearts sigh").

27 Mitsammen / together: The common German word would be *zusammen*, "together." *Mitsammen* is often used by Martin Buber and Franz Rosenzweig in their translation of the Bible (and by Buber in other of his writings). See, for example, Buber's "Zuhauf kommen dann die Söhne Jehudas / und die Söhne Jisraels mitsammen" ("Then the children of Judah and the children of Israel shall be gathered together") (Hosea 1:10; English from the King James Version).

"Ein Wurfholz" / "A boomerang"

Kermorvan, July 30, 1961.

1 Ein Wurfholz / A boomerang: See verse 16 of "Aber" / "But." In connection with this throwing weapon, see the motto to an early version of Mandelstam's *Requiem for Andrei Belyi*: "Between you and the land an icy link comes to be—So, fly, become younger, endlessly bending yourself straight. They shall not ask you, the young ones, the future ones, those, how you are doing over there, in the emptiness, in the pureness—you, the orphan!" (my translation via TCA/NR, p. 86); Celan's source was Grinberg's almanac (see the previous poem and commentary). See also an independent fragment of July 27, 1961, that links "A boomerang" with the following poem, "Havdalah": "Viel menschliches Unland in diesem Jahr. / Mit eigener / Hand Geschriebenes kommt, ein Wurfholz, / aus der Ferne zurück" / "much human unland in this year. / Writing by my own hand / returns / a boomerang,

/ from afar" (TCA/NR, p. 86, partial quote). Already on July 5, 1960, Celan had written to Otto Pöggeler: "So a poem goes out to people, it has to, as it follows this path, believe these people to be humans—we still are, to say it carefully, among hominids—, and already here it is, coming back, a missile [*Wurfgeschoss*], thrown by the hand it had 'reached'" (GA, #174).

1 auf Atemwegen / on breathroutes: See fragment #263 (MFV): "'What's on the lung, put on the tongue' my mother used to say—. . . on breathroutes it comes, the poem, it is there, pneumatic: for everyone. / In the mora meaning clarifies itself—" (TCA/MFV, p. 108).

8f. mit- / verwaisend / co- / orphaned: See above the final word of the planned Mandelstam motto.

10 Lapilli: Latin for "little stones," "pebbles"; see, in Ovid's *Metamorphoses* (Book 15): "Now, long ago / it was the custom to vote with pebbles, / black ones to declare the person guilty, / white ones to acquit, and in this case, too, / the harsh result was rendered in this way. / Every pebble placed in the cruel urn / was black, but then, when they tipped it over / and poured the pebbles out to tally them, / white. / So, through the sacred power of Hercules, / Alemon's son was favoured in the verdict and set free" (Ovid, *Metamorphoses,* translated by Ian Johnston, Richer Resources Publications, 2012, http://johnstoniatexts.x10host.com/ovid/ovid15html.html). See also the reading note from the time of *Sprachgitter / Speechgrille* that cites the word "Lapilli," among other geological terms for stones (TCA/SG, p. 115).

13 verbracht / displaced: See the first word of "Engführung" / "Stretto."

"Hawdalah" / "Havdalah"

Kermorvan, July 31, 1961.

T Hawdalah / Havdalah: From Hebrew *haḇdālāh*, "separation," "division." Havdalah is a Jewish religious ceremony that marks the symbolic end of Shabbat and ushers in the new week. The ritual involves lighting a special havdalah candle with several wicks, blessing a cup of wine, and smelling sweet spices. Shabbat ends on Saturday night after the appearance of three stars in the sky. Celan wrote the poem on a Monday that was not a holiday; the Celan family followed no religious rituals.

4 spinnst du / you spin, 5f. ins / Freie / into / the open: A reference to verses 5 and 11 of "Count the almonds."

5–7 ins / Freie, dahin, / ins Gebundne / into / the open, and on, / into the bound: A reference to verse 10 of "Threesome, foursome"; see also verses 12f. and 16f. of "I have cut bamboo."

9 Spindeln / spindels, 11f. ein / Licht geknüpft / a / light knitted: See the reading traces in Plato: "after going forward a day's journey, and they saw there at the middle of the light the extremities of its fastenings stretched from heaven; for this light was the girdle of the heavens like the undergirders of triremes, holding together in like manner the entire revolving vault. And from the extremities was stretched the spindle of Necessity, through which all the orbits turned. Its staff and its hook were made of adamant, and the whorl of these and other kinds was commingled" (Plato's Republic [10. 616c] translated by Paul Shorey, Cambridge, MA, Harvard University Press; London, William Heinemann Ltd. 1969. The underlinings reproduce those in Celan's German edition).

10 Unland / unland: See verse 1 of "A boomerang" and the quotation in the commentary. The word appears in Celan's oeuvre only during a limited time period: see verse 21 of "And with the Book from Tarussa," an uncollected poem beginning "Much human unland in this year," and his Yesenin translation "Ionien III."

13f. den leeren / Stühlen / the empty / chairs: At Jewish ceremonies, a chair is left empty for the prophet Elijah.

15 Sabbatglanz / sabbath radiance: See verse 17 of "Before a candle," and the blessing spoken at the extinguishing of the Sabbath candle linking Sabbath to light and other days to darkness. See also Gershom Scholem: "On the Sabbath the light of the upper world bursts into the profane world in which man lives during the six days of the week. The light of the Sabbath endures into the ensuing week, growing gradually dimmer, to be relieved in the middle of the week by the rising light of the next Sabbath" (p. 139).

"Le Menhir" / "Le Menhir"

Kermorvan, August 4, 1961.

T Le Menhir: menhir: from Breton *men* (stone) and *hir* (long): a tall upright stone erected in prehistoric (middle bronze Age) times in western Europe. The largest still standing menhir in Brittany is in Kerloas, close to Kermovan.

4 Steinblick / stone-gaze: The word had provisionally been considered as a possible title for the later volume *Lichtzwang / Lightduress*; see "Steinauge" / "stone eye" (verse 9 of "Im Zeitwinkel schwört" / "In Time's Corner" [*Breathturn into Timestead*, pp. 296–97]), and the late uncollected poem beginning "Befahrene Steinblicke" / "Frequented / navigated / eye-gazes" (PC, *Die Gedichte*, p. 543).

6 Weißheidewegen / wild-rosemary-paths: *Ledum palustre* or *Rhododendron tomentosum*, commonly known as marsh Labrador tea or wild rosemary, of the family Ericaceae, in German is also called *Weiße Heide*, "white heath," because of its white flowers.

9 Verkebstes, hierhergekarrt / Concubined, carted over here: *Kebse*, an antiquated word for "concubine," "paramour," but also (BW 2018, p. 816) "a reliquary." During the summer weeks in Kermovan Celan received twelve poems (without a referent letter) from Brigitta Eisenreich that show how Celan had hurt her. Celan already uses "Kebsehe" / "~concubine-marriage" in his translation of "mariage adultérin," an expression invented by Picasso in his play "Le désir attrapé par la queue" (GW IV, p. 10f.).

10f. Meer- / mühle mahlte / Sea- / mill milled: Quote of verse 30 from "White and Light."

13 Ginster / broom-bush, 18 Schoten / siliquae: See Celan's letter to Nelly Sachs from Kermovan the previous July: "We know that we can and may rely on you. With heather and centaury, with honeysuckly and foxglove and broom-bush (not stinging furze)" (PCNS #48, p. 32). The Faboideae broom has dark siliquae-like pulses.

14 Phaläne / night moth: See Jean Paul's *The Valley of Campan*: ". . . she raised from a projecting hairy potato stalk, a large moth [Phaläne], and showed it to us with a firm mouth, which should have been softened by a smile. / It was the so-called Death's-head. I stroked the flat, drooping wings, and said, 'It comes from Egypt, the land of mummies and graves; it bears a *memento mori* on its back, and a *miserere* in its plaintive voice'" (p. 99 in the English edition; with additional marginal marks in Celan's German edition, vol. 39, p. 52f.; see also the reading note of July 14, 1957, via Badiou).

15f. Schwarz, phylakterien- / farben, / Black, phylactery- / color, 17f. mit- / betenden Schoten / also- / praying siliquae: Philacteries, or Tefillin, are two small black boxes with black straps attached to them; Jewish men are required to place one box on their forehead and tie the other one on their left arm facing the heart, on weekday mornings for prayers. The text that is inserted inside the two boxes is handwritten by a scribe, and consists of the four sets of biblical verses in which Tefillin are commanded (Exod. 13:1–10, 11–16; Deut. 6:4–9, 11:13–21). See "Am weißen Gebetriemen" / "On the white philactery" (*Breathturn into Timestead*, pp. 30–31).

"Nachmittag mit Zirkus und Zitadelle" /
"Afternoon, with Circus and Citadel"

Brest–Kermorvan, August 15, 1961; written after a visit to a circus in the roadstead of Brest.

1 Brest: A major harbor town in Brittany and the most westerly city in continental Europe. Wiedemann suggests interestingly that this place-name, Brest, which harbors the French for "east," *est*, sets up a connection to the Russian elements of the poem and to Celan's own biography: the White Russian city of Brest-Litovsk, an important Jewish center before World War II, lies on the Western Bug River (see the poem from *Sand from the Urns* entitled "Nähe der Gräber" / "Nearness of the Graves," which opens with the lines "Do you still know the waters of the southern Bug? mother, the wave, the wounds it made?"). An early draft of the poem also calls the date of composition "Assumption Day," referring to verse 9 of "Zurich, Hotel zum Storchen." On that visit too, Celan (with GCL, son Eric, and Ingeborg Bachmann) had gone to a circus (PC/IB, #225, p. 190).

4 Mandelstamm / Mandelstam: This is the only time Celan uses the last name of Osip Mandelstam in a poem (see "Osip" in "Es ist alles anders" / "Everything is different" and the fragment "Bruder Ossip" / "Brother Osip" in BA, vol. 11, p. 476). See the dedication of the volume *NoOnesRose*, and also the marginal notes, underlinings, and markings of October 25, 1962: "x / Da sah ich dich, Mandelstamm!!" / "there I see you, Mandelstam," in André Néher's *L'essence du prophétisme* on page 337 next to: "Jérémie n'a rien vu qu'une branche d'amandier, mais, pour l'avoir vue, il en a pénétré la signification. À travers le reflet, il atteint la lumière" (Jeremiah saw only the branch

of an almond tree, but, for having seen it, he was able to understand its meaning. Through the reflection, he came to the light).

9f. Ich grüßte die Trikolore / mit einem russischen Wort / I greeted the tricolor / with a Russian word: See verse 45 of Mandelstam's poem "1 January 1924": "Moskau, aufs neue. Ach, ich grüß dich, wieder!" / "Moscow, anew. Ah, I greet you, again" (my translation of Celan's version [GW V, p. 146f.]; the original line is given as "Moscow is Moscow again. I say hello to her" in Clarence Brown and W. S. Merwin's version).

"Bei Tag" / "By Day"

Kermorvan, August 18, 1961.

1 Hasenfell-Himmel / Hare-pelt sky: See the description of the previous year's holiday dwelling to Nelly Sachs: "under clear skies in a little house on the edge of a huge park grown just wild enough for hares and also for people" (PCNS, #48, p. 32), and in a letter to Nani and Klaus Demus he writes how at quiet moments "we can eavesdrop on the hares as they converse in Breton with each other" (PC/KND, p. 322).

3 Auch ich, / I, too, 5f. kam / als ein Kranich / came / as a crane: See the last line of "Am letzten Tor" / "At the last gate," a poem from *SU*: "Let the stone be the cloud, let me be the crane."

"Kermorvan" / "Kermorvan"

August 21, 1961.

T Kermorvan: Celan's holiday house stood on the grounds of castle Kermorvan close to Trébabu (see also "The bright stones"). The Breton name means "sailor's house," composed of "ker" (house, village), "mor" (sea), and "van" (man, person, figure).

1 Tausendgüldenkraut-Sternchen / common-centaury-star, 4 Heimat / homeland: A reference to verse 2 of "Mute autumn odors." See also the letter to Nelly Sachs cited in the commentary to "Le Menhir."

2–4 du Erle, du Buche, du Farn: / mit euch Nahen geh ich ins Ferne,— / Wir gehen dir, Heimat, ins Garn / you alder, you beech, you fern: / with you, near ones, I go far away / we fall into your, homeland's, snare: Plants native to central and eastern Europe; the beech refers directly to Celan's "Bukovina,

Buchenland" which translates literally as "Beech-land, land of beeches." For alder and homeland, see verse 20 of "Hafen" / "Harbor" (*Breathturn into Timestead*, pp. 40–41) and verses 4–6 of "Lauter" / "Nothing but" (*Breathturn into Timestead*, pp. 270–71).

5 Kirschlorbeertraube / cherry laurel, 6 beim bärtigen Palmenschaft / near the bearded date-palm trunk: Because of mild Gulf Stream meteorological conditions, these heat-loving plants can be found in Brittany.

7 *Ich liebe, ich hoffe, ich glaube / I love, I hope, I believe*: See 1 Cor. 13:13: "And now abideth faith, hope, charity, these three; but the greatest of these is charity." Celan here uses a reversed order, drawing on Heinrich Heine's: "Die Eichen sind grün, und blau sind die Augen / Der deutschen Frauen; sie schmachten gelinde / Und seufzen von Liebe, Hoffnung und Glauben;— / Ich kann's nicht vertragen—es hat seine Gründe" ("Angelique V," verses 9–12, vol. 2, p. 37). In English in Emma Lazarus's translation: "The oak-tree there is green, the German women / Have soft blue eyes—tender they are and fair. / They whisper sighs of hope and truth and passion. / I have good cause—'tis more than I can bear" (Heinrich Heine, *Sämtliche Werke*, Bd. 2 Hg. v. Rudolf Frank, München und Leipzig, 1923; Emma Lazarus's translation: https://www.lieder.net/lieder/get_text.html?TextId=37825).

8 Steindattel klafft / stone-date gapes: Quotes verse 11 of "Matière de Bretagne."

10 *Servir Dieu est règner*, 12 Kannitverstan: The French means "To serve God is to rule"; it is the heraldic motto of the lords of Kermovan and is inscribed on plaques in the castle and the chapel. The French-German change of language is commented on by the reference to Johan Peter Hebel's story "Kannitverstan," in which a character who does not know Dutch interprets the expression for "I cannot understand" as a proper name.

1of ich kann / ihn lesen / I can / read it: Concerning reading, see verses 66 and 74 of "Stretto."

"Ich habe Bambus geschnitten" / "I have cut bamboo"

Kermorvan, August 22–23, 1961. The last poem written in Kermorvan, followed by several months of no writing due to mental health problems.

1 Bambus / bamboo: Even today bamboo grows in Kermorvan.

2 für dich, mein Sohn / for you, my son: The first direct reference to Celan's son Eric; however, see "Blume" / "Flower" and verse 3 of "Ein Holzstern" / "A woodstar," as well as the poem directly dedicated to him, "For Eric."

5f. sie / steht / it / stands, 14f. morgen / steht es noch immer / will still / stand, tomorrow: Concerning the concept of "standing," "to stand," etc., see the commentary to verse 27 of "A Gonif- and Gangster-Ditty," as well as a range of further comments.

8–10 in was für / Gefäße ich den / Sand um mich her tat, vor Jahren / into what kind of / vessels I put the sand around me: See the title of Celan's very first collection of poems, *Der Sand aus den Urnen / The Sand from the Urns*, and the poem by that title. According to Eric Celan these verses also reference Celan's time in a Romanian work camp, where he was doing forced labor in road construction.

"Kolon" / "Colon"

Rue d'Ulm, February 5, 1962. The elite École Normale Supèrieure (ENS), where Celan had taught since the 1959–1960 school year, is on rue d'Ulm. This is the first poem we know with certainty that he wrote there. The long pause in his writing since "I cut bamboo" is thematized in the poem.

T Kolon / Colon: from Greek plural *cola*: a rhythmical unit of an utterance; Celan defines the colon in *The Meridian* as "'Breath-units' (Buber); cola" (#269), and refers to it twice more: "In the 'mora and cola' the poem culminates.—" (# 218); "—Not the motif, but pause and interval, but the mute breath-auras, but the cola guarantee in the poem the truth of such an encounter" (#400).

T Kolon / Colon, 5f. sprachwahr in jeder / der Pausen / speechtrue in each of / the pauses: See *The Meridian*: "And then you stand with your falling silent thinking in the pause which reminds you of your heart, and don't speak of it. And, speak, later, of yourself. In this 'later,' in there remembered pauses, in the cola and mora, your word speaks" (#127).

1f. Wort- / Vigilie / word- / vigil: See *The Meridian*: "The poem—an endless vigil" (#47); "The poem as vigil" (#139); and "no oneiric qualities, but vigils" (#353). See also verse 12 of "La Contrescarpe."

IV

"Was geschah?" / "What happened?"

Paris, April 7, 1962–Moisville, June 14, 1962. This is the first poem written (partially) in Moisville (Eure Département), where the Celan family had bought a country place in the spring of 1962.

3 Neben-Erde: See the beginning of Jean Paul Richter's *Kampaner Thal*: "In my distilling process, I frequently precipitated the phlegma of our earth-ball—its polar deserts, its Russian forests, its icebergs—and from the sediments extracted a beautiful by-earth, a small satellite. If we extract and regulate the charms of this old world, we can form a delightful though minutely condensed world" (translated by Juliette Bauer; Project Gutenberg, eBook; see also the original, vol. 39, p. 13).

5 Wohin gings? Gen Unverklungen / Where did it lead? Toward unfaded: See verse 16 of "Es war Erde in ihnen" / "There was earth inside them."

7f. Zu schwer befunden. / Schwerer werden. Leichter sein / Judged too heavy. / Become heavier. Be lighter: See verse 3 of "Die Hand voller Stunden" / "The hand full of hours" and verses 35–37 of "In der Luft" / "In the air."

"In eins" / "In One"

January 23–May 24, 1962 [?]. The poem shows the use of fragments developed independently toward the "Parisian Elegy" project of January 23–28 and February 20, 1962, that were probably combined and expanded on May 24, 1962. The poem shows traces of Celan's reading of Mandelstam's posthumous poems in Grinberg's almanac (see "Anabasis").

T In eins / In One: See the reading traces in Helmuth v. Glasenapp's *Die Philosophie der Inder*: "Die Tendenz zur Reduktion geht aber noch weiter: auch für unser Empfinden ganz verschiedene Dinge glaubte man ineinssetzen zu können" ("But the tendency toward reduction goes even further: even things that for our understanding are very different, were believed to be able to be gathered into one") (my translation; further marginal notes, p. 26f.). See also verses 11 and 14 of Celan's translation of William Shakespeare's sonnet CV: "Fair, kind, and true, have often lived alone, Which three till now, never kept seat in one." / "Ich find, erfind—um sie in eins zu bringen" and "In Einem will ich drei zusammenschmieden" (GW V, p. 345).

T In eins / In One, 2 Schibboleth / shibboleth: See verses 17–20 of the following poem, "Hinausgekrönt" / "Crowned out." (In the book edition of *Die Niemandsrose* these poems were on facing pages.) For "shibboleth," see the poem with that title and its commentaries.

1 Dreizehnter Feber / February 13, 2 Schibboleth / Shibboleth, 4 *No pasarán*: "Feber" is the Austrian form of "Februar" / "February." See the title and verses 21 and 23 of "Schibboleth" / "Shibboleth." On February 13, 1962, eight demonstrators killed by the police—who violently broke up a demonstration at the Charonne metro station—were buried. Nearly a million people followed the funeral cortège from the Bourse du Travail (where the corpses of the killed had been kept) to the Père Lachaise Cemetery. Celan kept a flyer on which he had written "February 13th 1962" (Badiou's reference). The flyer ended with the lines "VIVE LA LIBERTE! LE FASCISME NE PASSERA PAS!" (in Celan's posthumous papers at Deutsches Literatur Archiv, Marbach). The not officially sanctioned demonstration was directed against the OAS (Organisation Armée Secrète, a right-wing terrorist organization of French colons, army officers, and soldiers opposed to the independence of Algeria), which tried with terrorist tactics to counter the attempts to bring the Algerian war of independence to a conclusion via negotiations.

3f. Peuple / de Paris: "Peuple de Paris" was the traditional address to the population of Paris during the 1871 Paris Commune uprising.

4 *No pasarán*: Spanish for "They will not pass," the motto of the International Brigades during the Spanish Civil War. See also verse 23 of "Shibboleth."

5 Schäfchen zur Linken / Lambs to the left: According to Gisèle Celan-Lestrange this is an allusion: depending on which side the sheep graze, they bring good or bad luck; Celan supposedly always tried to pass the sheep on the "correct" side.

5f. Abadias, / der Greis aus Huesca / Abadias, / the old man from Huesca: See Celan's letter to his friend Erich Einhorn: "In a few days we'll go to the countryside, to Normandy and a small village between Nonancourt and Damville [Moisville], where it is quiet and where there are simple, real people, among them a sheepherder from Huesca, a Spaniard brought to Normandy with Spanish republican refugees" (June 23, 1962, PC/EE, p. 6). Abadias is buried in the cemetery of the village.

7 Exil / exile: See also the theme of exile in the following poem.

11 Hirten-Spanisch: See verse 30 of "Shibboleth" and the commentary.

12 des Kreuzers "Aurora" / of the cruiser "Aurora": The warship Aurora's shots at the imperial palace on November 7, 1917, in St. Petersburg mark the beginning of the October Revolution.

13 Bruderhand / brotherhand: See the dedication of this volume and the earlier cited "Brother Osip."

15f. Petropolis, der / Unvergessenen Wanderstadt / Petropolis, the / unforgotten wander-city: Mandelstam used that name for St. Petersburg; see his poem from the volume *Tristia*—translated by Celan as "Petropolis, diaphan" / "Petropolis, diaphanous" (my translation of Celan's German version) (GW V, p. 93). Petropolis was also the name of a Russian-language exiled publishing house in Berlin where Mandelstam's *Tristia* was published in 1922, and of the place in Brazil where Stefan Zweig committed suicide.

17 toskanisch zu Herzen / tuscanly on your heart: See verses 9–12 of Osip Mandelstam's posthumous poem "Не сраеннеаў" ("Don't compare, the living are incomparable"; not translated by Celan), the Russian opening line of which Celan noted down several times, for example, as the epigraph for his "Walliser Elegie" (not reproduced here). The third, final stanza of that poem reads (in A. S. Kline's translation): "I'm ready to go—where there's more sky— / but pure longing now won't set me free / from the still-youthful hills of Voronezh, / to those, clear, and wholly-human, of Tuscany." In one of the Russian-German dictionaries Celan used, the word "тоска" (pronounced "toska") is given the meaning "harm, grief, sorrow, unrest of the heart . . . boredom." In reading Lev Shestov, Celan annotated the word in the margin as "angoisse" / "anguish."

18 *Friede den Hütten! / Peace to the huts!*: A part of the parole used by Georg Büchner at the start of his pamphlet "Der Hessische Landboten": "Friede den Hütten! Krieg den Palästen!" (Peace to the huts! War on the palaces!), which reverses the sequence of a call to arms during the French Revolution: "Guerre aux châteaux! Paix aux chaumières!"

"Hinausgekrönt" / "Crowned out"

Moisville, July 30, 1962. On October 26, 1965, Celan wrote to GCL: "do you remember: . . . 'and we sung the Warsowianka. With reeded lips, Petrarch,' it was, turned toward the Siberia of the exilees, of poetry, exile and ground of human pride, turned toward that 'Jewish bell, won't turn gray,' it was, enfolding us, with Eric, our most tenacious justification for existing" (PC/GCL, p. 297). With several "(here) too's" the poem refers to Celan's own oeuvre, while also showing his reading of Ilia Ehrenburg's *Memoirs: 1921–1941*.

5 graugeschlagenes Herzhammersilber / grayhammered hearthammersilver: See Rilke's Tenth Duino Elegy: "Daß von den klar geschlagenen Hämmern des Herzens / keiner versage an weichen zweifelnden oder / reißenden Saiten" / "Let not even one of the clear-struck hammers of my heart / fail to sound because of a slack, a doubtful / or a broken string" (verses 3–5, Bd. 1, S. 477; Stephen Mitchell's translation, p. 61).

6 Berenikes Haupthaar, auch hier / Berenice's mane, here too: Constellation named after the Egyptian queen Berenice II, who, to ensure the safe return of her husband, Ptolemy III, from the third Syrian War, offered locks of her hair to the goddess Aphrodite and placed them in the goddess's temple at Zephyrium. As the story goes, the hair offering disappeared when Ptolemy returned to Egypt, and was supposedly carried to the heavens and placed among the stars. The name Coma Berenices, or Berenice's hair, applied to a constellation, commemorates this incident. See also Celan's essay "Edgar Jené und der Traum vom Traume" / "Edgar Jené and the Dream of the Dream," in which he writes: "Ungläubig auch heute noch, wo doch das Haar der Berenike schon so lange unter den Sternen hängt" / "Incredulous even today, when Berenice's hair has been hanging among the stars for such a long time" (GW III, p. 159; translation by Rosmarie Waldrop, PCCP, p. 8); a poem ("Sternenlied" / "Starsong") from the early 1940s ends with the lines: "My heart beams wildly from the glorious awareness—your hair from the brightness of Berenice's hair" (BW, 2018, p. 355).

6 Haupthaar, auch hier,—ich flocht / mane, here too,—I braided: See verse 1 of "Strähne" / "Lock."

10 Blauschlucht / Blue ravine, 12 Huren / whores: Regarding the word-(part) "Schlucht" with sexual connotations, see verse 9 of "Dein vom Wachen" / "Your dream" (*Breathturn into Timestead*, pp. 12–13), and verse

13 of "Am weißen Gebetsriemen" / "On the white philactery" (*Breathturn into Timestead*, pp. 30–31).

17–20 auch sie in eins / geschmolzen, auch sie / phallisch gebündelt zu dir, / Garbe-und-Wort / they too fused / into one, they too / phallically bundled for you: See "Shibboleth" and "In One."

22 Exil / exile, 33f. Petrarca. / In Tundra-Ohren / Petrarch. / Into tundra-ears: In earlier drafts the phrase "by Vladivostok, he read" more clearly links this to Mandelstam; in a note to the poem "Walliser Elegie" on December 7, 1961, Celan had already made the connection: "Ehrenburg, Petrarch—Mandelstam / Siberia" (BA, vol. 11, p. 399). Ehrenburg reports that before his death in 1938 in the Siberian camp Mandelstam read Petrarch's sonnets.

32 Warschowjanka / Warszawianka: This is a revolutionary Polish song (1879). Osip Mandelstam was born in Warsaw.

"Wohin mir das Wort" / "Where the word"

Moisville, August 15, 1962 (Assumption Day).

4 Siebenstern / sevensisters' starflower: The German "Siebenstern" has two meanings: (1) It refers to a flower, *Trientalis europaea*, of the primrose family, usually called by one of its common names, chickweed wintergreen or arctic starflower. It is a small herbaceous perennial plant whose solitary white flowers (usually with six to eight white petals arrayed starlike around a yellow center) appear in midsummer; (2) The word (and its synonym *Siebengestirn*) can also refer to the constellation made by the seven visible stars that form the Pleiades, often called the Seven Sisters. The name Pleiades comes from the Greek *plein* (to sail), showing the importance of the constellation for sailors to orient themselves, but also in terms of delimiting the sailing seasons in the Mediterranean: rising early from May on and setting early from November on, the Seven Sisters indicated favorable and dangerous sailing times.

5 Im Nachthaus / In the binnacle: During this time Celan was reading Franz Schulze's treatise "Nautik," in which he came across the description of how the ship's compass is housed in a container called a "Nachthaus" (p. 16, with illustration), literally a "nighthouse," i.e., a binnacle. (Franz Schulze, *Nautik, Kurzer Abriß des täglich an Bord von Handelsschiffen angewandten Teils der Schiffahrtskund*e [Sammlung Göschen 84, Berlin und Leipzig, 1919], p. 16, with illustration).

7 ein aufrechtes Schweigen / an upstanding silence: See the range of commentaries regarding the verb "stehen" / "to stand," for example, the commentary to verse 27 of "Eine Gauner- und Ganovenweise" / "A Gonif- and Gangster-Ditty."

"Les Globes" / "Les Globes"

Date of composition uncertain; Celan marks one manuscript as "dated / before the trip to Brittany." Various word-cues suggest summer 1961 as the time of composition.

T Les Globes, 1 Augen / eyes, 2 die Sonnen-, die Herzbahnen / the sun's, the heart's ecliptics: The French word *globe*, here in the plural, refers to the (earth-) sphere, models thereof, and heavenly spheres, as well as to the eyeball. See Baudelaire's poem *Les Aveugles*: "Dardant on ne sait où leurs globes ténébreux. // Leurs yeux, d'où la divine étincelle est partie." / "Darting one knows not where their darkening eyeballs / Their eyes from which the divine spark has gone" (Charles Baudelaire, *Oeuvres complètes*, Editions Gallimard, Bibliothèque de la Pléiade, 1975, vol. 1, p. 92; my translation). In connection to the Brittany trip of 1961, Celan wrote to Beda Alleman: "Do you remember that in Tröbahu I told you about Kepler's quote I came across after my trip to Darmstadt. Here it is in his words: 'God is symbolyzed by the sphere; a section of the sphere produces a circle; this circle signifies the human being'" (March 27, 1962; Badiou's reference). See also the title of the Büchner Prize speech held in Darmstadt in 1960, *The Meridian*, and the various meanings of that term, including "a circle of constant longitude passing through a given place on the earth's surface and the terrestrial poles" and, in astronomy, "a great circle passing through the two poles of the celestial sphere and the zenith of a given observer. Also called celestial meridian, local meridian, vertical circle" (*American Heritage Dictionary*, 3rd Edition, New York: Houghton Mifflin, 1994, p. 1130).

"Huhediblu" / "Huhediblu"

Moisville, September 13, 1962. On that day Celan received a letter from Guntram Vesper, whom Celan mistook for the son of the Nazi poet Will Vesper, with the request for a critical appreciation of his poetry.

T Huhediblu: Regarding the title, James Hatley, after discussing the blasphematory accents of the poem, interestingly notes that the title word "purposefully omits those two vowels, the *alpha* and the *omega* cited in Revelations, the two vowels in which breath is given a Christian articulation and in which an absolute *arche* and *closure* to one's saying are intoned" (*Suffering Witness: The Quandary of Responsibility after the Irreparable* [Albany, N.Y.: SUNY, 2000], p. 183). But see also verses 41–44 of the poem, playing with those two vowels: "The tone, oh, / the Oh-tone, ah, / the *A* and the *O* / the Oh-these-gallows-already-again, the Ah-it-thrives."

5 die Bälge der Feme-Poeten / the Vehmic poets' bastard offspring, 6 lurchen und vespern / lurch and vesper, 7 episteln / epistle: "Feme" / "Vehmic," in Westphalian dialect, refers to a medieval secret tribunal and to "a secret Nazi organization intent upon seeking out and executing those considered enemies of National Socialism" (*Webster's Third New International Dictionary*, vol. 1, p. 835). In one of Vesper's poems, Celan circled the word "Olme" (also called *Schwanzlurche*), a kind of fire salamander.

13 Datum des Nimmermenschtags im September / date of the nolongerhumanday in September: Reference to the anti-Semitic and racist Nuremberg Laws enacted by the Reichstag on September 15, 1935, at a special meeting convened during the annual Nuremberg Rally of the Nazi Party (NSDAP). On September 29 and 30, 1941, German SS-Kommandos massacred thirty-four thousand Jews at Babi Yar (a ravine in the Ukrainian capital, Kiev). Yevgeny Yevtushenko wrote his poem "Babi Yar" in 1961, which was translated by Paul Celan in June 1962 (GW V, pp. 281–87). It was in September 1939 that Germany attacked Poland and World War II broke out; in September 1941 Romanian Nazis forced all Jews in Czernowitz to move into the ghetto and deported thousands to Transnistrian death camps.

September is the most often mentioned month in Celan's oeuvre; at least three poems have the month in their titles.

16–18 wann blühen die / when, / will they bloom, the [. . .] / [. . .] September- / rosen? / September- / roses? 63 Oh quand refleuriront, oh roses, vos septembres?: See the final verse of Paul Verlaine's sonnet "L'espoir luit comme un brin de paille dans l'étable," which Celan had translated in Czernowitz (Barbara Wiedemann, "Im alten Garten — Septemberrosen. Noch einmal zu Paul Celan und Paul Verlaine" in: *Celan Jahrbuch 5* 1993, p. 289).

19 Hüh, 61 (hott!): The German expressions "Hü!" and "Hott!" refer to

the opposite directions, left and right, you ask (and indicate by pulling on the reins) a horse to move. Celan plays on this in the drafts for the Meridian speech: "Die Geister rechts und links. Die Hü-und die Hott-Intellektuellen" / "The ghosts right and left. The 'this way-that way' intellectuals" and "Das Gedicht hört ebensowenig auf das Hüh der Engagierten, wie es auf das Hott der Aestheten—die Kybernetiker unter ihnen sind mitgemeint—hört; es bewegt sich auf anderen Bahnen; es horcht und es lauscht; und von seinem Horchen und Lauschen her spricht es sich, mit seinem Kummer und seinem Gram, dir zu—spricht es dich—endlich, d. h. vor dem Horizont seiner Unendlichkeit—dir selbst zu. Das Gedicht, ja, härmt sich für dich.— " / "The poem listens as little to the 'giddyap this way' of the politically engaged, as to the 'giddyap that way' of the aesthetes—the cyberneticists among them are also meant—; it moves along other trajectories; it harkens and listens; and from that harkening and listening it speaks itself, with its sorrow and its grief, toward you—it speaks you—finite, i.e. in front of the horizon of its infinitude—to yourself. The poem, yes, rues itself for you" (TCA/MFV, #645 and #644).

19 on tue: French for "they kill." An earlier draft had "on tue / les / poètes pour les citer après" / "they kill / the / poets to quote them later," and leads to Yevgeny Yevtushenko's poem "Verlaine," which Celan is probably quoting from memory as it appeared in the December 1961 issue of the magazine *Esprit* in a French translation by Tania Soucault.

22–24 Bruder / Geblendet, Bruder / Erloschen / Brother / Blinded, brother / Extinguished: In an early draft Celan had written " Brother Arnold, Brother / Osip," referencing the German-Jewish writer Arnold Zweig, who wrote the antifascist novel *The Axe of Wandsbek* (mentioned by Celan in a draft) and was deeply engaged in East German cultural politics after his return following World War II, and Osip Mandelstam, the dedicatee of the volume *Die Niemandsrose*.

33, 37 Achsenton / axistone: On August 17, 1961. Celan had underlined and copied the last verse of one of Mandelstam's poems from the Voronezh Notebooks (#61) and gives the following French and German translation-variations: "L'entendre, l'axe terrestre, l'axe terrestre" / "Der Erde Achse hören, sie, der Erde Achse" / "the earth's axis, to hear it, the earth's axis"

(Luftwege 58, Ralf Dutli 1996 *Ossip Mandelstamm: Die Woronescher Hefte. Letzte Gedichte 1935-1937*, hrsg. und übers. von Ralph Dutli, Zürich 1996. p. 137, note 125; here my translation; Andrew Davis's English translation (in *Osip Mandelstam: Voronezh Notebooks*, NYRB/Poets 2016) gives the line as "Hear the slipping earth, the slipping earth").

46 Alraunenfluren / mandrake-acres: The singular form had been used as provisional title for the poem. The mandrake is a plant belonging to the nightshade family (Solanaceae), containing poisonous and psychotropic chemicals, with a rich history in various belief systems, due especially to the resemblance of the root to the human figure. The German word *Alraune* is often linked to the verb *raunen*, to whisper, to speak lightly.

47 Beikraut / weed, 48 Beiwort / adjective-word, 49f. ad- / jektivisch / ad- / jectival: The German word *Beikraut* (also *Unkraut*) means "weed." Celan plays with the "bei," which when preceding "Wort" / "word" gives "Beiwort," i.e., literally "added word" (via Latin *adiacere*, to throw next to, to add)—thus gives our grammatical term "adjective."

56 kontemporan / up-to-date, 58 alibi-elbisch / alibi-elfish: See his letter to Erich Einhorn: "Don't let the literary prizes I'm awarded fool you: they are in the final analysis only the alibi of those who . . . in the shadow of such alibis, carry on with other, up-to-date, means what they had started, or else, continued, to do under Hitler" (August 10, 1962; PC/EE, p. 7).

57 Schinderhannes 59 Julchen / lil' Julia, 61 Fallbeil / guillotine: Johannes Bückler (c.1778–November 21, 1803), nicknamed Schinderhannes, was maybe the most famous legendary German outlaw. When his mistress, Juliana (Julchen) Blasius, was arrested and threatened with being charged as an accomplice, Schinderhannes testified against members of his gang, nineteen of whom were sentenced to death. Schinderhannes himself was guillotined on November 21, 1803, before the gates of Mainz. (See *Schinderhannes — Nichtnutz, Pferdedieb, Räuberhauptman?* by Mark Scheibe, especially the chapters "Julchen Blasius" and "Hinrichtung am 21 November 1803," 6. Auflage, Kelkheim, 2015.)

57 Schinderhannes, 59f. das Julchen: / daseinsfeist rülpst / lil' Julia / daseinsfat belches: See verse 9 and the final stanza of Guillaume Apollinaire's poem "Schinderhannes" in Celan's 1954 translation: "Das Julchen rülpst, daß

Gott bewahre—" / "Lil' Julia belches, may God keep—" and "So hält man Tafel rund im Kreise / und f . . . t und lacht beim Abendschmaus, / und wird ganz schwach, nach deutscher Weise, / und geht und bläst ein Leben aus" / "So one revels around the banquet table / and farts and laughs at dinner / and gets all mushy, in that German way / and goes out to take a life" (verses 9 and 29–32, GW IV, p. 787 f.). The connection with the Goll affair becomes clear via this unsent letter to Kurt Hirschfeld: "Die lachen sich nur allzuleicht und allzugerne den Ast, auf dem sie die Dichtung—das wohl schlechthin 'Artfremde'—ein zweites und ein drittes Mal aufknüpfen: 'Puis on s'amuse à l'allemande . . . après avoir assassiné'" / "All too easily and all too pleasurably do they laugh themselves a branch on which—for a second and third time—they lynch poetry, something clearly alien ["Artfremde": term used for "non-Aryan" in Nazi days]. 'And then they have fun in that German way . . . after having murdered'" (August 1, 1961; as cited by BW, 2018, p. 829).

61f. call it [. . .] / love: See Hans Magnus Enzensberger's poem "Call it Love," from his volume *Verteidigung der Wölfe* (S. 19).

"Hüttenfenster" / "Hutwindow"

Earlier than March 30, 1963; this date marks a title change (from "Hommage à Quelqu'un"). The poem is to a major extent an argument—even a skirmish—with the poet Johannes Bobrowski (1917–1965). Celan had been given the latter's volume *Schattenland Ströme* on May 30, 1962, in Stuttgart, and referred to it as "autre singerie" / "another aping" in his notebook, seeing how Bobrowski had imitated the diction of Celan's *Sprachgitter / Speechgrille* (BW, 2018, pp. 829–30).

T, 2 Hüttenfenster / Hutwindow: See verses 3–4 of the poem "Schneepart" / "Snowpart" in *Breathturn into Timestead*, pp. 334–35). Bobrowski's two books in Celan's possession show illustrations with huts and churches with onion domes. Both John Felstiner and David Young translate the title "Hüttenfenster" as "Tabernacle Window," thus linking the title to the Jewish feast of Sukkot, the name referring to the booths or huts in which Jews are supposed to dwell during the week of the festival that commemorates the forty years of wandering in the desert after escaping from slavery in Egypt. In this context I do not think this reference to be accurate.

6 Menschen-und-Juden / humans-and-Jews: See verses 8 and 14 of "Mandorla." Celan wrote to Gottfried Bermann Fischer: "das Jüdische—also eine der Gestalten des Menschlichen" / "the Jewish—thus one of the figures of the human" (December 14, 1963, PC/Fischer, p. 641). For "Juden" / "Jews" see also verse 5 of "A Gonif- and Gangster-Ditty."

7 das Volk-vom-Gewölk / the people-of-the-clouds / 15f. Engels- / schwinge / angels- / wing, 20 Witebsk / Vitebsk: See Bobrowski's poem "Die Heimat des Malers Chagall" / "The Homeland of the Painter Chagall," with its references to Chagall's representation of angels: "Und die Wolke Abend, / sinkend um Witebsk, aus eigener / Finsternis tönend" / "And the cloud Evening, / setting over Vitebsk, echoing / from its own darkness," and "bärtig, wie Engel, und zitternden Mundes, / mit Flügeln aus Weizenfeldern // Nähe des Künftigen, dieser / brennende Hörnerschall, / da es dunkelt, die Stadt / schwimmt durch Gewölk, / rot." / "bearded like angels and with trembling mouth, / with wings of wheatfields; // Closeness of the soon-to-be, this / burning horn-echo, / as it grows dark, the town / swims through clouds, / red" (verses 4–6 and 13–19; Johannes Bobrowski, *Sarmatische Zeit*, Union Verlag, 1967, p. 64; my translation).

23 mit mimetischer Panzerfaustklaue / with mimetic bazooka fist: "Klaue" / "claw" stands in opposition to Celan's concept of the hand and links in that sense to the Goll affair and to Celan's reverse accusations to contemporaries that they copied from him; see verse 40 of "La Contrescarpe." On June 20, 1962, he wrote to Paul Schallück: "But the lie rules, you know it, and it dominates, mimetically highly gifted as it is, the field and the fields," and further cites an Arabic proverb: "First they rob you, and then they weep with those who have been robbed" (PC/SSB, p. 323). Celan knew that Bobrowski had been a soldier in northern Russia (and thus had likely used a *Panzerfaust*) and that he had published in the Nazi magazine *Das Innere Reich*.

31 Eden: See "Ice, Eden."

38 Aleph und Jud / aleph and yod, 43 Aleph, bei Jud / Aleph with Yud: The first (*a*) and tenth (*y*) letters of the Hebrew alphabet. Ten is an important number in the formation of community (see verse 7 of "Marianne").

39 Davidsschild / Davidshield: Literal translation of the Hebrew expres-

sion for "Star of David," originally in the sense of a defensive weapon with a coat of arms.

47 Beth: Refers to *b*, the second letter of the Hebrew alphabet. The letter's name, "Beth," is also the word for "house"; see the poem title "Hut-window."

48f. wo der Tisch steht mit // dem Licht und dem Licht / where the table stands with // the light and the light: Two candles usually stand on the table for the Sabbath meal.

"Die Silbe Schmerz" / *"The Syllable Pain"*

September 16 and 19, 1962, Paris. On September 30, 1962, Celan wrote to GLC concerning the poem and an autumn crocus seen on a walk (French *colchique*; see verse 80 of "And with the Book from Tarussa"): "And then I had to think of the very last poem written after receiving the letter from Moscow in which Erich Einhorn said that he would spend his holidays 'in Colchis,' meaning on the Black Sea. 'Colchis,' that was, and it came to me only yesterday, only a secret echo of the 'Zeitlose' [literally: 'the timeless,' here the name of the colchique/autumn crocus: called up by reality]" (PC/GCL, p. 145). The poem also shows traces of Celan's reading of Lev Shestov's *In Job's Balances*, and Friedrich Behn's *Kultur der Urzeit*, as well as Nelly Sachs's *Fahrt ins Staublose* (the 1961 book gathering her poetry to that date, and which Celan told her on September 7, 1962, that he was rereading).

T Die Silbe Schmerz / The Syllable Pain, 44f. im Abgrund / buch-, buch-, buch- / in the abyss / book-, book-, book-: The word "pain" is but one syllable long, but see also the (here uncollected) poem "Wie das Ferne" / "Like the distant," whose seventh to ninth verses are: "there was / the word pain, a bowl, from which / arose for us the word / joy." See the connection between "abyss" and "homeland" in verse 3 of "Mute Autumn Odors." See also the play with cut-off syllables in "Huhediblu." The syllable cut off here—"buch-"—is from the word *buchstabiert*, which means "to spell out." But here "buch-" in its triple repetition recalls the *Buche*, the beech tree from Celan's homeland, the Bukovina, the "Beechtreeland." Of course the German *Buch* also means "book." The polysemy gets lost in the translation, though I think it worth evoking here.

T Schmerz / Pain, 28 Windrose / windrose: See Nelly Sachs, verses 1 and 5 of "Hiob" / "Job": "O du Windrose der Qualen!" / "Oh you, wind rose of torments!" and "Wo du stehst, ist der Nabel der Schmerzen" / "Where you stand is the navel of pain" (p. 95).

1 Es gab sich Dir in die Hand / It gave itself into Your hand: See Sachs's poem "In der Flucht" / "Fleeing": "Dieser Stein / mit der Inschrift der Fliege / hat sich mir in die Hand gegeben—" / "This stone / with the fly's inscription / gave itself into my hand—." The capitalized "Dir" / "You(r)," corrected thus by Celan, occurs only here.

21 Kolumbus / Columbus, 22f. die Zeit- / lose / the autumn-/ colchis, 25 Alles fuhr aus / Everything set forth, 27 entdeckerisch / discovery-eager: See Lev Shestov, p. 310: "To follow Alexander to India, to sail after Columbus into the West, or—if one may be pardoned for saying it—to sail with the Argonauts to Colchis in quest of the golden fleece, or to journey with the Jews to the promised land: to speak of such tasks today even in jest, seems improper to a scientist, still more to a philosopher. What Colchis, what promised land can there be?"

22–24 die Zeit- / lose im Aug, die Mutter- / Blume / eyeing the autumn- / colchis, the mother- / flower: See Celan's translation of Apollinaire's "Les Colchiques" / "Die Herbstzeitlosen": "Die Tochter ist und Mutter, die Herbstzeitlose, die / So schimmert wie dein Augenlid—die Kinder pflücken sie, / sie pflücken Augenlider im Wind, im irren Wind" / "That is daughter and mother, the autumn crocus that / shimmers like an eyelid—the children pick it, / they pick eyelids in the wind, in the erratic wind" (my retranslation). Apollinaire has: "Ils cueillent les colchiques qui sont comme des mères / Filles de leurs filles" / "They pick the autumn crocus that are like mothers / Daughters of their daughters." In the Middle Ages, the flower was known as *Filius ante patrem* (Son before the father), given that it turns the seasons backward: it develops its bloom in autumn, then in the spring its leaves and seeds. Which is also where the German term *Zeitlose*, "the timeless one," comes from. Another folk name is *Nackthure*, "naked whore," and in English—besides meadow saffron and autumn crocus—the flowers are known as "naked ladies."

32 Kanopen / canopic jars: See his reading of Behn's book on prehistoric

cultures, mentioning the canopic jars from the region of Chiusi, Italy (verse 3, p. 26, and reading note; Badiou's reference). See also other reading notes related to Behn (TCA/SG, p. 113). The Etruscan canopy jars mentioned in Behn are human-shaped urns for ashes with a human-head shaped cover.

33–35 die Kindlein / Jaspis, Achat, Amethyst—Völker, / Stämme und Sippen / little babes awoke: / jasper, agate, amethyst—peoples, / tribes and clans: See in Exod. 28:19–21 the description of the priestly "breastplate of judgment" with four rows of precious stones: "And the third row a ligure, an agate, and an amethyst. / And the fourth row a beryl, and an onyx, and a jasper: they shall be set in gold in their inclosings. And the stones shall be with the names of the children of Israel, twelve, according to their names, like the engravings of a signet; every one with his name shall they be according to the twelve tribes."

45 buch-, buch-, buch- / stabierte, stabierte. / book-, book-, book- / staved, staved: The German word *buchstabieren* means "to spell out," to say the names of the letters in a word. Celan's arrangement and repetition of the first syllable, "buch," cannot fail to bring to mind the German name for Celan's homeland, Buchenland, Bukovina, the land of the beech trees, but also the name of the concentration camp Buchenwald. The second part, "stabiert," is based on the word *Stab*, "stick" or "stave," referring to runic writing and the *Stab*, or stave, that is the central vertical line of most runes.

"La Contrescarpe" / *"La Contrescarpe"*

September 29–30, 1962 (Saint-Cergue, in the Nyon district, and Geneva)–March 13, 1963. The poem was started in Geneva, where Celan worked temporarily as translator at the International Labour Office. See PC's letter to GCL (PC/GCL #145, p. 141). Saint-Cergue lies in the Swiss Jura, above Lake Geneva; on September 29, 1962, starting from Geneva, Celan made an excursion to Nyon, of which he tells his wife in the long letter of September 30, 1962 (PC/GCL, p. 145).

T La Contrescarpe: French for counterscarp: the outer side of a ditch or moat used in fortifications. The Place de la Contrescarpe in Paris's fifth arrondissement is not far from the École Normale Supérieure (ENS), where Celan worked. The place has many cafés arranged around a paulownia tree at the center of the square. Celan liked to sit in one specific café on one of the corners of the square (pointed out to me in the early eighties by the poet Edmond Jabès, a friend of Celan's, who lived nearby).

12f. der Elends-, der Königs- / vigilie / the misery-, the kings- / vigil, 14 Kamen die Hände nicht mit, die wachten / Didn't they come along, the hands that guarded: See verse 1f. of "Kolon" / "Colon"; for "hand" see "Einiges Handähnliche" / "Something handlike."

29 Krakau // Kraków, 30f. Anhalter / Bahnhof / Anhalter / railway station, 31f. Rauch zu, / der war schon von morgen / smoke [. . .] / it already belonged to tomorrow: On his 1938 trip to Tours to study medicine, Celan passed through Kraków and the Anhalter railway station in Berlin just before the so-called Kristallnacht, the pogrom against Jews carried out by SA paramilitary forces and civilians throughout Nazi Germany on November 9–10, 1938. See also verse 3 of "Lila Luft" / "Lilac air" (*Breathturn into Timestead*, pp. 322–23).

33f. Unter / Paulownien / sahst du die Messer stehn / Under / paulownias / you saw the knives stand: This tree—originally Pavlovnia but now usually spelled paulownia—was named in honor of Anna Paulowna, the queen consort of the Netherlands (1795–1865) and the daughter of Tsar Paul I of Russia, but also contains Celan's first name, Paul. See verses 2–4 of "Entschlackt" / "Deslagged" (*Breathturn into Timestead*, pp. 182–83).

37f. Quatorze / juillets. Et plus de neuf autres: French for "Fourteen Julys. And more than nine others." July 14 (the day in 1789 when the revolutionary people of Paris stormed the Bastille prison, thus "Bastille Day") is the French national holiday, celebrated with dancing in the streets; it is on that day in 1948 that Celan arrived in Paris. Fourteen years had passed before he wrote this poem; and more than nine years lie between his first visit in November 1938 and July 1948.

51 Kristall / crystal: The poem "Kristall" / "Crystal" is among the very first poems written after his arrival in Paris.

"Es ist alles anders" / "Everything is different"

June 5, 1962, Paris. The poem is directly connected to Celan's signing of a contract with the Fischer-Taschenbuch publishers for *Drei Russische Dichter / Three Russian Poets*, which gathers his translations of Alexander Blok, Osip Mandelstam, and Sergei Yesenin.

2f. die Fahne weht noch, / die kleinen Geheimnisse sind noch bei sich / sie werfen noch Schatten / the flag still flutters, / the little secrets are still secret / they still throw shadows: This is a reference to short stories by Hans Daiber and Rolf Schroers in the *Deutsche Zeitung* of January 13, 1962, which Celan, in a state of deep psychic stress, thought referred to him. On the day the poem was written, Schroers tried to call Celan, but the latter refused to talk to him (see PC/SSB, p. 705) and called off a meeting with friends who wanted to mediate between him and Schroers. (Rolf Schroers had been a friend of Celan's since they met at the Gruppe 47 gathering in Niendorf in 1952. In 1961 Celan broke off the friendship, believing Hans Werner Richter's false accusations, according to which Schroers had supposedly taken part in hostage executions in 1943 in Italy and made anti-Semitic pronouncements in the mid-1950s [RF, p. 451 ff.].) See also verses 1f. and 10f. of "Ihn ritt die Nacht" / "Night rode him" (*Breathturn into Timestead*, pp. 236–37).

8 nach Rußland / to Russia, 9 die karelische Birke / the Karelian birch: *Karelische Birke* is the German translation of the Russian name for *Betula alba*, the white birch. Karelia, a Finnish-speaking territory in northwest Russia, was much fought over during World War II between Finland and the U.S.S.R. (See verse 7 of an early Celan poem, "The Hunter": "[my peace] lay under the birches of Karelia.") In the poems selected for the book of translations, the birch does not appear in Mandelstam's, but does in Yesenin's, as in the verse: "Birches, you, you stand, you stand together" (my translation of Celan's version).

17 da hast du sie, da nimm sie dir, da hast du alle beide / you have them now, so take them now, you have them both, 19 da nimm sie dir zum Unterpfand / take them as your pledge: Part of a *Klatschreim* (children's rhyming song) from H. M. Enzensberger's book *Allerleirauh*: "Scherenschleifen, Scherenschleifen, / Das ist die rechte Kunst. / Die rechte Hand, die linke Hand, / Die geb ich dir zum Unterpfand; / da hast du sie, da nimm du sie, / Da hast du alle beide. / Grinding knives, grinding knives, / That is a true art. / The right hand, the left hand, / I give them to you as a pledge; there you have it, there you take it, / there you now have both." On January 23, 1962, in relation to his poem "Matière de Bretagne" and to verse 59 of Mandelstam's "Griffelode" (GW V, p. 143; in my retranslation: "Two-handed, two-souled, I, / night's friend, day's companion . . .") Celan wrote to Norbert Koch:

“‘The hands’—: it is . . . the hands, both hands, the left and the right, it is—I quote Osip Mandelstam—our (everyone’s!) ‘Twohandedness’” (unsent letter). See the various poems and commentaries re “hand.” Wiedemann further suggests that in this exchange of hands also brings to mind the process of translation.

18 den Namen, den Namen, die Hand, die Hand / the name, the name, the hand, the hand: The name of the Israeli Shoah memorial and research center Yad Vashem (Hand-and-name) refers to Isa. 56:5: “And to them will I give in my house and within my walls a memorial and a name [Yad Vashem] . . . that will not be cut off” (World English Bible).

26 am Heck kein Warum / no Why at the stern: See verse 3f. of “Schuttkahn” / “Rubble Scow.”

26 Bug / bow: Besides its meaning as the front of a ship, the German word *Bug* is also the name of the river where the concentration camp Mikhaylovka was situated; Celan’s parents died there in the fall and winter of 1942–1943. (See stanza 1 of the poem “Nähe der Gräber” / “Nearness of the Graves,” from *SU*, not gathered here: “Does the water of the Southern Bug still know / mother, the wave that wounded you?”)

26–28 ein Widderhorn hebt dich / —*Tekiah!*— / wie ein Posaunenschall / a ram’s horn lifts you / —*Tekiah!*— / like a trumpet sound: A shofar is a musical instrument made of a ram’s horn and used in Jewish religious ceremonies, especially on Rosh Hashanah and at the end of Yom Kippur. “Tekiah” is one of the four long deep calls sounded on the shofar.

42 Wie das Wintermärchen / Like the Winter’s Tale, 44 das Dreijahreland deiner Mutter / your mother’s Three-Year-Land, 46 die Sprache / language, 50 Mährischen Senke / Moravian swale, 51 Prag / Prague, 59 Böhmen / Bohemia: On April 24, 1962, Celan wrote to Nina Cassian: “Quant à ma langue, la fidélité que je lui garde me vient de ma mère, qui, elle, l’avait cueillie en Bohème—(Concerning my language, my fidelity to it comes from my mother, who had gotten it in Bohemia—) but this is a Winter’s Tale, this is Bohemia” (English in the original letter, BW, 2018, p. 838), and on June 9, 1962, to the publisher and Kafka-specialist Klaus Wagenbach, an explanation for the map of “Behmen,” i.e., Bohemia, which he gave him as a gift: “You know, me too I am ‘böhmisch fixiert’ (fixated on Bohemia), in several ways, in fact, with me it started with Lubenec and Aussig on the Elbe [today: Ústí nad Labem in the

Czech Republic] where my mother spent several years as in exile, an experience decisive for me, the Ka(f)kanier* to be born later. (She was one of those Eastern Jewish refugees, of which K's journals have a lot to tell us.) Bohemia—: a land from the Winter's Tale. And the winter's tale again . . . old Harry Heine, a.k.a. 'the wound,' I can't get him out of my mind." (BW, 2018, pp. 838–39). Celan is thinking about Heine's poem "Deutschland, ein Wintersmärchen," and about Shakespeare's play, in which there is a Bohemia, "a desert country near the sea." Paul Celan himself was never in Prague, a city important to him because of Kafka.

49 den Kieselstein / the pebble , 51f. den dein Gedanke nach Prag trug, / aufs Grab, auf die Gräber, ins Leben / your thought carried to Prague, / to the grave, all the graves, into life: The Hebrew word for "pebble" is *tz'ror*—a word that also means "bond." When Jews recite the memorial prayer for the dead, "El maleh rahamim," they ask that the deceased be "bound up in the bond of life"—*tz'ror haHayyim*, which might also be translated as "the pebble of life." By placing the pebble, they signal that they have been there at the gravesite, and that the memory of the dead continues to live on in and through the living (via Ariel Resnikoff). Celan knew other explanations; see his note from 1957: "Vienna, Basil: Kafka's grave: the stones, the pebbles. The two explanations of the custom: a.) No flowers, but stones, so as not to attract animals b.) Stones as symbols of fertility" (TCA/SG, p. 116).

59 Normandie-Njemen—in Böhmen / Normandy-Niemen—in Bohemia: Celan wrote to Erich Einhorn on June 23, 1962: "when we were in Damville recently, the movie Normandy-Niemen played there." He is referring to director Jean Dréville's 1960 film with that title. Normandie-Niemen was the name of a fighter regiment of the French air force, which served on the Eastern Front of the European theater of World War II. The regiment is notable for being one of only three units from the Western Allied countries to see combat on the Eastern Front during World War II, and Normandie-Niemen was the only Western Allied unit to fight with the Soviet forces until the end of the war in Europe.

*Ka(f)kanier: Celan's neologism made up of Kafka's name and *Kakanier*—an old name for Austrians—derived, it seems, from the common abbreviation "k.k.," describing the Austrian-Bohemian Habsburg monarchy ("kaiserlich-königlich" = "Imperial-Royal").

66 ein Fluß / a river, 70 Alba: Besides being the Latin adjective for the *Betula alba*, the white birch (see verse 9), *alba* is the Latin word for "white" and for the river Elbe.

"Und mit dem Buch aus Tarussa" / "And with the Book from Tarussa"
September 20, 1962, Moisville and Paris. On September 10, 1962, Erich Einhorn sent Celan two books, which he must have received by the date of the writing: a selected poems volume by Konstantin Paustovsky, and the very rare anthology *Pages from Tarussa*, in which he tried to bring new writers to the public's attention and to publish writers suppressed during the Stalin years. There is a monument to him in Tarussa. On November 27, 1962, Celan thanked Einhorn explicitly for the "book from Tarussa," adding: "A new book has come into existence, poems again, and one of them was triggered by 'Pages from Tarussa'" (PC/EE, p. 9).

T Tarussa, 57 Oka, 74 Oka-Fluß / river Oka: Tarussa is a small Russian town situated on the left bank of the river Oka, a confluent of the Volga. Celan had learned from Einhorn that Osip Mandelstam's widow lived in Tarussa (November 6, 1962; PC/EE, p. 5).

M: See Marina Tsvetaeva's poem "Outside," from the longer "Poem of the End," has the line: "In this most Christian of all worlds, the poets are yids." Celan knew the poem via an anthology acquired on June 1, 1961, in which this line has a mark in the margins. Tsvetaeva, who had returned to Russia from France, committed suicide in 1941. According to Wiedemann, she had wanted to be buried in Tarussa, where her mother was from.

1–2 Vom / Sternbild des Hundes, / About / the constellation of the Dog, 6f. von / Pilgerstäben, auch dort, von Südlichem / about / pilgrim staffs, there too, about southern matters: See the reading traces in a Paustovsky short story marked by Celan: "About what was Maria speaking? About the constellation of the Great Dog, the guiding star for the pilgrims who travel to the grave of the Prophet? There it stood, fiery, glowing and low above the many wide spaces of this so barren and beloved land" (Konstantin Georgievic Paustovskij, Повесть о жизни [Geschichten über das Leben], Moscow, 1962; my translation via German; in the original p. 519, translation, p. 230). The poem, repeating "about" twenty-eight times, multiplies the answer to the narrator's rhetorical question. See Celan's use of the constellation's name as "Sternhund" / "stardog" in verse 11 of his translation of a 1931 poem by Mandelstam ("nachtlang der Sternhund am Himmel erblaut")—not a literal translation, as the original speaks rather of polar foxes. (In Lev Fridman's translation the line reads: "so all night the polar foxes may shine.")

2–4 Sternbild des Hundes, vom / Hellstern darin und der Zwerg- / leuchte / the constellation of the Dog, of / the brightstar in it and the dwarf- / light, 7 Pilgerstäben / pilgrim staffs, 65–67 den drei / Gürtelsternen Orions—Jakobs- / stab / to Orion's three / belt-stars—Jacob's / staff: See the Widmann/Schlüte book "Welcher Stern ist das?" (What star is this?) in Celan's library (Walter Widman and Karl Schütte, *Welcher Stern ist das? 60 Sternkarten zum Bestimmen der Sternbilder in allen Jahreszeiten* [Kosmos Naturführer: Stuttgart, 1955]): "The Great Dog contains the brightest star in the sky, Sirius, who follows Orion [. . .] Sirius is known and famous as a double star, although the companion star, because of the great difference in luminosity . . . is only visible through large instruments." About Orion: "The three stars of the belt . . . form the well-known Jacob's staff." See verse 9f. of "Dunkles Aug im September" / "Dark Eye in September," verse 2 of "Lilac air" (*Breathturn into Timestead*, pp. 322–23), and verse 1 of the early poem "The Hunter."

18 Herzsteine / heartstones: See verse 16 of "Sibirisch" / "Siberian."

21 Unland: See the commentaries to the poem "Ein Wurfholz" / "A boomerang," and verse 10 of "Havdalah."

35 skythisch / scythianly: See Behn's second chapter, "Eastern Europe: The Pontic Circle, Scythian Culture": "When the Greeks speak of Scythians, this ethnographic umbrella term includes all foreign, 'barbaric' peoples living northeast of the Greek lands." Behn goes on, referring to Herodotus: "He calls the culture-bearing ruling class as the 'Royal Scythians.' The scythian settlement area between the estuary of the Danube in the West and the Sea of Azov in the East included the basins of the rivers Pruth, Dniester, Bug and Dnieper" (vol. 3, pp. 36, 37, marked by Celan; see pp. 248–49 in Herodotus, *The Histories* [Penguin Classics, 1971]). Czernowitz lies on the Pruth; Celan's parents were murdered on the far shore of the Dniester, on the Southern Bug. A literary movement, founded shortly before the Russian Revolution, took the name "Скифы" / "Scythians." Yesenin and Blok, both translated by Celan, belonged to it; Blok in fact wrote a poem with this title. See also Celan's Man-

delstam translation "Die Zeiten, unbehaun": "Ein Gähnen, tierisch—Skythe, deine / Gestalt erkenn ich, dein Gesicht! // Wie einstmals er, Ovid, sie beide / in seinem Lied zusammentrug" / "A yawn, beastly—Scythian, I recognize your figure, your face! // Like long ago, he, Ovid, put them together in his song" (GW V, p. 83; my translation of Celan's version), and in Celan's radio play on Mandelstam: "The poet—the man for whom language is everything, origin and fate—is in exile with his language, 'among the Scythians'" (TCA/MFV 217).

47 Stummvölker-Zone / the mute-peoples' zone: The Russian word for "German," немецкий, shares a root with the word for "mute," немой.

56 Pont Mirabeau: A Seine bridge in Paris, in the fifteenth arrondissement.

57f. Et quels / amours!: French for "And what loves!" See verse 1f. of Guillaume Apollinaire's poem "Le Pont Mirabeau," from the book *Alcools*: "Sous le pont Mirabeau coule la Seine / Et nos amours."

58–60 Kyrillisches, Freunde, auch das / ritt ich über die Seine, / ritts übern Rhein / Cyrillic, friends, that too / I rode over the Seine, / rode it across the Rhine, 74 Ruderbank / rowing bench, 77 Ruderknecht / galley slave, 79 Dolle / oarlock: Already in verses 4–6 of the poem "Von Dunkel zu Dunkel" / "From Darkness to Darkness," the image of the translator as ferryman appears. See also in relation to his Russian translations, and to the translator as riding across rivers, this, from a letter to Nelly Sachs: "From time to time we rest, and I am then allowed to return to my Yesenin translation, thanks to Eric's instruction in riding, it also makes progress, not at full gallop perhaps, but at quite a reasonable speed at least" (August 11, 1960; PC/NS #55).

61f. Von einem Brief, von ihm. / Vom Ein-Brief, vom Ost-Brief / About a letter, about that. / About the One-Letter, the East-letter, 80 Kolchis / Colchis: See "Die Silbe Schmerz" / "The Syllable Pain," and the commentary on verse 2 of "Talglicht" / "Tallowlight."

"In der Luft" / "In the air"

Date of composition unknown. The poem shows traces of Celan's reading of Margaret Susman's book *Deutung biblischer Gestalten*, which he received probably together with her letter of January 7, 1963, and read immediately.

1 In der Luft, da bleibt deine Wurzel / In the air, there your root remains:

See the reading traces in Susman: "The tree of the people has been torn from its homeland earth, it no longer grows or roots. Ezekiel becomes conscious of this: the roots did not take. And now the monstrous happens: with a mighty hand the prophet grabs the tree hanging in emptiness, tears it completely from the old earth, tears out even the last rootlets that still stick full of yearning to the home soil, tears it around into the opposite direction and replants it in a monstrous reversal contrary to all natural growth, roots up high" (p. 62f., with marginal marks by Celan). See also verse 7 of "Ich hörte sagen" / "I Heard It Said."

4 Atem-und-Lehm / breath-and-clay: For the connection with the second creation story, see the commentary to verse 1 of "Psalm."

7f. ein Pommer, zuhause / im Maikäferlied / a Pomeranian, at home / in the Cockchafersong: See the well-known children's song, gathered in H. M. Enzensberger's *Allerleirauh*: "Maikäfer flieg! / Dein Vater ist im Krieg, / dein Mutter ist in Pommerland, / Pommerland ist abgebrannt, / Maikäfer flieg!" ("Cockchafer fly / Your father is at war / your mother's in Pomerania / Pomerania's burned down, / cockchafer fly!"), and the mention of "Pomerania" in verse 12 of the (not included) poem "Der Jäger" / "The hunter": ". . . and glows like the sky over Pomerania," in connection with the European war-torn regions.

14 Meridiane / meridians, 18 Mittagsspruch / noonday spell: About meridians, see Celan's Büchner Prize speech, especially the last lines: "I find something—like language—immaterial, yet terrestrial, something circular that returns to itself across both poles while—cheerfully—even crossing the tropics: I find . . . a meridian." And "Even in this here and now of the poem—for the poem itself, we know, has always only this one, unique, momentary present—even in this immediacy and nearness it lets the most essential aspect of the other speak: its time" (MFV, pp. 12, 9).

35–36 die / zu leicht, die zu schwer, die zu leicht / too light, too heavy, too light: See verse 7 of "Was geschah?" / "What happened?"

45 Klumpfuß der Götter / clubfoot of the gods: In Greek mythology, Hephaestus, blacksmith to the gods, had a clubfoot—as did Josef Goebbels, the Third Reich's propaganda minister.

Select Bibliography

EDITIONS OF PAUL CELAN

SINGLE VOLUMES

Der Sand aus den Urnen. Vienna: Sexl, 1948. Five hundred copies. With lithographs by Edgar Jené.

Mohn und Gedächtnis. Stuttgart: Deutsche Verlags-Anstalt, 1952. Includes twenty-six poems from *Der Sand aus den Urnen.*

Von Schwelle zu Schwelle. Stuttgart: Deutsche Verlags-Anstalt, 1955.

Sprachgitter. Frankfurt am Main: S. Fischer, 1959.

Die Niemandsrose. Frankfurt am Main: S. Fischer, 1963.

Atemwende. Frankfurt am Main: Suhrkamp, 1967. The first cycle of poems, *Atemkristall*, was published in a bibliophile edition of eighty-five copies, with etchings by Gisèle Celan-Lestrange (Paris: Brunidor, 1965).

Fadensonnen. Frankfurt am Main: Suhrkamp, 1968. The poem "Schlafbrocken," included in this volume, was first published, with an etching by Gisèle Celan-Lestrange, in a bibliophile edition of one hundred copies (Paris: Brunidor, 1967).

Lichtzwang. Frankfurt am Main: Suhrkamp, 1970. The first fourteen poems of this volume were published under the title *Schwarzmaut* in a bibliophile edition of eighty-five copies, with etchings by Gisèle Celan-Lestrange (Vaduz/Liechtenstein: Brunidor, 1969). The poem "Todtnauberg," also included in this volume, had been published in a bibliophile edition of fifty copies by Brunidor in 1968.

Schneepart. Frankfurt am Main: Suhrkamp, 1971.

Zeitgehöft. Frankfurt am Main: Suhrkamp, 1976. (Posthumous work; this is the one volume not compiled by Paul Celan himself.)

Gedichte 1938–1944. With a preface by Ruth Kraft. Frankfurt am Main: Suhrkamp, 1986.

COLLECTED VOLUMES

Gedichte in zwei Bänden. Frankfurt am Main: Suhrkamp, 1975. The first volume gathers the books *Mohn und Gedächtnis*, *Von Schwelle zu Schwelle*, *Sprachgitter*, and *Die Niemandsrose*; the second volume gathers the books *Atemwende*, *Fadensonnen*, *Lichtzwang*, and *Schneepart*. The posthumous volume *Zeitgehöft*, which came out in 1976, was thus not yet available for inclusion.

Gedichte aus dem Nachlaß. Edited by Bertrand Badiou, Claude Rambach, and Barbara Wiedemann. Annotations by Barbara Wiedemann and Bertrand Badiou. Frankfurt am Main: Suhrkamp, 1997.

Gesammelte Werke in sieben Bänden. Edited by Beda Allemann and Stefan Reichert in collaboration with Rolf Bücher. Frankfurt am Main: Suhrkamp, 2000.

- Volume I, subtitled *Gedichte 1*, contains *Mohn und Gedächtnis*, *Von Schwelle zu Schwelle*, *Sprachgitter*, and *Die Niemandsrose*.
- Volume II, subtitled *Gedichte 2*, contains *Atemwende*, *Fadensonnen*, *Lichtzwang*, and *Schneepart*.
- Volume III, subtitled *Gedichte 3, Prosa, Reden,* contains *Der Sand aus den Urnen*, *Zeitgehöft*, *Verstreute Gedichte*, and a number of uncollected poems, consisting of a first section of eleven poems stretching from 1948 to 1967 and a second section, the cycle *Eingedunkelt*, which also contains eleven poems, dating from 1968. The remainder of the volume gathers all the extant prose and speeches.
- Volume IV, subtitled *Übertragungen 1*, gathers all of Celan's translations from the French.
- Volume V, subtitled *Übertragungen 2*, gathers all of Celan's translations from the Russian, English, Italian, Romanian, Portuguese, and Hebrew. These two volumes gather only the poetry Celan translated, excluding his prose translations.
- Volume VI: subtitled *Das Frühwerk,* gathers chronologically all the early work under the categories "Bukovina," "Bucharest," and "Vienna."
- Volume VII: subtitled *Gedichte aus dem Nachlaß*, gathers all posthumous poems.

Die Gedichte: Kommentierte Gesamtausgabe in einem Band. Edited and with commentaries by Barbara Wiedemann. Frankfurt am Main: Suhrkamp, 2003. An expanded edition, *Neue kommentierte Gesamtausgabe*, came out in 2018. This is the edition used throughout the present volume, except when indicated otherwise. [BW 2003 and BW 2018]

Mikrolithen sinds, Steinchen. Die Prosa aus dem Nachlaß. Edited and with commentaries by Barbara Wiedemann and Bertrand Badiou. Frankfurt am Main: Suhrkamp, 2005.

SCHOLARLY EDITIONS

Paul Celan. Werke: Historisch-kritische Ausgabe. Prepared by Bonner Arbeitsstelle for the Celan-Ausgabe. Founded by Beda Allemann. Sixteen volumes. Frankfurt am Main: Suhrkamp, 1990–2017. [BA + volume and page number]

Paul Celan. Werke: Tübinger Ausgabe. Edited by Jürgen Wertheimer. Frankfurt am Main: Suhrkamp, 2004. Nine volumes. [TA + volume title abbreviation, for ex: TA/VS = *Von Schwelle zu Schwelle*]

Paul Celan. Der Meridian: Endfassung–Entwürfe–Materialien. Edited by Bernhard Böschenstein and Heino Schmull. Frankfurt am Main, 1999. [TCA/M]

TRANSLATIONS BY PAUL CELAN

The names of the translated authors are given in the German spelling (e.g., Sergej Jessenin, rather than Sergei Yesenin), as used by Celan and the various publications. All these are gathered in volumes 4 and 5 of the 1983 five-volume collected Celan edition.

Jean Cocteau. *Der Goldenen Vorhang. Brief an die Amerikaner.* Bad Salzig: Rauch, 1949.

Alexander Blok. *Die Zwölf.* Frankfurt am Main: S. Fischer, 1958.

Arthur Rimbaud. *Das Trunkene Schiff.* Wiesbaden: Insel, 1958.

Osip Mandelstam. *Gedichte.* Frankfurt am Main: S. Fischer, 1959.

Paul Valéry. *Die junge Parze.* Limited Edition. Wiesbaden: Insel, 1960.

Jean Cayrol. *Im Bereich einer Nacht.* Olten: Walter, 1961.

Sergei Jessenin. *Gedichte*. Frankfurt am Main: S. Fischer, 1961.

William Shakespeare. *Einundzwanzig Sonette*. Frankfurt am Main: Insel, 1967.

André du Bouchet. *Vakante Blut*. Frankfurt am Main: Suhrkamp, 1968.

Jules Supervielle. *Gedichte*. Frankfurt am Main: Insel, 1968.

Giuseppe Ungaretti. *Das verheißene Land / Das Merkbuch des Alten*. Frankfurt am Main: Insel, 1968.

TRANSLATIONS OF PAUL CELAN INTO ENGLISH

Speech-Grille and Selected Poems. Translated by Joachim Neugröschel. New York: E. P. Dutton, 1971. Contains all the poems of *Sprachgitter* and selected poems from the volumes *Mohn und Gedächtnis* through *Atemwende*.

Nineteen Poems. Translated by Michael Hamburger. Oxford: Carcanet Press; Chester Springs, PA: Dufour Editions, 1972. Poems from *Mohn und Gedächtnis* (11), *Von Schwelle zu Schwelle* (3), *Sprachgitter* (1), *Die Niemandsrose* (4).

Paul Celan: Selected Poems. Translated by Michael Hamburger and Christopher Middleton. Includes selected poems from the volumes *Mohn und Gedächtnis* through *Schneepart*. Harmondsworth, UK: Penguin Modern European Poets, 1972.

Breath Crystal (*Rigmarole of the Hours, 3*). Translated by Walter Billeter. Ivanhoe, Victoria, Australia: Ragman Productions, 1975.

Prose Writings and Selected Poems. Translated by Walter Billeter and Jerry Glenn. Carlton, Victoria, Australia: Paper Castle, 1977.

Poems. Translated by Michael Hamburger. New York: Persea Books; Manchester, UK: Carcanet Press, 1980.

65 Poems. Translated by Brian Lynch and Peter Jankowsky. Dublin: Raven Arts Press, 1985.

Last Poems. Translated by Katherine Washburn and Margret Guillemin. New York: North Point Press, 1986.

Paul Celan. Collected Prose. Translated by Rosmarie Waldrop. Manchester, UK: Carcanet Press, 1986. [PCCP]

Breathturn by Paul Celan. Translated by Pierre Joris. Los Angeles: Sun & Moon Press, 1995. (Reprinted in 2006 by Green Integer, Los Angeles.)

Glottal Stop: 101 Poems. Translated by Nikolai B. Popov and Heather McHugh. Middletown, CT: Wesleyan University Press, 2000.

Selected Poems and Prose of Paul Celan. Edited and translated by John Felstiner. New York: Norton, 2000.

Threadsuns by Paul Celan. Translated by Pierre Joris. Los Angeles: Sun & Moon Press, 2000. (Reprinted in 2005 by Green Integer, Los Angeles.)

Fathomsuns / Fadensonnen and Benighted / Eingedunkelt. Translated by Ian Fairley. Rhinebeck, NY: Sheepmeadow Press, 2001.

Lightduress by Paul Celan. Translated by Pierre Joris. Los Angeles: Green Integer, 2005.

Paul Celan: Selections. Edited and with an introduction by Pierre Joris. Berkeley: University of California Press, 2005. [PCS]

From Threshold to Threshold. Translated by David Young. Grosse Pointe Farms, MI: Marick Press, 2010.

The Meridian: Final Version–Drafts–Materials. Edited by Bernhard Böschenstein and Heino Schmull; translated by Pierre Joris. Palo Alto, CA: Stanford University Press, 2011. [TCA/MFV]

Language Behind Bars. Translated by David Young. Grosse Pointe Farms, MI: Marick Press, 2012.

Corona: The Selected Poems of Paul Celan. Translated by Susan Gillespie. Barrytown, NY: Station Hill Press, 2013.

Microliths They Are, Little Stones: Posthumous Prose. Translated by Pierre Joris. New York: Contra Mundum Press, 2020.

CORRESPONDENCE (IN ENGLISH)

Paul Celan, Nelly Sachs: Correspondence. Edited by Barbara Wiedemann. Translated by Christopher Clark. Rhinebeck, NY: Sheep Meadow Press, 1998. [PC/NS]

Correspondence: Paul Celan and Ingeborg Bachmann. Translated by Wieland Hoban. London/New York/ Calcutta: Seagull Books, 2010. [PC/IB]

The Correspondence of Paul Celan and Ilana Shmueli. Translated by Susan Gillespie. Rhinebeck, NY: Sheep Meadow Press, 2011. [PC/IS]

ON PAUL CELAN AND HIS WORK

BIOGRAPHICAL MATERIALS

Chalfen, Israel. *Paul Celan: A Biography of his Youth*. New York: Persea Books, 1991.

Eisenreich, Brigitta. *Celans Kreidestern: Ein Bericht*. Frankfurt am Main: Suhrkamp, 2010. [BE]

Felstiner, John. *Paul Celan: Poet, Survivor, Jew*. New Haven, CT: Yale University Press, 1995.

BOOK-LENGTH CRITICAL STUDIES

Cameron, Esther. *Western Art and Jewish Presence in the Work of Paul Celan: Roots and Ramifications of the "Meridian" Speech*. Lexington Books, 2014.

Carson, Anne. *Economy of the Unlost (Reading Simonides of Kos with Paul Celan)*. Princeton, NJ: Princeton University Press, 1999.

Colin, Amy D., ed. *Argumentum e Silentio: International Paul Celan Symposium*. Berlin: Walter de Gruyter, 1986. This edited volume gathers essays on Celan by Beda Alleman, Jean Bollack, Bernhard Böschenstein, Renate Böschenstein-Schäfer, Rolf Bücher, Amy D. Colin, Jacques Derrida, Hans-Georg Gadamer, Michael Hamburger, Alfred Hoelzel, John E. Jackson, James K. Lyon, Siegfried Mandel, Stéphane Mosès, Rainer Nägele, Elmar Tophoven, Alan Udoff, David E. Wellbery, Bernd Witte, and Shira Wolosky.

Connolly, Thomas C. *Paul Celan's Unfinished Poetics: Readings in the Sous-Oeuvre*. Cambridge, UK: Legenda, 2018.

Daive, Jean. *Under the Dome: Walks with Paul Celan* (*Serie D'ecriture*). Translated by Rosmarie Waldrop. Providence, RI: Burning Deck/Anyart, 2009.

Derrida, Jacques. *Sovereignties in Question: The Poetics of Paul Celan*. Edited by Thomas Dutoit and Outi Pasanen. Bronx, NY: Fordham University Press, 2005.

Fioretos, Aris, ed. *Word Traces: Readings of Paul Celan*. Baltimore: Johns Hopkins University Press, 1994.

Gadamer, Hans-Georg. *Gadamer on Celan: "Who Am I and Who Are You?"*

and Other Essays. Translated and edited by Richard Heinemann and Bruce Krajewski. Albany, NY: SUNY Press, 1997.

Glenn, Jerry. *Paul Celan*. New York: Twayne Publishers, 1973.

Hollander, Benjamin, ed. *Translating Tradition: Paul Celan in France*. San Francisco: *ACTS: A Journal of New Writing* (8/9), 1988. This volume, centered around Celan's work as a translator, with special reference to France, gathers essays by Maurice Blanchot, Dan Blue, Yves Bonnefoy, Bernhard Böschenstein, André du Bouchet, E. M. Cioran, Jean Daive, Robert Duncan, John Felstiner, Joel Golb, Hugo Huppert, Edmond Jabès, Pierre Joris, Robert Kelly, Roger Laporte, Leonard Olschner, and Marc Wortman; it also contains translations of fifteen poems from *Zeitgehöft* by Cid Corman and original writings and artwork by Tom Mandel, Joseph Siman, Claudio Spies, and Tim Trompeter.

Kligerman, Eric. *Sites of the Uncanny: Paul Celan, Specularity and the Visual Arts*. Berlin: Walter de Gruyter, 2007.

Lacoue-Labarthe, Philippe, and Jean-Luc Nancy. *Retreating the Political*. New York: Routledge, 1996.

Lyon, James K. *Paul Celan and Martin Heidegger: An Unresolved Conversation, 1951–1970*. Baltimore: Johns Hopkins University Press, 2006.

———, ed. "Special Issue on Paul Celan." *Studies in Twentieth Century Literature* 8, no. 1 (1983). Contains critical essays on Celan by John Felstiner, Jerry Glenn, James K. Lyon, Nicholas J. Meyerhofer, Joachim Schulze, and Howard Stern, as well as a section called "Encounters: American Poets on Paul Celan," with contributions by Paul Auster, Cid Corman, Clayton Eshleman, Jack Hirschman, David Meltzer, Jed Rasula, and Jerome Rothenberg.

Solomon, Petre, and Emanuela Tegla. *Paul Celan: The Romanian Dimension (Judaic Traditions in Literature, Music, and Art)*. Syracuse, NY: Syracuse University Press, 2019.

Szondi, Peter. *Celan Studies*. Translated by Susan Bernofsky with Harvey Mendelsohn. Palo Alto, CA: Stanford University Press, 2003.

Tobias, Rochelle. *The Discourse of Nature in the Poetry of Paul Celan: The Unnatural World*. Baltimore: Johns Hopkins University Press, 2006.

SELECTED ESSAYS

Foot, Robert. *The Phenomenon of Speechlessness in the Poetry of Marie Luise Kaschnitz, Günter Eich, Nelly Sachs, and Paul Celan*, 415. Bonn: Bouvier, 1982.

Fries, Thomas. "Critical Relation: Peter Szondi's Studies on Celan." *boundary 2* (November 3, 1983): 139–67.

Glenn, Jerry. "A Special Section on Paul Celan." *Sulfur* 11 (1984): 5–99.

———, and Edmund Remys. "Sergej Essenin in German: The Translations of Paul Celan and Alfred Gong." *Germano-Slavica* 5, nos. 1–2 (1985): 5–22.

Hamacher, Werner. "The Second of Inversion: Movements of a Figure Through Celan's Poetry." *Yale French Studies* 69 (1985): 276–314. Reprinted in *Word Traces: Readings of Paul Celan*, edited by Aris Fioretis, 219–63. Baltimore: Johns Hopkins University Press, 1994.

Lyon, James K. "Paul Celan's Language of Stone: The Geology of the Poetic Landscape." *Colloquia Germanica* 8 (1974): 298–317.

———, ed. *Paul Celan. Studies in Twentieth Century Literature* 8 (Fall 1983).

Melin, Charlotte. "Celan and Enzensberger on an Asian Conflict." *Germanic Notes* 18, nos. 1–2 (1987): 4–5.

Myers, Saul. "The Way through Human-Shaped Snow: Paul Celan's Job." *Studies in Twentieth Century Literature* 11, no. 2 (1987): 213–28.

Olschner, Leonard. "Anamnesis: Paul Celan's Translations of Poetry." *Studies in Twentieth Century Literature* 12, no. 2 (1988): 163–97.

Petuchowski, Elizabeth. "A New Examination of Paul Celan's Translation of Shakespeare's Sonnet 105." *Jahrbuch der Deutschen Shakespeare-Gesellschaft* (1985): 146–52.

Wolosky, Shira. "Paul Celan's Linguistic Mysticism." *Studies in Twentieth Century Literature* 10, no. 2 (1986): 191–211.

FURTHER BOOKS AND ESSAYS USED IN COMMENTARY

LPC: Abbreviation for references to Paul Celan's Library (as reconstructed in the PC archive in the Deutsches Literaturarchiv Marbach, Marbach am Neckar)

FAZ: Abbreviation for references to *Frankfurter Allgemeine Zeitung*
AHD: Abbreviation for references to American Heritage Dictionary
CJB: Abbreviation for references to the *Celan-Jahrbuch*

Paul Celan. *La bibliothèque philosophique*. Catalogue raisonné annotated by Alexandra Richter, Patrik Alac, and Bertrand Badiou. Lyon: ENS Éditions, 2004 [BPPC section x, entry #]

——— and Peter Szondi. *Briefwechsel*. Edited by Christoph König. Frankfurt am Main: Suhrkamp, 2005. [PC/PS]

——— and Franz Wurm. *Briefwechsel*. Edited by Barbara Wiedemann, with assistance by Franz Wurm. Frankfurt am Main: Suhrkamp, 2003. [PC/FW]

———. *Choix de poèmes*. Translated and edited by Jean-Pierre Lefebvre. Paris: Gallimard, 1998.

———. *Partie de neige*. Translated from the German and annotated by Jean-Pierre Lefebvre. Paris: Le Seuil, 2007. [PDN]

———. *Renverse de souffle*. Translated from the German and annotated by Jean-Pierre Lefebvre. Paris: Le Seuil, 2003. [RDS]

Anderson, Mark M. "The Impossibility of Poetry: Celan and Heidegger in France." *New German Critique* 53 (1991): 3–18.

Baer, Ulrich. *Remnants of Song: Trauma and the Experience of Modernity in Charles Baudelaire and Paul Celan*. Palo Alto, CA: Stanford University Press, 2000.

Barnert, Arno Albert. "*Die Insel des zweiten Gesichts* von Albert Vigoleis Thelen, gelesen von Paul Celan: 'une vraie oeuvre d'art.' " *Celan-Jahrbuch* 8 (2001/2002): 175–202.

Benjamin, Walter. *Selected Writings*. 4 volumes. Cambridge, MA: Belknap/Harvard University Press, 2003. [WBSW]

Ben-Porat, Ziva. "Forms of Intertextuality and the Reading of Poetry: Uri Zvi Greenberg's Basha'ar." *Prooftexts* 10, no. 2 (1990): 257–81.

Bilz, Rudolf. *Die unbewältigte Vergangenheit des Menschengeschlechts*. Frankfurt am Main: Suhrkamp, 1967.

Bonnefoy, Yves. "Paul Celan." *ACTS, a Journal of New Writing* (8/9) (1988): 9–14.

Böschenstein-Schäfer, Renate. "Traum und Sprache in der Dichtung Paul

Celans." In *Argumentum e Silentio: International Paul Celan Symposium*, edited by Amy D. Colin, 223–36. Berlin: Walter de Gruyter, 1986.

Brinkman, Roland. *Abriß der Geologie.* 2 volumes. 10th/11th edition, revised by Karl Krömmelbein. Stuttgart: Ferdinand Enke, 1977.

Broda, Martine. *Contre-Jour: Études sur Paul Celan.* In *Passages.* Paris: Éditions du Cerf, 1986.

Bücher, Rolf. "Erfahrenes Sprechen—Leseversuch an Celan-Entwürfen." In *Argumentum e Silentio.* Berlin: Walter de Gruyter, 1986.

Buhr, Gerhard. "Von der radikalen In-Frage-Stellung der Kunst in Celans Rede 'Der Meridian.' " CJB 2 (1988): 169–208.

Caputo, John D. *The Mystical Element in Heidegger's Thought.* Athens: Ohio University Press, 1978.

Celan, Paul. *Choix de poèmes (réunis par l'auteur).* Translated and edited by Jean-Pierre Lefebvre. Paris: Poésie/Gallimard, 1998. [JPL]

Derrida, Jacques. "Poetics and Politics of Witnessing." In *Sovereignties in Question: The Poetics of Paul Celan*, edited by Thomas Dutoit and Outi Pasanen, 65–96. Bronx, NY: Fordham University Press, 2005.

Eckhart, Meister. *Predigten: Die deutschen Werke.* Volume 1. Edited by Josef Quint. Stuttgart: W. Kohlhammer, 1958.

———. *Selected Writings.* Translated by Oliver Davies. London: Penguin, 1994.

Eis, Gerhard, ed. *Wahrsagetexte des Spätmittelalters. Aus Handschriften und Inkunabeln.* Berlin/Bielefeld/Münche: E. Schmidt, 1956. [LPC: acquired May 12, 1959]

Eshel, Amir. "Paul Celan's Other: History, Poetics, and Ethics." *New German Critique* 91 (2004): 57–77.

Faller, Adolf. *Der Körper des Menschen: Einführung in Bau und Funktion.* Stuttgart: Georg Thieme, 1966. [LPC]

Felstiner, John. " 'Ziv, that light': Translation and Tradition in Paul Celan." *New Literary History* 18, no. 3 (1987): 611–31.

Freud, Sigmund. *Beyond the Pleasure Principle.* New York: Bantam Books, 1967.

———. *The Interpretation of Dreams.* New York: Avon Books, 1965.

Hahn, Barbara. *The Jewess Pallas Athena: This Too a Theory of Modernity,* 233.

Translated by James McFarland. Princeton, NJ: Princeton University Press, 2005.

Hamacher, Werner. "Häm: Ein Gedicht Celans mit Motiven Benjamins." In *Jüdisches Denken in einer Welt ohne Gott. Festschrift für Stéphane Mosès*, edited by Jens Mattern, Gabriel Motzkin and Shimon Sandbank. Berlin: Verlag Vorwerk 8, 2000. [WHH]

———. "The Second of Inversion: Movements of a Figure through Celan's Poetry." In *Word Traces: Readings of Paul Celan*, edited by Aris Fioretis, 219-63. Baltimore: Johns Hopkins University Press, 1994.

Heidegger, Martin. *Holzwege*. Frankfurt am Main: Viktorio Klostermann, 2003.

———. *Unterwegs zur Sprache*. Tübingen: Neske, 1959.

Hellerstein, Kathryn Ann. "Moyshe Leyb Halpern's 'In New York': A Modern Yiddish Verse Narrative." Ph.D. diss. Stanford University, 1981.

Homer. *The Odyssey*. Translated by Charles Stein. Berkeley, CA: North Atlantic Books, 2008.

Husserl, Edmund. *Zur Phänomenologie des inneren Zeitbewusstseins (1893–1917)*. Edited by Rudolf Boehm. The Hague: Martinus Nijhoff, 1966.

Iiska, Vivian. "'Roots Against Heaven: An Aporetic Inversion in Paul Celan." *New German Critique* 91 (2004): 41–56.

Janz, Marlies. *Vom Engagement absoluter Poesie. Zur Lyrik und Ästhetik Paul Celans*. Frankfurt am Main: Athenaeum, 1976.

Joris, Pierre. "Paul Celan's Counterword: Who Witnesses for the Witness?" In *Justifying the Margins*, 79–86. Cambridge, UK: Salt Publishing, 2009.

Kafka, Franz. *Hochzeitsvorbereitungen auf dem Lande*. Collected Works. Frankfurt am Main: S. Fischer, 1976.

Kaufman, Walter. "Heidegger's Castle." Translated by Hugo Bergmann. *Iyyun: A Hebrew Philosophical Quarterly* 9, no. 1 (1958): 76–101.

King James Bible. The Official King James Bible Online. Oxford 1769 version. Web. October 3, 2010.

Klose, Barbara. "'Souvenirs entomologiques': Celans Begegnung mit Jean-Henri Fabre." In *Datum und Zitat bei Paul Celan*, edited by Bernd Witte and Chaim Shoam. Bern: Peter Lang, 1987.

Kluge, Friedrich, and Alfred Götze. *Etymologisches Wörterbuch der deutschen Sprache.* 16th edition. Berlin: Walter de Gruyter, 1953.

Konietzny, Ulrich. "All deine Siegel erbrochen?" *Celan-Jahrbuch* 2 (1988): 107–20.

Lyon, James K. "Ganz und gar nicht hermetisch: Zum 'richtigen' Lesen von Paul Celans Lyrik." In *Psalm und Hawdalah: Zum Werk Paul Celans*, edited by Joseph P. Strelka, 185–89. Bern/Frankfurt am Main/ New York/ Paris: Peter Lang, 1987.

———. "Paul Celan's Language of Stone: The Geology of the Poetic Landscape." *Colloquia Germanica* 8 (1974): 298–317.

May, Markus, Peter Goßens, and Jürgen Lehmann, eds. *Celan Handbuch: Leben–Werk–Wirkung*. Stuttgart: J. B. Metzler, 2008. (CH)

Mendes-Hohr, Paul. *German Jews: A Dual Identity.* New Haven, CT: Yale University Press, 1999.

Oelmann, Ute Maria. *Deutsche poetologische Lyrik nach 1945: Ingeborg Bachmann, Günter Eich, Paul Celan.* Stuttgart: H. D. Heinz Akademischer, 1980.

Petuchowski, Elizabeth. "Bilingual and Multilingual *Wortspiele* in the Poetry of Paul Celan." *Deutsche Vierteljahrsschrift für Literaturwissenschaft und Geistesgeschichte* 52 (DVjs) (1978): 635–51.

Pöggeler, Otto. "Mystical Elements in Heidegger's Thought and Celan's Poetry." In *Word Traces: Readings of Paul Celan*, edited by Aris Fioretis, 75–109. Baltimore: Johns Hopkins University Press, 1994.

———. "'Schwarzmaut': Bildende Kunst in der Lyrik Paul Celans." In *Die Frage nach der Kunst: Von Hegel zu Heidegger.* Munich/ Freiburg im Breisgau: Karl Alber, 1984.

———. *Spur des Wortes.* Munich: Karl Alber, 1986. [SPUR]

———. *Der Stein hinterm Aug. Studien zu Celans Gedichten.* Munich: Wilhelm Fink, 2000. [STEIN]

Rabinbach, Anson. Introduction to *The Correspondence of Walter Benjamin and Gershom Scholem 1932–1940*, edited by Gershom Scholem. Translated by Gary Smith and Andre Lefevere, vii-xxxviii. Cambridge, MA: Harvard University Press, 1992.

Rebien, Kristin. "Politics and Aesthetics in Postwar German Literature:

Heinrich Böll, Hans Erich Nossack, Paul Celan." Ph.D. diss., Stanford University, 2005.

Reichel, Hans, and Adolf Bleichert. *Leitfaden der Physiologie des Menschen*. Stuttgart: Ferdinand Enke, 1966.

Reschika, Richard. *Poesie und Apokalypse: Paul Celans Jerusalem-Gedichte aus dem Nachlassband Zeitgehöft*. Pfaffenweiler: Centaurus, 1991.

Santner, Eric. *Creaturely Life: Rilke, Benjamin, Sebald*. Chicago: University of Chicago Press, 2006.

Scholem, Gershom. "Mystische Motive in Paul Celans Gedichten." *Poetica* 3 (1970): 472–509.

———. *On the Kabbalah and Its Symbolism*. New York: Schocken, 1996.

———. *On the Mystical Shape of the Godhead: Basic Concepts in the Kabbalah*. Translated by Joachim Neugröschel. New York: Schocken, 1997.

———. *Ursprung und Anfänge der Kabbala*. Berlin: Walter de Gruyter, 1962.

———. *Von der mystischen Gestalt der Gottheit: Studien zu Grundbegriffen der Kabbala*. Zurich: Rhein-Verlag, 1962.

Schulze, Joachim. *Celan und die Mystiker: Motivtypologische und quellenkundliche Kommentare*. Bonn: Bouvier, 1976.

Shmueli, Ilana. *Sag, daß Jerusalem ist*. Aachen: Rimbaud Verlag, 2010. [IS]

Spector, Scott. *Prague Territories: National Conflict and Cultural Innovation in Franz Kafka's Fin-de-Siècle*. Berkeley: University of California Press, 2000.

Speier, Hans-Michael. "Paul Celan, Dichter einer neuen Wirklichkeit: Studien zu *Schneepart*." *Celan-Jahrbuch* 1 (1987): 65–79.

Steinecke, Hartmut. "Lieder . . . jenseits der Menschen?" In: *Psalm und Hawdalah: Zum Werk Paul Celans*, edited by Joseph P. Strelka. Bern: Peter Lang, 1987.

Weidner, Daniel. *Gershom Scholem: Politisches, esoterisches und historiographisches Schreiben*. Munich: Wilhelm Fink, 2003.

Wiedemann, Barbara. *Paul Celan: Die Goll-Affäre*. Frankfurt am Main: Suhrkamp, 2000. [GA]

Witte, Bernd. "Der zyklische Charakter der *Niemandsrose* von Paul Celan." In *Argumentum e Silentio*. Berlin: Walter de Gruyter, 1986.

Index of Titles and First Lines in German

Index of Titles and First Lines in English

www.ingramcontent.com/pod-product-compliance
Lightning Source LLC
LaVergne TN
LVHW090430230725
816804LV00022B/781
9780374603236